Your

CW00780424

Visitor Discount Card

HOW TO USE YOUR VISITOR DISCOUNT CARD

Please remove the card carefully and sign your name on the signature panel on the reverse. Your card is now valid to be used in 100's of attractions listed in the guide. The more you use it the more money you'll save. Keep it safe in your purse or wallet.

Lookout for the **1998** *Visitor Discount Card* symbol under the entries this means these attractions accept the *Visitor Discount Card*. The discount offer is shown in the entry listing text for example;

Discount Card Offer: Admit two for the price of one

Every participating attraction has been supplied with a *Visitor Discount Card* sticker to display at their paypoint, look out for it when visiting.

In the unlikely event that you encounter any problems using your card please telephone us on 01604 711994 or write to the above address, and we will help.

BEST GUIDES CREDITS

Alyson Spark
...ers: Debora Stone, Leisa Griggs
Database Programming: David White
Administration: Jayne Moore
Publisher: Martin Spark

Thi... ...blished February 1998.
Typeset in FF Meta+ and FF Providence
Film output by Harpur Phototypesetters, Northampton
Printed & bound by Benham & Company Ltd, Colchester and Stones the Printers
Distributed in the UK by Biblios, Star Road, Partridge Green, West Sussex RH13 8LD
T 01403 710971
Sales by Best Guides Ltd P O Box 427 Northampton NN2 7YJ England T 01604 711994
F 01604 722446 email *info@bestguides.demon.co.uk*
Internet address *www.thisislondon.com*

© *BEST GUIDES LTD 1998*

A catalogue record for this book is available from the British Library

ISBN 1 901258 07 6

FRONT COVER PHOTO CREDITS *Warwick Castle*

The Best Guide to DAYS OUT ever!

50 MILES AROUND
BIRMINGHAM 98/99

BEST GUIDES

GOING OUT Guides for *OUTGOING* People

FACILITY SYMBOLS

To help you in deciding where to go we have created 29 symbols shown here in enlarged format. They can also be found at the bottom of every listing page for immediate reference.

Suitable for pushchairs	Historic Scotland
Mother & baby facilities	CADW Welsh Monuments
Suitable for wheelchairs	Guided tours available
1998 Visitor discount card accepted	Refreshments
No dogs: except guide dogs	Photography allowed
Parking on site	Beach/coastal area
Parking nearby	VISA Visa accepted
£ Charged parking	Mastercard accepted
Picnic areas	C All major cards accepted
Cafè-restaurant	Corporate facilities
Licensed	Wedding ceremonies
Special events listed	Educational packs
National Trust	Celebration catering
National Trust for Scotland	Gift shop
English Heritage	

GOING OUT Guides for **OUTGOING** People

LISTING GUIDE

CLASSIFICATION HEADING
we have over 300 to choose from to make your decision easier

ADDRESS AND LOCATION
Item in brackets is the location which can vary from a tube station to a full description for way out locations

VENUE NAME

TELEPHONE AND FAX

Caves

Wookey Hole Caves and Papermill
Wookey Hole Wells Somerset BA5 1BB (J22 M5, A39, A38, A371)
Tel: 01749 672243 Fax: 01749 677749
Web Site: www.wookey.co.uk
The caves are the main feature of Wookey Hole. Visitors are guided through the Chambers seeing the amazing stalagmites and stalactites including the famous Witch of Wookey. There is also a Victorian Papermill where handmade paper is still made in the traditional way.
Visitor Comments: 'best caves I've seen' 'walk to the top for a brilliant view'
All year Mar-Oct 10.00-17.00, Nov-Feb 10.30-16.30. Closed 17-25 Dec inclusive
Last Admission: Summer 17.30, Winter 16.30
A£6.70 C£3.60
Discount Card Offer: 50p Off Full Admission Price For A Maximum Of 6 People, not with Family Tickets

1998

INTERNET ADDRESS
If you are connected to the Internet you should be able to find out much more about the venue

DESCRIPTION
Varies between 20-100 words to give a flavour of what's in store

VISITOR COMMENTS
your views and comments

OPENING TIMES
Months, days and hours of opening

LAST ADMISSION
The time the last ticket is sold, if not detailed last admission is closing time

FACILITY SYMBOLS
A full list with their explanations are shown at the front of the guide and at the bottom of each listing page for quick reference

VISITOR DISCOUNT CARD
Describes the offer you may claim on presentation of your card

QUEUING TIMES
Expected for venue admission at peak times. If not detailed queuing is not likely

ADMISSION PRICES
A= Adult C= Child etc
OAPs = Old age pensioners
A Family Ticket normally is 2 adults and 2 children but some venues allow up to 3 or 4 children, we suggest you check before visiting. Many venues offer group and school rates if not detailed call the venue

INTRODUCTION

Welcome to the 98/99 edition of our best selling guide. New for this year is our **Visitor Discount Card** which entitles you to admission and other discounts throughout the season. You can claim these discounts every time you visit, full details on the use of the card can be found on the first page in the guide.

An extended Special Events section includes, all the National Trust and English Heritage events taking place in 1998 and early 1999 as well as many hundreds more to give you even more choice. Full classified and venue name A-Z indexes have now been added to make it even easier to navigate the guide.

In partnership with Associated Newspapers, publishers of the London Evening Standard and the Mail on Sunday, Best Guides information can now be accessed on the Internet @ *www.thisislondon.com* Our listings and special events can be found under the section *Things to Do*, updated daily this site covers London, during 1998 our listings and events for the rest of the UK, including the '50 miles Around Birmingham' area, will appear on other sites currently under development. We recommend a visit to the site, it's one of the best on the net!

Listings
How to locate your choice of day out?
Check the regional map for main towns etc, look in the classified index for the type of day out you would like to have, then choose your venue. Alternatively you can use the venue name A-Z index located at the back of the guide. Each listing has been checked for accuracy and 98/99 prices however some venues had not set their price structure before we went to press (Jan 98!) and in some cases we have stated that the prices are 1997's, any price increases encountered will probably only be small. We have extended our venue listings to over 1,000, a larger selection than any other regional guide, giving you more choice.

Special Events
This guide also lists over 1,000 special events in a calendar format. All the dates have been supplied by the attractions concerned and were correct at press time, however due to their nature we would suggest telephoning before attending an event to check that the date has not been moved and that the event is still being held. A particular date to watch out for is July 12th 1998 which is FIFA World Cup Final day.

Our Special Events calendars are listed in *start date* order however please note that whilst some events only last one day many last 2-3 days and some exhibitions may last months, so please check the *end date* as well. For example if you are looking under the June events calendar there may still be some exhibitions running in June, and not shown in the June calendar, but are listed under the April calendar which is the date when they started.

The venue information shown on these pages is limited to the venue name, telephone number and classification under which the full venue information can be found.

We want your opinion

This year we have introduced a visitor comments line in all our listings and we would like you to help us complete these for our 99/2000 Millennium guides available in February 1999. Everyone who participates in this annual survey of the views of attraction visitors receives a **free copy** of the following year's regional guide in the area in which they live as a 'thank-you' for taking part. If you would like to participate in our 1998 survey, send your name and address on a postcard to: Survey Registrations Best Guides PO Box 427 Northampton NN2 7YJ. or email us on *survey@bestguides.demon.co.uk* Please register by the 31st August 1998.

Looking ahead

Many venues have recently, or soon will be, celebrating lottery grants and have embarked upon a programme of refurbishment, redevelopment and purchase of significant works of art. A number of Millennium projects open this year and early 1999 and, whilst they may not yet be open, we have listed them to keep you up to date with the latest developments.

Photo '98 is a programme of exhibitions, commissions and public art events, which will include the opening of the new Photography Gallery at the *Victoria and Albert Museum* in London and many events in the Midlands art and photographic galleries. *Chatsworth House* opens a fantastic new kids adventure playground and *Alton Towers* new £12 million white-knuckle ride 'Secret Weapon 4' opens in March and promises to make Nemesis seem tame.

The details on these venues and events can be found in the guide. We hope you enjoy using the guide during the year and we look forward to providing you with a packed Millennium regional guide for your area and an 'Around Britain' Millennium special **double issue,** for those travelling to other parts of the country. These guides are published in February 1999, to reserve your copy please see the details on the inside back cover.

50 Miles Around Birmingham

Including:
Derbyshire
Nottinghamshire
Leicestershire
Staffordshire
Shropshire
Hereford
Worcester
West Midlands
Warwickshire
Gloucestershire
Northamptonshire

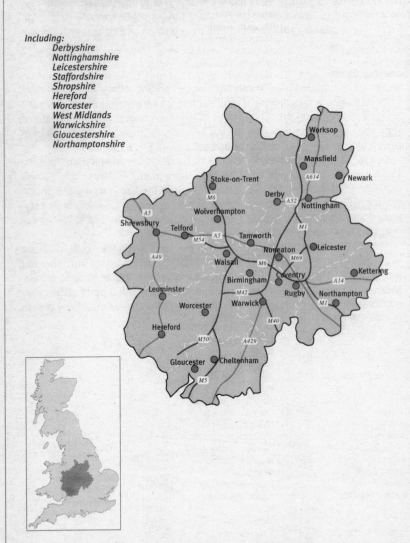

Abbeys

Hailes Abbey

nr Winchcombe Cheltenham Gloucester GL54 5PB
(2m NE of Winchcombe off B463)
Tel: 01242 602398
In the Middle Ages this 13th century Cistercian abbey, set in woodland pastureland, was one of the main centres of pilgrimages in Britain due to a phial possessed by the monks said to contain the blood of Christ. The museum displays include some fine high quality medieval sculpture and floor tiles.
1 Apr-31 Oct daily 10.00-16.00 dusk in Oct. 1 Nov-31 Mar Sat & Sun 10.00-16.00. Closed 24-26 Dec
A£2.50 C£1.30 Concessions£1.90, personal stereo tour included in admission price

Halesowen Abbey

Halesowen West Midlands *(off A456 Kidderminster road 6m W of Birmingham city centre. Bus: West Midlands Travel 9/19 Birmingham / Stourbridge. BR: Old Hill 2.5m)*
Tel: 01604 730320
Remains of an abbey founded by King John in the 13th century, now incorporated into a 19th century farm.
July-Aug weekends only 10.00-18.00
A£1.00 C£0.80 OAP£0.50

Lilleshall Abbey

Abbey Road Lilleshall Newport Shropshire TF10 9HW *(on unclassified road off A518 4m N of Oaken gates)*
Tel: 01604 730320
Some of the most evocative ruins in Shropshire stand in the beautiful grounds of Lilleshall Hall. Lilleshall Abbey was founded shortly before the middle of the 12th century and from the high west front visitors can look down the entire 228ft length of the abbey church.
22 Mar-31 Oct Weekends only 10.00-18.00. Closed 13.00-14.00
A£1.10 C£0.60 Concessions£0.80

Prinknash Abbey

Cranham Gloucester Gloucestershire GL4 8EX *(take A6 or J11A M5)*
Tel: 01452 812066 Fax: 01452 812066
The abbey has become famous for its pottery in the 20th century, but its origins lie in the Middle Ages. The old abbey building is a 12th to 16th century house used by Benedictine monks and guests until 1539. Set in one of the most breathtaking beauty spots in Gloucestershire, many come for the views, some for the solitude and tranquility, some for the friendly shops & tearoom. Prinknash Pottery allows visitors to view the factory via a guided tour and the young ones can try their hand at painting their own plate. A low cost and memorable day out for all ages.
Abbey: daily 05.00-20.00. Shop & Tearoom: daily 09.30-17.00
Last Admission: Shop 17.00, Abbey 20.00
Viewing gallery fee: A£1.00 C£0.50. Sept-Feb £Free, (No guide)
Discount Card Offer: 10% Off Pottery Firsts

Strata Florida Abbey

Ffair Rhos Ystrad Meurig Dyfed SY25 6BT
Tel: 01974 831261
Little remains of the Cistercian abbey founded in 1164, except the ruined church and cloister. Strata Florida was an important centre of learning in the Middle Ages, and it is believed that the 14th century poet Dafyd ap Gwilym was buried here.
1 May-30 Sept daily 10.00-17.00
A£1.70 C(0-5)£Free Family Ticket (A2+C3)£4.00 Concessions£1.20

Amphitheatres

Cirencester Amphitheatre

Cirencester Gloucestershire *(next to bypass W of town. Access from town or along Chesterton Lane from W end of bypass onto Cotswold Avenue Park next to obelisk. BR: Kemble 4m)*
Tel: 0117 975 0700
A large well-preserved Roman amphitheatre.
Any reasonable time
Admission Free

Amusement Parks

American Adventure Theme Park

Pit Lane Ilkeston Derbyshire DE7 5SX *(follow tourist signposts from M1 and major trunk roads)*
Tel: 01773 769931 Fax: 01773 530238
Fully themed park based on legend of whole continent. Widely varied experiences from heartpounding action of Missile Rollercoaster in Spaceport USA, to the wet and wild excitement of the Great Niagara Falls log Flume and many more.
End Mar-end Nov daily 10.00-17.30
Last Admission: 16.30
All £1.99 rides wristbands £7.99 over 1.22m, £5.99 under 1.22m

Animal Farms

THE WHITE POST MODERN FARM CENTRE

The White Post Modern Farm Centre

Mansfield Road Farnsfield Newark Nottinghamshire
NG22 8HL *(12m N of Nottingham on A614)*
Tel: 01623 882977 Fax: 01623 883499
A modern working farm with over 3000 friendly animals (half indoors) including llamas, deer, rheas, piglets, owls, cattle and lambs (all year!)
Experience the Green Farm Barn, the Night-Time Walk, the New Beach Barn and the Pet Learning Centre. Winner of numerous national awards.
All year Mon-Fri 10.00-17.00, Sat & Sun 10.00-18.00
Last Admission: 16.00
A£3.95 C(0-4)£Free C(4-16)&OAPs£2.95. School Parties C(3+)£2.45, Teachers, accompanying adults (1:5 ratio) & coach drivers £Free. Price includes a Guide for each class for entire 4.5hr visit. Booking is essential
Discount Card Offer: 10% Off Admissions Plus A FREE Bag Of Animal Feed Per Child - Guaranteed To Work!

Arboreta

Batsford Arboretum

Batsford Moreton-In-Marsh Gloucestershire GL56 9QF *(1.5m NW off A44)*
Tel: 01608 650722 Fax: 01608 650290
This arboretum of some 50 acres overlooking the Vale of Evenlode boasts one of the largest private collections of woody plants in Great Britain. There are many rare and unusual trees.
Mar-Nov daily 10.00-17.00
A£3.00 C&OAPs£2.50

Westonbirt Arboretum

Tetbury Gloucestershire GL8 8QS *(3m S Tetbury on A433)*
Tel: 01666 880220 Fax: 01666 880559
Westonbirt is a wonderful world of trees. There are

18,000 of them dating from 1829, including 96 'champions' (the tallest, oldest etc). Set in 600 acres with 17 miles of paths, it is famous for its Autumn colour, but is beautiful at any time of the year.

All year daily 10.00-20.00 or sunset if sooner

Last Admission: Dusk

A£3.50 C£1.00 Concessions£2.50, Group rates A£2.50 OAPs£1.50

Archaelogical Sites

Creswell Crags

Craigs Road Welbeck Worksop Nottinghamshire S80 3LH *(between A616 /A60, 1m E of Creswell village)*

Tel: 01909 720378

The deep narrow gorge of Creswell Crags is honeycombed with caves and rock shelters which were used as seasonal camps by Ice Age hunters who preyed on mammoth, reindeer, bison and other animals that roamed nearby. The most northerly place on earth to be inhabited during the Ice Age. A visitor centre with audio visual programme and display tells the story of life in the Ice Age. Woodland and lakeside trail through the gorge. Regular cave tours and other events.

All year Feb-Oct daily 10.30-16.30, Nov-Jan Sun only 10.30-16.30

Cave tour: A£1.95 C£1.45

Littledean Hall

Newnham Road Littledean Cinderford Gloucestershire GL14 3NR *(from Gloucester A48 towards Chepstow M5 /M4 A4151 Elthon Corner)*

Tel: 01594 824213

The largest know Roman temple in rural Britain was unearthed here in 1984. The manor itself was built in Norman times. The house has always been lived in and remains relatively untouched since the 19th century.

House Grounds & Archaeological Site please telephone for opening times

Please telephone for admission prices

🐿 suitable for pushchairs   🍼 mother & baby facilities   ♿ suitable for wheelchairs   🎁 gift shop
🤝 corporate facilities   🚫 no dogs: except guide dogs   🚗 parking on site   🅿 parking nearby
£ charged parking   ☕ café-restaurant 🍸 licensed   🎂 special events 📚 educational pack

Art Galleries

MANOR HOUSE MUSEUM

Alfred East Art Gallery and Manor House Museum

The Coach House Sheep Street Kettering Northamptonshire NN16 0AN *(A6 A43 Town Centre)*
Tel: 01536 534381/534219 Fax: 01536 534370
Frequent family events and a "hands-on" approach to history make the Manor House Museum an exciting place to visit, while the Gallery hosts around 20 temporary exhibitions annually featuring national, regional and local art, craft and photography.
All year Mon-Sat 09.30-17.00. Closed Bank Hol
Last Admission: 16.45
Admission Free

Astley Cheetham Art Gallery

Trinity Street Stalybridge Cheshire SK15 2BN *(from Manchester A635, or A672 from Oldham, signposted within town centre)*
Tel: 0161 338 2708/343 1978 Fax: 0161 339 8246
This Victorian gallery was founded in 1901 by John Cheetham, a local mill-owner, who bequeathed his private collection of renaissance paintings and watercolours to the gallery. Throughout 1998, the gallery will be mounting a variety of exhibitions featuring: contemporary painting, textiles, sculptures and work by local amateur and professional artists.
All year Mon, Tue, Wed & Fri 13.00-19.30, Sat 09.00-16.00. Closed Thur, Sun and Bank Hol
Admission Free

Bilston Art Gallery and Museum

Mount Pleasant Bilston West Midlands WV14 7LU *(follow A41 out of Wolverhampton to Bilston)*
Tel: 01902 409143 Fax: 01902 353440
Changing programme of temporary exhibitions focusing on contemporary crafts. Bilston enamels; story of the town and its people; workshops and events; sculpture garden featuring Amber the fire breather - carved dragon. Changing programme of temporary exhibitions focusing on contemporary crafts and popular culture.
All year Mon-Thur 11.00-17.00, Sat 11.00-16.00, Fri group visits by arrangement
Admission Free

Borough Museum and Art Gallery

Brampton Park Newcastle Staffordshire *(2m from J15 M6)*
Tel: 01782 619705
The Museum and Art Gallery has permanent displays of Staffordshire pottery and glass, weapons, toys and social history, including a recreated Victorian street scene. There is also a frequently changing temporary exhibition programme of fine art and crafts, drawn both from the gallery's permanent collection and touring exhibitions.
Mon-Sat 10.00-17.30, Sun 14.00-17.30. Closed Bank Hol and May Day Mon
Admission Free

Castle Park Arts Centre

Castle Park Estate Frodsham Cheshire WS6 6SE *(J12 M56 A56 Runcorn / Chester)*
Tel: 01928 735832
Created from the repair and conversion of the 1852 clock tower building of the Castle Park Estate. Housing 3 galleries, one showing a permanent Heritage Exhibition, the other 2 having monthly and bi-monthly changing exhibitions, the largest gallery space in Cheshire for changing exhibitions. Sponsored by Cheshire County Council. Also housing official Tourist Information Centre.
All year Tue-Sun 10.00-12.30 & 14.00-16.30, Winter closing 16.00
Last Admission: Summer 16.25, Winter 15.50
Admission Free Donations appreciated

Central Museum and Art Gallery

Guildhall Road Northampton Northamptonshire NN1 1DP *(J15 M1, signposted town centre)*
Tel: 01604 39415 Fax: 01604 238720
The Central Museum and Art Gallery reflects Northampton's proud standing as Britain's boot and shoe capital by housing a collection of boots and shoes considered one of the finest in the world. Also on display are Northampton's history, decorative arts, The Art Gallery and the Leathercraft Gallery.
All year Mon-Sat 10.00-17.00, Sun 14.00-17.00. Closed 25 Dec & 1 Jan
Admission Free

City Museum and Art Gallery

Chamberlain Square Birmingham West Midlands B3 3DH *(J5&6 M42, J5,6&7 M6, J1,2,3&4 M5. City centre location)*

Tel: 0121 235 2834 Fax: 0121 235 1343

One of the world's best collections of Pre-Raphaelite paintings can be seen here, including important works by Burne-Jones, a native of Birmingham. The wide-ranging archaeology section has prehistoric, Greek and Roman antiquities, and also objects from the Near East, Mexico and Peru.

All year Mon-Thur & Sat 10.00-17.00, Fri 10.30-17.00, Sun 12.30-17.00. Closed 25-27 Dec & 1 Jan

Admission Free

Djanogly Art Gallery

The University of Nottingham Arts Centre University Park Nottingham Nottinghamshire NG7 2RD *(situated at the S entrance to University Park off University Boulevard A6005)*

Tel: 0115 951 3192 Fax: 0115 951 3194

Web Site: www.nottingham.ac.uk/artscentre

Temporary exhibition programme (see Special Events) incorporating contemporary and historical art, workshops, educational activities, craft cabinets, café and bookshop.

All year Mon-Fri 10.00-18.00, Sat 11.00-18.00, Sun & Bank Hol 14.00-17.00

Admission Free

Leamington Art Gallery and Museum

Avenue Road Leamington Spa Warwickshire CV31 3PP *(J13&14 M40, A452 Leamington Spa, signposted from A452)*

Tel: 01926 426559 Fax: 01926 317867

Art Gallery with themed displays of works by major British and Dutch artists, 17th-early 19th century English drinking glasses and British pottery from the 18th-20th centuries. The world of art can also be explored through interactive games and toys for children and adults. Discover the history of Leamington Spa and its people in the Local History gallery.

Closing Jan 98 until May 98. All Year Mon Tue Thur-Sat 10.00-13.00 & 14.00-17.00, Thur 18.00-20.00 Last Admission: 16.55

Admission Free

Ombersley Gallery

Church Terrace Ombersley Worcestershire WR9 0EP *(J6 M5 off the A449 to Kidderminster)*

Tel: 01905 620655 Fax: 01905 620655

Set in the heart of a picturesque Worcestershire village, a Craft Council selected Gallery enjoying an enviable reputation for attracting the work of internationally renowned artists and fine crafts people. Regular exhibitions featuring painters, ceramic artists and other crafts.

All year Tue-Sat daily 10.00-17.00

Admission Free

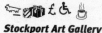

Shire Hall Gallery

Market Square Stafford Staffordshire ST16 2LD *(town centre location)*

Tel: 01785 278345 Fax: 01785 278327

A fine gallery housed in the 18th century Shire Hall one of Staffordshire's most magnificent buildings. Exhibitions of contemporary arts, historic courtrooms and a Crafts Council selected craft shop.

All year Mon-Fri 10.00-17.00, Sat 10.00-17.00

Admission Free

Stockport Art Gallery

War Memorial Building Greek Street / Wellington Road South Stockport Cheshire SK3 8AB *(main A6 Manchester to Buxton Road. 5mins walk from Stockport railway and bus stations)*

Tel: 0161 474 4453 Fax: 0161 480 4960

Changing exhibitions of contemporary art, photography and craft with emphasis on complementary events - practical workshops for children and adults, lectures etc. 'Artlink' scheme for purchasing or borrowing contemporary works of art including paintings, sculpture, photographs and craft work.

Mon Tue Thur Fri 11.00-17.00, Sat 10.00-17.00. Closed Wed & Sun

Admission Free

The Barber Institute Of Fine Arts

Edgbaston Birmingham West Midlands B15 2TS *(Edgbaston Park Road off Bristol Road)*

Tel: 0121 414 7333 Fax: 0121 414 3370

An outstanding collection of Old Master and modern paintings including major works by Bellini, Rubens, Poussin, Murillo, Gainsborough, Rossetti and Whistler.

All year Mon-Sat 10.00-17.00, Sun 14.00-17.00. Closed 25-26 Dec, New Year, Good Fri-Easter Mon

Admission Free

Discount Card Offer: Purchase The Gallery Handbook For £4.50 - A Saving Of £2.45

 suitable for pushchairs   mother & baby facilities   suitable for wheelchairs   gift shop   corporate facilities   no dogs: except guide dogs   parking on site   parking nearby   £ charged parking   café-restaurant   licensed   special events   educational pack

THE HARLEY GALLERY

The Harley Gallery

Welbeck Nr. Worksop Nottinghamshire S80 3LW
(5m S of Worksop on A60)
Tel: 01909 501700 Fax: 01909 488747
A unique award winning gallery situated in the
heart of The Dukeries. Built on the site of the
Welbeck Estate former gasworks and set in a land-
scaped courtyard. Regular seasonal exhibitions of
contemporary art and crafts. Also Treasury housing
historic fine art and crafts.
28 Mar-1 Nov Thur-Sun & Bank Hol Mon 11.30-17.00
A£1.50 C(0-5)£Free Concessions£0.50. Season
Ticket A£6.00. Pre-booked groups 10+ guided tours
- call for details
Discount Card Offer: 50p Off Admission Price For
Full Paying Adult/s (Up To Two Per Card). Not
Applicable To Concessions, Concerts Or Special
Events

Walsall Museum and Art Gallery

Lichfield Street Walsall West Midlands WS1 1TR
(signposted from M6 and A34)
Tel: 01922 653116 Fax: 01922 32824
One of the liveliest and friendliest galleries in the
country with a regular programme of exciting exhi-
bitions and events. Also the home of the stunning
Garman Ryan Collection - with works by Van Gogh,
Rembrandt, Matisse, Epstein and many more. No
dogs are allowed except guide dogs.
All year Tue-Sat 10.00-17.00, Sun 14.00-17.00.
Closed Mon
Admission Free

Wolverhampton Art Gallery and Museum

Lichfield Street Wolverhampton West Midlands WV1
1DU *(easy road access from M6 M5 or M54)*
Tel: 01902 552055 Fax: 01902 552054
Outstanding collections of contemporary fine art
and sculpture, 18th & 19th century paintings in
beautifully restored galleries, local history and
geology displays. Exciting programme of temporary

exhibitions. New "ways of seeing" Gallery offers a
new way of looking at art with lots of things to see
and do.
Mon-Sat 10.00-17.00. Please telephone for Bank
Hol openings
Last Admission: 16.30
Admission Free

Worcester City Museum and Art Gallery

Foregate Street Worcester Worcestershire WR1 1DT
(Worcester City Centre J6 or J7 M5)
Tel: 01905 25371 Fax: 01905 616979
The gallery has temporary art exhibitions from both
local and national sources; while the museum
exhibits cover geology, local and natural history,
including River Severn displays and activities. Of
particular interest is a complete 19th-century
chemists shop. There are collections relating to the
Worcestershire Regiment and the Worcestershire
Yeoman Cavalry.
All year Mon Tue Wed & Fri 09.30-18.00, Sat 09.30-
17.00. Closed Good Friday
Admission Free

Art Gallery- Open Air

Forest of Dean Sculpture Trail

Beechenhurst Picnic Site Gloucestershire *(B4226 E*
of J with B4234 between Coleford and Cinderford)
Tel: 01594 833057 Fax: 01594 833908
A four-mile sculpture trail by artists including
Magdelena Jetelova, Carole Drake, Tim Lees, David
Nash, Keir Smith, Ian Hamilton Finlay, Peter Randal
Page, Miles Davis, Bruce Allan, Kevin Atherton,
Cornelia Parker and Peter Appleton.
Summer 10.00-18.00, Winter every weekend but
limited on weekdays
Admission Free. Car Parking £1.50

Balloon Festivals

Northampton Balloon Festival

Race Course Park Northampton Northamptonshire
NN2 7BL *(1m N of town on the Kettering Rd)*
Tel: 01604 238791 Fax: 01604 238796
Over 200,000 people visited the 1997 festival making it one of the most successful ever held. Three
days of Balloon glows, flights, fireworks and festival fun.
14-16 Aug 06.00-22.00
Early Bird Ticket from 06.00: £2.00. Parking on site
after 08.00: £7.50, Park & Ride Scheme: £0.50

---

return per person from Sixfields, Delapre & Nene College

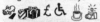

Battlefields

Bosworth Battlefield Visitor Centre and Country Park

Ambion Hill Sutton Cheney Market Bosworth Leicestershire CV13 0AD *(2.5m S of Market Bosworth)*

Tel: 01455 290429 Fax: 01455 292841

The Battle of Bosworth Field was fought in 1485 between the armies of Richard III and the future Henry VII. The visitor centre gives the viewer a comprehensive interpretation of the battle by means of exhibitions, models and a film theatre. Also illustrated trails around battlefield and medieval special events.

Country Park & Battle trails all year during daylight hours. Visitor Centre: Apr-Oct Mon-Fri 13.00-17.00. July-Aug from 11.00, weekends Bank Hol Mon & Good Fri 11.00-18.00

Visitor Centre A£2.30 C&OAPs&UB40£1.50. Special charges on Event days

Bird Centres

Birdland

Rissington Road Bourton-on-the-Water Cheltenham Gloucestershire GL54 2BN *(on A429)*

Tel: 01451 820480 Fax: 01451 822398

Set in 7 acres of landscaped gardens, rivers and waterways. The garden contains a fine collection of penguins, new aviaries, a tropical house and birds at liberty, including macaws, parrots, cockatoos, lorikeets and flamingos. Children's play area available.

Apr-Oct daily 10.00-18.00, Nov-Mar 10.00-16.00 Last Admission: 1 hr before closing

A£3.75 C£2.00 OAPs£2.75. Groups 10+ 10% discount

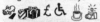

Folly Farm Waterfowl

Bourton-on-the-Water Cheltenham Gloucestershire GL54 3BY *(2.5m W on A436)*

Tel: 01451 820285

Two miles from Bourton, this conservation centre in the Cotswolds has a series of pools and lakes with over 2,500 birds. Waterfowl, ducks, geese and poultry, including many rare and endangered species. There is an undercover pets area where hand reared animals and birds may be stroked. Domestic breeds of ducks and geese for sale. Trees, shrubs and lavender available from the gar-

den centre.

Apr-Sept daily 10.00-18.00, Oct-Mar daily 10.00-16.00

A£3.00 C£1.60 OAPs£2.50. Price increase likely in April 1998

Tropical Birdland

Lindridge Lane Desford Leicestershire *(signposted off A47, bus: regular)*

Tel: 01455 824603

Experience birds of the rainforest on your doorstep. Over 85 species, walk through aviaries, chick room, woodland walk, koi ponds, bird shop.

Easter-end Oct daily 10.00-17.00

A£3.00 C&OAPs£2.00. Group discounts available

Birds of Prey Centre

The National Birds of Prey Centre

Great Boulsdon Newent Gloucestershire GL18 1JJ *(B2415 from Gloucester, J3 M50)*

Tel: 01531 820286 Fax: 01531 821389

Founded in 1967 the Centre now run by Jemima Parry-Jones has over 230 birds. See Eagles, Vulture Hawks and Falcons flying free at the daily demonstrations. An experience the whole family will never forget. Allow at least 2 hours or stay all day!

Feb-Nov daily 10.30-17.30 or dusk if earlier Last Admission: Summer 16.15, Winter 15.30

A£4.50 C£2.50 Family Ticket £12.50. Group Rates call for details

Birth Places

D H Lawrence Birthplace Museum

8a Victoria Street Eastwood Worksop Nottinghamshire NG16 3AW *(J26 or 27 M, A610)*

Tel: 01773 763312 Fax: 0115 943 1452

House furnished as at the time of the Lawrence family occupation and D H Lawrence's birth 1885. Audio-visual presentation, craft centre in renovated cottages nearby.

All year daily Apr-Oct 10.00-17.00, Nov-Mar 10.00-16.00. Closed 24 Dec-1 Jan Last Admission: 30mins before closing

A£1.75 C&OAPs£1.00

Holst Birthplace Museum

4 Clarence Road Pittville Cheltenham Gloucestershire GL52 3JE *(just off A435 Evesham Road N of town centre)*

Tel: 01242 524846 Fax: 01242 262334

Composer of 'The Planets', Gustav Holst, was born

🦃 *suitable for pushchairs* 🍼 *mother & baby facilities* ♿ *suitable for wheelchairs* 🎁 *gift shop* 🤝 *corporate facilities* 🐕 *no dogs: except guide dogs* 🚗 *parking on site* 🅿️ *parking nearby* £ *charged parking* 🍴 *café-restaurant* 🍷 *licensed* 🎪 *special events* 📚 *educational pack*

at 4 Clarence Road in 1874 and made this Regency house his home where he composed much of his music till his death. The museum contains unique displays from the life of the musician including his original piano, with the rooms being carefully restored.

All year Tue-Sat 10.00-16.20

A£1.50 Concessions£0.50

Jerome K Jerome Birthplace Museum

Belsize House Bradford Street Walsall

Tel: 01922 653116

The famous author of 'Three Men in a Boat' was born in Walsall in 1859. His birthplace now houses a small museum about his life and work.

Opening times limited, call before making a special journey

Admission Free

Boat Hire

Ashby Boat Company

Canal Wharf Station Road Stoke Golding Hinckley Leicestershire CV13 6EY

Tel: 01455 212671

Steer yourself along the picturesque lock free Ashby Canal. Three fully equipped traditional narrowboats provide comfort for 2-12 people. Weekly narrowboat hire. Canalside Tea Room, Souvenir Shop and Chandlery.

All year daily Mar-Oct 09.00-17.00

From £50.00 per day inclusive. Day Boats for 7.5 hours 09.30-17.00/10.00-17.30 please reserve

Blisworth Tunnel Boats

Gayton Road Blisworth Northampton Northamptonshire NN7 3BN *(off the A43 in the village of Blisworth)*

Tel: 01604 858868

Enjoy a relaxing day out with your family and friends aboard one of our self-steer narrow boats. Navigate the Blisworth Tunnel and Stoke Bruerne locks, or just potter gently through the Northamptonshire countryside.

Mar-Oct 9.30-18.00

£95.00 inclusive for a whole day for a max of 12 on each boat. Weekdays £80.00 per day. Half day

£48.00: 09.30-13.15 or 14.15-18.00

North Kilworth Narrowboats

Kilworth Marina Nr Market Harborough Kilworth Leicestershire *(on A4304 (A427) towards Lutterworth)*

Tel: 01858 880484

Self Steer day boat hire for 8-10 people. Cruise a picturesque lock free section of the Grand Union Canal in our Picnic Boat, or NEW for this year our 20ft Cabin Cruiser.

Mar-Nov daily 10.00-17.00

From £45.00 per day inc VAT and fuel

Boat Trips

NARROWBOAT CABIN, GLOUCESTER LEISURE CRUSIE

Gloucester Leisure Cruise

The National Waterways Museum Llanthony Warehouse Gloucester Docks Gloucester Gloucestershire GL1 2EH *(follow historic dock signs from motorway and A roads)*

Tel: 01452 318054 Fax: 01452 318066

Built in 1936 as a River Thames passenger boat, the Queen Boadicea II is certificated and inspected for up to 145 passengers and is piloted by trained certified skippers. All trips depart from and return to Merchants Quay. Short Cruises: A 45min trip on the Gloucester and Sharpness on board QBII from Merchants Quay, travel down the canal from the old Port of Gloucester and return. Full commentary on the buildings and scenery enroute. On board there is a licensed bar with light refreshments and toilet facilities. Noon, Sunset & Disco Cruises: This trip takes you up towards Tewkesbury on the majestic River Severn, past the old village of Ashleworth and Wainlodes Hill, licensed bar, hot drinks and snacks available on evening trips. All Day Cruises: Running through a quiet rural landscape the River Severn offers a very pleasant trip, going through locks and a short visit to the old town of Tewkesbury. Also Canal trips to Sharpness. Three hour Sunset cruises on Wednesdays during June, July and August offer a peaceful voyage on the River Severn for individuals, parties and small groups. King Arthur, a boat new to Gloucester Docks, offers covered accommodation for larger groups and a range of party options from educational lecture theatre to discos. Food ranging from finger buffets to barbecues are available. A venue with a difference for a wedding reception or an office party, or family get together.

45min trips: Weekends only from Feb- Easter then daily to 31 Oct; Noon Cruises: July & Aug Wed 11.30-14.30; Sunset Cruises: May-Sept Wed 19.00-22.00, 9-30 Aug Sun 18.00-21.00; Disco Cruises: Fri 22 May, 26 June & 24 July 20.00-24.00, All Day Cruises (Tewkesbury): 5 Apr-4 Oct (call for dates) 10.00-17.00, (Sharpness): 18 Apr-20 Sept (call for dates) 10.00-17.00, (Gloucester): 16 May & 8 Aug 10.00-17.00. Call to confirm dates

Short Cruises: A£2.50 C(5-16)&OAPs£2.00 Pre-booked Groups £0.50 discount; Noon Cruises A£6.00 C(5-16)&OAPs£5.00 Family Ticket (A2+C2)£15.00. Disco Cruises: A£10.00. All Day Cruises: A£12.00 C(5-16)&OAPs£10.00 Family Ticket (A2+C2)£30.00. Sunset Cruise: A£6.00 C(5-16)&OAPs£5.00 Family Ticket (A2+C2)£15.00

Indian Chief Cruises

The Boat Inn Stoke Bruerne Towcester Northamptonshire NN12 7SB *(in village centre just off A508)*

Tel: 01604 862428

Take a leisurely cruise along the picturesque Grand Union Canal in the hospitable narrow boat Indian Chief. Trips available from 25 mins to 6hrs. Light buffet meals and teas by arrangement.

Easter-Sept and Santa Cruises in Dec, for public trips call for daily schedule

Prices vary, please call for details

Breweries

The Bass Museum

Horninglow Street Burton-On-Trent Staffordshire DE14 1YQ *(A50 from Stoke-on-Trent to Leicester)*

Tel: 01283 511000 Fax: 01283 513509

In the heart of England, in Britain's brewing capital of Burton-On-Trent, The Bass Museum brings together a unique collection of artifacts and memorabilia tracing the fascinating history of both the brewing industry and the family of William Bass, one of the world's most famous brewing dynasties. Using a mixture of audio-visual presentations and original brewing apparatus we explain the fascinating history of brewing. The art of coopering is kept alive in an authentic reconstruction. Wandering through these historic buildings you come across four of the most famous horses in the land. This history collection is presented on three floors of the old Joiners's Shop and includes many beautiful models, interactive displays and reconstructions. And So Much More...

All year Mon-Fri 10.00-17.00, Weekends 10.30-17.00

Last Admission: 16.00

A£3.75 C£2.00 Family Ticket £9.95, call for details on Educational Visits, hiring the venue for special occasions, Children's parties, pre-booked group tours, function rooms etc

Discount Card Offer: One Child Free With Each Paying Adult

THE BASS MUSEUM

Butterfly Farms

Stratford-Upon-Avon Butterfly Farm

Swans Nest Lane Stratford-Upon-Avon Warwickshire CV37 7LS *(south bank of River Avon opposite RSC)*

Tel: 01789 299288 Fax: 01789 415878

Web Site: www.stratford.co.uk/butterfly

Europe's largest live Butterfly and Insect Exhibit. Hundreds of the world's most spectacular and colourful butterflies. Insect city one of the worlds largest collections. Arachnoland features the 'dealers in death' There is also an outdoor British butterfly garden in the summer.

Summer daily 10.00-18.00. Winter 10.00-dusk. Closed 25 Dec

🧒 suitable for pushchairs 👶 mother & baby facilities ♿ suitable for wheelchairs 🛍 gift shop
🤝 corporate facilities 🐕 no dogs: except guide dogs 🅿 parking on site 🅿 parking nearby
£ charged parking ☕ café-restaurant 🍷 licensed 🎪 special events 📚 educational pack

A£3.25 C£2.25 Family Ticket £9.95
Concessions£2.75. Special school tours can be
arranged

Castles

Ashby-De-La-Zouch Castle

South Street Ashby-De-La-Zouch Leicestershire
LE65 1BR *(in Ashby de la Zouch 12m S of Derby on
A50, Bus: Stevensons 9 / 27 Burton-on-Trent -
Ashby-de-la-Zouch. BR: Burton-on-Trent 9m)*

Tel: 01530 413343

The impressive ruins of this late medieval castle
are dominated by a magnificent tower, over 24
metres (80 feet) high, which was split in two during
the Civil War. There are panoramic views of the surrounding countryside.

*1 Apr-31 Oct daily 10.00-18.00 (or dusk if earlier in
Oct), 1 Nov-31 Mar Wed-Sun 10.00-16.00, closed
13.00-14.00 in winter. Closed 24-26 Dec*
A£2.30 C£1.20 Concessions£1.70

Belvoir Castle

Belvoir Grantham Lincolnshire NG32 1PD *(between
A52 and A607)*

Tel: 01476 870262 Fax: 01476 870443

Home of the Dukes of Rutland for many centuries,
the turrets, battlements, towers and pinnacles of
the house are a 19th century fantasy. Featuring
paintings by Van Dyke, Murillo, Holbein and others.
Includes the museum of the Queens Royal Lancers.
The terraced gardens feature sculptures. Regular
jousting tournaments

*Apr-Sept Tue-Thur & Sat-Sun & Bank Hol 11.00-
17.00*
Last Admission: 16.00
*A£4.55 C£3.00 Family Ticket (A2+C2)£13.00
OAPs£3.50*

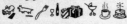

Berkeley Castle

Berkeley Gloucestershire GL13 9BQ *(on B4509
1.5m W of A38.)*

Tel: 01453 810332

Home of the Berkeley's for almost 850 years, the
castle is all one might expect - a great rambling
place surrounded by 14ft thick walls, with a
Norman keep, a great hall, medieval kitchens and
some splendid apartments. It is famous for the
dungeon where Edward II was gruesomely murdered in 1327.

*Apr & May daily 14.00-17.00, June-Sept Tue-Sat
11.00-17.00, Sun 14.00-17.00, July-Aug Mon-Sat
11.00-17.00*
Last Admission: 16.30

A£4.80 C£2.50 Family Ticket £13.00 OAPs£3.80.
Price increase due April 1998

Bolsover Castle

Castle Bungalows Castle Street Bolsover
Chesterfield Derbyshire S44 6PR *(J29 M1 6m E of
Chesterfield on A632)*

Tel: 01246 823349

Built on the site of a Norman Castle this is largely
seventeenth century mansion, explore the romanticism of the 'Little Castle' a unique celebration of
Jacobean romanticism and the impressive internal
seventeenth century riding school.

*22 Mar-31 Oct daily 10.00-18.00 or dusk, 1 Nov-31
Mar Wed-Sun 10.00-16.00. Closed 24-26 Dec*
A£2.95 C£2.20 OAPs&Students&UB40£1.50

Clun Castle

Clun Shropshire *(in Clun off A488 18m W of Ludlow,
Bus: Midland Red West 741-5/773 from Ludlow, BR:
Hopton Heath 6.5m)*

Tel: 01604 730320

The remains of a four-storey keep and other buildings of this border castle.

Any reasonable time
Admission Free

✠

Croft Castle

Croft Leominster Herefordshire HR6 9PW *(5m NW
of Leominster 9m SW of Ludlow approach from
B4362 turning N at Cock Gate between Bircher and
Mortimer's Cross signposted from Ludlow /
Leominster road A49 and from A4110 at Mortimer's
Cross. BR: Leominster)*

Tel: 01568 780246

Home of the Croft family since Domesday with a
break of 170 years from 1750. The walls and corner
towers date from 14th/15th centuries, while the
interior is mainly 18th century. Avenue of 350 year
old Spanish chestnuts runs through the park and
an Iron Age fort (Croft Ambrey) may be reached by
footpath.

*29-30 Mar 13.30-16.30, Apr Sat-Sun 13.30-16.30,
May-Sept Wed-Sun & Bank Hol Mon 13.30-17.30,
Oct Sat-Sun 13.30-16.30. Grounds, car park, Croft
Ambrey open all year*
Last Admission: 30mins before closing
*A£3.20 C£1.60 Family Ticket £8.00, Car park £1.50
per car, £10 coaches*

Eastnor Castle

Eastnor Ledbury Herefordshire HR8 1RL *(1.5m E on A438)*

Tel: 01531 633160 Fax: 01531 631776

A magnificent Georgian castle in a fairytale setting with a deer park, arboretum and lake. Inside tapestries, fine art and armour. The Italianate and Gothic interiors have been restored to a superb standard. There is a children's adventure playground and delightful nature trails and lakeside walks. Homemade teas are available.

Easter-4 Oct Sun & Bank Hol Mon 11.00-17.00, July-Aug Sun-Fri 11.00-17.00
Last Admission: 16.30
Castle & Grounds: A£4.50 C£2.00. Family Ticket £11.00. Grounds: A£2.50 C£1.00. Groups 20+ £3.50, Guided Tours £4.75

Goodrich Castle

Goodrich Ross-on-Wye Worcestershire HR9 6HY *(5m S of Ross-on-Wye off A40)*

Tel: 01600 890538

Goodrich Castle towers majestically over an ancient crossing of the River Wye. The castle was built here in medieval times and saw much action during the Civil War, when a locally made cannon called 'Roaring Meg' was used to bombard the Royalist garrison ending a long siege. The cannon can still be seen at Hereford Cathedral.

1 Apr-31 Oct daily 10.00-18.00 or dusk if sooner, 1 Nov-31 Mar 10.00-16.00. Closed 13.00-14.00. Closed 24-26 Dec & 1 Jan
A£2.95 C£1.50 Concessions£2.20

Hartlebury Castle State Rooms

Stourport Road Hartlebury Kidderminster Worcestershire DY11 7XX *(5m S of Hartlebury)*

Tel: 01299 250410

The elegant interior of this castle, the seat of the Bishops of Worcester since 850, reveals little of its long and sometimes troubled history. Its present Gothic appearance dates from the 18th century.

Easter Mon-1 Sept 1st Sun in month plus Bank Hol Mon & Tue 14.00-17.00. Also Wed Easter-Aug 14.00-16.00
A£0.75 C&OAPs£0.50

Kenilworth Castle

Castle Green Kenilworth Warwickshire CV8 1NE *(at W end of Kenilworth town)*

Tel: 01926 852078

The largest castle ruin in England - its massive walls tower over the peaceful Warwickshire landscape. The grim Norman keep featuring twenty foot thick walls was already nearly 500 years old when Elizabeth I visited in 1575. John of Gaunt's Great Hall is second only in width and grandeur to Westminster Hall. Fine views from the tower.

1 Apr-31 Oct daily 10.00-18.00 or dusk if sooner, 1 Nov-31 Mar 10.00-16.00. Closed 24-26 Dec
A£3.10 C£1.60 Concessions£2.30

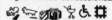

Kirby Muxloe Castle

Oakcroft Avenue Kirby Muxloe Leicestershire LE9 9DM *(off B5380 4m W of Leicester)*

Tel: 01604 730320

Picturesque ruined fortified manor house with moat, gatehouse and towers. Brick built started 1480 by Lord Hastings - executed in 1483, building never completed.

Any reasonable time. Closed 24-26 Dec & 1 Jan
A£1.75 C£1.30 OAPs£0.90

Longtown Castle

Abbey Dore Hereford and Worcester *(4m of Abbey Dore)*

Tel: 01604 730320

An unusual cylindrical keep built c.1200 with walls 4.5 metres (15 feet) thick.

Any reasonable time
Admission Free

Ludlow Castle

Castle Square Ludlow Shropshire SY8 1AY *(0.75 m from A49, located in centre of Ludlow, road runs out at Castle)*

Tel: 01584 873355

Ludlow Castle dates from about 1086 and was greatly extended as ownership passed through the de Lacy and Mortimer families to the Crown. In 1473 Edward IV sent the Prince of Wales and his brother to Ludlow and Ludlow Castle became a seat of government with the establishment there of the Council for Wales and the Marches. To bring ancient and modern together the Holodeck - a permanent hologram exhibition consisting of a wide range of holographic images. Giant Kaleidosphere, Face to Face Illusion. Plus much more for the whole family to see and do. Entry to Shop free of charge. Dogs welcome on leads.

May-Sept daily 10.30-17.00, Oct-Dec & Feb-Apr 10.30-16.00, Jan Weekends only 10.30-16.00
Last Admission: 30mins before closing
Castle: A£2.50 C(6-16)£1.50 C(0-6)£Free Family Ticket (A2+C2)£7.50 OAPs£2.00. School parties by arrangement, 10% discount on parties of 10+.

🏃 suitable for pushchairs   👶 mother & baby facilities   ♿ suitable for wheelchairs   🎁 gift shop
🤝 corporate facilities   🐕 no dogs: except guide dogs   🅿 parking on site   🅿 parking nearby
£ charged parking   🍴 café-restaurant   🍷 licensed   🎂 special events   📚 educational pack

Holodeck: A£1.50 C£0.50, All children must be accompanied by an adult

Newark Castle

Castle Gate Newark Nottinghamshire NG24 1BG *(in Port Glasgow on the A8)*
Tel: 01636 611908 Fax: 01636 611274
Newark Castle stands proudly on the River Trent in the pretty market town of Newark-on-Trent. Built in the early 12th Century, the Castle has the finest Norman gatehouse in England. 'The Castle Story' exhibition, in the nearby Gilstrap Heritage Centre, unlocks the 800 year history of this historic monument.
Any reasonable time
Admission Free

Nottingham Castle Museum and Art Gallery

Nottingham Nottinghamshire NG1 6EL *(near city centre on A52)*
Tel: 0115 915 3687 Fax: 0115 915 3653
Sited on a high rock, Nottingham Castle commands spectacular views over the city and once rivalled great castles of Windsor and the Tower of London with all kings from William the Conqueror to Henry VIII staying there at one time. Now houses magnificent fine art, silver, ceramic, ethnographic and social history collections.
All year daily 10.00-17.00. Museum 13.00-17.00.
Closed 25-26 Dec & Fri during Nov-Mar
Mon-Fri £Free, Weekends & Bank Hol A£1.50
C&Concessions£0.75

Oakham Castle

Market Place Oakham Leicestershire *(off Market Place)*
Tel: 01572 723654 Fax: 01572 757576
An exceptionally fine Norman Great Hall of a 12th century fortified manor house. Earthworks, walls and remains of an earlier motte can be seen along with medieval sculptures and unique presentation horseshoes fortified by peers of the realm and royalty to the Lord of the Manor.
All year. Grounds: daily 10.00-17.30, late Oct-late Mar 10.00-16.00. Great Hall: Tue-Sat & Bank Hol Mon 10.00-13.00 & 14.00-17.30 Sun 14.00-17.30, late Oct-late Mar 10.00-16.00. Closed Mon, Good Fri & Christmas
Admission Free

Peveril Castle

Market Place Castleton Hope Valley South Yorkshire S33 8WQ *(on S side of Castleton, 15m W of Sheffield on A625)*
Tel: 01433 620613
William Peveril, one of William the Conqueror's most trusted Knights, guarded the King's manor in the peak from this natural vantage point. Today's visitor is greeted with spectacular views across the Hope valley and beyond. The site is a Site of Special Scientific Interest.
22 Mar-31 Oct daily 10.00-18.00 or dusk if sooner, 1 Nov- 31 Mar Wed-Sun 10.00-16.00. Closed 24-26 Dec
A£1.60 C£0.80 Concessions£1.20, Special Event days: A£2.50 C£1.50 Concessions£2.00

ROCKINGHAM CASTLE

Rockingham Castle

Rockingham Castle Estate Rockingham Market Harborough Leicestershire LE16 8TH *(2m N of Corby, 9m from Market Harborough, 14m from Stamford on A427, visitors entrance on A6003 S of J with A6116)*
Tel: 01536 770240 Fax: 01536 771692
Set on a hill overlooking three counties, Rockingham Castle was built by William the Conqueror. The castle was a royal residence for 450 years. Then in the 16th century Henry VIII granted it to Edward Watson.
Easter Sun-18 Oct Thur, Sun, Bank Hol Mon & following Tue also Tue in Aug 13.00-17.00, daily for pre-booked parties and schools. Grounds: Sun & Bank Hol Mon 11.30. Light refreshments from 12.00. Winter months daily by appointment for pre-booked parties and schools only
House & Garden: A£4.00 C£2.60 Family Ticket (A2+C2)£11.00 OAPs£3.60. Group rates (minimum of £70.00: A&OAPs£3.60 Students£1.70. Grounds: All £2.50

Shrewsbury Castle and Shropshire Regimental Museum

Castle Gates Shrewsbury Shropshire SY1 2AT
(Shrewsbury Town Centre)
Tel: 01743 358516 Fax: 01743 358411
Re-opened in 1995 after a two year closure, the museum of The King's Shropshire Light Infantry and The Shropshire Yeomanry is housed within the main surviving building of Shrewsbury Castle. This was a Norman fortification commanding the historic town of Shrewsbury. Thomas Telford was responsible for alterations to the castle in the 18th century.
Tue-Sat 10.00-16.30 & Sun from Easter-Sept & Bank Hol Mon. Castle grounds open Mon. Closed Dec 1997-Feb 1998
Last Admission: Museum 16.30 Castle 17.00
A£2.00 C£0.50 Student&OAPs£1.00. Inclusive ticket to Rowley's House, Clive House & Regimental Museum A£4.00 C£1.00 Student&OAPs£2.00

St Briavel's Castle

St Briavel Gloucestershire *(in St Briavel 7m NE of Chepstow off B4228)*
Tel: 01604 730320
A splendid 12th-century castle now used as a youth hostel, which is appropriate for a building set in such marvellous walking country.
Exterior: Any reasonable time. Bailey: 1 Apr-30 Sept daily 13.00-16.00
Admission Free

STAFFORD CASTLE

Stafford Castle

off Newport Road Stafford Staffordshire ST16 1DJ
(off the A518 Newport Road, SW of Stafford)
Tel: 01785 257698 Fax: 01785 257698
The site of a Norman timber fortress, now covered by the ruins of a 19th century Gothic Revival building. The Visitor Centre contains an audio-visual display, model reconstructions. Limited access for wheelchairs to visitor centre only.
Visitor Centre: Apr-Oct Tue-Sun 10.00-17.00, Nov-Mar Tue-Sun 10.00-16.00. Closed Mon except Bank Hol, call for Christmas and New Year opening

A£1.75 Family Ticket (A2+C2)£4.00 Concessions£1.10

Stokesay Castle

Stokesay Craven Arms Shropshire SY7 9AH *(7m NW of Ludlow off A49)*

Tel: 01588 672544

Wonderfully preserved and little altered, this 13th-century manor house has a romantic setting in peaceful countryside. Special features are the timber-framed Jacobean gatehouse, the great hall and, reached by an outside staircase, a solar with 17th-century panelling. Parish church nearby.

1 Apr-31 Oct daily 10.00-18.00 or dusk if sooner, 1 Nov-31 Mar Wed-Sun 10.00-16.00. Closed 24-26 Dec. Closed 13.00-14.00 in Winter

A£2.95 C£1.50 Concessions£2.20. Personal stereo included in admission price

Sudeley Castle and Gardens

Winchcombe Cheltenham Gloucestershire GL54 5JD
(from Bristol or Birmingham J9 M5 then A438 to Stow on The Wold, 8m NE of Cheltenham on B4632)

Tel: 01242 602308 Fax: 01242 602959

Sudley Castle, one of England's most delightful historic houses was once the palace of Katherine Parr, who is buried in the Chapel; Henry VIII, Anne Boleyn, Lady Jane Grey and Elizabeth I stayed here. The Queens Garden is famous for its rose collection. A wildfowl sanctuary, exhibition centre and plant centre are other features of Sudley.

Gardens, Plant Centre & Shop: Mar Tue-Sun 11.00-16.30. Castle & Gardens: 1 Apr-31 May Tue-Sun & Bank Hol Mon 11.00-17.00, 1 June-13 Sept daily 11.00-17.00, Gardens 11.00-17.30, 14 Sept-31 Oct Tue-Sun 11.00-17.00, closed 9 & 10 May. Shop, Gardens & Church: 28 Nov-20 Dec Thur-Sun 11.00-15.30

Castle & Gardens: Weekends: A£5.95 C£3.00 OAPs£4.95, Bank Hol: A£5.95 C£3.95 OAPs£4.95. Gardens only: Weekends: A£4.45 C£1.95 OAPs£3.45 Bank Hol: A£4.45 C£1.95 OAPs£3.45. Group rates available.

🛒 suitable for pushchairs 👶 mother & baby facilities ♿ suitable for wheelchairs 🎁 gift shop
🤝 corporate facilities 🐕 no dogs: except guide dogs 🚗 parking on site 🅿 parking nearby
£ charged parking ☕ café-restaurant 🍴 licensed 🎉 special events 📚 educational pack

TAMWORTH CASTLE

Tamworth Castle

The Holloway Tamworth Staffordshire B79 7LR *(J10 M42, signposted off A51 and A5)*
Tel: 01827 63563 Fax: 01827 56567
Web Site: www.zipmail.co.uk/tbc
A mixture of Norman, Gothic, Tudor, Jacobean and early 19th century architecture. Starting as a Norman motte-and-bailey shell-keep, with walls 10ft thick at the base; outer walls and gatehouse added in the 13th century. Tudor period brought a splendid timber-roofed great hall and a warder's lodge. Outside floral terraces with adventure playground and much more.
All year Mon-Sat 10.00-17.30, Sun 14.00-17.30.
Closed 24-26 Dec
Last Admission: 16.30
A£3.40 C&Concessions£1.75 Family Ticket £8.55
NB: Wheelchair users confined to ground floor: for this reason special prices apply

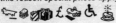

Warwick Castle

Castle Hill Warwick Warwickshire CV34 4QU *(J15 M40 then A429 into Warwick)*
Tel: 01926 406600 Fax: 01926 401692
One Castle, Many Eras: The Mediaeval Period 1068-1485, Kingmaker - a preparation for battle, 1471, Armoury, Dungeon and Torture Chamber, Tower and Ramparts. The Tudor and Jacobean Period 1485-1625, The Ghost Tower - refurbished in Easter 1997. The 17th and 18th Centuries, The Great Hall, State Rooms and Chapel, Grounds and Gardens. The Victorian Period 1837-1091, Royal Weekend Party 1989, Victorian Rose Garden.
Visitor Comments: 'don't miss the jousting tournaments'
All year daily 10.00-18.00, Nov-Mar 10.00-17.00.
Closed 25 Dec
Last Admission: 30mins before closing
A£9.25 C£5.60 Family Ticket £26.00 OAPs£6.65
June-Aug A£9.95 C£5.95 Family Ticket £27.00

Wigmore Castle

Hereford and Worcester *(11m NW of Leominster 14m SW of Ludlow off W side of A4110 BR: Leominster 11m)*
Tel: 01604 730320
There has been a castle at Wigmore since the 1060's and the present ruins date from the late 13th and early 14th centuries, when the Mortimers were at the height of their power. The castle was dismantled in 1643 by parliamentary troops during the Civil War.
Telephone for details
Admission Free

Cathedrals

Coventry Cathedral and Visitor Centre

Priory Row Coventry West Midlands CV1 5ES *(signposted from M6 M69 A45 & A46)*
Tel: 01203 227597 Fax: 01203 631448
Coventry's old cathedral was bombed during an air raid of November 1940 which devastated the city. The remains have been carefully preserved. The new cathedral was designed by Sir Basil Spence and consecrated in May 1962. There is also an opportunity to enjoy an audio-visual display in the visitor's centre.
All year daily Easter-Sept 09.30-18.00, Oct-Easter 09.30-17.30. Visitor Centre: restricted opening Oct-Apr
Visitors Centre A£1.25 C(0-6)£Free C(6-16)Students & OAPs£0.75 Camera charge £1.00. Video charge £3.00

Hereford Cathedral

Cathedral Close Hereford Herefordshire HR1 2NG *(J7 M5, A4103 Worcester, venue signposted around the City)*
Tel: 01432 359880 Fax: 01432 355929
The Seat of Hereford is one of the oldest in England, the first bishop having been appointed in 676AD. The cathedral is mainly Norman with a 13th-century Lady Chapel. It also contains the Diocesan Treasure and the St. Thomas Becket Reliquary. The Cathedral Guides provide tours at 11.30 and 14.30
Cathedral daily 08.00-18.00, Mappa Mundi & Chained Library Exhibition Mon-Sat 10.00-16.15, Sun 12.00-15.15
Last Admission: 16.15
Mappa Mundi & Chained Library Exhibition: A£4.00 Concessions£3.00 Family Ticket £10.00 Party 10+ A£3.50 Concessions£2.50 School Groups 10+

Primary £1.00 p/h Secondary £2.00 p/h

Lichfield Cathedral

The Close Lichfield Staffordshire WS13 7LD *(from North: J12 M6 then A5/A461; from South: J4 M6 to M42 then A38; from North: J28 M1 then A38; from South: J17 M1 to M6 then route as before signpost-ed from A38 and A5)*

Tel: 01543 306240 Fax: 01543 306109

Web Site: www.lichfield-cathedral.org

An 800 year old Gothic Cathedral with three spires, dedicated to St Chad and set in unspoilt Close. See Lichfield Gospels - an 8th century illuminated man-uscript; 16th century Flemish glass; sculptures by Chantry and Epstein and a modern silver collection. Venue for Lichfield International Music Festival.

All year daily 07.45-18.00

Suggested donation A£3.00

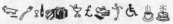

Worcester Cathedral

College Green Worcester Worcestershire WR1 2LH

Tel: 01905 28854/21004 Fax: 01905 611139

Worcester Cathedral with its 200 foot tower stands majestically beside the River Severn. The Crypt, built by St. Wulstan in 1084, is a classic example of Norman architecture. The 12th century Chapter House and Cloisters are a reminder of the cathe-dral's monastic past. King John and Prince Arthur are buried near the High Altar.

All year daily 7.30-18.00

Admission Free: Invite donation of A£2.00. Groups essential to book in advance

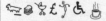

Caverns

Blue-John Cavern and Mine

Buxton Road Castleton Sheffield S30 2WP *(on the A625 at the foot of Mam-Tor)*

Tel: 01433 620638 Fax: 01433 621586

The cavern is a remarkable example of a water-worn cave, and measures over a third of a mile long, with chambers 200ft high. It contains 8 of the 14 veins of Blue John stone and has been the major source of this unique form of fluorspar for nearly 300 years.

All year daily 09.30-18.00 or dusk if sooner. Winter: weather permitting

A5.00 C(5-15)£3.00 OAPs&Students£4.00. Group rates on application

Peak Cavern

Peak Cavern Road Castleton Hope Valley Derbyshire S33 8WS *(on an A625, 15m W of Sheffield, 25m E of Manchester, in centre of Castleton village)*

Tel: 01433 620285 Fax: 01433 620285

The Peak Cavern is the largest natural cavern in Derbyshire, and has the largest entrance to any cave in Britain. A village once existed inside the cave entrance, built and inhabited by rope makers, who carried out their craft in the cave for over 300 years.

Apr-Oct daily 10.00-17.00, Nov-Mar Sat & Sun 10.00-16.00

Last Admission: 1 hour before closing

A£4.00 C(5-15)£2.00 Family Ticket (A2+C2)£10.50. Additional children £1.50 Concessions£3.00. Group rates: A£2.50 C£1.30. School Parties: Teacher Free C£1.30

Poole's Cavern and Buxton Country Park

Green Lane Buxton Derbyshire SK17 9DH *(A515 Ashbourne road 15min walk from Buxton town cen-tre)*

Tel: 01298 26978 Fax: 01298 26978

Limestone rock, water and millions of years created this magnificent natural cavern. Rich in spectacular formations including Derbyshire's largest stalactite and the unique Poached Egg chamber. Set in 100 acres of beautiful woodland with walks to a panoramic viewpoint tower at 1440ft.

Mar-Oct daily 10.00-17.00

Last Admission: 17.00

Queuing Times: 20mins

A£3.80 C£2.00 Concessions£3.00

Discount Card Offer: One Child Or Adult Free With One Full Paying Adult

Speedwell Cavern

Castleton Sheffield South Yorkshire S30 2WA *(off A625 0.5m W of Castleton Village)*

Tel: 01433 620512 Fax: 01433 621888

🡒 suitable for pushchairs 🍼 mother & baby facilities ♿ suitable for wheelchairs 🎁 gift shop
🤝 corporate facilities 🐕 no dogs: except guide dogs 🚗 parking on site 🚙 parking nearby
£ charged parking 🍴 café-restaurant ‖ licensed 🎂 special events 📖 educational pack

Visitors descend 105 steps to a boat which takes them on a one-mile underground exploration of the floodlit cavern with its 'bottomless pit.'
All year daily, Summer: 09.30-17.00, Winter: 10.00-16.00
A£5.00 C£3.00 Concessions£4.00. Group rates on application

The Heights of Abraham Cable Cars Cavern and Country Park

Upperwood Road Matlock Bath Matlock Derbyshire DE4 3PD *(on A6 N of Derby)*
Tel: 01629 582365 Fax: 01629 580279
High above the village of Matlock Bath are the Grounds of the Heights of Abraham. Cable cars provide a spectacular way of reaching the top.
Two famous show caverns provide fascinating tours.
There is also a nature trail, owl maze, the explorers challenge and landscaped water gardens. Allow 3 hrs minimum.
Easter-Oct 10.00-17.00, later in high season
Last Admission: Last cable car advertised at office
A£6.20 C£4.10 OAPs£5.20. Groups rates 10+
A£5.20 C£3.60 OAPs£4.10

Treak Cliff Cavern

Buxton Road Castleton Hope Valley Sheffield S33 2WP *(Castleton is situated at the centre of the Peak National Park on the A625. 16m from Sheffield and 29m from Manchester within easy reach of the M1 and M6)*
Tel: 01433 620571 Fax: 01433 620519
Web Site: www.bluejohnstone.com
Discover the rich deposits of the rare and beautiful Blue John Stone and fine stalactite's and stalagmites on a guided tour of the Caverns, which are illuminated by electric lighting and have safe clean footpaths. School workpack free on application.
Mar-Oct daily 09.30-17.30, Nov-Feb daily 10.00-16.00. Later at weekends and Bank Hol. Closed 25 Dec
Last Admission: Last tour 40mins before closing
A£4.95 C(5-15)£2.25 Family Ticket £13.00 Concessions£3.95. Discounts for pre-booked groups

Caves

Clearwell Caves Ancient Iron Mines

Coleford Royal Forest of Dean Gloucestershire GL16 8JR *(1.5m S of Coleford town centre on B4228 signposted from Coleford Town Centre)*
Tel: 01594 832535 Fax: 01594 833362

The mines have worked from Iron Age times, 2500 years ago. Today nine large caverns can be explored. Visitors descend 100 feet underground. Deeper trips can be arranged for the more adventurous. Geological and mining displays, blacksmith's shop, Ochre Room, shop and tearoom. Working continues today.
Mar-Oct daily 10.00-17.00, all other times by arrangement only
Last Admission: 17.00
A£3.00 C£2.00 Concessions£2.50

THE CAVES OF NOTTINGHAM

The Caves of Nottingham

Drury Walk Broad Marsh Centre Nottingham Nottinghamshire NG1 7LS *(within Broadmarsh Shopping centre)*
Tel: 0115 924 1424
Step down into the past and explore 'Tigguo Cobavc' - a city of caves. Listen to the unique audio tape as it guides you through 700 year old manmade caves. See the medieval tannery, beer cellars, air raid shelters and the remains of Drury Hill, one of the most historic streets in Nottingham.
All year Mon-Sat 10.00-17.00, Sun 11.00-17.00. Closed 25-26 Dec
Last Admission: 1 hour before closing
A£2.95 Family Ticket £8.50 Concessions£1.95
Discount Card Offer: 45p Off Admissions

Churches

St Mary's Church

Kempley Gloucestershire *(1m N of Kempley off B4024, 6m NE of Ross-on-Wye)*
Tel: 01604 730320
A Norman church with superb wall paintings from the 12th-14th centuries.
1 Apr-30 Sept daily 10.00-18.00. 1 Oct-31 Mar 10.00-16.00. Closed 24-26 Dec & 1 Jan

Admission Free

Staunton Harold Church

Staunton Harold Ashby-de-la-Zouch Leicestershire *(5m NE of Ashby-de-la-Zouch W of B587)*
Tel: 01332 863822 Fax: 01332 865272
One of the very few churches to be built dating the Commonwealth. The interior retains its original 17th century cushions and hangings, and includes fine panelling and painted ceilings. The wrought-iron screen was designed by Robert Bakewell. In attractive parkland and stands next to Staunton Hall.
Apr-Sept Sat-Wed & Bank Hol Mon 13.00-17.00 or sunset if sooner. Oct Sat & Sun only 13.00-17.00. Closed Good Fri
Donations of £1.00, collection box. Voluntary vehicle charge may be requested on busy Summer Sun & Bank Hol Mon

Churches & Chapels

Langley Chapel

Acton Burnell Shropshire *(1.5m S of Acton Burnell on unclassified road off A49. 9.5m S of Shrewsbury. Bus: Boultons / Midland Red Church Stretton / Shrewsbury Sat only to within 1.5m. BR: Shrewsbury 7.5m)*
Tel: 01604 730320
A delightful medieval chapel, standing alone in a field, with a complete set of early 17th century wooden fittings and furniture.
All year any reasonable time. Closed 24-26 Dec
Admission Free

Odda's Chapel

Deerhurst Gloucestershire *(in Deerhurst off B4213 nr River Severn at Abbots Court SW of parish church)*
A rare Saxon chapel was built by Earl Odda and dedicated in 1056. It was discovered attached to a half-timbered farmhouse and has been restored.
Easter-30 Sept daily 10.00-18.00. 1 Oct-Easter daily 10.00-16.00. Closed 24-26 Dec & 1 Jan
Admission Free

Rotherwas Chapel

Hereford Hereford and Worcester *(1.5m SE of Hereford on B4399 Bus- Hereford Hopper 110/1/8 from City Centre BR: Hereford 3.5m)*
Tel: 01604 730320
This Roman Catholic chapel dates from the 14th and 16th centuries and features an interesting mid-

Victorian side chapel.
Any reasonable time. Key-keeper at nearby filling station
Admission Free

City Tours

Guide Friday in Birmingham

14 Rother Street The Civic Hall Stratford-upon-Avon Warwickshire
Tel: 01789 294466 Fax: 01789 414681
"Europe's Meeting Place" with a wealth of tourist attractions based on its rich industrial heritage. Tour highlights include Cadbury World, National Sea Life Centre, Bournville Village, The Botanical Gardens and Jewellery Quarter. For booking please telephone 01789 294466.
Daily 17 May-14 Sept. Please phone for times and departure points.
A£7.50/£6.50, C£2.00/£1.50, OAPs&Students£5.50. Pre-booking discount of up to £2.50 on each tour ticket.

Guide Friday in Bourton-on-the-Water

14 Rother Street The Civic Hall Stratford-upon-Avon Warwickshire
Tel: 01789 294466 Fax: 01789 414681
Explore Bourton-on-the-Water, Upper and Lower Slaughter and picturesque Cotswold Villages by Open Top single decker bus. For booking please telephone 01789 294466.
Sun & Bank Hol 31 Mar-14 June, daily 14 June-7 Sept, 13&14 Sept only. Please phone for times and departure points.
No pre-booking discounts available. Please phone for prices.

Guide Friday in Europe

14 Rother Street The Civic hall Stratford-upon-Avon Warwickshire CV37 6LU
Tel: 01789 294466 Fax: 01789 414681
Discover the best of Spanish architecture, including the Spanish Square, the Cathedral and 13th Century Golden Tower. This is a taped tour. For booking please telephone 01789 294466.
All year daily. Please phone for times and departure points.
No pre-booking discounts available on this tour. Please phone for prices.

Guide Friday in Europe

14 Rother Street The Civic Hall Stratford-upon-Avon Warwickshire CV37 6LU

Tel: 01789 294466 Fax: 01789 414681
See the remains of the infamous wall. Unterden Linden (Berlin's most beautiful boulevard), Brandenburg Gate and The Reichstag. For booking please telephone 01789 294466.
All year daily. Telephone for times and departure points.
No pre-booking discounts available - please phone for prices

Guide Friday Ltd
14 Rother Street The Civic Hall Stratford-upon-Avon Warwickshire CV37 6LU
Tel: 01789 294466 Fax: 01789 414681
The best way to see Britain's historic towns and cities. The world's largest open top sightseeing tour bus operator over 700 tours daily nationwide. Tickets valid all day so you can get off as you please at places of interest with frequent stops all round the circular route. All tours include principal sights. Your tour ticket also provides discounts at many major attractions and places to visit, restaurants and retailers.
All year daily . See separate listings for details.
Up to £2.50 pre-booking discount on certain tours, please see separate listings for individual prices

Guide Friday Stratford-upon-Avon
14 Rother Street The Civic Hall Stratford-upon-Avon Warwickshire CV37 6LU
Tel: 01789 294466 Fax: 01789 414681
Web Site: www.stratford.co.uk
Home of the Bard of Avon. A beautiful market town with the Shakespeare Houses giving a fascinating insight into Elizabethan life. Tour highlights include the Shakespeare Houses, The Royal Shakespeare Theatre, Holy Trinity Church, where Shakespeare is buried and the River Avon. For booking please telephone 01789 294466.
All year daily. Please phone for times and departure points.
A£8.00 C£2.50 OAPs&Students£6.50. Pre-booking discount available. Group rates on request

Country Estates

Dinmore Manor
Dinmore Hereford Herefordshire HR4 8EE *(off A49 1.5m)*
Tel: 01432 830322 Fax: 01432 830503
The manor enjoys outstanding views of the surrounding countryside. The cloister's, South Room, Roof Walk, Chapel, Music Room (Great Hall), and Grotto are all open to the public. The chapel, dating

back to the 12th century, is in a unique setting next to the rock garden, pools, the collection of old acers, and the 1200-year-old yew tree.
All year daily 10.00-17.30
A£2.50 Accompanied C(0-14)£Free

Rode Hall
Scholar Green Congleton Cheshire ST7 3QP *(5m SW of Congleton between A34 & A50 BR: Alsager 2.25m)*
Tel: 01270 873237 Fax: 01270 882962
18th century country house with Georgian stable block set in a Humphrey Reaton landscape. Later alterations by L Wyatt and Darcy Braddell. Large walled kitchen garden.
3 Apr-25 Sept Wed & Bank Hol 14.00-17.00. Garden only Tue & Thur 14.00-17.00
House, Garden & Kitchen Garden: A£3.50. Garden & Kitchen Garden A£2.00

SHUGBOROUGH ESTATE

Shugborough Estate
Shugborough Milford Stafford Staffordshire ST17 0XB *(6m E of Stafford off A513. J13 M6 on A513 Stafford /Lichfield Road)*
Tel: 01889 881388 Fax: 01889 881323
The 900 acre seat of the Earls of Lichfield. The 18th century mansion house contains fine collections of ceramics, silver, paintings and french furniture. Other attractions include Grade I listed garden, county museum, laundry, kitchens and coach houses. Rare breeds farmstead with fully restored working corn mill. Children's parties at Shugborough: activities available on request to include a cart ride and a birthday feast. Minimum 10, call for details.
28 Mar-27 Sept daily 11.00-17.00, Oct Sun only. Open all year to pre-booked parties
Mansion: A£3.50 C&OAPs&UB40s£2.50. County Museum: A£3.50 C&OAPs&UB40s£2.50. Park Farm: A£3.50 C&Concessions£2.50. Combined ticket: A£8.00 C&OAPs&UB40s£6.00 Family Ticket £18.00. Car Parking: £1.50

Sudbury Hall and The Museum of Childhood

Sudbury Ashbourne Derbyshire DE6 5HT *(6m E of Uttoxeter at the crossing point of A50 Derby /Stoke and A515 Lichfield /Ashbourne roads)*

Tel: 01283 585305 Fax: 01283 585139

One of the most individual and richly decorated late 17th century country houses with superb wood carvings and plasterwork. The great staircase is one of the finest in England. The Museum of Childhood contains fascinating displays about growing up in Victorian and Edwardian times. 'Sweep sized' visitors can try the chimney climb before admiring the fine collections of toys and dolls.

Hall & Museum: 1 Apr-1 Nov Wed-Sun & Bank Hol Mon 13.00-17.30. All weekends throughout season & all Open Days in July & Aug 12.30-17.00. Closed Good Fri. Shop open as Hall. Coach House Tea Room 12.30-17.30

Last Admission: 30mins before closing

House: A£3.50 C£1.60 Family Ticket £8.60. House & Museum: A£5.50 C£2.70 Family Ticket £13.70

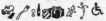

Country Leisure Parks

Billing Aquadrome Limited

Crow Lane Little Billing Northampton Northamptonshire NN3 9DA *(follow the Billing Aquadrome signs from J15 M1 - just 15mins away via dual carriageway - or pick up the signed routes from Northampton which is just 10 minutes away)*

Tel: 01604 408181 Fax: 01604 784412

Renowned for a wide range of leisure facilities, incl. a swimming pool and licensed bars offering tempting meals and a variety of amusements. For children there are plenty of free play areas, a safe paddling pool, walks and bicycle rides, and an exciting range of family amusements. Anglers can try their luck on the river or the lakes within our natural wildlife environment. Within the Park complex we have a funfair, jet-ski's, a supermarket, a wide variety of fast-food outlets, a caravan / camping accessory shop, a launderette, public telephones. Many sites have electrical hook-up points and are all within easy reach of modern and fully equipped toilet blocks.

All year daily 17 Mar-6 Jan '99

Day Visitor Charges: Mon-Sat £4.00 per car, Sun & Bank Hol Mon at all times £5.00 per car, Mon-Thur at all other times £2.00 per car, Pedestrians £1.00 at all times, additional cars will be charged at £4.00. Caravan charges vary according to duration etc.

MINIATURE TRAIN AT BILLING AQUADROME

Country Parks

Beacon Hill Country Park

Beacon Road Woodhouse Eaves Loughborough Leicestershire *(B591 off A6)*

Tel: 01509 890048

180 acres of undulating heathland, bracken, woods, rhododendrons, and rocky summit with superb views. Remains of Bronze Age settlement near summit. New Nature Tree collection.

All year daily during daylight hours

Admission Free

Broadway Tower Country Park

Broadway Worcestershire WR12 7LB *(off A44 5m SE of Evesham, 1m E of Broadway)*

Tel: 01386 852390 Fax: 01386 858829

This unique folly tower, situated high on top of the Cotswold ridge, was built in 1799 and offers spectacular views over 12 Counties. There are exhibitions on its illustrious history and inhabitants, including William Morris, the famous designer. Family fun for all ages includes: adventure playground, free use of BBQs, animal enclosures and more.

Good Fri-31 Oct daily 10.00-18.00 (or dusk if earlier)

Last Admission: 17.15 for Tower

A£3.00 C£2.20 Family Ticket £9.00 OAPs£2.50

Passport Tickets (Free admission for one year)

A£9.00 C£6.60 Family Ticket £27.00 OAPs£7.50

Burton Dassett Hills Country Park

Northend Leamington Spa Warwickshire *(J12 M40 in Northend)*

Tel: 01827 872660 Fax: 01827 875161

Web Site: www.warwickshire.gov.uk

The Country Park, covering about 100 acres, is situated on a spur of rugged hills projecting into a relatively flat plain, as a result the hills provide magnificent views in all directions. The Church of All

Saints nearby and the Brecon Tower, an ancient monument and the focal point of the hills, provide additional interest while the old worked-out quarries provide excellent places for exploration by children. The openness of the hills encourages picnicking, walking, kite and model glider flying etc. and of course just sitting and sunbathing; when it snows the hills are ideal for tobogganing and skiing. Roads and footpaths across the hills are unfenced and the public have had access for many years. The hills were purchased by the County Council in 1971 with assistance from the Countryside Commission, and the aim has been to retain the countryside character; consequently facilities are limited to toilets (suitable for the disabled). The hills remain in agricultural use being grazed by sheep (dogs must be kept under control). A modest parking fee is charged.

All year daily any reasonable time
Admission Free

Coombe Country Park

Brinklow Road Binley Coventry Warwickshire CV3 2AB *(on B4027 6.5m between Coventry & Rugby)*
Tel: 01203 453720 Fax: 01203 635350
400 acres of historic parkland offer a memorable countryside experience. Plant, bird and animal life reside in abundance with each change of season offering it's own natural focus. Most of the parkland is classified as a Site of Special Scientific Interest.

All year daily dawn-dusk
Admission Free

Draycote Water Country Park

Kites Hardwick Rugby Warwickshire *(on A426, S of Rugby)*
Tel: 01827 872660 Fax: 01827 875161
The country park, covering an area of 21 acres on the southern side of Draycote Water, was established in 1972 by the County Council with assistance from the Countryside Commission. Hensborough Hill is an excellent vantage point for watching the sailing activities on the reservoir and for viewing the surrounding countryside, with the open slopes being popular for walking and kite flying. From the hilltop car park a short footpath now leads down to the reservoir, and along to new picnicking areas created by Severn Trent Water on the water's edge. For hygiene reasons, dogs are not allowed in these areas. The adjoining lower area has proved very attractive for casual car parking, picnicking and informal games, and is available by reservation for small caravan rallies. The adventure playground is always very popular, even for those watching from the seats alongside. The aim is to

retain the countryside character of the area, and facilities are thus limited to toilets (suitable for the disabled) and a small hard surface car park for wet weather. A nominal car parking fee is charged as a contribution towards the continuous maintenance which is required. The hill overlooking the reservoir is grazed by sheep to avoid the expense of grass cutting on this large and steep area. The sheep are used to people and will ignore you, but please keep dogs under control.

All year daily, variable hours according to season
Admission Free

Elvaston Castle Country Park

Borrowash Road Elvaston Derby Derbyshire DE72 3EP *(signposted from A6 and A52)*
Tel: 01332 571342 Fax: 01332 758751
200 acre park landscaped early 19th century. Restored after 30 years of neglect. Topiary gardens, walled kitchen garden, herbaceous borders, roses and scented herbs. Take a step back in time at our Estate Museum. Nature trails, caravaning and campsites.

All year daily dawn-dusk. Museum: Easter-Oct Wed-Sat 13.00-16.30, Sun & Bank Hol 11.00-16.30. Café:
All year daily 10.00-16.00
Museum: A£1.20 C£0.60 Family Ticket £3.00. Car Park: £1.20 Sat-Sun & £0.60 Mon-Fri

Foxton Locks Country Park

Gumley Road Foxton Market Harborough Leicestershire LE16 7RA *(on the A6 signposted)*
Tel: 0116 265 6913/265 6962 Fax: 0116 265 6722
Landscaped car park and picnic site with woodland footpath to Grand Union Canal towpath, long flight of locks and remains of barge lift on inclined plane.

All year daily during daylight hours
Admission Free

Hartshill Hayes Country Park

Hartshill Nuneaton Warwickshire *(between A5 / B4114 at Hartshill, near Nuneaton)*
Tel: 01203 395141 Fax: 01827 875161
Web Site: www.warwickshire.gov.uk
The country park encompasses 137 acres of woodland, and open hilltop on a ridge overlooking the Anker Valley. It was opened in 1978 by the County Council with assistance from the Countryside Commission. In 1996 the Park was presented with the Forestry Authority's Centre of Excellence Award for public access and growing timber in environmentally sound ways. The open hilltop offers panoramic views across four counties, and on a

clear day it is possible to see the Derbyshire Peaks, Charnwood Forest and Drakelow Power Station. The valley below has always been a major transport route; today you can see the Watling Street roman road (now the A5), the London to Manchester railway line, and the Coventry Canal. St Lawrence's Wood is named after a small chapel built close by in the 10th century dedicated to this 3rd century martyr. It is a mixed woodland of sycamore and pine, with large open glades of bracken and gorse. The Hayes is over 100 acres of woodland, but with many easily walkable footpaths amongst many different species of trees.

All year daily, hours according to season
Admission Free

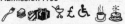

Himley Country Park

Himley Park Himley Dudley West Midlands DY3 4DF *(off A449 on B4176 4m W of Dudley)*
Tel: 01902 324093 Fax: 01384 415599
Extensive parkland offering a range of attractions including a nine hole golf course and coarse fishing. The hall is only open to the public during exhibitions. Permanent orienteering course, a charge is made for the maps.
Mid June-Sept daily 06.00-30mins before dusk, Oct-15 June daily 07.30-30mins before dusk. Hall: 24 Mar-30 Sept daily hours vary call for details
Admission Free, Car Park £0.70

ILAM PARK

Ilam Park

Ilam Ashbourne Derbyshire DE6 2AZ *(4.5m NW of Ashbourne)*
Tel: 01335 350245/350503 Fax: 01335 350503
Attractive park and woodland on both banks of the River Manifold in the South Peak Estate, with magnificent views towards Thorpe Cloud and the entrance to Dovedale. Limited access for wheelchairs. Dogs on leads only. Hall let to YHA, not open to the public.
Grounds & Park: all year daily during daylight hours. Shop & Information Centre: Jan-end Mar

Weekends 11.00-16.00, Easter- Oct daily 11.00-17.00, Nov-20 Dec Weekends 11.00-16.00
Admission Free. Car Park charge for non National Trust members. No coaches on Sun or Bank Hol. Guided Tours for pre-booked groups

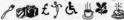

Kingsbury Water Park

Bodymoor Heath Sutton Coldfield West Midlands B76 0DY *(J9 M42 off A4097)*
Tel: 01827 872660 Fax: 01827 875161
A family day out in the countryside, miles of waterside and woodland walks, picnic areas, adventure playground, fishing, shop, cafe. Lots of birdlife and wildlife in 600 acres within 30 lakes.
All year daily, hours variable according to season
Admission Free. On site parking charge £2.00

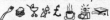

Lickey Hills Country Park

Visitor Centre Warren Lane Rednal Birmingham Hereford and Worcester B45 8ER *(J4 M5, A38 B4096 to Rednal, J1 M42 B4096 to Rednal, 9m SW of Birmingham A38 B4096)*
Tel: 0121 447 7106
Lickey Hills Country Park comprises of a mosaic of diverse habitats including deciduous and coniferous woodlands, heathland and wet areas as well as formal parkland. Rich in wildlife. Visitor centre, playground, golf, tennis and bowls. Led educational visits by arrangement.
All year daily, Summer: 10.00-19.00, Winter: 10.00-16.30
Admission Free

Market Bosworth Country Park

The Park Nuneaton Leicestershire *(off B585 on outskirts of Market Bosworth)*
Tel: 01455 290118
87 acres of rural park, including 11 acre arboretum. Children's Adventure Playground, lake, June-March, Day tickets for fishing available.
All year daily during daylight hours
Admission Free

Rufford Abbey and Country Park

Rufford Abbey Rufford Newark Nottinghamshire NG22 9DF *(just off A614, 2m S of Ollerton roundabout)*
Tel: 01623 824153 Fax: 01623 824840
Tour the restored 12th century Cistercian Abbey set in beautiful parklands. Visit our renowned gallery and craft shops. Enjoy plant and herb centres, restaurants, formal gardens, newly restored Orangery and Heritage Centre. Various Special

---

events telephone for details.

Park: all year dawn-dusk. Craft Centre, Gallery, Rufford Abbey and Mill: all year daily 10.30-17.00. Buttery Restaurant: all year Mon-Fri 12.00-14.30, Sat & Sun 12.30-15.30. Coach House Restaurant: all year daily 10.00-16.00. Facilities close pm on 24 Dec & re-open 27 Dec

Last Admission: 16.30

Admission Free. Car Park during weekends and school holidays £1.00 per vehicle (except coaches)

Ryton Pools Country Park

Ryton Road Bubbenhall Coventry West Midlands *(off the A445 S of Ryton-on-Dunsmore, near Coventry)*

Tel: 01203 305592 Fax: 01827 872660

Web Site: www.warwickshire.gov.uk

The new 100 acre Country Park was opened on 16 August 1996 by the Chairman of the County Council and represented the culmination of 5 years work to transform the former landfill site into a new and exciting Country Park. During that time two million tonnes of rubbish from Rugby, Warwick and Leamington Spa have been covered in clay and top soil and over 2,500 trees and shrubs have been planted. Over the coming years the site's character will change as the trees and shrubs grow and the site develops into both a haven for wildlife and an ideal place to walk or picnic.

All year daily, hours according to season

Admission Free

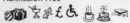

Sheldon Country Park

Ragley Drive Church Road Sheldon Birmingham B26 3TU

Tel: 0121 742 0226

Sheldon Country Park covers 296 acres of mixed habitats. The focal point is the Urban Farm where a variety of animals can be seen. Children's play area, disabled toilets.

All year daily, Summer 10.00-18.00, Winter 10.00-16.00

Admission Free

Styal Country Park

Estate Office 7 Oak Cottages Styal Wilmslow Cheshire SK9 4JQ *(1.5m N of Wilmslow off B5166, 2.5m from J5 M56, 10m S of Manchester. BR: Styal)*

Tel: 01625 523012

Part of the valley of the River Bollin, combining natural beauty with historic interest. There are pleasant riverside walks in fine woodlands. The Country Park includes Quarry Bank Cotton Mill, the factory colony village of Styal and associated farmland.

Guided tours of woodlands and village from main car park on 2nd Sun in month at 14.30.

All year during daylight hours

Admission charge per car to country park £1.50

The Greenway

Seven Meadows Road Stratford-upon-Avon Warwickshire *(near the racecourse)*

Tel: 01827 872660 Fax: 01827 875161

Web Site: www.warwickshire.gov.uk

The Greenway is nearly five miles of what was the Old Honeybourne Railway Line, running south from Stratford-upon-Avon to Long Marston on the border with Gloucestershire. Warwickshire County Council, in partnership with the charity SUSTRANS, removed and sold the ballast to help pay to renovate the derelict line and it was opened to walkers, cyclists and horseriders (Milcote to Lone Marston only) in 1989. In addition to five miles of enjoyable walking, there are two picnic sites, one by the Milcote car park and the other a pleasant three-quarter mile stroll along The Greenway from the Stratford car park on the banks of the Avon.

All year daily, any reasonable time

Admission Free

Ufton Fields Nature Reserve

Ufton Southam Warwickshire *(between the A425 / B4452 near Harbury, Southam)*

Tel: 01827 872660 Fax: 01827 875161

Web Site: www.warwickshire.gov.uk

A special place for wildlife and for you to enjoy 78 acres of grassland, lakes, marsh and woodland. Easy Going Trail gives access to everyone. Two bird hides with easy access. Regular guided walks.

All year Sun & Bank Hol 12.00-16.00

Admission Free

Watermead Country Park

off Wanlip Road Syston Leicestershire *(off A6 via bypass and Syston then B673)*

Tel: 0116 267 1944

230 acres of Country Park, with lakes, nature reserve, woodland walks, footpaths. Access to River Soar and canal.

All year daily during daylight hours

Admission Free

Woodgate Valley Country Park

Woodgate Valley Visitor Centre Clapgate Lane Bartley Green Birmingham B32 3DS *(from Birmingham just 10mins from J3 M5 - along Clapgate Lane, Visitor Centre and car park on the*

---

right)
Tel: 0121 421 7575 Fax: 0121 421 7575
A 450 acre area of meadows, hedgerows, woods and streams on the western edge of Birmingham. A safeguarded haven for wildlife, and a great place for a day out in the countryside. The Visitor Centre contains displays and exhibits with a wide range of souvenirs. A whole host of events are organised by the Rangers throughout the year. Hole Farm Pony Trekking is just a few minutes walk from the Visitor Centre call 0121 422 2400 for details.
Country Park: all year daily during daylight hours. Visitor Centre: All year daily Summer 10.00-19.00, Winter 10.00-16.30. Car Park: Summer 07.30-19.00, Winter 07.30-16.30
Admission Free

Craft Galleries

Rufford Craft Centre
Rufford Abbey Rufford Newark Nottinghamshire NG22 9DF *(A614, 16m N of Nottingham)*
Tel: 01623 822944 Fax: 01623 824702
Situated in Rufford country Park an estate built in the 17th century sited in the Stable block. The Gallery has 6 exhibitions a year and 3 sculpture exhibitions a year.
Jan-Feb 11.00-16.00. All other times 10.30-17.00
Admission Free

The Ferrers Centre for Arts and Crafts
Staunton Harold Ashby de la Zouch Leicestershire LE65 1RU *(J23 M1 along A512 until Ashby de la Zouch, out towards Melbourne on B587)*
Tel: 01332 865408 Fax: 01332 865408
Situated within the beautiful lakeland countryside of the Staunton Estate and home to 14 crafts people working in studios in the 18th century stable blocks. A 3 floor crafts council selected gallery represents some 300 British makers.
All year Tue-Sun 10.30-17.00
Admission Free

Exhibition Centres

Lichfield Heritage Exhibition and Treasury
Market Street Lichfield Staffordshire WS13 6LG *(J11 M6, A51-A38)*
Tel: 01543 256611 Fax: 01543 414749
Experience: the sights and sounds of the Civil War. Enjoy: A Walk through History. Admire: the art of the silversmith in one of Britain's finest small treasuries. Enjoy: magnificent views of the City, Cathedral and surrounding countryside from our 40

meter high viewing platform. A photographers' delight!
All year daily 10.00-17.00. Closed 25-26 Dec & Jan 1 Last Admission: 16.14
A£1.30 C&Students&OAPs£0.80 Family Ticket £3.30. Parties welcome, call for details

National Exhibition Centre
Birmingham West Midlands B40 1NT *(J4 M6, J6 M42. BR: Birmingham International)*
Tel: 0121 780 4141 x2604 Fax: 0121 780 2517
Main UK Exhibition Centre holding over 100 events throughout the year which are listed in our Specials Events section.
Depending on Events
Admission varies depending on event.

Factory Shops

Aynsley China Factory Shop
Sutherland Road Longton Stoke-on-Trent Staffordshire ST3 1HS
Tel: 01782 593536 Fax: 01782 599498
Aynsley is recognised as one of the early pioneers of the high class china trade in Stoke-on-Trent. The company is now one of the world's leading fine bone china giftware manufacturers.
All year Mon-Sat 09.00-17.30, Sun 11.00-16.00
Admission Free

Tutbury Crystal Glass
Burton Street Tutbury Burton upon Trent Staffordshire DE13 9NG
Tel: 01283 813281 Fax: 01283 813228
Factory tours by appointment to see Traditional Glassmaking by skilled craftsmen. Factory shop with a vast range of quality crystal at discount prices, plus tea room.
All year Mon-Sat 09.00-17.00 Sun 11.00-16.00
Factory Tours A£0.50

Moorcroft
Sandbach Road Burslem Stoke-on-Trent Staffordshire ST6 2DQ
Tel: 01782 207943 Fax: 01782 283455
During our centenary year (1897-1997) visit the Moorcroft Factory. Tours show the hand made process which has become the unique hallmark of Moorcroft so eagerly collected around the world.
Factory Shop/Museum: All year Mon-Fri 10.00-17.00, Sat 09.30-16.30, Factory Tours: All year Mon, Wed, Thur 11.00 only
Factory Shop/Museum: Admission Free, Factory

Tours: A£2.50 C&OAPs£1.50

Factory Tours and Shopping

Denby Pottery Visitor Centre

Denby Ripley Derbyshire DE5 8NX *(8m N on B6179 just off A38)*

Tel: 01773 740799 Fax: 01773 570211

Guided factory tours show the intricate skills of the potters craft, including throwing, turning, glazing and decorating. The museum illustrates the history of Denby Pottery. There is a large factory shop selling Denby Products. Self service restaurant, Dartington Crystal Factory shop, florist and children's play area. Check tour times prior to visit.

All year. Full factory tours: Mon-Thur 10.30 & 13.00. Craftroom from 10.00, Factory Shop: Mon-Sat 9.30-17.00, Sun 10.00-16.30

Last Admission: Craftroom 15.30

Factory tour: A£3.75 C&OAPs£2.50. Craftroom: A£2.75 C&OAPs£1.75

ROYAL DOULTON VISITOR CENTRE

Royal Doulton Visitor Centre

Nile Street Burslem Stoke-On-Trent Staffordshire ST6 2AJ *(J15/16 M6, follow A500, Royal Doulton is then signposted)*

Tel: 01782 292434 Fax: 01782 292424

Visit the home of the Royal Doulton Figure, featuring the world's largest public display, live demonstration area including a 'hands-on' area, museum, restaurant and retail shop. Factory tours are available Mon-Fri (expect factory holidays), prior booking is advised.

All year Mon-Sat 09.30-17.00, Sun 10.00-16.00. Factory tours by appointment, Closed factory holidays, Christmas and New Year

Visitor Centre: A£2.50, £5.00 with factory tour. Concessions available

Discount Card Offer: One Child Free When Accompanied By A Full Paying Adult

ROYAL WORCESTER

Royal Worcester

Severn Street Worcester Worcestershire WR1 2NE *(J7 M5 take A44 turn left at 3rd set of traffic lights near the Cathedral)*

Tel: 01905 23221 Fax: 01905 23601

Established in 1751, Royal Worcester is Britain's oldest continuous producer of Porcelain and is world famous for its Fine Bone China. Factory Tours available Monday to Friday. Visitor Centre open Mon-Sun. Shops and family restaurant also on site. Other attractions to open in Spring 1998 are: Museum, Craft demonstrations and an area in the Visitor Centre.

Factory Tours all year Mon-Fri 09.00-17.30

Last Admission: Mon-Thur 15.30, Fri 14.30

A£3.50 C£2.50 Concessions£4.50

Stuart Crystal

Wordsley Stourbridge West Midlands DY8 4AA *(on the A491 Stourbridge /Wolverhampton road)*

Tel: 01384 71161 Fax: 01384 70463

Fine glass has been made in the area since the beginning of the 17th century when French glass makers arrived in the area. The 200 year old Redhouse Glass Cone and associated building have recently been restored in the first stage of creating a museum. On the site there is also a factory shop.

All year daily 10.00-17.30. Closed 25-26 Dec & 1 Jan

Last Admission: Last Factory Tour: 16.00, Shop:

17.00

A£2.00 C£1.00 Family Ticket (A2+C2)£5.00
Concessions£1.50. Groups rates: A£1.50 C£0.75
Concessions£1.00

Wedgwood Visitor Centre

Barlaston Stoke-On-Trent Staffordshire ST12 9ES
(J15 M6, signposted)

Tel: 01782 204141/204218 Fax: 01782 373146

Web Site: www.wedgwood.co.uk

A complex including: art gallery with works by
Reynolds, Stubbs and Romney, and a reconstruction of Wedgwood's original 18th century Etruria
workshops. Demonstrations of the traditional skills
in the production of Wedgwood ware, and a museum containing a comprehensive collection of the
works of Josiah Wedgwood from 1750.

*All year Mon-Fri 09.00-17.00, Sat 10.00-17.00, Sun
10.00-16.00. Closed Christmas & 1 Jan*

*A£3.25 Family Ticket£7.95 Concessions£1.60,
Connoisseur Tours £7.25 pre booked only*

Falconry Centre

Cotswold Falconry Centre

Batsford Park Moreton-in-Marsh Gloucestershire
GL56 9QB (on A44)

Tel: 01386 701043

The Cotswold Falconry gives daily demonstrations
in the art of falconry. There is an emphasis on
breeding and conservation, eagles, hawks, owls
and falcons may be seen flying.

Mar-Nov daily 10.30-17.30

Last Admission: 17.00

A£3.00 C£1.50 OAPs£3.00

The Falconry Centre

Kidderminster Road South Hagley West Midlands
DY9 0JB (off A456 in Hurrans Garden Centre)

Tel: 01562 700014 Fax: 01562 700014

The centre houses some 80 birds of prey including
Hawk, Owls and Falcons. It is also a rehabilitation
centre for sick and injured birds of prey. Regular flying demonstrations daily from midday. Falconry
courses available throughout the year.

All year daily 10.00-17.30. Closed 25 & 26 Dec

A£2.50 C&OAPs£1.50 Disabled£1.00

Family Attraction

TALES OF ROBIN HOOD

Tales of Robin Hood

30-38 Maid Marian Way Nottingham
Nottinghamshire NG1 6GF (J25 M1 Southbound, J26
M1 Northbound, follow signs for the City)

Tel: 0115 948 3284 Fax: 0115 950 1536

Travel back in time to re-live the legend of Robin
Hood, in sight, sound and smell. A long gone world
of storytelling and adventure recreated beneath the
City Streets.

*All year daily Summer: 10.00-18.00, Winter: 10.00-
17.00*

Last Admission: 90mins before closing

*A£4.50 C£3.50 Family Ticket (A2+C2)£13.95
OAPs&Students£4.00*

**Discount Card Offer: One Child Admitted Free With
One Paying Adult**

Family Theme Park

Wickstead Park

Kettering Northamptonshire NN15 6NJ (outskirts of
Kettering. Follow signs from J10 off A14)

Tel: 01536 512475 Fax: 01536 518948

148 acres of parkland and lakes, 40 rides and
attractions, incl. roller coaster, pirate ship, train
ride, Mississippi river boat, large free playground
and many junior rides.

Mar-Oct daily 10.00-18.00 (19.00 peak periods)

Free playground, rides charged

🚼 suitable for pushchairs 👶 mother & baby facilities ♿ suitable for wheelchairs 🎁 gift shop
🤝 corporate facilities 🚫🐕 no dogs: except guide dogs 🅿️ parking on site 🅿️ parking nearby
£ charged parking 🍴 café-restaurant 🍷 licensed 🎆 special events 📚 educational pack

Farm Parks

COTSWOLD FARM PARK

Cotswold Farm Park

Guiting Power Stow on the Wold Cheltenham
Gloucester GL54 5UG *(J9 M5 off B4077 Tewkesbury /Stow road)*
Tel: 01451 850307 Fax: 01451 850423
The home of Rare Breed Conservation. Over 50 breeding flocks and herds of our rarest British Farm animals on top of the Cotswold hills. Pets Corner, Touch barn, Adventure Playground, Woodland Walk, Farm Nature Trail, Viewing Tower, Lambing, Shearing and other seasonal. Daily milking July-September 11.00-16.00.
28 Mar-4 Oct Mon-Sat 10.30-17.00, Sun & Holidays 10.30-18.00
Last Admission: 16.30
A£3.50 C£1.80 OAPs£2.50. Group rates 10% discount

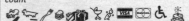

ST AUGUSTIN'S FARM

Farmworld

Stoughton Farm Park Gartree Road Oadby
Leicestershire LE2 2FB *(signposted off A6 /A47)*
Tel: 0116 271 0355 Fax: 0116 271 3211
Farmworld is a working farm that offers a feast of fun and surprises for all the family. Children will enjoy the Children's Farmyard and the playground, while parents might appreciate the Edwardian Ale-House and the craft workshops and demonstrations. Also Shire horse and cart rides, lakeside and woodland walks, nature trails and a collection of rare farm animals, and a toy tractor park with 'real'

play-on tractors.
All year daily Summer: 10.00-17.30 Winter: 10.00-17.00. Closed 25 Dec-3 Jan
Last Admission: 17.00
A£4.00 C£2.50 Family Ticket £12.00 OAPs£3.25. Groups rates call for details. Schools welcome.
Discount Card Offer: One Child Free With Two Full Paying Adults

Sherwood Forest Farm Park

Lamb Pens Farm Edwinstowe Mansfield
Nottinghamshire NG21 9HL *(A6075 midway between Edwinstowe /Mansfield Woodhouse)*
Tel: 01623 823558 Fax: 01623 823558
Large display of many rare breeds of cattle, sheep, pigs, goats and horse in attractive lakeside setting. Beautiful gardens, waterfowl lakes, aviaries, Pets Corner, picnic and play areas.
4 Apr-27 Sept daily, also Sat & Sun Oct 10.30-17.15
A£3.75 C£2.25 C(0-3)£Free OAPs£2.75. Group rates

FARMWORLD

St Augustine's Farm

Arlingham Gloucester Gloucestershire GL2 7JN
(between Gloucester and Bristol, M5 J3 to A38, 0.5m S turn right and follow brown signs onto B4071)
Tel: 01452 740277
A lovely place to visit with children, said to be the most authentic working farm open to the public. A traditional 110 acre farm, situated in the horseshoe bend of the River Severn, where our family has

farmed for 200 years. Help feed the animals. Watch the milking every afternoon. Farm trail. Bygones, Play area. Cows, sheep, pigs, goats, ducks and other animals.

Mar-Oct Tue-Sun & Bank Hol 11.00-17.00
A£3.00 C£2.00 OAPs£2.50, 20% discount for booked parties 15+
Discount Card Offer: 10% Discount Off Admission

Tumbledown Farm
Spinney Road Melton Mowbray Leicestershire LE14 4SB *(1m from Melton Mowbray signposted from A607 between Melton Mowbray / Grantham)*
Tel: 01664 481811
A traditional family run working farm set in unspoiled countryside. We breed animals, milk cows, sheep and goats and grow cereal crops. All year round you can watch us work with the animals and the land. Adventure field, Indoor play barn, Vintage machinery and much more.
All year daily Summer: 10.00-17.00, Winter: 10.00-16.00. Closed 24-26 Dec
All £2.95 C(0-2)£Free

Farm- Flower

Naturescape Wildflower Farm
Coachgap Lane Langar Nottingham Nottinghamshire NG13 9HP *(from Nottingham A52 on Bingham by pass signed Langar. Pass Langar village on right and continue towards Harby, Coach Gap Lane on left)*
Tel: 01949 851045/860592 Fax: 01949 850431
Range of Wildflowers in bloom over 40 acres of fields which attract associated butterflies, birds and mammals. Wildlife garden featuring many habitats to provide ideas for visitors.
28 Mar-30 Sept daily 11.00-17.30
Last Admission: 17.00
Fields: 15 June-15 Aug A£1.95 C£Free OAPs£1.50, other areas Admission Free

Farms

Acton Scott Historic Working Farm
Wenlock Lodge Acton Scott Church Stretton Shropshire SY6 6QN *(signposted off the A49, approximately 17m S of Shrewsbury, 14m N of Ludlow)*
Tel: 01694 781306/7 Fax: 01694 781569
Living history in the Shropshire Hills. Experience daily life on an upland farm at the turn of the century. The waggoner and his team of heavy horses work the land with vintage farm machines. In the cottage the farmer's wife goes about her chores. This working farm museum gives a vivid introduction to traditional rural life. Children will love the cows, pigs, poultry and sheep in the farmyard and fields. There are Tamworth pigs and Shropshire sheep amongst the rarer breeds. Daily demonstrations of rural crafts complete the picture of estate-life a hundred years ago. Guided tours of the farm are available. New for 1998 is a cartwheel maze play area and holiday activities. NO DOGS
31 Mar-1 Nov Tue-Sun & Bank Hol 10.00-17.00.
Last Admission: 16.30
A£3.25 C(0-5)£Free C£1.50 Family Ticket £10.00
OAPs£2.75 UB40s£Free. Group Rate: A£3.00
C£1.25 OAPs£2.50. Season Ticket (To the Farm, Ludlow and Much Wenlock Museums) A£8.00
C£4.00. Guide: A£7.50 per 20, C£5.50 per 20. One A£Free for every 10 paying Children. £Free admission to helpers of disabled groups where a one to one, or a wheelchair pusher is required.

ACTON SCOTT HISTORIC WORKING FARM

Bentley Fields Open Farm
Bentley Fields Alkmonton Cubley Derbyshire DE6 3DJ *(7m from the A52 or on A515 turn at Cubley)*
Tel: 01335 330240
A working farm with rare and commercial breeds of sheep and cattle. Milking 13.00 and 16.00 daily, Pets Corner and Play Area. Enjoy the chaos of Easter lambing or take a stroll among a wide variety of cattle, sheep, pigs and poultry.
Easter-mid April, May Day Sun & Mon, end May-beg June, July-Aug Sun only & Bank Hol Mon 11.00-18.00
A£1.50 Concessions£0.80

Children's Farm
Ash End House Farm Middleton Lane Middleton Tamworth Staffordshire B78 2BL *(A4091)*
Tel: 0121 329 3240 Fax: 0121 329 3872
Small family owned farm with lots of friendly animals to feed and stroke. Play areas, picnic barns,

🏃 *suitable for pushchairs* 👶 *mother & baby facilities* ♿ *suitable for wheelchairs* 🎁 *gift shop*
corporate facilities 🐕 *no dogs: except guide dogs* 🚗 *parking on site* 🚙 *parking nearby*
£ *charged parking* 🍴 *café-restaurant* 🍷 *licensed* *special events* *educational pack*

"have a go Sundays" lots of undercover activities for the children during school holidays and weekends including "make a memento" to take home, ie. Friendship bands, colouring cards etc. Bookings also taken from schools, playgroups, clubs and Birthday Parties on the farm. Every Sunday from March to November there are wool spinning demonstrations and "Have-A-Go" yourself on the spinning wheel.

All year daily 10.00-17.00 dusk in Winter. Closed 25-27 Dec, 1 Jan

Last Admission: 60mins before closing

A£1.80 C£3.60

Old Dairy Farm Centre

Upper Stowe Nr Weedon Northampton NN7 4SH *(J16 M1, signposted off A5 N of Towcester)*

Tel: 01327 340525

The Old Dairy Farm Centre is a mixed arable and sheep farm with animals on view in beautiful countryside. Antiques, craft workshops, gifts, clothes and a farm shop with homemade food. Traditional Sunday Lunches in licensed relaxing surroundings.

All year Jan-Feb daily 10.00-16.30, Mar-Dec 10.00-17.30. Closed 2 weeks at Christmas

Admission Free

Forest Visitor Centres

Sherwood Forest Country Park and Visitor Centre

Edwinstowe Mansfield Nottinghamshire NG21 9HN *(20m N of Nottingham, just off A614)*

Tel: 01623 823202 Fax: 01623 823202

Visit the legendary home of England's most famous outlaw - Robin Hood. Over 450 acres of ancient oak woodland, including the famous Major Oak. Enjoy the hands on exhibition, video on the history of the former Royal Hunting Forest, heritage and gift shops and restaurant. Explore woodland paths, picnic in forest glades and enjoy a year-round programme of events and activities.

Country Park: all year daily dawn-dusk. Visitor Centre: Apr-Oct 10.30-17.00, Nov-Mar 10.30-16.30

Admission Free, Car Park charge Easter-Oct Sat-Sun and Bank Hol and all of Aug

SHERWOOD FOREST COUNTRY PARK AND VISITOR CENTRE

Wyre Forest Visitor Centre

Wyre Forest Callow Hill Beudley Nr Kidderminster Worcestershire DY14 9XQ *(3m W of Beudley on A456, follow brown tourist signs)*

Tel: 01299 266929 Fax: 01299 266302

The beautiful Wyre Forest is a stimulating family day out. The new café and Visitor area is a delight to behold with its wholefood restaurant and natural displays of the forest. There is an all ability trail and forest walks which wind through this unique mixed woodland with wildlife in abundance.

All year Forest dawn-dusk, Café 11.00-16.00

Last Admission: 16.00

Admission Free

Forests

Rockingham Forest

Rockingham Forest Tourism Association 30 Leys Avenue Desborough Northamptonshire NN14 2PY *(N of Northamptonshire)*

Tel: 01536 760582

The Rockingham Forest was first designated a Royal Hunting forest by William the Conqueror over 900 years ago. It was never just woodland but always contained many small villages, and areas of grass and parkland vital for grazing deer. It is an area rich in history and has a distinct identity. Many countryside, culture and craft events organised throughout the year within this area of Northamptonshire.

Admission Free

Forts

Old Oswestry Hill Fort

Oswestry Shropshire *(1m N of Oswestry accessible from unclassified road off A483)*

Tel: 01604 730320

This Iron Age hill-fort covers 68 acres, has five ramparts and an elaborate western portal. It is abutted by part of the prehistoric Wat's Dyke.

Any reasonable time
Admission Free

Gardens

Barnsdale Plants and Gardens

The Avenue Exton Oakham Leicestershire LE15 8AH *(turn off A606 Oakham / Stamford road at Barnsdale Lodge Hotel, then 1m on the left)*

Tel: 01572 813200 Fax: 01572 813346

11 acres of Gardens laid out as part of Barnsdale television gardens. All told, there are 25 individual gardens in every possible style-each a living stage from which visitors can glean ideas. The Reclaimed Garden, Country Paradise Garden & The Ornamental Vegetable garden are but three. All were the inspiration of Geoff Hamilton.

TV Garden& small Nursery: 1 Mar-31 Oct daily 10.00-17.00, Nursery only: 1 Nov-28 Feb 10.00-16.00. Closed Christmas and New Year
T.V. Garden & small Nursery: A&OAPs£4.50 C£Free. Group rates 10+ £3.50. Nursery £Free

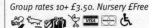

Barnsley House Garden

Barnsley Village Cirencester Gloucestershire GL7 5EE *(3m NE of Cirencester on B4425)*

Tel: 01285 740281 Fax: 01285 740281

This lovely garden is the creation of Rosemary Verey, who since 1960 has transformed the older garden that was here. There are herbs, a knot garden and a vegetable garden to include mixed borders. The garden is not purely for show all produce is picked and used by the family.

All year 10.00-18.00 Mon Wed Thur & Sat
A£3.00 OAPs£2.00 Parties must book.

Biddulph Grange Garden

Biddulph Grange Biddulph Stoke-On-Trent Staffordshire ST8 7SD *(off A527 0.5m N of Biddulph)*

Tel: 01782 517999

An exciting and rare survival of a high-Victorian garden, acquired by the Trust in 1988 and focus of an extensive restoration project. Conceived by James Bateman, the 6ha are divided into a number of small gardens designed to house specimens from his extensive and wide-ranging plant collection. An Egyptian Court, Chinese Pagoda, Joss House, Bridge and Pinetum, together with many other settings, all combine to make the garden a miniature tour of the world. Picnics in the car park only.

1 Apr-1 Nov Wed-Fri 12.00-18.00, Weekends & Bank Hol Mon 11.00-18.00, 7 Nov-20 Dec Weekends 12.00-16.00 or dusk if sooner. Closed Good Fri Last Admission: 17.30 or dusk
April-Oct: A£4.00 C£2.00 Family Ticket £10.00, Nov-Dec: A£2.00 C£1.00 Family Ticket £5.00. Pre-booked groups or educational visits welcome

Bourton House Garden

Bourton On The Hill Gloucestershire GL56 9AE *(2m W of Moreton-in-marsh on A44. BR: Moreton-in-Marsh)*

Tel: 01386 700121

An imaginatively planted garden, largely created under the present ownership, enhances a handsome circa 18th century Cotswold Manor House (not open). Unusual plants for sale.

29 May-24 Oct, Bank Hol, May-Aug Sun & Mon, 25-26 May & 24-25 Aug
A£2.50 C£Free

Burford House Gardens

Tenbury Wells Worcestershire WR15 8HQ *(off A456, 1m W of Tenbury Wells, 8m from Ludlow)*

Tel: 01584 810777 Fax: 01584 810673

Set in South Shropshire's picturesque landscape, this early Georgian House looks over 4 acres of sweeping lawns and serpentine borders containing the National Clematis Collection of more than 200 varieties and over 2,000 other kinds of plants.

All year daily 10.00-17.00 or dusk if sooner
A£2.50 C£1.00. Group rate 10+ £2.00
Discount Card Offer: Two For The Price Of One Into Gardens

Castle Ashby Gardens

Castle Ashby Northampton Northamptonshire NN7 1LQ *(situated off A428 between Northampton / Bedford)*

Tel: 01604 696696 Fax: 01604 696516

Castle Ashby's 25 acres of gardens include a Victorian terrace and romantic Italian gardens. An elegant conservatory leads through a triumphal arch, past a gloriette and camellia house to a series of lakes, that form part of the 200 acre parkland designed by Capability Brown.

All year daily 10.00-dusk
A£2.50 C(0-10)£Free C(10+)&OAPs£1.00 Family Ticket £6.00.

🕑 *suitable for pushchairs* 🍼 *mother & baby facilities* ♿ *suitable for wheelchairs* 🎁 *gift shop*
🍬 *corporate facilities* 🐕 *no dogs: except guide dogs* 🚗 *parking on site* 🚙 *parking nearby*
£ *charged parking* ☕ *café-restaurant* 🍷 *licensed* 🎂 *special events* 📦 *educational pack*

Castle Bromwich Hall Gardens

Chester Road Castle Bromwich Birmingham West Midlands B36 9BT *(1m from J5 M6 northbound, J6 M6 southbound follow A38 /A452. 4m E of Birmingham City centre, well signposted)*

Tel: 0121 749 4100 Fax: 0121 749 4100

Restored 18th century walled gardens featuring a variety of rare and historic plants. Highlights include The Orangery, Music Room, Holly Maze (with an escape route!) and Batty Langley Vegetable Garden. Guided tours available on Wednesday, Saturday and Sunday call for details. Coffee and gift shops.

Apr-Sept Mon-Thur 13.30-16.30, Sat & Sun 14.00-18.00

A£2.00 C£0.50 OAPs&Concessions£1.50. Group rates on application, School Groups £Free

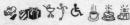

Cholmondeley Castle Garden

Cholmondeley Malpas Cheshire SY14 8AH *(off A49 / A41. BR: Crewe)*

Tel: 01829 720383 Fax: 01829 720383

The extensive pleasure gardens are dominated by a romantic Gothic Castle built in 1801. The gardens are imaginatively laid out with fine tress and water gardens, herbaceous borders, a rose and lavender garden, lovely lakeside and woodland walks, rare breeds of farm animals and an ancient private chapel. Gift shop, tea room and plants for sale.

1 Apr-30 Sept Wed & Thur only 12.00-17.00, Sun & Bank Hol 11.30-17.30

A£2.50 C£0.75 OAP£2.00. Groups welcome, call for details

Coton Manor Garden

Coton Northampton Northamptonshire NN6 8RQ *(10m N of Northampton, 11m SE of Rugby, follow tourist signs on A428 and A50. BR: Northampton / Long Buckby)*

Tel: 01604 740219 Fax: 01604 740838

Traditional old English garden set in Northamptonshire countryside, with yew and holly hedges, extensive herbaceous borders, rose garden, water garden, herb garden, woodland garden, famous bluebell wood early May and exotic wildfowl collection. Large plant nursery.

Apr-Sept Wed-Sun 12.00-17.30

Last Admission: 17.00
A£3.00 C(0-16)£1.50 OAPs£2.50

Hare Hill Garden

Over Alderley Nr Macclesfield Cheshire SK10 4QB *(between Alderley Edge / Prestbury off B5087 at Greyhound Road. Link path to Alderley Edge 2m in each direction)*

Tel: 01625 828981

A woodland garden surrounding a walled garden with pergola, rhododendrons and azaleas, parkland, link path to Alderley Edge. Ample parking for disabled, but on a slope, gravel paths, strong companion advisable. Wheelchair available. No dogs in the garden, elsewhere on leads.

Apr-Oct Wed, Thur, Weekends & Bank Hol Mon 10.00-17.30. May-June daily 10.00-17.30 for Rhododendrons & Azaleas. Closed Nov-Mar

A£2.50, Car £1.50 refundable on entry to the garden. Groupss by written appointment c/o Garden Lodge at the above address

Hergest Croft Gardens

Kington Herefordshire HR5 3EG *(0.25m W of Kington, off A44)*

Tel: 01544 230160 Fax: 01544 230160

From spring bulbs to autumn colour, this is garden for all seasons. One of the finest collections of trees and shrubs surround the Edwardian house, an old fashioned kitchen garden has spring and summer borders and Park Wood, a hidden valley, has rhododendrons up to 30ft tall.

10 Apr-1 Nov daily 13.30-18.30
A£2.75 C£Free
Discount Card Offer: Two For The Price Of One, Not Valid For May Flower Fair

Hidcote Manor Garden

Hidcote Bartrim Chipping Campden Gloucestershire GL55 6LR *(4m NW of Chipping Camden, 1m E of B4632 originally A46 off B4081. BR: Honeybourne)*

Tel: 01386 438333 Fax: 01386 433817

One of the most delightful gardens in England, created by the great horticulturist Major Lawrence Johnston. A series of small gardens separated by walls and hedges. Hidcote is famous for rare shrubs, trees, herbaceous borders, 'old' roses and interesting plant species. Limited access for disabled visitors, contact to arrange assistance. Shop additionally open 1 Nov-14 Dec Sat-Sun 12.00-16.00 *1 Apr-31 Oct Wed-Thur Sat-Mon 11.00-18.00. July Wed-Mon 11.00-18.00. Closed Good Fri.*

Last Admission: 1 hour before closing
A£5.50 C£2.70 Family Ticket £13.80. No group con-

cessions

Hodges Barn Gardens

Shipton Moyne Tetbury Gloucestershire GL8 8PR
*(J17 M4, 1.75m off A433 between Tetbury /
Westonbirt)*
Tel: 01666 880202 Fax: 01666 880373
One of the finest private gardens in England. Spring
bulbs, Magnolias and flowering trees are followed
by a superb collection of old fashioned and climb-
ing roses with many mixed shrub and herbaceous
beds.
Easter-21 Aug Mon Tue Fri 14.00-17.00
Last Admission: 15mins before closing
A£2.50 C£Free

Hodnet Hall Gardens

Hodnet Market Drayton Shropshire TF9 3NN
*(Shrewsbury / Market Drayton road A442. Telford /
Whitechurch road J12 & J15 M6, J3 M54)*
Tel: 01630 685202 Fax: 01630 685853
Sixty acres of landscaped gardens offer tranquility
among pools, lush plants and trees. Big game tro-
phies adorn the 17th-century tea rooms, and plants
are usually for sale in the kitchen gardens. The
house, rebuilt in Victorian-Elizabethan style, is not
open.
*Good Fri-Sept Tue-Sat 14.00-17.00, Sun & Bank Hol
Mon 12.00-17.30*
A£2.80 C£1.00 OAPs£2.30. Groups on application

Hodsock Priory Gardens

Blyth Worksop Nottinghamshire S81 0TY *(less than
2m from A1 at Blyth off B6045 Blyth to Worksop
road)*
Tel: 01909 591204 Fax: 01909 591578
Share the beauty and peace of a romantic traditional 5-acre private garden on the historic Domesday
site bounded by a dry moat and Grade 1 listed brick
gatehouse c.1500. Sensational snowdrops and
woodland walk. A profuse planting for year-round
beauty.
*4 weeks Feb-Mar daily 10.00-16.00 best show
depends on weather call before travelling. 1 Apr-31
Aug Tue-Thur 13.00-17.00*
*A£2.50. No charge for accompanied children & visi-
tors in wheelchairs. Summer proceeds all for
Charities.*

How Caple Court Gardens

How Caple Hereford Herefordshire HR1 4SX *(B4224
Ross on Wye 4.5m to Hereford 9m)*
Tel: 01989 740612 Fax: 01989 740611

11 acres overlooking the River Wye. Formal
Edwardian gardens, extensive plantings of mature
trees and shrubs, water features and a sunken
Florentine garden undergoing restoration. Norman
church with 16th century Diptych. Specialist nursery plants and old variety roses for sale.
*All year Mon-Sat 09.30-17.30, Apr-Nov Sun 09.00-
17.00. Closed Sat Oct-Feb*
A£2.50 C1.25. Groups welcome by appointment

Kiftsgate Court Garden

Mickleton Chipping Campden Gloucestershire GL55
6LW *(0.5m S off A46 adjacent Hidcote Garden)*
Tel: 01386 438777 Fax: 01386 438777
This magnificently situated house has a garden
which is open to the public. The main attraction lies
in its collection of old-fashioned roses, including
the largest rose in England the R Filipes Kiftsgate.
*Apr-May &Aug-Sept Wed Thur Sun 14.00-18.00,
June-July Wed Thur Sat Sun 12.00-18.00*
A£3.50 C£1.00

LEA GARDENS

Lea Gardens

Lea Matlock Derbyshire DE4 5GH *(3m SE Matlock
off A6)*
Tel: 01629 534380 Fax: 01629 534260
Three and a half acres of attractive woodland gar-
dens with rhododendrons, azaleas and rock plants
are open for public enjoyment. A Music Day on 14th
June 1998, plant sales to reflect garden content and
a tea shop specialising in home baking.
Mar-July daily 10.00-19.00
A£3.00 C£0.50 Disabled£Free, Season Ticket £4.00
**Discount Card Offer: Children Free With One
Paying Adult**

Lydney Park Gardens

Lydney Park Estate Lydney Gloucestershire GL15
6BU *(0.25m W of Lydney on A48 Gloucester /
Chepstow. BR: Lydney)*
Tel: 01594 842844 Fax: 01594 842027

🖎 suitable for pushchairs   ⚶ mother & baby facilities   ⚑ suitable for wheelchairs   ⛁ gift shop
🤝 corporate facilities   🐾 no dogs: except guide dogs   ⚶ parking on site   🅿 parking nearby
£ charged parking   ☕ café-restaurant ⚱ licensed   🎂 special events   🎓 educational pack

Extensive Woodland Garden with lakes and a wide selection of rhododendrons and azaleas, fine shrubs and trees. Roman Temple Site and Roman Museum with artifacts from the site. Picnic area in the Deer Park.
Easter-14 June Sun Wed & Bank Hol 11.00-18.00, 25-30 May daily
A£2.40 C£Free, Wed: A£1.240. Group rates 25+ on application

Misarden Park Gardens

Misarden Stroud Gloucestershire *(in Misarden 7m from Gloucester, Cheltenham, Stroud & Cirencester. 3m off A417)*
Tel: 01285 821303 Fax: 01285 821530
Spring flowers, shrubs, fine topiary (some designed by Sir Edwin Lutyens) and herbaceous borders within a walled garden, roses and fine specimen trees. 17th century Manor House (not open), standing high overlooking Golden Valley.
1 Apr-30 Sept Tue Wed Thur 09.30-16.30 Nurseries: Tue-Sun
A£2.50 C£Free. Group rates 20+ by appointment. Guided tour extra

PAINSWICK ROCOCO GARDEN

Painswick Rococo Garden

The Stables Painswick House Gloucester Road

Painswick Stroud Gloucestershire GL6 6TH *(on B4073)*
Tel: 01452 813204 Fax: 01452 813204
This beautiful Rococo garden is the only one of its period to survive completely and nearing the end of an ambitious restoration programme. It consists of contemporary buildings, woodland walks, and magnificent vistas. Charitable Trust No. 299792.
2nd Wed in Jan-30 Nov Wed-Sun & daily during July & Aug 11.00-17.00
A£3.00 C£1.60 OAPs£2.70
Discount Card Offer: Two For The Price Of One

Priory Gardens

The Priory Kemerton nr Tewkesbury Gloucestershire GL20 7JN *(5m N of Tewkesbury on B4080 Evesham Rd)*
Tel: 01386 725258
4 acre garden with a collection of rare trees and shrubs, long herbaceous borders planned in colour groups. Stream, fern and sunken garden, raised beds planted with alpine and many other unusual and interesting plants. Remains of 16th century ruins with large clipped yew of same date. Refreshments on Special Sundays only when home-made Cream-Teas are served. Guided Tours by arrangement. Dogs on leads only.
May-Sept Thur 14.00-18.00. Special Sundays call for dates
June: A£1.50, July-Sept: A£2.00 C(0-7)£Free. Groups by arrangement

Pureland Relaxation and Meditation Centre

Japanese Garden Pureland North Clifton Newark Nottinghamshire NG23 7AT *(3m from Dunham Bridge halfway between Newark / Gainsborough off A1133)*
Tel: 01777 228567
The garden reflects the natural landscape of Japan; Harmony of Nature and Peace of Man. The Centre offers relaxation and meditation tuition all the year round.
Apr-Oct Tue-Fri 12.00-17.30, Sat, Sun & Bank Hol 10.30-17.30
A£3.00 C£1.50 OAPs£2.50

RHS Regional Centre Pershore

Pershore College of Horticulture Avonbank Pershore Worcestershire WR10 3JP
Tel: 01386 554609 Fax: 01386
Although the RHS Centre at Pershore was originally intended for members in the West Midlands, its extensive range of courses and events have proved

too popular that it attracts members and non-members from all over the country. With a strong emphasis on practical involvement, specialists are on hand to teach visitors everything from creating a scree garden, to making a wormery. The 180 acre campus is maintained by the college and includes decorative and tropical glasshouses, landscaped gardens, orchards, plant collections and an arboretum.

Depending on course or event

Depending on course or event. RHS members are entitled to reduced price tickets. All courses must be booked in advance

Ryton Organic Gardens

Wolston Lane Coventry West Midlands CV8 3LG *(on B4029)*

Tel: 01203 303517 Fax: 01203 639229

Ten acres of glorious gardens show how to grow in harmony with nature. Award winning organic restaurant on site. Large shop, conference facilities. Coaches and groups welcome by prior arrangement.

All year 10.00-17.00. 1 Nov-Good Fri 10.00-dusk. Closed Christmas week

A£2.50 C£1.25 Concessions£2.00. 1 Nov-Good Fri & Winter: A£1.25 C£0.60 Concessions£1.00. RHS members free

Discount Card Offer: One Child Free When Accompanied By A Full Paying Adult

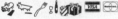

Spetchley Park Gardens

Spetchley Worcester Worcestershire WR5 1RS *(3m E of Worcester off A422)*

Tel: 01905 345213/345224

The 110-acre deer park and the 30-acre gardens surround an early 19th-century mansion (not open), with sweeping lawns and herbaceous borders, a rose lawn and enclosed gardens with low box and yew hedges. There is a large collection of trees, shrubs and plants, many of which are rare or unusual.

Apr-Sept Tue-Fri 11.00-17.00, Sun 14.00-17.00, Bank Hol Mon 11.00-17.00. Other days by appointment

A£2.90 C£1.40. Groups 25+ £2.70

The Dorothy Clive Garden

Willoughbridge Market Drayton Shropshire TF9 4EU *(on A51 between Nantwich /Stone. 3m S of Bridgemere Garden World)*

Tel: 01630 647237 Fax: 01630 647902

In the small village of Willoughbridge is a 200 year old gravel quarry converted into a delightful woodland garden, which is at the top of a small hill and

the garden cover over 8 acres. It has fine views of the countryside and adjoining counties. Among the tall oak trees are daffodils, rhododendrons and azaleas.

Apr-Oct daily 10.00-17.30

Last Admission: 17.00

A£2.80 C(0-11)£Free C(11-16)£1.00 OAPs£2.40

The Herb Garden

Chesterfield Road Hardstoft Pilsley Chesterfield Derbyshire *(A6039 Holmewood /Tibshelf road, 3m from J29 M1, follow brown tourist signs from A6175 and B6014)*

Tel: 01246 854268

One of the foremost herb gardens in the country. Four display gardens; the Mixed Herb Garden which includes an established parterre. The Physic Garden houses a comprehensive collection of medicinal plants from all over the world and the Pot Pourri Garden illustrates a collection of plants which dry well for pot pourri and flower arranging.

Mar-Sept daily 10.00-18.00. Tearoom 10.00-17.30

Admission Free

The Jubilee Park

Whitchurch Ross-On-Wye Herefordshire HR9 6DA *(200 meters from A40 at Whitchurch Junction)*

Tel: 01600 890360 Fax: 01600 890058

The Jubilee Park houses the Jubilee Maze, built to celebrate the Queen's Jubilee in 1977, and the celebrated Museum of Mazes showing paths of mazes and labyrinth through the ages. The World of Butterflies, has hundreds of colourful butterflies from all over the world flying free in their large tropical indoor garden.

Good Fri-Sept daily 11.00-17.30, Winter Weekends & daily during half term 12.00-16.00. Closed Dec & Jan and in bad weather

Last Admission: 30mins before closing

A£2.80 C(0-4)£Free C(5yrs+)£1.80 Family Ticket (A2+C3) or (A1+C4)£8.50 Concessions&OAPs£2.25. Price change due 1 May 1998

The Weir Gardens

Swainshill Hereford Herefordshire HR4 7QF *(5m W of Hereford on A438)*

Tel: 01684 850051

Delightful riverside garden particularly spectacular in early spring when there are lovely displays of naturalised bulbs set in woodland and grassland walks. Cliff garden walks can be taken here, with fine views of the River Wye and the Welsh hills. No WC. Dogs in car park only. Not advisable for wheelchair users.

🏃 suitable for pushchairs   👶 mother & baby facilities   ♿ suitable for wheelchairs   🎁 gift shop
🤝 corporate facilities   🐕 no dogs: except guide dogs   🚗 parking on site   🚗 parking nearby
£ charged parking   🍴 café-restaurant   🍷 licensed   🎂 special events   📖 educational pack

Feb-Oct Wed-Sun Bank Hol Mon & Good Fri 11.00-18.00
A£1.50 C£0.75

Gardens- Botanical

BIRMINGHAM BOTANICAL GARDENS AND GLASSHOUSES

Birmingham Botanical Gardens and Glasshouses

Westbourne Road Edgbaston Birmingham West Midlands B15 3TR *(2m W of City Centre)*
Tel: 0121 454 1860 Fax: 0121 454 7835
Tropical, Mediterranean and desert glasshouse contain a wide range of exotic and economic flora. 15 acres of beautiful gardens with the finest collection of plants in the Midlands. Children's adventure playground, aviaries, gallery and plant centre.
All year daily Mon-Sat 09.00-19.00 or dusk if sooner, Sun 10.00-20.00 or dusk if sooner. Closed 25 Dec
A£3.80, Summer Sundays A£4.20
Concessions£2.10

Grange Cottage Herb Gardens
4 Grange Cottages Grange Lane Nailstone Nuneaton Warwickshire CV13 0QN *(from Leicester take the A47 towards Hinckley. After 5m turn right into the B582 towards Ibstock. After 7m the garden is on the right)*
Tel: 01530 262072 Fax: 01530 262072
Ornamental and medicinal herb gardens. Plants, books and herbal products for sale.
Apr-June Fri Sat Sun and Bank Hol Mon 10.00-17.00 Admission Free

Kayes Garden Nursery
1700 Melton Road Rearsby Leicester Leicestershire LE7 4YR *(just inside Rearsby village NE of Leicester on A607 on left hand side approaching from Leicester)*
Tel: 01664 424578
Hardy herbaceous perennials and good selection of

climbers and shrubs. The garden and nursery are in Rearsby, in the Wreake Valley countryside North East of Leicestershire. Once an orchard, the one acre garden houses an extensive selection of herbaceous plants and climbers. New extensive stream and water garden.
Mar-Oct Tue-Sat 10.00-17.00, Sun-10.00-12.00. Nov-Feb Fri-Sat 10.00-16.00. Closed 25 Dec-31Jan
A£2.00 accompanied C£0.10
Discount Card Offer: Half Price Admission

KAYES GARDEN NURSERY

Stone House Cottage Gardens
Stone Kidderminster Worcestershire DY10 4BG *(2m SE on A448)*
Tel: 01562 69902
A beautiful walled garden with towers provides a sheltered area of about one acre for rare shrubs, climbers and interesting herbaceous plants. Adjacent to the garden is a nursery with a large selection of unusual plants.
Gardens & Nursery: Mar-Sept Wed-Sat 10.00-17.30
A£2.00 C£Free

University of Leicester Botanic Gardens
Beaumont Hall Stoughton Drive South Oadby Leicester Leicestershire LE2 2NA *(3m SE on A6)*
Tel: 0116 271 7725
The grounds of four houses, now used as student residences and not open to the public, make up this 16 acre garden. A great variety of plants in different settings provide a delightful place to walk, including rock, water and sunken gardens, trees, borders, heathers and glasshouses.
All year Mon-Fri 09.00-15.30. Closed Bank Hol Admission Free

Gardens- Roses

Dorothy Clive Garden
Willoughbridge Market Drayton Shropshire TF9 4EU *(on A51 road midway between Nantwich / Stone and 3m S of Bridgemere Garden World)*

Tel: 01630 647237

8 acre woodland and rhododendron garden; shrub roses; water garden and a large scree in a fine landscape setting. Good herbaceous plantings are a summer feature autumn colour. Spectacular waterfall, many interesting and less usual plants.
Garden only: Apr-Oct daily 10.00-17.30
A£2.60 C£1.00

Gatehouses

City East Gate

Gloucester City Museum & Art Gallery Broomswick Road Gloucester Gloucestershire GL1 1HP *(located at junction of Eastgate St / Brunswick Rd in City centre)*
Tel: 01452 524131 Fax: 01452 410898
At City East Gate there are Roman and medieval gate towers and a moat in an underground exhibition chamber.
May-Sept Sat 10.15-13.00 & 14.15-16.45
A£1.25 C£0.50 Concessions£Free

Heritage Centres

Dean Heritage Centre

Camp Mill Soudley Cinderford Gloucestershire GL14 2UB *(on B4227 between Blakeney / Cinderford)*
Tel: 01594 822170
Located in the heart of the Forest of Dean, the centre is set around a restored corn mill and its mill pond. It tells the fascinating story of this unique area. There are informative museum displays and adventure playground. Woodland walks nearby.
Feb-Mar daily 10.00-17.00, Apr-Sept 10.00-18.00, Oct 10.00-17.00
Last Admission: 45mins before closing
A£3.30 C(5+)£2.00 Family Ticket (A2+C4)£9.50 OAPs £2.80. Groups: A£2.80 C£1.50 OAPs£2.30

Droitwich Heritage Centre

Victoria Square Droitwich Spa Worcestershire WR9 8DS
Tel: 01905 774312
Originally the St Andrew's Brine Baths, the building has been carefully converted into a local history museum, exhibition hall and tourist information centre. The town's history display depicts the fascinating development of Droitwich from Iron Age salt town to present day luxury spa resort.
Summer: Mon-Fri 09.30-17.00, Winter: Mon-Fri 10.00-16.00, Sat 10.00-16.00

Admission Free

Gilstrap Heritage Centre

Castle Gate Newark Nottinghamshire NG24 1BG *(in the Newark Castle grounds)*
Tel: 01636 611908
Visit the Castle Story exhibition and unlock the 800 year history of Newark Castle. Newark at the crossroads exhibition. Local Artists varying throughout the year.
All year 10.00-17.00, Summer: 10.00-18.00. Closed 25-26 Dec & 1 Jan
Admission Free

QUARRY BANK MILL AND STYAL COUNTRY PARK

Quarry Bank Mill and Styal Country Park

Styal Wilmslow Cheshire SK9 4LA *(1.5m N of Wilmslow, off B5166 2.5m from J5 M56)*
Tel: 01625 527468 Fax: 01625 539267
Quarry Bank Mill is the best preserved Georgian cotton mill in the Country. Set in the beautiful grounds of Styal Country Park. The Power Project 1998 will make us the only place in the world where visitors can actually see water and steam power working together. Apprentice House tours reveal how the young pauper apprentices lived. Regular new exhibitions, interactive children's drama and craft workshops, provide great family entertainment.
All year Apr-Sept daily 11.00-18.00, Oct-Mar Tue-Sun 11.00-17.00
Last Admission: 90mins before closing
Mill & Apprentice House: A£4.70 C£3.20, Mill: A£3.70 C£2.50 Family Ticket £12.00. Apprentice

House & Garden: £3.20 per car, Styal Country Park:
£1.50 per car

Historic Buildings

Ashleworth Tithe Barn
Ashleworth Gloucester Gloucestershire (6m NW of
Gloucester, 1.25m E of Hartpury A417 on W bank of
Severn SE of Ashleworth)
Tel: 01684 850051
A 15th century tithe barn with two projecting porch
bays and fines roof timbers with queenposts.
*Apr-Oct daily 09.00-18.00 or sunset if sooner. Other
times by prior appointment through the Regional
Office*
£0.60

Bredon Barn
Bredon Tewkesbury (3m NE of Tewkesbury just N of
B4080. BR: Pershore)
Tel: 01684 850051 Fax: 01684 850090
A 14th century barn approximately 44 metres long
with fine porches, one of which has unusual stone
chimney cowling. The barn was restored with tradi-
tional materials after a fire in 1980. Contact Severn
Regional Office for other visiting times.
*Apr-Nov Wed Thur Sat & Sun 10.00-18.00 or sunset
if sooner Dec-Feb by prior appointment through the
Regional Office*
£0.60

Cwmmau Farmhouse
Brilley Whitney-on-Wye Hereford Herefordshire HR3
6JP (4m SW of Kington between A4111 /A438
approach by a narrow lane leading S from Kington-
Brilley road at Brilley Mountain)
Tel: 01497 831251
Early 17th century timber-framed and stone-tiles
farmhouse. Arrange viewing with Mr D Joyce. No
facilities but tearoom run by the tenant.
May-Aug Wed 14.00-17.30
A£2.00 £1.00. Not suitable for coaches

Delapre Abbey and Garden
London Road Northampton Northamptonshire NN4
8AT
Tel: 01604 761074
Open public gardens originally a monastery abbey,
formal internal gardens, grapevines, herbs etc.
*All year Mar-Sept 08.00 to sunset Oct-Feb 08.00-
15.30*

Admission Free

Eastwood
8a Victoria Street Eastwood Nottingham
Nottinghamshire NG16 3AW (follow signs on A610)
Tel: 01773 763312 Fax: 0115 943 1452
Birthplace of DH Lawrence, 11th September 1885,
surroundings influenced his writing. Restored
house gives insight into his working class childhood. Audio-visual presentations held, and two
new exhibition rooms show a model of The Country
of my Heart and Lawrence's travels round the
world. There are craft workshops adjacent.
*All year Apr-Oct daily 10.00-17.00, Nov-Mar 10.00-
16.00. Evenings by arrangement. Closed 24 Dec-1
Jan*
A£1.75 Concessions£1.00

Guildhall
Guildhall Lane Leicester Leicestershire LE1 5FQ
(central Leicester)
Tel: 0116 253 2569
Built in 1390 for the Corpus Christi Guild, later used
as Leicester's Town Hall. This is a building of
national importance containing a Great Hall, Lord
Mayor's Parlour, 19th century police cells and the
Old Town Library. A feast of vernacular architecture.
*All year Mon-Sat 10.00-17.30, Sun 14.00-17.30.
Closed 24-26 Dec & Jan 1*
Admission Free

Haughmond Abbey
Upton Magna Offington Shrewsbury Shropshire
SY4 4RW (1m NE of Shrewsbury off B5062)
Tel: 01743 709661
Extensive remains of this 12th century Augustinian
abbey include the Chapter House, which retains its
late-medieval timber ceiling and some fine
medieval sculpture
22 Mar-31 Oct daily 10.00-18.00. Closed 13.00-14.00
A£1.60 C£0.80 Concessions£1.20

Hawford Dovecote
Hawford Worcester (3m N of Worcester 0.5m E of
A449. BR: Worcester Foregate Street & Worcester
Shrub Hill)
Tel: 01684 850051
A 16th century half-timbered dovecote. Access on
foot via the entrance to adjoining house.
*Apr-Oct daily 09.00-18.00 or sunset if sooner. Other
times by prior appointment through the
Regional Office*

❀ *National Trust* **❦** *National Trust for Scotland* **▦** *English Heritage* **▮** *Historic Scotland* **✦** *CADW*
✦ guided tours available **◉** *picnic areas* **♨** *refreshments* **▦** *photography allowed* **1998** *visitor discount
card offer* **❦** *beach/coastal area* **VISA** *Visa accepted* **▭** *Mastercard accepted* **C** *All cards accepted*

£0.60

Kinwarton Dovecote

Kinwarton Nr Alcester Warwickshire *(1.5m NE of Alcester just S off B4089. Bus: for Coughton Court but alight Alcester 1.5m except on the 228 which passes the Dovecote. BR: Wilmcote not Sun except May to Sept 5m, Wootton Wawen not Sun 5m)*

Tel: 01684 850051

A circular 14th-century dovecote, with fine ogee doorway. It retains its potence - a rare feature.
Apr-end Oct daily 09.00-18.00 or sunset if sooner. Closed Good Fri. Other times by prior appointment only with Severn Regional Office on above number. Key obtainable from Glebe Farm next door
A£0.60

Leigh Court Barn

Hereford and Worcester *(5m W of Worcester on unclassified road off A4103. BR: Worcester Foregate 5m)*

Tel: 01604 730320

Magnificent 14th century timber-framed barn, built for the monks of Pershore Abbey. It is the largest of its kind in Britain.
1 Apr-30 Sept Thur-Sun 10.00-18.00
Admission Free

Lord Leycester Hospital

High Street Warwick Warwickshire CV34 4BH *(1m N J15 M40 on A429)*

Tel: 01926 492797

These lovely half-timbered buildings were built in the late 14th century and adapted into almshouses by the Earl of Leycester in 1571. The Hospital is still a home for ex-servicemen and their wives. Originally it was built as a Guildhouse and the old Guildhall, Great Hall, Chapel and Courtyard remain. The Queen's Own Hussars Regimental Museum is housed here. The historic masters garden has been restored and is now open from 10.00-16.00 Tue-Sun Easter-Sept
All year Tue-Sun & Bank Hol 10.00-17.00, 16.00 in Winter. Closed Good Fri & 25 Dec
A£2.50 C£1.50 OAPs£1.75

Newark Town Hall

Market Place Newark Nottinghamshire NG24 1DU *(Market Place Newark located on A1 /A46. BR: Newark Castle, Northgate)*
Tel: 01636 640100 Fax: 01636 640967
One of the finest Georgian Town Halls in the country, the building has recently been refurbished in sympathy with John Carr's original concept. On display is the Town's collection of Civic Plate, silver dating generally from the 17th and 18th century, including the 'Newark Monteith' and the Newark Siege Pieces.
All year Mon-Fri 10-12.00 14.00-16.00, Closed Sat Sun Bank Hol Mon and Tue following and Christmas week, open at other times for groups by appointment
Admission Free

Shrewsbury Quest

193 Abbey Foregate Shrewsbury Shropshire SY2 6AH *(opposite Shrewsbury Abbey)*

Tel: 01743 243324 Fax: 01743 244342

An opportunity to experience the sights sounds and smells of medieval England. The Quest is based on 12th-century England in general and monastic life in particular, including a part dedicated to the world famous monk detective of fiction, Brother Cadfael. Recreated on Shrewsbury Abbey's original grounds, it makes use of Scheduled Monuments and Grade II listed buildings.
Apr-Oct 10.00-18.30, Nov-Mar 10.00-17.30
Last Admission: Apr-Oct 17.00, Nov-Mar 16.00
A£3.95 C£2.50

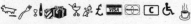

St Mary's Guildhall

Baylby Lane Coventry CV1 5QP *(next to the Cathedral ruins in Baylby Lane)*

Tel: 01203 832381 Fax: 01203 832410

An important medieval Guildhall steeped in the social, industrial and political past of Coventry. Wonder at craftsmanship displayed in stone, glass, timber and thread. Soak up the historic atmosphere, discover the fascinating myths and legends, imagine splendid royal banquets and meetings of powerful guilds. Learn of this great building's role in Coventry's history.
Easter-Sept Sun-Thur 10.00-16.00
Admission Free

Stoke Park Pavilions

Stoke Bruerne Towcester Northamptonshire NN12 7RZ *(Stoke Bruerne village; 7m S of Northampton, W of Stoney Stratford, A508 Northampton Road)*
Tel: 01604 862172
Two pavilions and colonnade. Built in 1630 by Inigo Jones. Exterior only on view
June July & Aug Sat Sun & Bank Hol 14.00-18.00
A£1.00

🐾 suitable for pushchairs 👶 mother & baby facilities ♿ suitable for wheelchairs 🎁 gift shop 🤝 corporate facilities 🐕 no dogs: except guide dogs 🚗 parking on site 🚗 parking nearby £ charged parking ☕ café-restaurant licensed special events educational pack

THE COMMANDERY

The Commandery

Sidbury Worcester Worcestershire WR1 2HU
(Worcester city centre, A44 from J7 M5)

Tel: 01905 355071

This delightful 15th century timber-framed building
was the headquarters of Charles II's army during
the Battle of Worcester in 1651. It has an impressive
Great Hall with fine examples of 15th century
stained glass. The building contains fascinating
Civil War displays including audio-visuals. A varied
events programme all year.

*All year Mon-Sat 10.00-17.00, Sun 13.30-17.30.
Closed 24-28 Dec & 1 Jan*

Last Admission: 16.30

*A£3.40 C£2.30 Family Ticket £9.00, price increase
likely 1/4/98*

***Discount Card Offer: One Child Free When
Accompanied By A Full Paying Adult***

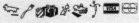

Wichenford Dovecote

Wichenford Worcester Worcestershire *(5.5m NW of
Worcester N of B4204. BR: Worcester Foregate
Street & Worcester Shrub Hill)*

Tel: 01684 850051 Fax: 01684 850090

This large 17th-century dovecote has nearly 600
nesting boxes and is unusual in its timber-framed,
wattle and daub construction, which was rarely
used for dovecotes. The gabled roof appears to
have a chimney, but it is actually an entrance for
the birds.

*Apr-Oct daily 09.00-18.00 or sunset if sooner. Other
times by appointment only through the Regional
Office.*

£0.60

WOODCHESTER MANSION

Woodchester Mansion

Woodchester Park Nympsfield Stonehouse
Gloucestershire GL10 3TS *(by Coaley Peak Picnic
Site on B4066 Stroud to Dursley, 0.5m from
Nympsfield Village. Parking is in the field above the
Mansion, but there is a free bus which runs down
to the Mansion)*

Tel: 01453 750455 Fax: 01453 750457

Hidden in a secluded woodland valley near Stroud
in Gloucestershire is a unique Victorian building.
Mysteriously unfinished and almost untouched for
over 120 years it is one of Britain's most fascinating
country houses. Fantastic gargoyles adorn the
imposing Gothic architecture whilst inside the
bones of the building are laid bare to reveal the
superb craftsmanship of a bygone age.

*Easter-Oct 1st full weekend in each month (Sat &
Sun) and Bank Hol Weekends (Sat-Mon) 11.00-
16.00*

*A£3.50 C£1.00 Students£2.50. Group visits by
arrangement Tel: 01453 860531/860661*

Historic Houses

Adcote

Adcote Little Ness Shrewsbury Shropshire SY4 2JY
(7m NW of Shrewsbury off A5)

Tel: 01939 260202 Fax: 01939 261300

Adcote is the most controlled, coherent and mas-
terly of the big country houses designed by
Norman Shaw (Mark Girouard, Country Life Oct

🌸 *National Trust* 🏴 *National Trust for Scotland* 🏛 *English Heritage* 🏴 *Historic Scotland* 🟢*CADW*
🍵 *guided tours available* 🖼 *picnic areas* ☕*refreshments* 📷 *photography allowed* 1998 *visitor discount
card offer* 🏖 *beach/coastal area* VISA *Visa accepted* 💳 *Mastercard accepted* C *All cards accepted*

970)
Apr-July 14.00-17.00, re-open Sept-Oct. All other times by appointment
Admission Free

Adlington Hall

Mill Lane Adlington Macclesfield Cheshire SK10 4LF
(5m N of Macclesfield on the Stockport / Macclesfield road (A523). BR: Adlington 0.5m)
Tel: 01625 820875 Fax: 01625 828756
A Cheshire Manor home of the Leghs since 1315. The Great Hall was built between 1450 and 1505, the Elizabethan 'Black and White' in 1581 and the Georgian South Front in 1757. A Bernard Smith Organ installed circa 1670. Follies include a chinese bridge, Temple to Diana, Tig House and Shell Cottage.
All year daily to groups by prior arrangement only
A£4.00 C£1.50. Group rates 25+ £3.50

ANCIENT HIGH HOUSE

Ancient High House

Greengate Street Stafford Staffordshire ST16 2HS (J14 M6)
Tel: 01785 214668 Fax: 01785 240204
Built in 1595. Period room settings, changing Exhibitions.
Apr-Oct Mon-Fri 09.00-17.00, Sat 10.00-16.00. Nov-Mar 10.00-15.00

A£1.75 Family Ticket (A2+C2)£4.00
Concessions£1.10

ANNE HATHAWAY'S COTTAGE

Anne Hathaway's Cottage

Shottery Stratford upon Avon Warwickshire CV37 9HH *(off A422)*
Tel: 01789 204016 Fax: 01789 296083
Before her marriage to William Shakespeare, Anne Hathaway lived in this substantial 12-roomed thatched Tudor farmhouse with her family. Famous Hathaway bed and other furniture owned by the family. Shop and garden centre, traditional English Cottage garden. Home to descendants of the Hathaway family until 19th century. Enjoy the near-by Shakespeare Tree Garden, where the many different species of tree are grown mentioned in Shakespeare's plays. Limited wheelchair access, teas and lunches available in The Thatch nearby.
All year 20 Mar-19 Oct Mon-Sat 09.00-17.00, Sun 09.30-17.00, 20 Oct-31 Dec Mon-Sat 09.30-16.00, Sun 10.00-16.00. Closed 23-26 Dec
A£3.50 C£1.50, group concessions available 01789 201806

Arbury Hall

Arbury Nuneaton Warwickshire CV10 7PT *(5M SW of Nuneaton off B4102 Meriden road)*
Tel: 01203 382804 Fax: 01203 641147
The 16th century Elizabethan house, Gothicised in the 18th century, has been the home of the Newdegate family for over 450 years. The finest complete example of Gothic revival architecture in the country. Fine furniture, glassware and portraits. Spectacular plaster work ceilings.
House: Easter-Sept 14.00-17.30 Sun & Bank Hol only. Gardens as House plus Wed in May June July
Last Admission: 17.00
A£4.00 C£2.50 Gardens only A£2.50 C£1.50

🧸 suitable for pushchairs   👶 mother & baby facilities   ♿ suitable for wheelchairs   🎁 gift shop
💼 corporate facilities   🐕 no dogs: except guide dogs   🚗 parking on site   🅿 parking nearby
£ charged parking   ☕ café-restaurant   🍷 licensed   ✨ special events   📚 educational pack

Belgrave Hall

Church Road Belgrave Leicester Leicestershire LE4 5PE *(off Thurcaston Road)*

Tel: 0116 266 6590

A delightful three-storey Queen Anne house dating from 1709 with beautiful period and botanic gardens. Authentic room settings contrast Edwardian elegance with Victorian cosiness and include the kitchen, drawing room, music room and nursery.

All year Mon-Sat 10.00-17.30, Sun 14.00-17.30. Closed 24-26 Dec & Jan 1

Admission Free

BELGRAVE HALL

Belton House

Grantham Lincolnshire NG32 2LS *(3m NE of Grantham on A607 Grantham /Lincoln road easily reached and signposted from A1 BR: Grantham)*

Tel: 01476 566116 Fax: 01476 579071

Built 1685-88 for Sir John Brownlow. The rooms contain portraits, furniture, tapestries, oriental porcelain, family silver and Speaker Cust's silver. Formal gardens, an Orangery and a magnificent landscaped park with a lakeside walk and the Bellmount Tower. Adventure playground, miniature train rides in summer.

House: 1 Apr-1 Nov Wed-Sun & Bank Hol Mon 13.00-17.30. Garden & Park: 11.00-17.30. Shop & Restaurant: 12.00-17.30

Last Admission: 17.00

House & Garden: A£4.80 C£2.40 Family Ticket £12.00 (July & Aug £10.00). Reductions for pre-booked parties

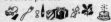

Benthall Hall

Benthall Broseley Shropshire TF12 5RX *(1m NW of Broseley on B4375, 4m NE of Much Wenlock, 1m SW of Ironbridge)*

Tel: 01952 882159

A 16th century stone house with mullioned windows and moulded plaster brick chimneys. The interior includes an intricately-carved oak staircase,

decorated plaster ceilings and oak panelling; also family collections of furniture, ceramics and paintings. Carefully restored plantsman's garden. Restoration church.

Easter-Sept Wed, Sun & Bank Hol Mon 13.30-17.30 House and/or garden at other times by appointment for groups only

Last Admission: 17.00

House: A£3.00 C£1.00. Garden only: A£2.00, reduced rates for pre-booked parties

Boscobel House

Boscobel Lane Bishop's Wood Shropshire ST19 9AR *(on unclassified road between A41 /A5, 8m NW of Wolverhampton)*

Tel: 01902 850244

Fully refurbished and restored the panelled rooms, secret hiding places and pretty gardens lend this seventeenth century timber-framed hunting lodge a truly romantic character. King Charles II hid in the house and in the nearby oak after the battle of Worcester in 1651. House not suitable for wheelchairs, access to gardens only.

22 Mar-31 Oct daily 10.00-18.00 or dusk if sooner. 1 Nov-31 Mar Wed-Sun 10.00-16.00. Tearooms: 1 Apr - 31 Oct Tues-Sun 11.00-17.00. Closed 24-26 Dec and Jan

Last Admission: 30mins before closing

A£3.95 C£2.00 Concessions£3.00

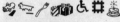

Canons Ashby House

Canons Ashby Daventry Northamptonshire NN11 3SD *(J11 M40, A422 exit then left along unclassified road or J16 M1 signposted from A5, 2m S of Weedon crossroads)*

Tel: 01327 860044

Home of the Dryden family since the 16th century, this manor house was built circa 1550, added to in the 1590's and altered in the 1630's and circa 1710; largely unaltered since. Within the house, Elizabethan wall-paintings and outstanding Jacobean plasterwork are of particular interest. A formal garden includes terraces, walls and gate piers of 1710. There is also a mediaeval priory church and a 28 hectares park.

House & Garden: Easter-Oct Sat-Wed 13.00-17.30 or dusk if sooner. Closed Thur & Fri

Last Admission: 17.00

A£3.50 C£1.80 Family Ticket £8.80

Discount Card Offer: Pre-Booked Groups A£3.00 C£1.50

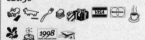

apesthorne Hall

apesthorne Siddington Macclesfield Cheshire
K11 9JY (J18 /J19 M6 J6 M56 approx 10m from
ther motorway, A34 between Congleton /
ilmslow)
el: 01625 861221 Fax: 01625 861619

ating back to the Domesday times, Capesthorne
ontains a great variety of sculptures, paintings, &
ther contents including a collection of American
olonial furnishings. There are gardens, a nature
ail & woodland walks.
arden: Mar-Oct daily 12.00-18.00. Hall: Mar-Oct
'ed Sun & Bank Hol 13.30-15.30
ast Admission: Gardens 16.30 Hall 15.30
ardens: A£2.25 C£1.00. Hall & Gardens: A£4.00
£1.50 OAPs£3.50 Family Ticket £8.00. Groups 25+
all for details

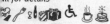

havenage

havenage Tetbury Gloucestershire GL8 8XP *(1m*
ff A48, 7m SE of Stroud, 2m NW of Tetbury sign-
osted off B4014)
el: 01666 502329 Fax: 01453 832700

uilt in 1576, this unspoilt Elizabethan house con-
ains some stained glass from the 17th century and
arlier, as well as some good furniture and tapes-
ies. Hear stories of The Ghosts of Chavenage
ncluding the Headless Coachman.
May-Sept Thur & Sun & Bank Hol 14.00-17.00
£3.00 C£1.50

hurchill House Museum and Hatton Art Gallery

enns Lane Hereford Herefordshire HR1 1DE *(A49,*
5 M5 and A4103)
el: 01432 267409 Fax: 01432 342492

he museum is laid out in a Regency house with
ine grounds, and has 18th and early 19th-century
ooms, displays of costume, and a gallery devoted
o works by the local artist Brian Hatton who was
killed in the first world war.
All year Apr-Sept Tue-Sun, Oct-Mar Tue-Sat, Bank
Hol Mon 14.00-17.00
A£1.00 C&OAPs£0.40, Joint ticket with Old House
A£1.60 C&OAPs£0.75

Deene Park

Deene Park Deene Corby Northamptonshire NN17
3EW *(0.5m off A43, between Kettering /Stamford)*
Tel: 01780 450223/450278 Fax: 01780 450282
Mainly 16th century house of great architectural
importance and historical interest. Home of the
Brudenell family since 1514 including the 7th Earl of
Cardigan who led the Charge of the Light Brigade.

Extensive gardens with old-fashioned roses, rare
trees and shrubs.
Easter, May, Spring & Aug Bank Hol Sun & Mon.
June-Aug Sun 14.00-17.00. Group bookings for 20+
at other times by prior arrangement
House & Garden: A£4.50 C(10-14)£2.00. Garden
only: A£2.50 C(0-10)£Free with accompanying
Adult C(10-14)£1.25

Donington-le-Heath Mnor House

Manor Road Donington le Heath Coalville
Leicestershire LE67 2FW *(A50)*
Tel: 01530 831259 Fax: 0116 247 3011

This is a rare example of a medieval manor house,
tracing its history back to about 1820. It has now
been restored as a period house, with fine oak furnishings. The surrounding grounds include rose
and herb gardens, and the adjoining stone barn is
home to a tempting tea shop.
Wed before Easter-30 Sept 14.00-18.00
Admission Free

FORD GREEN HALL

Ford Green Hall

Ford Green Road Smallthorne Stoke-On-Trent
Staffordshire ST6 1NG *(NE of Stoke on Trent on the*
B5051 between Burslem and Endon)
Tel: 01782 233195 Fax: 01782 233194

This timber-framed farmhouse was built in 1624 for
the Ford family and extended in the early 1700's.
Furnished with items and utensils used by a farm-
ing family from the 16th to 19th centuries. 17th cen-
tury style period gardens in grounds. Wheelchair
access limited to ground floor only.
All year Sun-Thur 13.00-17.00. Closed Christmas-
New Year
Last Admission: 16.45
A£1.50 Concessions£1.00. Wheelchair users and
C(0-4)£Free. Groups & Coaches by appointment
Discount Card Offer: Two For The Price Of One

✗ suitable for pushchairs ✗ mother & baby facilities ♿ suitable for wheelchairs 🎁 gift shop
✎ corporate facilities ✎ no dogs: except guide dogs ✎ parking on site ✎ parking nearby
£ charged parking ✎ café-restaurant ⚲ licensed ✎ special events ✎ educational pack

Gawsworth Hall

Church Lane Gawsworth Macclesfield Cheshire SK11 9RN *(2.5m S of Macclesfield on A536. BR: Macclesfield)*
Tel: 01260 223456 Fax: 01260 223469
This fine Tudor black & white manor house was the birthplace of Mary Fitton (allegedly the 'Dark Lady' of Shakespeare's sonnets). Pictures & armour can be seen in the house, which also has a tilting ground, thought to be a rare example of an Elizabethan pleasure garden.
Mar-Oct 14.00-17.30. Evening parties call for details A£3.80 C£1.90. Groups 20+ £2.80

Grantham House

Castlegate Grantham Lincolnshire NG31 6SS *(E of Grantham Church. BR: Grantham)*
Tel: 01909 486411
The house dates from 1380, but has been extensively altered and added-to throughout the centuries, resulting in a pleasant mixture of architectural styles. The walled gardens run down to the river, and on the opposite bank Sedgwick Meadows. By written appointment only with tenant Major-General Sir Brian Wyldebore-Smith. No toilet facilities.
Ground floor only 30 Mar-end Sept Wed 14.00-17.00, by written appointment only with the tenant £1.50 limited space parties should not exceed 7

Haddon Hall

Bakewell Derbyshire DE45 1LA *(1.5m S of Bakewell off A6)*
Tel: 01629 812855 Fax: 01629 814379
Originally held by the illegitimate some of William the Conqueror, Haddon has been owned by the Dukes of Rutland since the 16th Century. The present house, built over 600 years ago, has escaped the ravages of time. Film location for Zeffirelli's "Jane Eyre" and the B.B.C.'s "Prince and the Pauper."
Apr-Sept daily 11.00-17.45, Aug Mon-Sat 11.00-17.45
Last Admission: 17.00
A£4.75 C£2.95 OAPs£3.90 Family Ticket £13.50 Party 20+

Hagley Hall

Hagley Stourbridge West Midlands DY9 9LG *(just off A456 Birmingham to Kidderminster, 12m from Birmingham within easy reach M5J 3 or 4 M6 or M42)*
Tel: 01562 882408 Fax: 01562 882632
The last of the great Palladian Houses, designed by

Sanderson Miller and completed in 1760. The House contains the finest example of Rococo plasterwork by Francesco Vassali, and a unique collection of 18th century furniture and family portraits.
24 Mar-2 Apr, 23-29 May, 22-29 Aug 14.00-17.00.
Garden open May-Aug
A£3.50 C£1.50 OAPs£2.50 Pre-booked groups by arrangement

HALL'S CROFT

Hall's Croft

Old Town Stratford-Upon-Avon Warwickshire *(town centre location)*
Tel: 01789 204016 Fax: 01789 296083
This impressive 16th-century house, with Jacobean additions, was named after Dr John Hall, who married Shakespeare's daughter Susanna in 1607. It is likely they lived here until moving to New Place after Shakespeare died, in 1616. Hall's Croft is near Holy Trinity Church, where Shakespeare is buried. Admire the outstanding 16th and 17th century furniture and paintings. View Dr Hall's 'consulting room' and exhibition about medicine in Shakespeare's time. Walk round the lovely old walled garden. Take tea in the shade of a 200-year-old mulberry tree.
All year 20 Mar-19 Oct Mon-Sat 09.30-17.00, Sun 10.00-17.00. 20 Oct-19 Mar 10.00-16.00, Sun 10.30-16.00. Closed 23-26 Dec
A£3.00 C(5-17)£1.50. Joint Tickets: 3 town houses A£7.00 C(5-17)£3.50 Family Ticket(A2+C3)£18.00 Concessions£6.00. 5 houses: A£10.00 C(5-17)£5.00 Family Ticket(A2+C3)£26.00 Concessions£9.00

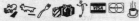

Hardwick Old Hall

Doe Lea Chesterfield Derbyshire S44 5QJ *(9.5m SE of Chesterfield off A6175 from J29 M1, BR: Chesterfield 9.5m, Bus: E Midland / Trent X2-63 Chesterfield / Nottingham to within 1.5m)*
Tel: 01246 850431
This large ruined house, finished in 1591, still displays Bess of Hardwick's innovative planning and interesting decorative plasterwork. The views from

---

the top floor over the country park and 'New Hall are spectacular.

22 Mar-31 Oct Wed-Sun 10.00-18.00 or dusk
A£2.30 C£1.70 OAPs£1.20

Hardwicke Court

Bristol Road Hardwicke Gloucester Gloucestershire GL2 4RS *(5m S of Gloucester on A38 between M5 access, J12 S only and J13)*
Tel: 01452 720212
Late Georgian house designed by Robert Smirke, built 1816-1817. Entrance Hall, Drawing Room, Library and Dining Room open.
Easter Mon-Sept Mon 14.00-16.00 other times by prior written appointment
A£1.00

HARVARD HOUSE

Harvard House

High Street Stratford-Upon-Avon Warwickshire CV37 6HB *(A3400 Birmingham)*
Tel: 01789 204016 Fax: 01789 296083
The most ornate house in Stratford, Harvard House is a fine example of an Elizabethan town house, containing many architectural features. Rebuilt in 1596, it was the home of Katherine Rogers, mother of John Harvard, founder of Harvard College. It was presented in 1910 to Harvard College by Edward Morris, a famous Chicago millionaire. The rooms,

with their flagstone floors and period furniture are an appropriate setting for the recently-acquired, nationally important, Neish Collection of Pewter, which ranges from Roman times to the 19th-century and includes many domestic items which would have been familiar to the inhabitants of Harvard House over the centuries.
Summer daily Mon-Sat 09.30-17.00, Sun 10.00-17.00
Last Admission: 16.00
A£2.00 C£1.50 Concessions£10.00 (for 20+)

Harvington Hall

Harvington Hall Lane Harvington Kidderminster Worcestershire DY10 4LR *(3m SE of Kidderminster, 0.5m from junction of A448 and A450 at Mustow Green)*
Tel: 01562 777846 Fax: 01562 777190
Moated medieval and Elizabethan manor-house containing secret hiding-places and rare wall-paintings. Georgian Chapel in garden with 18th century altar, rails and organ.
Mar-Oct 31 Sun, Tue, Wed, Thur, 11.30-17.30. Closed at other times except by appointment
A£3.50 C£2.00 OAPs£2.50. Private tours wedding receptions by arrangement

Honington Hall

Honington Shipston-On-Stour Warwickshire CV36 5AA *(10m S of Stratford-on-Avon 0.5m E off A3400)*
Tel: 01608 661434 Fax: 01608 663717
Originally built by the Parker family in 1680. Contains fine 18th century plasterwork.
Jun Jul Aug Wed & Bank Hol Mon 14.30-17.00
Parties by appointment
A£2.75 C£1.00

KEDDLESTON HALL AND PARK

Kedleston Hall and Park

Derby Derbyshire DE22 5JH *(5m NW of Derby, signposted from roundabout where A38 crosses A52 close to Markeaton Park. BR: Duffield & Derby)*

🏃 suitable for pushchairs 🧸 mother & baby facilities ♿ suitable for wheelchairs 🎁 gift shop
💼 corporate facilities 🐕 no dogs: except guide dogs 🅿️ parking on site 🅿️ parking nearby
£ charged parking ☕ café-restaurant 🍽 licensed 🎪 special events 🎒 educational pack

Tel: 01332 842191 Fax: 01332 841972

The house has the most complete and least altered sequence of Robert Adam interiors in England. The Indian Museum houses objects collected by Lord Curzon from his time as Viceroy of India. An Adam bridge and fishing pavilion in the park, a garden & pleasure grounds.

House: 28 Mar-1 Nov Sat-Wed 13.00-17.30, Bank Hol 11.00-17.30. Closed Good Fri. Garden 11.00-18.00. Park: Apr-Oct daily 11.00-18.00. Nov-Dec Sat & Sun 12.00-16.00

Last Admission: 17.00

A£4.70 C£2.40 Family Ticket £11.50. Reduced rates for booked parties. Park & Garden: A£2.00 refundable on purchase of tickets for house. Vehicle entry charge for park only Thur-Fri £2.00

Kelmscott Manor

Kelmscott Lechlade Gloucestershire GL7 3HJ *(2m SE of Lechlade off the Lechlade /Faringdon road)*

Tel: 01367 252486 Fax: 01367 253754

Kelmscott Manor was the country home of William Morris, poet, craftsman and socialist from 1871 until his death in 1896. The house contains a collection of he possessions and works of Morris and his associates including furniture, textiles carpets and ceramics.

Apr-Sept Weds 11.00-13.00 14.00-17.00 & Third Sat in each month 14.00-17.00 Thur & Fri by appointment

Last Admission: 16.30

Queuing Times: 1 hour

A£6.00 C&Students£3.00

Kirby Hall

Deene Corby Northamptonshire NN17 5EN *(on unclassified road off A43 4m NE of Corby)*

Tel: 01536 203230

Begun in 1570 this beautiful Elizabethan manor house boasts an unusual richness and variety of architectural detail in the Renaissance style. The extensive gardens - currently being restored - were among the finest in England at their peak during the 17th century.

22 Mar-31 Oct daily 10.00-18.00 or dusk, 1 Nov-21 Mar Wed-Sun 10.00-16.00. Closed 13.00-14.00 Closed 24-26 Dec

A£2.30 C£1.70 OAP£1.20

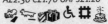

Little Dean Hall

Newnham Road Littledean Cinderford Gloucestershire GL14 3NR *(12m W of Gloucester 2m E of Cinderford 400yds from A4151 Littledean / Newnham-on-Severn road)*

Tel: 01594 824213

Reputedly England's oldest inhabited house with the reputation for being "one of the most haunted houses in the British Isles." The site is steeped in the myth and legend of the Celtic West and Arthurian Age. The Hall is sparsely furnished and presented as a low key museum. Informal grounds.

1 Apr-31 Oct Sun-Fri 14.00-17.30. Other times for parties by appointment

Admission costs please call for details

Little Fleece Bookshop

Bisley Street Painswick Stroud Gloucestershire *(3m N of Stroud A46 6m SE of Gloucester, B4073 off main High Street Painswick. BR: Stroud)*

Tel: 01452 812103

17th century building in heart of Painswick, originally part of Great Fleece Inn. An exemplary restoration carried out 1935 with the advice of Sir George Oakley, enhancing the existing 17th century features and character. Ground floor room only open as bookshop.

4 Apr-31 Oct Tue-Sat 10.00-13.00 & 14.00-17.00, Nov & Dec Sat only 10.00-13.00 & 14.00-17.00 Closed Good Fri

Lower Brockhampton

Brockhampton Bringsty Worcester Worcestershire WR6 5UH *(2m E of Bromyard on Worcester road A44 reached by a narrow road through 1.5m of woods and farmland)*

Tel: 01885 488099

A late 14th century moated manor house, with an attractive detached half-timbered 15th century gatehouse, a rare example of this type of structure. Also, the ruins of a 12th century chapel. Gatehouse and upper floor not accessible to wheelchairs

Medieval Hall & Parlour, gatehouse & chapel: 29 Mar-Sept Wed-Sun & Bank Hol Mon 10.00-17.00. Closed Good Fri, Oct Wed-Sun 10.00-16.00

A£1.60 C£0.80 FamilyTicket £4.00

Lyddington Bede House

Bluecoat Lane Lyddington Uppingham Oakham Rutland LE15 9LZ *(in Lyddington 6m N of Corby, 1m E of A6003)*

Tel: 01572 822438

Elaborate 16th century timbered ceiling first floor. Set amongst picturesque golden stone cottages beside the handsome parish church of St. Andrew, the Bede House was originally a medieval palace of the Bishops of Lincoln. It was later converted to an almshouse in 1602.

22 Mar-31 Oct daily 10.00-18.00. Closed 13.00-14.00

Lyme Park

Lyme Park Disley Stockport Cheshire SK12 2NX *(off A6)*

Tel: 01663 762023/766492 Fax: 01663 765035
Home of the Legh family for 600 years and the largest house in Cheshire, the house is set in historic gardens. There is a 1400 acre park, home to red & fallow deer with magnificent views of the Pennine Hills & Cheshire Plain. Children's play area with multi-play apparatus.
Park: Apr-Oct daily 08.00-20.30, Nov-Mar 08.00-18.00 Gardens: 3 Apr-31 Oct daily Fri-Tue 11.00-17.00, Wed-Thur 10.00-17.00. Hall: 3 Apr-31 Oct Fri-Tue Telephone for winter opening hours
Last Admission: House 16.30
House & Garden: A£4.00 Family Ticket £10.00, Garden only: A£2.00, Park only: £3.30 per car, House only: A£3.00

Melbourne Hall

Church Square Melbourne Derbyshire DE73 1EN *(9m S of Derby on A514)*

Tel: 01332 862502 Fax: 01332 862263
1133 saw Henry I give the manor of Melbourne to the first Bishop of Carlisle, sold to Sir John Coke (Charles I's Secretary of State in 1628) and still owned by his descendants. Converted over time to a grander residence, the home of two Prime Ministers Palmerston and Melbourne, now houses collections of art and antiques with formal gardens laid out in the french style.
Gardens: Apr-Sept Wed, Sat, Sun & Bank Hol Mon 14.00-18.00. House: Aug only Tue-Sat 14.00-17.00. Sun & Bank Hol Mon (No Guided Tours)
Last Admission: Gardens 17.30 House 16.30
House Guided Tour: A£2.50 C£1.00 OAPs£2.00. House: A£2.00 OAPs£1.50 C£0.75. House & Garden: Aug only A£4.50 OAPs£3.50 C£2.50. Garden only: A£3.00 OAPs£2.00 Family Ticket £8.00

Middle Littleton Tithe Barn

Middle Littleton Evesham Worcester *(3m NE of Evesham, E of B4085. BR: Honeybourne /Evesham)*

Tel: 01684 850051 Fax: 01684 850090
Magnificent 13th century tithe barn, built of blue lias stone, and still in use as a farm building.
Apr-Oct daily 14.00-17.00. Access by key only, see notice at property
£0.60

Moat House

Longnor Shrewsbury Shropshire SY5 7PP *(8m S of Shrewsbury E off A49 through village left into lane)*

Tel: 01743 718434 Fax: 01743 718434
Fine example of a timber framed manor house of circa 1463. The hall exhibiting unique timber work and wooden masks. Surrounded by its moat of circa 1250. Accommodation available.
Apr-Sept Thur & Spring & Summer Bank Hol 14.30-17.00 other times, by arrangement for groups 20+
Last Admission: 16.30
A£3.00

THE KING'S BEDROOM AT MOSELEY OLD HALL. © NT PHOTO LIBRARY/ANDREAS VON EINSIEDEL

Moseley Old Hall

Moseley Old Hall Lane Fordhouses Wolverhampton Staffordshire WV10 7HY *(4m N of Wolverhampton, S of M54 between A449 /A460. From N J11 M6, then A460. From S J10A M6 & J1 M54. Coaches must approach via A460 to avoid low bridge)*

Tel: 01902 782808
An Elizabethan house with later additions. Charles II hid here after the Battle of Worcester, and the bed in which he slept is on view, as well as the hiding place he used. A special exhibition in the barn tells the story of the King's escape using contemporary accounts. The small garden has been reconstructed in 17th century style with formal box parterre; 17th century plants only are grown. Optional Free guided tours, wheelchair access limited to ground floor (3 rooms) and garden only. Braille and large-print guides. Tearoom in 18th century barn, teas served as house opening details 13.30-17.30, light lunches Bank Hol Mon also Sundays in July & August from 13.00. The property holds three Sandford Heritage Education Awards.
28 Mar-13 Dec. Mar & May Weekends, Bank Hol Mon and Tue following except Tue 5 May. June-Oct Wed Weekends Bank Hol Mon and following Tue; also Tue in July & Aug. 13.30-17.30, Bank Hol Mon 11.00-17.00. Nov-Dec Guided Tours only Sun 13.30-16.30. Pre-booked groups at other times including

---

🚼 suitable for pushchairs 🍼 mother & baby facilities ♿ suitable for wheelchairs 🎁 gift shop
💼 corporate facilities 🐕 no dogs: except guide dogs 🚗 parking on site 🚗 parking nearby
£ charged parking ☕ café-restaurant 🍷 licensed 🎆 special events 📑 educational pack

evening tours
Last Admission: Last tour 30 mins before closing
A£3.60 C£1.80 Family Ticket £9.00. Groups rates
15+ call for details

Museum of Local Life

Friar Street Worcester Worcestershire WR1 2NA
(Central Worcester 5mins walk from the Cathedral)
Tel: 01905 722349
This interesting 500-year timber-framed house has
a squint and an ornate plaster ceiling. It is now a
museum of local life featuring a children's room, an
Edwardian bathroom and displays of the Home
Front of World War II. There is a change of pro-
gramme of temporary exhibitions and events.
All year Mon-Wed & Fri-Sat 10.30-17.00
A£1.50 Concessions£0.75 school's £0.60

NASH'S HOUSE AND NEW PLACE

Nash's House and New Place

Chapel Street Stratford-Upon-Avon Warkwickshire
CV37 6EP *(next door to Shakespeare Hotel.*
Opposite Falcon Hotel)
Tel: 01789 292325
Step aside from the bustle of Chapel Street into the
tranquility of Nash's House which dates from the
16th-century. It was owned by Thomas Nash who
married Shakespeare's grand-daughter Elizabeth
Hall in 1626. As well as exceptional furnishings of
Shakespeare's time it has displays on the history of
Stratford. From Nash's House go outside to explore
the site of New Place, the house where
Shakespeare lived from 1597 until he died in 1616.
The house was pulled down in 1759 but its founda-
tions and grounds can be seen. Visit the colourful
Elizabethan style Knott Garden.
All year 20 Mar-19 Oct Mon-Sat 09.30-17.00, Sun
10.00-17.00. 1 Jan-19 Mar & 20 Oct-31 Dec Mon-Sat
10.00-16.00, Sun 10.30-16.00. Closed 23-26 Dec
A£3.00 C£1.50 Joint Ticket (with Shakespeare's
Birthplace and Halls Croft) A£7.00 C£3.50 Family

Ticket £18.00 Students&OAPs£6.00. Joint Ticket (as
above plus Anne Hathaway's Cottage and Mary
Arden's House) A£10.00 C£5.00 Family Ticket
£26.00 Students&OAPs£9.00

Owlpen Manor

Owlpen Dursley Gloucestershire *(3m E of Dursley*
off B4066 signposted)
Tel: 01453 860261 Fax: 01453 860819
A romantic Tudor manor house dating from 1450 to
1616. Housing unique 17th century painted cloth
wallhangings, furniture, textiles and pictures. Set in
formal terraced gardens and part of a picturesque
Cotswold manorial group including a watermill, a
Victorian church and medieval tithe barn.
Easter-Sept Tue-Sun 14.00-17.00, July-Aug Tue-Sun
14.00-17.00 also Bank Hol Mon
A£3.75 C£2.00

Pickford's House Social History Museum

41 Friargate Derby Derbyshire DE1 1DA *(signposted*
5m walk W of the city centre)
Tel: 01332 255363
The house built in 1770 by architect Joseph
Pickford as a workplace and home, and stands in
Derby's most handsome street. House shows
domestic life at different periods, with Georgian
reception rooms and service areas and a 1930's
bathroom. Other galleries have temporary exhibi-
tions on social history, textiles and costume
themes. Display on growth of Georgian Derby and
Pickford's contribution to Midland architecture. The
garden has been reconstructed in the Georgian
style.
All year Mon 11.00-17.00, Tue-Sat 10.00-17.00 Sun
& Bank Hol 14.00-17.00. Closed Christmas
Last Admission: 30 mins before closing
Admission Free

Revolution House

High Street Old Whittington Chesterfield Derbyshire
S41 9LA *(on B6052 off A61 signposted)*
Tel: 01246 453554 Fax: 01246 345720
Originally the Cock and Pynot alehouse, this 17th
century cottage was the scene of a meeting
between local noblemen to plan their part in the
Revolution of 1688. The house is now furnished in
17th century style. A video relates the story of the
Revolution and there is a small exhibition room.
Apr-Nov daily 10.00-16.00. Christmas opening call
for details
Admission Free

🌺 *National Trust*   🌷 *National Trust for Scotland*   🏛 *English Heritage*   ▮ *Historic Scotland*   ✛*CADW*
🎋 *guided tours available*   🍴 *picnic areas*   ☕ *refreshments*   📷 *photography allowed*   1998 *visitor discount*
card offer 🏖 *beach/coastal area*   VISA *Visa accepted*   💳 *Mastercard accepted*   C *All cards accepted*

Rushton Triangular Lodge

Rushton Kettering Northamptonshire NN14 1RP *(1m W of Rushton on unclassified road 3m from Desborough on A6)*

Tel: 01536 710761

Almost every detail of the lodge completed by Sir Thomas Tresham in 1593. Sir Thomas was a devout Roman Catholic, imprisoned for his beliefs, who built Rushton Triangular Lodge as an expression of his faith.

22 Mar-31 Oct daily 10.00-18.00. Closed 13.00-14.00
A£1.30 C£1.00 Concessions£0.70

Stanford Hall

Lutterworth Leicestershire LE17 6DH *(M1 J1819 from N. M6 exit at A14/M1(N) signposted off A426, A4304, A50, A5, A14. 1.5m from Swinford)*

Tel: 01788 860250 Fax: 01788 860870

Beautiful William and Mary (1690's) house set in an attractive Park besides Shakespeare's River Avon. The house contains antique furniture, fine pictures (including the Stuart Collection) and family costumes. In the Grounds there is a Motorcycle Museum (extra charge), Craft Centre and Pottery (most Sundays), Walled Rose Garden, Nature Trail and a full-size replica of Percy Pilcher's 1898 Flying Machine, 'The Hawk.'

Easter Sat-end Sept Sat Sun Bank Hol Mon & Tue following 14.30-17.30. Bank Hol and Event days
Grounds: 12.00. House: 14.30
Last Admission: 17.00
House & Grounds: A£3.80 C£1.90. Grounds only: A£2.10 C£1.00. Motorcycle Museum: A£1.00 C£0.35

Stanway House

Stanway Cheltenham Gloucestershire GL54 5PQ *(0.5m E of B4632 on the B4077)*

Tel: 01386 584469 Fax: 01386 584688

A thoroughly lived-in Jacobean manor house with unusual furniture, set in formal landscaped parkland. There is also a tithe barn and gatehouse.

June-Sept limited days only, call for details
A£3.50 C£1.00 OAPs£3.00. Group rates 15+ £3.00

The Fleece Inn

Bretforton Evesham Worcester *(4m E of Evesham on B4035. BR: Evesham)*

Tel: 01386 831173

A medieval farmhouse in the centre of the village, containing family collection of furniture. It became a licensed house in 1848 and remains largely unaltered. Car parking in village square, coaches by written appointment only.

During normal public house licensing hours

Admission Free

The Greyfriars

Friar Street Worcester Worcestershire WR1 2LZ *(in centre of Worcester. BR: Worcester Foregate Street)*

Tel: 01905 23571

Built in 1480, with early 17th century and late 18th century additions, this timber-framed house was rescued from demolition at the time of the WWII and has been carefully restored and refurbished, interesting textiles and furnishings add character to the panelled rooms. An archway leads through to a delightful garden. No toilet facilities.

Easter-Oct Wed-Thur Bank Hol Mon 14.00-17.00
A£2.20 C£1.10 Family Ticket £5.50

The Old House

High Town Hereford Herefordshire HR1 2AA *(approx 0.5m from A49)*

Tel: 01432 364598 Fax: 01432 342492

This good example of a Jacobean house was built in around 1621, and was once in a row of similar houses. The hall, kitchens, and a bedroom with a four-poster bed can be seen along with a number of wall paintings.

May-Sept (incl Easter Sun) Tue-Sat 10.00-17.30, Sun 10.00-16.00, Apr-Sept Mon 10.00-13.00 Bank Hol Mon 10.00-17.00. Closed 13.00-14.00 each day
A£1.00 C&OAPs£0.40. Joint ticket with Churchill Gardens Museum A£1.60 C&OAPs£0.75

The Old Manor

Norbury Ashbourne Derbyshire DE6 2ED

A stone built 13-15th century hall with a rare king-post roof, undercroft and cellars; the hall is of specialist architectural interest only. Also a late 17th century red-brick manor house, incorporating fragments of an earlier Tudor house. The church is well worth a visit.

Mar-Sept Tue Wed & Sat. Medieval Hall by written appointment only with tenant Mr C Wright
A£1.50

Upton Cressett Hall

Bridgnorth Shropshire *(4m W of Bridgnorth, 18m SE of Shrewsbury off A458)*

Tel: 01746 714307 Fax: 01746 714506

Elizabethan Manor House and magnificent Gatehouse in beautiful countryside by Norman church. Unusually fine medieval timber work and interesting brick and plaster work; 14th century Great Hall. Self catering accommodation available in Gatehouse.

🖒 suitable for pushchairs 🍼 mother & baby facilities ♿ suitable for wheelchairs 🎁 gift shop
🍬 corporate facilities 🐕 no dogs: except guide dogs 🚗 parking on site 🚙 parking nearby
£ charged parking ☕ café-restaurant 🍴 licensed 🎉 special events 📚 educational pack

By appointment only. Groups welcome throughout the year
A£2.50 C£1.00

Whitmore Hall

Whitmore Road Whitmore Newcastle Staffordshire ST5 5HW *(4m from Newcastle-under-Lyme on the A53 Road to Market Drayton)*
Tel: 01782 680235 Fax: 01782 680049
Carolinian Manor House, owner's family home for over 800 years. Family portraits dating back to 1624. Outstanding Tudor Stable Block. The house has recently been refurbished.
May-Aug Tue & Wed & Bank Hol 14.00-17.30
Last Admission: 17.00
A£2.50 C£0.50 no reduction for groups

Wightwick Manor

Wightwick Bank Wolverhampton West Midlands WV6 8EE *(3m W of Wolverhampton, up Wightwick Bank, off A454 beside the Mermaid Inn)*
Tel: 01902 761108
Begun in 1887, the house is a notable example of the influence of William Morris, with many original Morris wallpapers and fabrics. Also of interest are Pre-Raphaelite pictures, Kempe glass and de Morgan ware. The Victorian/Edwardian garden has yew hedges and topiary, terraces and two pools. Dogs in garden only, on leads. No guided tours over Bank Holidays Weekends. Wheelchair access (via steps to ground floor) to 5 rooms and garden (site slopes; strong companions necessary).
*House: Mar-Dec Thur & Sat 14.30-17.30, also Bank Hol Weekends 14.30-17.30 (ground floor only, no guided tours). Pre-booked groups Wed-Thur and special evening tours. School visits Wed-Thur.
Garden: Wed-Thur 11.00-18.00 Bank Hol Sun & Mon 13.00-18.00, other days by appointment only
Last Admission: Timed ticket
A£4.80 C&Students£2.40 Gardens only £2.20, parking for one coach only*

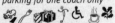

Wilderhope Manor

Easthope Longville Much Wenlock Shropshire TF13 6EG *(7m SW of Much Wenlock, 7m E of Church Stretton, 0.5m S of B4371)*
Tel: 01694 771363
This limestone house stands on the southern slopes of Wenlock Edge in remote country with views down to Corvedale. Dating from 1586, it is unaltered but unfurnished; features include remarkable wooden spiral staircase, unique bow rack and fine plaster ceilings. Let to the YHA, circular walk through farmland and woods. Wheelchair access to house via steep section of path (strong

companion needed) the ground floor accessible.
*Apr-end Sept Wed & Sat 14.00-16.30, Oct-end Mar Sat only 14.00-16.30
All £1.00, no reduction for groups*

Wingfield Manor

Garner Lane South Wingfield Derbyshire *(17m N of Derby 11m S of Chesterfield on B5035, 0.5m S of South Wingfield. From J28 M1 W on A38 /A615 at Alfreton and turn onto B5035 after 1.5m. BR: Alfreton and Mansfield Parkway 4m)*
Tel: 01773 832060
Huge, ruined medieval country mansion built in mid-15th century. Mary Queen of Scots was imprisoned at Wingfield in 1569. Most of the manor has been unoccupied since the 1770's but the late-Gothic Great Hall and the 'High Tower' are fine testaments to Wingfield in its heyday. Used as a film location for 'Peak Practice' and Zeffirelli's 'Jane Austen.'
*1 Apr-31 Oct Wed-Sun 10.00-18.00 or dusk if sooner, 1 Nov-31 Mar Wed-Sun 10.00-16.00. Closed 13.00-14.00. Closed 24-26 Dec
A£2.95 C£1.50 Concessions£2.20*

Winkburn Hall

Winkburn Newark Nottinghamshire NG22 8PQ *(off A617 8m W of Newark 4m N of Southwell)*
Tel: 01636 636465 Fax: 01636 636717
William and Mary Hall undergoing restoration. Interesting sopraporte. Hall is next to church with box pews and monuments unaltered since early 18th century
*By appointment only
A£4.00*

Woolsthorpe Manor

23 Newton Way Woolsthorpe-by-Colsterworth Nr Grantham Lincolnshire NG33 5NR *(7m S of Grantham. 0.5m NW of Colsterworth, 1m W of A1. Leave A1 at Colsterworth roundabout via B676 at second crossroads turn right following NT signs. BR: Grantham)*
Tel: 01476 860338 Fax: 01476 8630338
This small 17th centry farmhouse was the birthplace and family home of Sir Isaac Newton. Some of his major work was formulated here, during the Plague years; an early edition of his Principia Mathematica 1687 is on display. The orchard includes a descendant of the famous apple tree.
*Mar-Oct Wed-Sun & Bank Hol Mon 13.00-17.30. Closed Good Fri
Last Admission: 17.00
Queuing Times: peak weekends*

A£2.50 C£1.20 Family Ticket £6.20. No reduction for parties which must pre-book

Historic Houses & Gardens

Althorp House and Park

Althorp Northampton Northamptonshire NN7 4HG (J16 M1, A45 to Northampton, A428 Northampton / Coventry Road, approx 5m NW of Northampton)
Tel: 01604 592020 tickets Fax: 01604 770042
Web Site: www.althorphouse.co.uk
Althorp House, the final resting place of Diana, Princess of Wales. The house was built in the 16th century, but has been changed since, most notably by Henry Holland in the 18th century. Recently restored by the present Earl, the house is in immaculate condition. Open only (during 1998) from Diana, Princess of Wales' birthday to the eve of the anniversary of her death by prior ticket purchase only by calling the above number.
1 July-30 Aug 1998 daily. Limited tickets available
A£9.50 C£5.00 OAPs£7.00

Ashorne Hall Nickleodeon

Ashorne Hill Nr Warwick Warwickshire CV33 9QN (J13 M40, 13m N of Banbury)
Tel: 01926 651444
Mar-Oct Sun, July & Aug Fri-Sun, Bank Hol & Easter Tue 13.30-15.00. Also open most weekday afternoons for Musical Tea Parties pre-booking only please

Attingham Park

Attingham Park Shrewsbury Shropshire SY4 4TP (4m SE of Shrewsbury on B4380)
Tel: 01743 709203 Fax: 01743 709352
An elegant Neo-classical mansion of the late 18th century with magnificent state rooms, built for the 1st Lord Berwick. His eldest son added a top-lit picture gallery by Nash to display his Grand Tour collection. The 3rd Lord Berwick contributed splendid Regency Silver, Italian Neo-classical furniture and more pictures, making this one of the richest displays of Regency taste to survive. The park was landscaped by Humphrey Repton; there are attractive walks along the river and through the deer park. Prior notice of wheelchair visitors is appreciated as access to house is by rear lift with staff assistance. No dogs in deer park, on leads in the immediate vicinity of the house.
House: 4 Apr - 1 Nov Sat-Wed & Good Fri 13.30-17.00, Bank Hol Mon 11.00-17.00. Deer Park & Grounds: Mar-Oct daily 08.00-21.00, Nov-Feb daily

08.00-17.00 Tearoom & Shop: 4 Apr - 1 Nov Sat-Wed & Good Fri 12.30-17.00, daily in Aug, Nov & Dec Sat & Sun 12.30-16.00. Closed 25 Dec
Last Admission: House 16.30
House & Park: £4.00 Family Ticket £10.00, Park and Grounds only: £1.50, pre-booked parties £3.00
Discount Card Offer: Free Entry For Children Under 16 To The Park Only

ATTINGHAM PARK. PHOTOGRAPH MIKE WILLIAMS

Baddesley Clinton House

Rising Lane Baddesley Clinton Village Knowle Solihull West Midlands B93 0DQ (0.75m W off A4141)
Tel: 01564 783294 Fax: 01564 782706
A romantically sited medieval moated house, dating from the 14th century changed little since 1634. Features family portraits, priest holes, chapel, garden, ponds and lake walk.
House: 4 Mar-1 Nov Wed-Sun & Bank Hol Mon, closed Good Fri. Mar & Apr, Oct-1 Nov 13.30-17.00. May-end Sept 13.30-17.30. Grounds: from 12.00. Shop days as House, Mar, Apr & Oct 12.00-17.00. May-end Sept 12.00-17.30, also 4 Nov-13 Dec Wed-Sun 12.00-16.30. Restaurant: days as House, Lunches 12.00-14.00, Teas 14.30-17.30, Mar, Apr & Oct 17.00, also 4 Nov-13 Dec Wed-Sun 12.00-16.30
Last Admission: 30mins before closing
A£4.80 C£2.40 Family Tickets £12.00. Grounds,

restaurant and shop only: £2.40

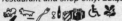

BADDESLEY CLINTON HOUSE

BERRINGTON HALL. © NT PHOTO LIBRARY/JOHN BLAKE

Berrington Hall

Berrington Nr. Leominster Herefordshire HR6 0DW *(3m N of Leominster 7m S of Ludlow on W side of A49. BR: Leominster)*

Tel: 01568 615721 Fax: 01568 613263

An elegant neo-classical house of late 18th century set in a park landscaped by Capability Brown. Formal exterior belies the delicate interior with beautifully decorated ceilings and fine furniture. Nursery, Victorian laundry and Georgian dairy. Attractive garden and historic apple orchard. Children's quizzes indoor and outdoor. Servants Hall Licensed Restaurant and Edwardian Tea Room.

House: Apr Fri-Sun & Bank Hol Mon, closed Good Fri. May-June Wed-Sun & Bank Hol Mon. July-Aug daily. Sept Wed-Sun all 13.30-17.30. Oct-1 Nov Fri-Sun 13.30-16.30. Garden: as House 12.30-18.00, Oct 17.30. Park Walk: July-Oct same days and times as House. Shop: Same as House 13.00-17.30, also 7 Nov-13 Dec Sat-Sun 13.00-16.30. Servants Hall Licensed Restaurant: as House, Lunch: 12.30-17.30. Oct 12.30-16.30, also 7 Nov-13 Dec Sat-Sun 12.30-

16.30. Edwardian Tea Room: Bank Hol weekends and pre-booked groups
Last Admission: 30mins before closing
A£4.00 C£2.00 Family Ticket £10.00. Grounds: £1.80

Boughton House

Living Landscape Trust Kettering Northamptonshire NN14 1BJ *(3m N of Kettering on A43 access from A14)*

Tel: 01536 515731 Fax: 01536 417255

Northamptonshire home of the Dukes of Buccleuch and their Montagu ancestors since 1528. 50-year-old Tudor monastic building enlarged around seven courtyards until the French-style addition of 1695. Many art treasures, Armoury, park with lake.

House: 1 Aug-1 Sept 14.00-17.00, Grounds: 1 May-15 Sept Sun-Thur 13.00-17.00
Last Admission: 16.30
House: A£4.00 C&OAPs£3.00 Grounds: A£1.50 C&OAPs£1.00

Brobury House Garden & Gallery

Brobury Hereford Herefordshire HR3 6BS *(from Hereford A438 W towards Brecon for 10m, turn left at the Brobury /Bredwardine sign, Brobury House is 1m further on left)*

Tel: 01981 500229 Fax: 01981 500229

Victorian Gentleman's Country House set in 8 acres of magnificent gardens, with stunning view over the Wye Valley. Overnight accommodation and self catering cottages available. Art gallery with antique maps & prints on site.

All year 1 Apr-31 Oct Mon-Sat 09.00-16.30, 1 Nov-31 Mar 09.00-16.00. Closed Christmas and New Year
A£2.00 C£1.00

Burton Court

Eardisland Leominster Herefordshire HR6 9DN *(5m W of Leominster signposted on A44)*

Tel: 01544 388231

A typical squire's house, built around the surprising survival of a 14th century hall. The East Front re-designed by Sir Clough Williams-Ellis in 1912. An extensive display of European and Oriental costume, natural history specimens, and models including a working model fairground. Pick your own soft fruit in season.

Spring Bank Hol-end Sept Wed Thur Sat Sun & Bank Hol Mon 14.30-18.00
A£2.50 C£2.00. Coach parties £2.00
Discount Card Offer: Two For The Price Of One

Calke Abbey

Ticknall Derbyshire DE73 1LE *(10m S of Derby on A514 at Ticknall between Swadlincote & Melbourne. BR: Derby & Burton on Trent)*
Tel: 01332 863822 Fax: 01332 865272
Calke Abbey is a baroque house built in 1703-4 for Sir John Harpur and contains rooms almost unchanged since the 1880s. Extensive natural history collections. Chinese silk state bed. Other features include: walled garden, pleasure ground, Orangery, stables with collection of carriages, church, restaurant and shop, landscape park.
House, Garden & Church: Apr-Oct Sat-Wed & Bank Hol Mon. Closed Good Fri and 15 Aug 98. House & Church: 12.45-17.30 Garden: 11.00-17.30. Ticket Office 11.00-17.00
Last Admission: 14.45
Queuing Times: Considerable queues at peak times
All sites: A£4.90 C£2.45 Family Ticket £12.25. Garden only: £2.20. Discount for parties. Refundable vehicle charge on entry to house when open

CHARLECOTE PARK. © NATIONAL TRUST

Charlecote Park

Charlecote Warwick Warwickshire CV35 9ER *(5m E of Stratford-upon-Avon on N side of B4086)*
Tel: 01789 470277 Fax: 01789 470544
Home of the Ivay family since 1247 the present house was built in the 1550s and later visited by Queen Elizabeth I. Landscaped by 'Capability' Brown the park has a herd of red and fallow deer, reputedly poached by Shakespeare, and a flock of Jacob sheep first introduced in 1756. Principal rooms are decorated in Elizabethan Revival style.
House: 3 Apr-1 Nov Fri-Tue 12.00-17.00, closed Good Fri. Shop: as House 11.00-17.00. Orangery Restaurant: 12.00-17.00
Last Admission: 30mins before closing
A£4.80 C£2.40 Family Ticket £12.00

Chatsworth

Chatsworth Bakewell Derbyshire DE45 1PP *(8m N of Matlock off B6012. 16m from J29 M1 signposted via Chesterfield. 30m from J19 M6. BR: Chesterfield)*
Tel: 01246 582204/565300 Fax: 01246 583536
Chatsworth is the palatial home of the Duke and Duchess of Devonshire and has one of the richest collections of fine and decorative arts in private hands. Garden with fountain and maze. The park is one of the finest in Britain, laid out by Capability Brown. NEW for 1998 the NEW adventure playground. The thrilling new playground has been built to conform to the highest international safety standards. Young children will enjoy the sand and water play areas, while older children will be able to test their skills and daring on the towers, ropewalks, spiral slide and commando wire.

Visitor Comments: "a whole day to visit" "beautiful house, amazing antiques" "you will be left gasping" "gardens are wonderful - in hot weather you can walk up the waterfall steps" "the maze was a real challenge"

18 Mar-1 Nov House: 11.00-17.30. Garden: 11.00-18.00 June-Aug Garden opens at 10.30. Farmyard & Adventure Playground: 10.30-17.30. House & Garden open 5 & 6 Sept for Country Fair Visitors as a reduced rate

Last Admission: 16.00-17.30

House & Garden: A£6.25 C£3.00 Family Ticket £16.00 OAPs&Students£5.00. Extra for Scots Bedroom A&OAPs&Students£1.00 C£0.50 Family Ticket £2.00. Garden: A£3.60 C£1.75 Family Ticket £9.00 OAPs&Students£3.00. Farmyard & Adventure Playground: A&C£3.00 C(0-3)£Free. Groups 5+ £2.50 each. Car Park £1.00. Family Pass £25.00 for all attractions. Pre-Booked Groups: A£5.75 OAPs&Students£4.50 incl Scots Bedroom + £1.00. Pre-booked Guided Tours: details on request call above number

CHATSWORTH HOUSE

Clumber Park

Clumber Gardens Clumber Park Worksop
Nottinghamshire S80 3AZ *(4.5m SE of Worksop, signposted from A1)*
Tel: 01909 476592 Fax: 01909 500721
1538 hectares of parkland, farmland, lake and
woodlands. The mansion was demolished in 1938,
but the fine Gothic Revival Chapel, built 1886-89 for
the 7th Duke of Newcastle, survives. Park includes
the longest double lime avenue in Europe and a
superb 32 hectares lake. Also Classical bridge, tem-
ples, lawned Lincoln Terrace, pleasure grounds and
the stable block with restaurant, shop and information room. Walled Garden including Victorian
Apiary, Vineries and Tools exhibition. Clumber
Conservation Centre near Cricket Ground. Guided
walks may be booked for groups throughout the
summer.
Park: All year during daylight hours. Walled
Garden, Victorian Apiary, Fig House, Vineries and
Garden Tools Exhibition: Apr-end Sept Weekends &
Bank Hol Mon 10.00-17.00. Conservation Centre:
Apr-Sept Weekends & Bank Hol Mon 13.00-17.00.
Chapel: Wed-Sun 10.00-16.00. Closed 25 Dec
Last Admission: 16.30
Pedestrians Free, Car motorbikes & caravenettes
£3.00 (with the exception of NT members)
Individual attractions charged, call for details

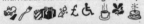

VIEW OF THE CHAPEL FROM THE LAKE SHORE AT CLUMBER
PARK. © NT PHOTO LIBRARY/JERRY HARPUR

Cottesbrooke Hall

Cottesbrooke Northampton Northamptonshire NN6
8PF *(10m N of Northampton near Creaton on A50*
near Brixworth on A508. A14 /A1 /M1 link road)
Tel: 01604 505808 Fax: 01604 505619
Magnificent Queen Anne house, reputed pattern for
Jane Austen's 'Mansfield Park,' with fine picture,
furniture and porcelain collections. Celebrated gardens include fine old cedars, specimen trees, glorious herbaceous borders, courtyards and water gardens. All set in a remarkable landscaped park with

vistas and lakes.
Easter Mon-End Sept House: Thur & Bank Hol Mon
14.00-17.30 Sept Sun 14.00-17.30, Gardens: Wed-Fri
& Bank Hol Mon 14.00-17.30 Sept Sun 14.00-17.30
Last Admission: 17.00
House & Gardens: A£4.00 C£2.00 OAPs£4.00
Gardens only: A£2.50 C£1.25 OAPs£2.50

WEST FRONT AND GATEHOUSE. COUGHTON COURT © NT

Coughton Court

Coughton Alcester Warwickshire B49 5JA *(2m N of*
Coughton, on E side of A435)
Tel: 01789 762435 Fax: 01789 765544
An impressive central gatehouse dating from 1530.
During the Civil War this formerly moated and
mainly Elizabethan house was attacked by both
sides. Also has strong connections with the Gun
Powder Plot. Featuring some notable furniture,
porcelain, portraits and memorabilia of the
Throckmorton family resident since 1409. Two
churches, tranquil lake, riverside walk and newly
created formal gardens. Photography allowed in
grounds only.
14 Mar-Apr Sat-Sun 11.30-17.00, Easter Mon-Wed
11.30-17.00, May-Sept Sat-Wed 11.30-17.00, July-
Aug Fri-Wed 11.30-17.00, 3-18 Oct Sat-Sun 11.30-
17.00. Grounds: 11.00-17.30
Last Admission: 30mins before closing
Queuing Times: Timed entry tickets for busy days
A£5.90 C£2.95 Family Ticket £18.50. Grounds:

£3.90. New walled garden: £2.00 charge for NT members only

Discount Card Offer: Two Adults (@ £5.90) For The Price Of One. Not Valid Saturdays, Sundays Or Bank Holiday Mondays

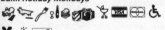

Dudmaston

Quatt Bridgnorth Shropshire WV15 6QN *(4m SE of Bridgnorth on A442)*

Tel: 01746 780866

The 17th-century flower paintings which belonged to Francis Darby of Coalbrookdale are exhibited in this house of the same period, with modern works, botanical art and fine furniture. The house stands in an extensive parkland garden and there are dingle and lakeside walks; two estate walks starting from Hampton Loade, of 3.5 and 5 miles. Light lunches for pre-booked groups on Wednesday and Thursdays, otherwise home-made teas 14.00-17.30. Dogs in Dingle and estate only, on leads.

30 Mar-28 Sept Wed & Sun 14.00-17.30, Pre-booked groups only Thur 14.00-17.30

Last Admission: 17.00

House & Garden: A£3.50 C£2.00 Family Ticket £8.00 Garden only: £2.50, Guided Tours for pre-booked groups

FAMILY GATHERING AT EYAM HALL

Eyam Hall

Eyam Hope Valley Derbyshire S32 5QW *(approxi-* mately 10m from Sheffield / Chesterfield / Buxton. Eyam Hall is off the A623 which runs between Stockport / Chesterfield in the centre of the village past the church)

Tel: 01433 631976 Fax: 01433 631603

Robert and Nicola Wright welcome you to their family home, Eyam Hall and hope you will enjoy your visit to this fascinating 17th century house, with its collections of portraits, tapestries, costumes and family memorabilia. Tours of the house give a very personal interpretation of the domestic and social history of previous Wright ancestors inhabiting the Hall. Extend your stay with a visit to the Craft Centre within the restored buildings of the Hall Farm and housing seven working craft shops, including stained glass design, stenciling, leatherwork and musical instrument making. Don't leave without indulging yourself at The Buttery which offers an exceptional menu of home-made cakes (Mary's Russian Cake is a must!) and unusual delicious light lunch dishes such as Spinakopita.

House: 1 Apr-1 Nov Wed Thur Sun & Bank Hol 11.00-16.30. Craft Centre & Buttery: 28 Feb-20 Dec every day except Mon 10.30-17.30

Craft Centre: Admission Free. House: A£3.50 Family Ticket £10.50 Concessions£3.00

Discount Card Offer: Two For The Price Of One

Frampton Manor

Gloucester Gloucestershire *(3m from J13 M5)*

Tel: 01452 740698/787

Medieval/Elizabethan timber framed Manor House with walled garden. Reputed 12th century birthplace of 'Fair Rosamund' Clifford mistress of King Henry II. 15th century Wool Barn and Granary with dovecote.

House & Garden all year by written appointment. Garden open 20 Apr-6 July 14.00-17.00

House & Garden £2.50 Garden only £1.50

Fulbeck Hall

Lincoln Road Fulbeck Grantham Lincolnshire NG32 3JW *(on A607 between Grantham and Lincoln)*

Tel: 01400 272205 Fax: 01400 272205

Fine family house since 1632. House mainly 18th century with alterations and additions. Collection includes furniture, pictures, porcelain and embroidery. Headquarters of 1st Airborne Division during WWII and now home of the Arnhem Museum. 11 acres of picturesque gardens.

12 Apr, 13 Apr, 4 May, 25 May, 28 June - 10 July & 13-26 July daily, 24 Aug 14.00-17.00

House and Garden:A£3.50 C£1.50 Family Ticket £9.50 OAPs£3.00 Garden Only: A&OAPs£1.50

🛒 suitable for pushchairs   👶 mother & baby facilities   ♿ suitable for wheelchairs   🎁 gift shop
🤝 corporate facilities   🐕 no dogs: except guide dogs   🅿️ parking on site   🚗 parking nearby
£ charged parking   ☕ café-restaurant ⛤ licensed   🎆 special events   📚 educational pack

C£1.00

Hanbury Hall

School Road Hanbury Droitwich Worcestershire WR9 7EA *(4.5m E of Droitwich, 1m N of B4090, 6m S of Bromsgrove, 1.5m W of B4091. BR: Droitwich)*
Tel: 01527 821214 Fax: 01527 821251
William & Mary-style red-brick house, completed in 1701. Hanbury is a typical example of an English country house built by a prosperous local family, with outstanding painted ceilings and staircase by Thornhill. The Watney Collection of porcelain is also on display in the house. No dogs in garden allowed on leads in park.
29 Mar-28 Oct Sun-Wed 14.00-18.00. Evening guided tours for pre-booked parties (May-Sept)
Last Admission: 17.30 or dusk if sooner
House & Garden: A£4.30 C£2.00 Family Ticket £10.50, Garden only: A£2.50
Discount Card Offer: Two for One. One Adult Free When Accompanied By A Paying Adult For House & Garden @ £4.30

Hanch Hall

Lichfield Staffordshire WS13 8HH *(4m NW on B5014)*
Tel: 01543 490308
Twelve rooms of this small country mansion are open to the public. There is a Jacobean staircase, the unusual window in the Great Hall mentioned in Pepys Diary, and cellars dating back to the 12th century. Gardens include a 40ft model of Lichfield Cathedral, Chapel and an Elizabethan Wall.
House: Apr-Sept Sun & Bank Hol Mon 11.00-17.00, Tea Rooms & Gardens: Sun Tue Thur Fri & Bank Hol Mon 11.00-17.00
Last Admission: Tour of house 16.00
House A£2.00 Tea Rooms & Gardens A£1.50 Party 20+ call for details

HARLAXTON MANOR GARDENS

Harlaxton Manor Gardens

The Garden House Grantham Lincolnshire NG32 1AG *(1m from A1 on A607 Grantham / Melton Mowbray road main gates on left after 2m)*
Tel: 01476 592101 Fax: 01476 592131
Magnificent Fairy-Tale Chateau in 110 acres of gardens and grounds currently being restored by TV gardener and garden designer Alan Mason. Built on seven terraces with Italian, French and Dutch influences. Six and a half acre walled garden containing show gardens. (Gardens only- House open by appointment only).*Apr-Oct Tue-Sun & Bank Hol Mon 11.00-17.00. Groups by appointment A£2.50 C£1.25 OAPs£2.00*

HOLDENBY HOUSE, GARDENS AND FALCONRY CENTRE

Holdenby House, Gardens and Falconry Centre

Holdenby Northampton Northamptonshire NN6 8DJ *(7m NW of Northampton off A428 & A50 approx. 7m from J15a/16/J18 M1)*
Tel: 01604 770074 Fax: 01604 770962
Once the largest house in Elizabethan England, Holdenby secured its place in history when it became the prison of Charles I during the Civil War. Visit the Holdenby Falconry Centre and Children's Farm.
Gardens & Falconry Centre: Apr-end Sept Mon-Fri 14.00-18.00, Sun 14.00-18.00, Bank Hol Sun & Mon 13.00-18.00. Closed Sat
House & Gardens (Bank Hol Mon only): A£4.00 C£2.00 OAPs£3.75. Garden: A£3.75 C£1.75 OAPs£2.25

Holme Pierrepont Hall

Holme Pierrepont Nottingham Nottinghamshire NG12 2LD *(5m SE from centre of Nottingham follow signs for National Water Sports Centre on A52 A6011 and continue for 1.5m)*

Tel: 0115 933 2371

Early Tudor brick Manor house. Fine medieval timber-work and lodgings with original fireplaces. Family furniture and pictures 17th century to present. 19th century Courtyard garden with box hedges.

June Sun 14.00-18.00, July Thur & Sun 14.00-18.00, Aug Tues Thur-Fri & Sun 14.00-1800, Easter Hol weekend and May Bank Hol 14.00-18.00, Bank Hol Sun-Tue 14.00-18.00

A£3.00 C£1.00 OAPs£3.00. Pre-booked groups

KELMARSH HALL

Kelmarsh Hall

Kelmarsh Northampton Northamptonshire NN6 9LU *(12m N of Northampton, 5m S of Market Harborough on A508 /A14 J2)*

Tel: 01604 686543 Fax: 01604 686543

1732 Palladian house designed by James Gibbs and built by Smiths of Warwick. Chinese room with wallpaper from 1940. Entrance lodges by Wyatt. Interesting gardens with lake and woodland walks. Herd of British White cattle. Guided tours of the house. Home made cream teas.

Easter-end Aug Sun & Bank Hol Mon 14.30-17.00
Last Admission: 16.30
House & Garden: A£3.50 C£2.00 OAPs£2.00. Gardens: £2.00

Lamport Hall and Gardens

Lamport Hall Trust Northampton Northamptonshire NN6 9HD *(J15 16 18 20 M1 on A508 between Northampton and Market Harborough)*

Tel: 01604 686272

17th/18th century country house, home of Isham family, mainly John Webb and Francis Smith. High room (1655) fine library (1732). Garden home to the first gnome in England.

Easter-end Sept Sun & Bank Hol Mon 14.15-17.15, Aug Mon-Sat one tour at 16.30, 24-25 Oct 14.15-

17.15
Last Admission: 16.00
A£3.80 C£2.00 OAPs£3.30

Little Malvern Court and Gardens

Little Malvern Malvern Worcestershire WR14 4JN *(3m S of Great Malvern on Upton-on-Severn Road (A4104))*

Tel: 01684 892988 Fax: 01684 893057

14th century Prior's Hall once attached to 12th-century Benedictine Priory, with Victorian addition by Hansom. Family and European paintings and furniture. Collection of 18th and 19th century needlework. Home of the Berington family by descent since the Dissolution. 10 acres of former monastic grounds. Magnificent views, lake, garden rooms, terrace.

15 Apr-16 July Wed Thur 14.15-17.00 Parties by prior arrangement
Last Admission: 16.30
House & Garden A£4.00 C£2.00 House or Garden only A£3.00 C£1.00

Ludford House

Ludford Ludlow Shropshire SY8 1PJ *(0.5m S of Ludlow B4361 road Ludlow Station)*

Tel: 01584 872542 Fax: 01584 875662

House dating back to 12th century
Grounds and exterior by written permission with limited inspection of interior
£3.00

Marston Hall

School Lane Marston Grantham Lincolnshire NG32 2HQ *(A1 1.5m in the village turn right at pub)*

Tel: 01400 250225

Tudor manor house with Georgian interiors, held by Thorold family since 14th century; interesting pictures and furniture. Romantic garden with long walks and avenues, high hedges enclosing herbaceous borders and vegetables. Gothic gazebo and ancient trees.

Open 3 times a year 2nd-3rd & 4th Sun in June 14.00-18.00
House & Garden A£2.50 Society and private visits by appointment

Middleton Hall

Middleton Tamworth Staffordshire B78 2AE *(J9 M42 on A4091 Belfry /Tamworth road, follow brown signs)*

Tel: 01827 283095 Fax: 01827 285717

🦘 suitable for pushchairs   👶 mother & baby facilities   ♿ suitable for wheelchairs   🎁 gift shop
🍬 corporate facilities   🐕 no dogs: except guide dogs   🚗 parking on site   🚙 parking nearby
£ charged parking   🍴 café-restaurant   🍷 licensed   🎆 special events   🎒 educational pack

Once the home of two great 17th century natural-
ists, Francis Willughby and John Ray, the Hall shows
several architectural styles, from circa 1300 to an 11
bay Georgian west wing. The grounds include a
nature reserve, lake, meadow, orchard and woodland - all sites of special scientific interest plus two
walled gardens and a craft centre. Reg. Charity No.
510564.

House & Gardens: Sun & Bank Hol 14.00-17.00.
Craft Centre & Coffee Shop: All year Wed-Sun inclu-
sive 11.00-17.00
A£2.00 Concessions£1.00. Craft Centre Only: £Free

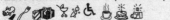

MIDDLETON HALL

Moccas Court

Moccas Hereford Herefordshire HR2 9LH *(10m E of*
Hay on Wye 13m W of Hereford on the River Wye 1m
off B4352
Station: Hereford)
Tel: 01981 500381
Built by Anthony Keck in 1775 overlooking the River
Wye, decoration by Robert Adam including the
round room and oval stair. Scene of famous 17th
century romance and destination of epic night ride
from London. Set in 'Capability' Brown parkland
with an attractive walk to The Scar Rapids.
House and Gardens Apr-Sept Thurs 14.00-18.00
£1.95

Morville Hall

Westgate Bridgnorth Shropshire WV16 5BN *(Bus:*
Midland Red West 436/7. BR: Bridgnorth)
An Elizabethan house of mellow stone converted in
the 18th century. The hall sits in a fine setting with
three gardens. Guided tours available for pre-
booked parties. Wheelchair access to ground floor
and most of garden.
By written appointment only with tenant
Charge may be levied by tenant

Newark Park

Ozleworth Wotton-Under-Edge Gloucestershire

GL12 7PZ *(1.5m E of Wotton-under-Edge 1.75m S of*
junction of A4135 & B4058 BR: Stroud)
Tel: 01684 850 051 Fax: 01684 850 090
Tudor 'standing' or hunting lodge built of the edge
of a cliff By the Poyntz family, made into a four-
square castellated country house by James Wyatt
1790. Restoration work on the garden and house is
in progress.
By prior appointment only please call 01684
850051
A£2.00 C£1.00 No reduction for parties, not suit-
able for coaches

Newstead Abbey House and Grounds

Newstead Abbey Park Nottingham Nottinghamshire
NG15 8GE *(J27 M1 12m N of Nottingham on A60)*
Tel: 01623 793557 Fax: 01623 797136
Beautiful historic house set in parklands, home of
poet Lord Byron. Byrons own room and mementoes
on display, and rooms from Medieval to Victorian,
splendidly decorated. 300 acres of grounds include
waterfalls, water gardens and japanese gardens.
Disabled access limited to ground floor.
Grounds all year daily 09.30-18.00 House Apr-Sept
daily 12.00-18.00
Last Admission: 17.00
House & Grounds A£3.50 C£1.00 OAPs & Students
£2.00 Grounds only A£1.60 Concessions£1.00

Packwood House

Packwood Lane Lapworth Solihull West Midlands
B94 6AT *(2m EW of Hockley Heath on A3400)*
Tel: 01564 782024
The house, originally 16th century, is a 20th century
evocation of domestic Tudor architecture. Created
by Graham Baron Ash, its interiors reflect the peri-
od between the world wars and contain a fine col-
lection of 16th century textiles and furniture.
Important gardens with renowned herbaceous bor-
ders.
Car Park: 1 Mar-22 Mar Sat & Sun 12.00-16.00. 25
Mar-end Sept Wed-Sun & Bank Hol Mon; Car park:
12.00-18.00, Garden: 13.30-18.00, House: 14.00-
18.00. Closed Good Fri. Oct-1 Nov Wed-Sun 12.30-
16.30. Shop: as House
Last Admission: 30mins before closing
A£4.20 C£2.10 Family Ticket £10.30. Garden: £2.10.
Car park: £2.00 refunded on entry to House &
Garden

Papplewick Hall

Main Street Papplewick Nottingham
Nottinghamshire NG15 8FE *(6m N Nottingham off*
A60 2m from J27 M1)

🦋 *National Trust* 🏴 *National Trust for Scotland* ✠ *English Heritage* ▌ *Historic Scotland* 🏴 CADW
🌿 *guided tours available* 🅿 *picnic areas* ♨ *refreshments* 📷 *photography allowed* 1998 *visitor discount*
card offer 🏖 *beach/coastal area* VISA *Visa accepted* 💳 *Mastercard accepted* C *All cards accepted*

Tel: 0115 963 3491

Fine Adam house built 1784 with lovely plasterwork ceilings. Park and woodland garden, particularly known for its rhododendrons. Accommodation and conference facilities available. *All year by appointment only*
On request

Ragley Hall

Alcester Warwickshire B49 5NJ *(1.5m SW off A435 near Alcester)*

Tel: 01789 762090 Fax: 01789 764791

Set in four hundred acres of parkland and gardens, the Great Hall contains some of England's finest baroque plasterwork designed by James Gibbs. Features an adventure playground, maze, woodland walks and a sculpture trail in the gardens. Relax in the delightful landscape designed by Capability Brown where peacocks freely roam, enjoy tea overlooking the Rose Gardens, or enjoy the tranquillity of a lakeside picnic. Dogs are welcome on leads in the Park and on the Woodland Walk but NOT in the House, Garden, or Adventure Wood.

*Apr-Oct Thur-Sun & Bank Hol Mon 10.00-18.00.
Park open July-Aug daily 10.00-18.00.
Last Admission: 16.30*
A£4.50 C£3.00 OAPs£4.00

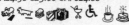

Rodmarton Manor

Rodmarton Manor Rodmarton Cirencester Gloucestershire GL7 6PF *(off A433 6m W of Cirencester)*

Tel: 01285 841253 Fax: 01285 841298

One of the last great country houses to be constructed entirely by hand from local material between 1909-1929. Most of the furniture was made for the house and there are fine examples of decorated pottery, applique, rugs and curtains. Superb gardens with greatest impact in June.
*All year to groups by prior written appointment
Garden Sat 17 May-30 Aug 14.00-17.00 and by appointment all year
Tour of house with un-conducted tour of garden
A£4.50 C£2.20 Minimum group charge £31.50
Garden only £2.00 Sat 14.00-17.00 and £2.50 any other time accompanied children free*

Sandon Hall

Sandon Stafford Staffordshire ST18 0BZ *(5m NE of Stafford on A51 10mins from J14 M6)*

Tel: 01889 508004

Neo-Jacobean ancestral home containing family museum situated in the heart of Staffordshire

amidst 400 acres of superb parkland and a notable arboretum.

Throughout the year to booked groups only
Guided Tour A£3.00 Concessions £2.50 Gardens A£1.50 Concessions £1.00

SHIPTON HALL

Shipton Hall

Shipton Much Wenlock Shropshire TF13 6JZ *(in Shipton 6m SW of Much Wenlock, J B4376 & B4368)*

Tel: 01746 785225 Fax: 01746 785125

Delightful Elizabethan stone manor circa 1587 with Georgian additions. Interesting Rococo and Gothic plasterwork by T.F. Pritchard. Family Home. Stone walled garden, medieval dovecot, and Parish Church dating from late Saxon period. Refreshments by prior arrangement for groups of 20+.

Easter-end Sept Thur, Bank Hol Sun & Mon, except Christmas and New Year 14.30-17.30 also by appointment for groups of 20+ any time of year
House and Garden: A£3.00 C£1.50. Special rate for parties

Snowshill Manor

Snowshill Broadway Worcestershire WR12 7JU *(3m SW of Broadway approach only from turning off the A44 by Broadway Green BR: Moreton -in-Marsh)*

Tel: 01386 852410 Fax: 01386 852410

A Tudor house with a circa 1700 façade, best known for Charles Paget Wades' collections of craftsmanship and design, including musical instruments, clocks, toys, bicycles, weavers' and spinners' tools, Japanese armour. A 10min walk along undulating country path. Timed tickets for house. Liable to overcrowding at peak times.

1 Apr-1 Nov Wed-Mon 13.00-17.00. Visitor facilities open from 12.00. Closed Good Fri & Tue
Last Admission: 45mins before closing
A£5.50 C£2.75 Family Ticket £13.70. Grounds

👶 suitable for pushchairs 👶 mother & baby facilities ♿ suitable for wheelchairs 🎁 gift shop
🐕 corporate facilities 🐕 no dogs: except guide dogs 🚗 parking on site 🚗 parking nearby
£ charged parking ☕ café-restaurant 🍷 licensed 🎆 special events 📚 educational pack

restaurant & shop £2.50

SNOWSHILL MANOR

The Manor House

Manor Road Donington le Heath Coalville
Leicestershire LE67 2FW *(off B585, signposted from
A50)*
Tel: 01530 831259 Fax: 01530 831259
Medieval manor house of early 13th century with
16th-17th century alterations. Rooms have 16th-
17th century oak furniture. The gardens are current-
ly being returned to 15th-16th century style with a
Maze, flower gardens and trees all of which were
grown throughout those centuries. Refurbishment
of restaurant facilities. Herb garden.
*Wed before Easter, then Easter-30 Sept Wed-Sun &
Bank Hol 14.00-18.00*
Admission Free

Thrumpton Hall

Main Street Thrumpton Nottingham
Nottinghamshire NG11 0AX *(7m S of Nottingham
3m E of J24 M1 1m from A453)*
Tel: 0115 983 0333
Fine Jacobean house, built 1607, incorporating ear-
lier manor house. Priest's hiding hole, magnificent
Charles II carved staircase carved and panelled

saloon and other fine rooms, containing beautiful
17th and 18th century furniture and many fine portraits. Large lawns separated from landscaped park
by ha-ha and by lake.
*All year including evenings by appointment only for
parties of 20+*
*House and Gardens: A£5.00 C£2.50 Minimum
charge of £90.00 per party*

WALCOT HALL

Walcot Hall

Walcot Lydbury North Shropshire SY7 8AZ
Tel: 0171 581 2782 Fax: 0171 589 0195
Built by Sir William Chambers for Lord Clive of
India. The Georgian House possesses a free-stand-
ing and recently restored Ballroom, stableyard with
matching clock towers and extensive walled garden, in addition to its ice house, meat-safe and
dovecote. There is an Arboretum, noted for its
rhododendrons and azaleas, specimen trees, pools
and a lake. Food available at Powis Arms.
*End May Bank Hol Sun-Mon. Other days by prior
arrangement*

WESTON PARK

Weston Park

Weston-under-Lizard Shifnal Shropshire TF11 8LE
(7m W of J12 M6, 3m N of J3 M54)
Tel: 01952 850207 Fax: 01952 850430
Built in 1671, this fine mansion stands in elegant
gardens and a vast park designed by Capability
Brown. Three lakes, a miniature railway and a
woodland adventure playground are to be found in

the grounds. The house is open to the public for special gourmet dinner evenings. Call for details.

Park & House: 11-14 Apr, 15 Apr-14 June weekends, Bank Hol & Whit Week (23-31 May), 15 June-26 July Tue-Thur & Weekends, 27 July-6 Sept daily, 6-20 Sept weekends only Park 11.00-17.30, House 13.00-17.00. Closed 18 July & 15-16 Aug

Last Admission: Park 17.00, House 16.30

Park & Gardens: A£3.50 C£2.00 OAPs£2.50. House, Park & Gardens: A£5.00 C£3.00 OAPs£3.75

Discount Card Offer: One Child Free With Full Paying Adult

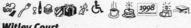

Witley Court

Great Witley Worcester Worcestershire WR6 6JT *(10m NW of Worcester on A443)*

Tel: 01299 896636

This is one of the most spectacular country house ruins. An earlier Jacobean house was converted in the 19th century into a vast Italianate Mansion by John Nash. The gardens, William Nesfield's 'master work' contain immense stone fountains, including the Poseidan Fountain currently being restored to working order.

1 Apr-31 Oct daily 10.00-18.00 dusk if sooner 1 Nov-31 Mar Wed-Sun 10.00-16.00. Closed 13.00-14.00. Closed 24-26 Dec

A£3.10 C£1.60 Concessions£2.30

Historical Remains

Acton Burnell Castle

Acton Burnell Shrewsbury Shropshire SY5 7PE *(on unclassified road, 8m S of Shrewsbury)*

Tel: 01604 730320 Fax: 01604 730321

Now ruined, this fortified manor house was built in the late 13th century by Robert Burnell, the Chancellor of the time. It consisted of a central block with towers to the corners and a great hall and chapel on the upper floor. By 1420 the house was no longer being used.

Any reasonable times

Admission Free

Blackfriars

Ladybellegate Street Gloucester Gloucestershire *(in Ladybellegate Street off Southgate Street & Blackfriars Walk. BR: Gloucester)*

Tel: 0117 975 0700

A small Dominican priory church. Most of the original 13th century church remains, including a rare scissor-blade roof.

Call for details

Call for Admission details

Buildwas Abbey

Iron Bridge Telford Shropshire TF8 7BW *(on S bank of River Severn on B4378, 2m W of Iron Bridge)*

Tel: 01952 433274 Fax:

The beautiful, ruined, Cistercian abbey was founded in 1135, and stands in a picturesque setting. The church with its stout round pillars is roofless but otherwise almost complete.

1 Apr-31 Oct daily 10.00-18.00 or dusk if sooner

A£1.75 C£0.90 Concessions£1.30

Chichele College

Higham Ferrers Northamptonshire *(in Higham Ferrers on A6. Bus- Stagecoach United Counties 46/A/X94 from Wellingborough. BR: Wellingborough 5m)*

Tel: 01933 317182

Parts of a quadrangle remain of this college for secular canons, founded in 1422.

Quadrangle: any reasonable time. For Chapel: please contact key-keeper Mrs. C. Jones

Admission Free

Croxden Abbey

Uttoxeter Staffordshire *(5m NW of Uttoxeter off A522 BR: Uttoxeter 6m)*

Tel: 01604 730320

Remains of a Cistercian abbey founded in 1176.

All year any reasonable time

Admission Free

Edvin Loach Old Church

Hereford and Worcester *(4m N of Bromyard on unclassified road off B4203)*

Tel: 01604 730320

Peaceful and isolated 11th century church remains.

Any reasonable time

Admission Free

Greyfriars

Gloucester *(on Greyfriars walk behind Eastgate Market off Southgate St. Bus: From surrounding areas Tel: 01452 425543. Train: Gloucester 0.50m)*

Remains of a late 15th, early 16th century Franciscan friary church.

Any reasonable time

Admission Free

Iron Bridge

Ironbridge Shropshire *(in Ironbridge adjacent to A4169. BR: Telford Central 5m)*

Tel: 01604 730320

The world's first iron bridge and Britain's best-known industrial monument. Cast in Coalbrookdale by local ironmaster Abraham Darby, it was erected across the River Severn in 1779.

Any reasonable time

Admission Free

Kingswood Abbey Gatehouse

Kingswood Gloucestershire *(in Kingswood off B4060 1m SW of Wotton-under-Edge. BR: Yate 8m)*

Tel: 01604 730320

The 16th-century gatehouse, with a richly carved mullioned window, is all that remains of the Cistercian abbey.

Exterior: any reasonable time. Key for interior obtainable from shop nearby during opening hours

Admission Free

Kinver Edge

The Warden's Lodge The Compa Kinver Stourbridge West Midlands DY7 6HU *(5m W of Stourbridge, 6m N of Kidderminster, 2.5m off A458)*

Tel: 01384 872418

Wood and heath covered sandstone ridge from which views across Shropshire and the West Midlands are excellent. Rock houses inhabited until the 1950's, one rebuilt in 1993 for resident tenants but not open to the public. Wheelchair access limited. No toilet facilities. Dogs on leads in rock house grounds.

Kinver Edge: all year during daylight hours, Rock House grounds: Apr-Sept daily 09.00-19.00, Oct-Mar daily 09.00-16.00

Admission Free

Lunt Roman Fort

Baginton Coventry CV1 5QP *(in Baginton village near Coventry Airport Brown tourist signs give directions)*

Tel: 01203 832381 Fax: 01203 832410

Once inhabited by the Roman Army, this ancient site provides a fascinating snapshot of Roman military life. Setting the scene for a unique historical experience are the timber gateway, 350 feet of ramparts, granary building and Gyrus. All are faithfully reconstructed from archaeological evidence.

Easter-Oct Sat Sun & Bank Hol Mon, 19 July-7 Sept daily 10.00-17.00

A£2.50 C£1.25 Concessions£1.25. Group booking essential

Mattersey Priory

Nottinghamshire *(rough access down drive 0.75m long - 1m E of Mattersey off B6045 - 7m N of East Retford BR: Retford 7m)*

Tel: 01604 730320

Remains of a small Gilbertine monastery founded in 1185.

All year any reasonable time

Admission Free

Morton Corbet Castle

Moreton Corbet Shropshire *(in Moreton Corbet off B5063 7m NE of Shrewsbury)*

Tel: 01604 730320

A small 13th-century keep and the ruins of an impressive Elizabethan house are all that remain: the house was destroyed when the Parliamentary forces captured it in 1644.

Any reasonable time

Admission Free

Nine Ladies Stone Circle

Stanton Moor Derbyshire *(from unclassified road off A6 5m SE of Bakewell . BR: Matlock 4.5m)*

Tel: 01604 730320

Once part of the burial site for 300-400 people, this Early Bronze Age circle is 15 metres (50 feet) across.

Any reasonable time

Admission Free

Offa's Dyke

Chepstow Gloucestershire *(3m NE of Chepstow off B4228. Access via Forestry Commission Tidenham car park 1m walk down to Devil's Pulpit on Offa's Dyke)*

Tel: 01604 730320

Three-mile section of the great earthwork built by Offa, King of Mercia 757-96, from the Severn estuary to the Welsh coast as a defensive boundary to his kingdom. Access suitable only for those wearing proper walking shoes - not suitable for very young or old or infirm.

Any reasonable time

Admission Free

White Ladies Priory

Shropshire *(1m SW of Boscobel House off unclassified road between A41 and A5 - 8m NW of*

Wolverhampton BR: Cosford 2.5m)
Tel: 01604 730320
The ruins of the late 12th century church of a small priory of Augustinian canonesses.
Any reasonable time
Admission Free

Whiteladies Priory (St Leonards Priory)

Shropshire *(1m SW of Boscobel House)*
Tel: 01604 730320
Only the ruins are left of this Augustinian nunnery, which dates from 1158 and was destroyed in the Civil War. After the Battle of Worcester Charles II hid here and in the nearby woods before going on to Boscobel House.
Any reasonable time
Admission Free

Humps & Bumps

Arbor Low Stone Circle and Gib Hill Barrow

Monyash Derbyshire *(0.5m W of A515 2m S of Monyash. BR: Buxton 10m)*
Tel: 01604 730320
A fine Neolithic monument, this 'Stonehenge of Derbyshire' comprises many slabs of limestone, surrounded by an unusually large ditch. Site managed by the Peak Park joint planning board
All year daily 10.00-18.00 or dusk
Farmer who owns right of way to site may levy a charge

Arthur's Stone

Dorstone Hereford and Worcester *(7m E of Hay-on-Wye off B4348 near Dorstone. Bus- Stagecoach Red & White 39 Hereford-Brecon to within 0.75m)*
Tel: 01604 730320 Fax: 01604 730321
Prehistoric burial chamber formed of large blocks of stone.
All year any reasonable time
Admisison Free

Belas Knap Long Barrow

Nr Winchcombe Gloucestershire *(2m S of Winchcombe near Charlton Abbots 0.5m on Cotswold Way. BR: Cheltenham)*
A good example of a Neolithic long barrow, with the mound still intact and surrounded by a stone wall. The chamber tombs, where the remains of 31 people were found, have been opened up so that visitors can see inside.
Any reasonable time

Admission Free

Cantlop Bridge

Berrington Shropshire *(0.75m SW of Berrington on unclassified road off A458 BR: Shrewsbury)*
Tel: 01604 730320
Single-span cast-iron road bridge over the Cound Brook, designed by the great engineer Thomas Telford.
Any reasonable time
Admission Free

Eleanor Cross

Geddington Northamptonshire *(in Geddington off A43 between Kettering and Corby. BR: Kettering 4m)*
Tel: 01604 730320
One of a series of famous crosses erected by Edward I to mark the resting places of the body of his wife, Eleanor, when brought for burial from Harby in Nottinghamshire to Westminster Abbey.
Any reasonable time
Admission Free

Hob Hurst's House

Beeley Derbyshire *(off B6012, 2m SE Beeley.)*
Tel: 01604 730334
A rectangular prehistoric burial mound, surrounded bya ditch with an outer bank situated half mile N of unclassified road off B6012.

Mitchell's Fold Stone Circle

Shropshire *(16m SW of Shrewsbury W of A488 Bus-Minsterley 553 Shrewsbury-Bishop's Castle BR: Welshpool 10m)*
Tel: 01604 730320
An air of mystery surrounds this Bronze Age stone circle, set on dramatic moorland and consisting of some 30 stones of which 15 are visible.
Any reasonable time
Admission Free

Notgrove Long Barrow

Notgrove Gloucestershire *(1.5m NW of Notgrove on A436)*
Tel: 01604 730320
A Neolithic burial mound with chambers for human remains opening from a stone-built central passage.
Any reasonable time

🏹 suitable for pushchairs 🐾 mother & baby facilities ♿ suitable for wheelchairs 🛍 gift shop
🍬 corporate facilities 🐕 no dogs: except guide dogs 🚗 parking on site 🚙 parking nearby
£ charged parking ☕ café-restaurant ⚖ licensed 🎉 special events 📚 educational pack

Admission Free

Nympsfield Long Barrow

Nympsfield Gloucestershire *(1m NW of Nympsfield on B4066)*
Tel: 01604 730320
A chambered Neolithic long barrow 30 metres (90 feet) in length.
Any reasonable time
Admission Free

Uley Long Barrow Hetty Pegler's Tump

Uley Gloucestershire *(3.5m NE of Dursley on B4066)*
Tel: 01604 730320
Dating from around 3000 BC, this 55 metre (180 foot) long Neolithic chambered burial mound is unusual in that its mound is still intact.
Any reasonable time
Admission Free

Industrial Heritage

Black Country Living Museum

Tipton Road Dudley West Midlands DY1 4SQ *(3m from J2 M5, follow brown signs from motorway, on A4037 opposite Dudley Guest Hospital)*
Tel: 0121 557 9643 Fax: 0121 557 4242
Web Site: www.bclm.co.uk
Friendly costumed demonstrations bring reconstructed original cottages, shops and workshops to life on a 26 acre site. Features include; underground 1850's coalmine experience, 1930's Fried Fish Shop, electric trams, Olde Tyme Fairground and 1920's Cinema. Regularly changing programme of working exhibits.
All year Mar-Oct daily 10.00-17.00. Nov-Feb Wed-Sun 10.00-16.00. Closed 25 Dec
A£6.95 C(5-17)£4.50 Family Ticket (A2+C3)£19.50 OAPs£5.95. Group rates 20+ call for details

Snibston Discovery Park

Ashby Road Coalville Leicestershire LE67 3LN *(10mins from M1 J22, M42/A42 J13)*
Tel: 01530 510851/813256 Fax: 01530 813301
All weather 'hands-on' science and industrial heritage museum where visitors of all ages can discover the wonders of science or explore our rich industrial heritage. Other attractions include lively surface tours of Snibstons colliery buildings conducted by ex-miners and a outdoor science and playground.

Visitor Comments: "exhibits are clean and well maintained" "truly brilliant for all ages" "restaurant light and airy with a well priced menu" "picnic area was beautiful and calming on such a hot day"
Apr-Aug daily 10.00-18.00, Sept-Mar daily 10.00-17.00. Closed 25-26 Dec
A£4.00 C£2.75 Concessions£2.95 Family Ticket £10.00. Group rates 10+ A£3.25 Concessions£2.00

Temple Mine

The Pavilion Matlock Bath Matlock Derbyshire DE4 3NR *(off A6 At S end of Matlock Bath 200yds up Temple Rd)*
Tel: 01629 583834
In the process of being restored to how it was in the 1920/30's, this old lead Fluorspar workings makes interesting viewing. A self-guided tour illustrates the geology, mineralisation and mining techniques.

Open all year Apr-Oct daily 10.00-17.00, Nov-Mar daily 11.00-16.00 (visits at 12.00 and 14.00 only)
Last Admission: 30 mins before closing
Museum and Mine A£3.00 Family Ticket £7.00 Concessions£2.25 Museum or Mine only A£2.00 Family Ticket £4.00 Concessions£1.50

WIRKSWORTH HERITAGE CENTRE

Wirksworth Heritage Centre

Crown Yard Market Place Wirksworth Nr Matlock Derbyshire DE4 4ET *(on B5023 off A6 signposted from Wirksworth Market Place)*
Tel: 01629 825225
The Centre has been created in an old silk and velvet mill. The three floors of the mill have interpretative displays of the town's past history as the hub of a prosperous lead-mining industry. Each floor offers many features of interest. Unusual local customs are explained as well as workshops showing the skills of a cabinet maker and a silversmith.
Feb-June & Oct-Nov 11.00-16.00, closed Mon, Sun morning & some Tue, July-Sept daily 10.00-17.00

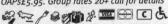

Last Admission: 45mins prior to closing
A£1.00 C&OAPs£0.80 Family Ticket £2.80. Parties
20+ call for details

Industrial Sites

Magpie Mine

Sheldon Bakewell Derbyshire DE *(3m W off B5055
Macclesfield Road)*
Tel: 01629 583834
The surface remains of the mine are the best exam-
ple in Britain of a 19th century lead mine. It was
last worked (unsuccessfully) in 1958 and then sta-
bilised in the 1970's.
Any reasonable time
Free Admission

Kite Festivals

Shrewsbury Kite Festival

Sundorne Playing Fields Shrewsbury SY4 *(on
B5062 2m E of Shrewsbury)*
Tel: 01743 235068 Fax: 01743 358681
Now in it's 14th year this event is held in three
fields including one for Boomerang throwing. In
1992 this event witnessed the world record throw
of 149.12 meters! Over 5,000 people attend.
4-5 Jul 09.00-dusk
Admission Free

Leisure Facilities

Hayfield Cycle Hire

Hayfield Picnic Site Station Road Hayfield High
Peak Derbyshire SK22 2ES *(signed off Chinley-
Glossop Road)*
Tel: 01663 746222
Cycle Hire Centre based on the Sett Valley Trail.
16.00
All Day A£7.70 C£5.80 Half DayA£5.40 C£4.300

Middleton Top Cycle Hire

Middleton Top Visitor Centre Middleton by
Wirksworth Derbyshire DE4 4LS *(0.5m S from
B5036 signed A6 in Cromford J28 M1 12mm)*
Tel: 01629 823204 Fax: 01629 825336
Cycle Hire Centre based upon High Peak Trail with
17.5 miles of traffic free route.
*Spring Bank Hol-mid Sept daily 09.30-18.00. Mid-
Sept-mid-Dec weekends 09.30-dusk. Closed Mid-
Dec-Feb*
Queuing Times: 30mins at times

All day: A£8.00 C(14inch)£5.50. 3 Hours:A£5.70
C(14inch)£4.00. 2 Hours: A£4.00 C(14inch)£4.00.
School Groups: All day £5.80. 3 Hours All £4.00.
Tandems: All day £24.00. 3 Hours £16.00. Child's
Trailers: All day £6.00. 3 Hours £4.50. Child Seats:
All day £2.50. 3 Hours £1.20. Deposits: upto 9
bikes £20.00 10 or more bikes £50.00

MIDDLETON TOP CYCLE HIRE

Leisure Pools

Waterworld

Festival Park Stoke-on-Trent Staffordshire ST1 5PU
Tel: 01782 283838 Fax: 01782 201815
The UK's No.1 Indoor Water Theme Park with 17
major attractions including Nucleus, a 350ft indoor
water roller coaster. There's a water edge restau-
rant, and 86F tropical temperature all year!
All year daily
A£4.50 C£3.75

Lived Here

Izaak Walton's Cottage

Worston Lane Shallowford Nr Stafford *(Shallowford
off the A5013 5m N of Stafford)*
Tel: 01785 760278 Fax: 01785 240204
Thatched timber-framed cottage bequeathed to
Stafford by Izaak Walton, author of the 'Compleat
Angler' Now has period room settings and a small
fishing museum.
Apr-Oct Tue-Sun 11.00-16.30
A£1.75 Family Ticket (A2+C2)£4.00

🏃 suitable for pushchairs   🍼 mother & baby facilities   ♿ suitable for wheelchairs   🎁 gift shop
🤝 corporate facilities   🐕 no dogs: except guide dogs   🚗 parking on site   🅿 parking nearby
£ charged parking   🍴 café-restaurant   🍷 licensed   🎂 special events   📚 educational pack

Concessions £1.10

IZAAK WALTON'S COTTAGE

MARY ARDEN'S HOUSE AND THE SHAKESPEARE COUNTRY SIDE MUSEUM

Mary Arden's House and the Shakespeare Countryside Museum

Station Road Wilmcote Stratford-Upon-Avon Warwickshire CV37 9UN *(3m NW off A34)*
Tel: 01789 204016 Fax: 01789 296083
Mary Arden was William Shakespeare's mother, and this picturesque, half-timbered Tudor house was her childhood home. The house is the main historic feature of an extensive complex of farm buildings which house displays of farming and country life, including a remarkable dovecote, a smithy and cooper's workshop.
All year 20-Mar 19 Oct Mon-Sat 09.30-17.00, Sun 10.00-17.00, 1 Jan-19 Mar & 20 Oct-31 Dec Mon-Sat 10.00-16.00, Sun 10.30-16.00. Closed 23-26 Dec A£4.00 C£2.00 FamilyTicket £11.00. Groups 20+ 10% discount. All five houses: A£10.00 C£5.00 Family Ticket £26.00 OAPs£9.00

Mr Straw's House

7 Blyth Grove Worksop Nottinghamshire S81 0JG *(in Worksop follow signs for Bassetlaw General Hospital BR: Worksop)*
Tel: 01909 482380
A semi-detached house built at the turn of the cen-

tury belonging to William Straw and his brother Walter. The interior has been preserved since the death of their parents in the 1930's with 1920's wallpaper, furnishings and local furniture. Wheelchair access is poor.
Mar-Oct daily 11.00-16.30
Last Admission: 16.00
A£3.00 C£1.50 Family Ticket £7.50

SHAKESPEARE'S BIRTHPLACE

Shakespeare's Birthplace

The Shakespeare Centre Henley Street Stratford upon Avon Warwickshire CV37 6QW *(J15 M40, A46 to Stratford upon Avon)*
Tel: 01789 204016 Fax: 01789 296083
The half-timbered house where William Shakespeare was born in 1564 continued as a family home until the 19th century. It has welcomed visitors for well over 250 years, and has many fascinating architectural features and 16th-and 17th-century furniture. Come in through the Visitors' Centre and see the highly-acclaimed exhibition William Shakespeare: His Life and Background. Enjoy the traditional English garden. Stand in the rooms where Shakespeare grew up. Read the signatures of famous visitors cut in the window panes. See how the walls were made of wattle and daub. Choose from the selection of gifts in the Birthplace Shop. Browse in the Shakespeare Bookshop (opposite the Birthplace).
All year Mon-Sun. Closed 23-26 Dec Last Admission: Summer 17.00, Winter 15.00 A£4.50 C£2.00 Family Ticket (A2+C3)£12.00, Joint Tickets 3 in-town houses: A£7.00 C£3.50 Family Ticket(A2+C3)£18.00 Concessions£6.00, All 5 houses: A£10.00 C£5.00 Family Ticket(A2+C3)£26.00

Monuments

Over Bridge

Gloucester Gloucestershire *(1m NW of Gloucester city centre at J of A40 & A419)*
Tel: 01604 730320

🦋 National Trust   🏴 National Trust for Scotland   ♯ English Heritage   🏛 Historic Scotland   ⬤ CADW
🎋 guided tours available   🌳 picnic areas   ♨ refreshments   📷 photography allowed   1998 visitor discount
card offer   🦶 beach/coastal area   VISA Visa accepted   ⬭ Mastercard accepted   C All cards accepted

A single-arch masonry bridge spanning the River Severn, built by Thomas Telford 1825-27.
Any reasonable time
Admission Free

Moorlands

Carding Mill Valley and Long Mynd

Chalet Pavilion Carding Mill Valley Church Stretton Shropshire SY6 6JG *(15m S of Shrewsbury, W of Church Stretton valley and A49. Bus: Midland Red West 435, BR: Church Stretton)*
Tel: 01694 722631
236 hectares of historic moorland, part of the Long Mynd extends for 4 miles including Carding Mill Valley. The land rises to some 560 metres and there are wonderful views of the Shropshire and Cheshire plains and the Black Mountains. Dogs must be kept under control on the moorland. Guided walks during summer months
Moorland: all year, Chalet Pavilion café, shop and information centre: Mar-Sept daily 11.00-17.00.
Car park: £1.50 per car, coaches £10.00,reduction for pre-booked coaches

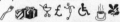

Motor Racing Circuit

Mallory Park

Church Road Kirkby Mallory Leicester Leicestershire LE9 7QE *(just of A47 between Leicester and Hinkley)*
Tel: 01455 842931 Fax: 01455 848289
Web Site: www.excim.co.uk/mallorypark/
Motor racing circuit staging mainly motor cycle and car races. Alternative phone number 0891 884445.
See Special Events for details.
Varies on meeting call for details

Silverstone Circuit

Towcester Northamptonshire NN12 8TN *(0.75m from Silverstone between Towcester and Brackley on A43)*
Tel: 01327 857271 Fax: 01327 857663
Web Site: www.silverstone-circuit.co.uk
Britains premier motor racing circuit. Hosts the British Grand Prix. Booking line 01327 857273.
See special events for dates and times
See Special events for details

Motor Sports

Santa Pod Raceway

Airfield Road Podington Wellingborough Northamptonshire NN29 7XA *(M1 J14. In the village of Podington. Follow RAC signs)*
Tel: 01234 782828 Fax: 01234 782818
'The Home of European Drag Racing' Santa Pod Raceway established for over 30 years in North Bedfordshire is the home of European Drag Racing - the fastest motorsport on earth! Sited on what was once an American airbase, Santa Pod attracts over 200,000 visitors each season (March to November) to watch one of America's great motor sports. This is motor racing at it's fastest and the season's calendar comprises over 35 different car/bike related events. These range from 3 day International Drag Racing Championships to specialist events including VW's, Minis and Public Test Days where the public try their hand at racing too from just £10.00! All major race meetings provide a great family day and weekend entertainment with free camping for weekend ticket holders, show cars, fun fair rides, night racing, bars and a wide selection of food.
March-Nov weekend race meetings 10.00-21.00
Day ticket prices start from A£13.00 C(0-11)£Free C(12-16)£Half Price. Prices vary according to the event, please call to clarify prices.

Museum- Aerospace

Midland Air Museum

Coventry Airport Baignton Coventry Warwickshire
Tel: 01203 301033 Fax: 01203 301033
Over 40 aircraft from diminutive Gnat jet fighter to giant Vulcan bomber and Argosy freighter. Sir Frank Whittle Jet Heritage Centre - exhibition building contains displays on work of the Coventry born jet pioneer.
All year Mon-Sat 10.30-17.00, Sun 10.30-18.00
A£3.00 C£2.00 Family Ticket £8.50 OAPs£2.25.
Group rates on application

The Aerospace Museum

Cosford Shifnal Shropshire TF11 8UP *(on the A41, only 1m from J3 on the M54)*
Tel: 01902 374872/374112 Fax: 01902 374813
Web Site: www.uk-guide.com/west-mid/aerospac.htm
One of Britain's largest and best kept aviation collections with extensive displays: over 50 rockets and missiles from the deadly experimental types to current state-of-the-art technology; aero engines include power plants from early piston engined aircraft to the modern jet. Exhibitions include British, German, Japanese and American war planes including the Spitfire, Hurricane, Mosquito, Liberator and

🦒 suitable for pushchairs 🍼 mother & baby facilities ♿ suitable for wheelchairs 🎁 gift shop
🤝 corporate facilities 🐕 no dogs: except guide dogs 🚗 parking on site 🚙 parking nearby
£ charged parking ☕ café-restaurant 🍷 licensed 🎂 special events ✈ educational pack

Lincoln, along with the mighty post-war bombers and fighters such as Vulcan, Victor and Lightning. Research and development aircraft from the early days of 1941 when the first British jet aircraft made it maiden flight, through the post-war years, the advancement of aviation technology made thrilling and fascinating strides. The Aerospace Museum is the home to many huge retired civil and military transport aircraft which tell the story of passenger carrying by air from the early days to the present time. All of this in three fully heated hangers. The Aerospace Museum provides a unique venue for corporate entertaining and private parties. A range of events can be accommodated. Call for further information.

All year daily 10.00-17.00. Closed 24-26 Dec & 1 Jan
Last Admission: 16.00
A£5.00 C£3.00 Family Ticket £12.00 OAPs£3.50
Party rates for 20+ and educational parties available on application

Museum- Art

Aston Hall

Trinity Road Aston Birmingham West Midlands B6 6JD
Tel: 0121 327 0062
This splendid Jacobean mansion built between 1618 and 1635, was the scene of a Civil War siege. Scars left by cannon-shot can still be seen on its magnificent Great Stairs. The hall is finely decorated with elaborate plasterwork freizes and ceilings, and has a spectacular Long Gallery. There are more than twenty furnished rooms containing paintings, furniture, textiles and metalwork.
Apr-Oct daily 14.00-17.00
Admission Free

Cheltenham Art Gallery and Museum

Clarence Street Cheltenham Gloucester GL50 3JT *(M5 J10 then A4019 & J11then A40, also A435 and A46 meet at Cheltenham, in town centre near the bus station)*
Tel: 01242 237431 Fax: 01242 262334
This museum close to the town centre of Cheltenham has an outstanding collection relating to the Arts and Crafts Movement made famous by William Morris. The Art Gallery contains Dutch and British paintings from the 17th century to present day.
All year Mon-Sat 10.00-17.20. Closed Bank Hol
Admission Free

Hereford City Museum and Art Gallery

Broad Street Hereford Herefordshire HR4 9AU *(A49 /J6 M5 A4103)*
Tel: 01432 364691 Fax: 01432 342492
A selection from the wide range of the city museum's collections are displayed, usually including archaeology, social history, natural history decorative and fine art. The Art Gallery has an interesting programme of temporary exhibitions, occasionally showing works from the permanent collections. Exhibitions change regularly.
All year Wed & Fri 10.00-18.00, Thur 10.00-17.00, Sat 10.00-17.00, Apr-Sept Sat 10.00-16.00, Oct-Mar Sun May-Sept 10.00-16.00. Closed Mon ex Bank Hol
Admission Free

Nature in Art

Wallsworth Hall Twigworth Gloucester Gloucestershire GL2 9PA *(on A38 from village follow tourist signs)*
Tel: 01452 731422 Fax: 01452 730937
Dedicated to art inspired by nature, from Picasso to David Sheppard there are myriads of outstanding exhibits including sculpture, tapestries and ceramics. There is a comprehensive 'artist in residence' programe for ten months of year. A current collection includes the work by over 450 artists from nearly 50 countries, spanning 1500 years.
All year Tue-Sun & Bank Hol 10.00-17.00, Mon by arrangement. Closed 24-26 Dec
A£2.95 C&OAPs&Students£2.10 C(0-8)£Free Family Ticket £9.50

Museum- Aviation

NEWARK AIR MUSEUM

Newark Air Museum

Winthorpe Showground Lincoln Road Newark Nottinghamshire NG24 2NY
Tel: 01636 707170 Fax: 01636 707170
The museum's collection of more than forty five aircraft and helicopters covers all aspects of aviation:

jet fighters; bombers; transport; trainers; civilian; and light aircraft. Large under cover Display Hall, Engine Hall, Artefact Displays, large shop and café. Anyone wishing to fly-in to the Museum should call in advance for Briefing Sheets and approval contacts.

All year Apr-Sept Mon-Fri 10.00-17.00 Sat, Sun & Bank Hol 10.00-18.00. Oct & Mar daily 10.00-17.00. Nov-Feb daily 10.00-16.00. Closed 24-26 Dec

A£3.50 C£2.00 Family Ticket (A2+C2)£9.00 OAPs£2.75. Special rates for concessions and Groups 10+ available

Discount Card Offer: Party Rate Admission, Equivalent to 50p Per Person In A Group

Museum- Canal

Birchalls Canal Museum

Old Birchalls Walsall Birmingham *(signposted from A454 and A34)*

Tel: 01922 645778

Small museum housed in a former Boatman's Mission about life on Walsall's canals.

Tue & Wed 09.30-12.30, Thur-Sun 13.00-16.00

Admission Free

Foxton Locks Canal Museum

Foxton Boat Services Ltd Bottom Lock Foxton Market Harborough Leicestershire LE16 7RA *(3m N of Market Harborough, follow brown tourist signs. BR: Market Harborough)*

Tel: 0116 279 2285 Fax: 0116 279 2188

In the heart of the beautiful Leciestershire coutrnyside - Historic flight of 10 locks on busy working canal. Site of the Inclined Plane: Victorian steam-powered boat lift, now under restoration. Pub, Shop, Museum, Boat Trips, Boat Hire, Working Boatyard, Interesting local walks. Watch the boats go by, feed the ducks. Site open every day.

Museum: all year daily 10.00-17.00, Easter-Oct 11.00-16.00, Oct-Easter closed Mon & Tue. Site open all year daily 24hrs

The Canal Museum

Bridge Road Stoke Bruerne Towcester Northamptonshire NN12 7SE *(4m S of J15 M1 off A508)*

Tel: 01604 862229 Fax: 01604 862229

Visit Stoke Bruerne with its famous Canal Museum and discover 200 years of colourful history and tra-

ditions. There are traditional 'Roses and Castles' painting demonstrations on selected dates, Blisworth Tunnel, flight of seven locks, boat trips and countryside walks.

Easter-Oct daily 10.00-18.00, Oct-Easter daily Tue-Sun 10.00-16.00

Last Admission: 30 mins before closing

A£2.70 Family Ticket£6.30 Concessions£1.80

Museum- Ceramics

Jackfield Tile Museum

Jackfield Telford Shropshire *(on S side of river Severn)*

Tel: 01952 882030 Fax: 01952 432204

Web Site: www.igmt@vtel

Housed in the former Craven Dunnill Tileworks contains a most beautiful display of tiles. Tile manufacture may be seen. Geology Gallery called The Great Rock Sandwich.

All year daily 10.00-17.00

Last Admission: 16.30

A£3.50 or on passport ticket to Ironbrige Museums: A£9.00 C&Students£5.30 Family Ticket (A2+C5)£28.00 OAPs£8.00

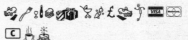

Museum- Childhood

Museum of Childhood

Sudbury Hall Sudbury Ashbourne Derbyshire DE6 5HT *(On A50 between Derby and Uttoxetter)*

Tel: 01283 585337 Fax: 01283 585139

Housed in the service wing of the 17th century hall. Room sets shows extremes of 19th century life from the poverty of the cellar dwelling to the luxury of a wealthy nursery. Child at work area incl chimney climb and mine tunnel. Features Victorian schoolroom and handling collection of old fashioned playground games. Features the Betty Cadbury toy collection.

29 Mar-2 Nov Wed-Sun 13.00-17.30, Nov-21 Dec Sat-Sun 12.00-16.00. Closed Good Fri

Last Admission: 17.00

A£3.00 C£1.50 Family Ticket£7.50 Joint Ticket (with Sudbury Hall) A£5.00 C£2.50 Family Ticket £12.50

Museum- Costume

WYGSTON'S HOUSE MUSEUM OF COSTUME

Wygston's House Museum of Costume

12 Applegate Leicester Leicestershire LE1 5LD

Tel: 0116 247 3056 Fax: 0116 247 3011

Behind a Georgian street front hides a beautiful late medieval building which houses selections from our extensive collections of costumes and textiles. The exhibits include a recreation of a 1920's draper's shop and fashionable outfits from 1805 to the present day. A children's gallery and temporary exhibitions throughout the year.

All year Mon-Sat 10.00-17.30, Sun 14.00-17.30. Closed 24-26 Dec & Jan 1

Admission Free

Museum- Country

John Moore Countryside Museum

41 Church Street Tewkesbury Gloucestershire GL20 5SN *(signposted on the A38)*

Tel: 01684 297174

Countryside collections and natural history. Also The Little Museum, restored Medieval merchant's cottage. Reproduction furniture, Living history days at various times throughout the year.

Apr-end Oct Tues-Sat 10.00-13.00 14.00-17.00
A£1.00 C£0.50 Concessions£0.75 Family Ticket £2.50 School groups £0.40 per pupil

Museum- Doll

Warwick Doll Museum

Oken's House Castle Street Warwick Warwickshire CV34 4BP *(next to Warwick Castle)*

Tel: 01926 495546

Displays on dolls and their houses, puzzles and games. A timber framed house famed for it's collection of 100's of dolls and toys from days gone by also a video showing how the mechanical toys work in the collection.

Easter-end Sept Mon-Sat 10.00-17.00, Sun 13.00-17.00, Sept-Easter Sat only 10.00-16.00
A£1.00 Concessions£0.70

Museum- Farms

Blakesley Hall

Blakesley Road Yardley Birmingham West Midlands B25 8RN *(on the A4040 off the A45)*

Tel: 0121 783 2193

A delightful timber framed Elizabethan farmhouse, built around 1590 in old Yardley, with furnishings that can be traced back to 1684. Staff in historic costume bring the house to life. Includes herb garden, barn and historical vehicles.

Apr-Oct daily 14.00-17.00
Admission Free

Museum- Folk

Millgate Folk Museum

Mill Gate Newark Nottinghamshire NG24 4TS *(off Millgate leading into the town)*

Tel: 01636 79403 Fax: 01636 613279

Fascinating displays including streets, shops and rooms in period settings. Agriculture gallery and 1st and 2nd World War displays.

Mon-Fri 10.00-17.00, Sat Sun 13.00-17.00.
Closed 25-26 Dec
Last Admission: 16.30
Admission Free

Museum- Food & Drink

Cadbury World

Bournville Birmingham West Midlands B30 2LD *(1m S of A38 Bristol Road on A4040 Ring Road)*

Tel: 0121 451 4180 Info line Fax: 0121 451 1366

Cadbury World is a wonderful chocolate experience of sights, sounds, tastes and smells for all the family - an absolute treat for chocolate lovers. New for 1997 experience Cadabra - a magical Cadbury journey - a colourful Beanmobile ride into a fairytale chocolate wonderland inhabited by the Bean Team an their friends.

8 Jan-6 Feb Wed Thur Sat & Sun 10.00-16.00, 8 Feb-2 Nov daily 10.00-16.00, 5 Nov-21 Dec Wed Thur Sat & Sun 10.00-16.00 then 27-28 10.00-17.00

A£6.00 C£4.30 Family Ticket(A2+C2)£17.80
OAPs£5.00 Mon-Fri only Weekends OAPs£6.00

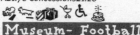

Cider Museum and King Offa Distillery
Pomona Place Whitecross Road Hereford
Herefordshire HR4 0LW *(off A438 to Brecon)*
Tel: 01432 354207
Housed in a former cider works, the museum tells
the fascinating story of cidermaking through the
ages. Displays include advertising material, prints,
huge English and French beam presses, farm cider
house, travelling cidermakers' tack, champagne
cider cellars, press house and early bottling equip-
ment. A varied programme of temporary exhibi-
tions and events is held throughout the year.
*All year Easter-Oct daily 10.00-17.30, Nov-Mar Mon-
Sat 13.00-17.00. Pre-booked groups at any time*
*A£2.20 C&OAPs&Students £1.70 Group rates 15+
A£1.70 Concessions£1.20*

Museum- Football

THE JAMES GILBERT RUGBY FOOTBALL MUSEUM

The James Gilbert Rugby Football Museum
St. Matthews Street Rugby Warwickshire CV21 3BY
*(from South M1, M45 & A426, from North M1 & M6
& A426)*
Tel: 01788 542426 Fax: 01788 540795
An intriguing collection of Rugby football memora-
bilia is housed in the shop in which Gilbert's have
made their world famous Rugby balls since 1842.
Free demonstrations of leather ball manufacturer
by master craftsmen.
*All year Mon-Fri 10.00-17.00, Sat 10.00-16.00
Last Admission: 10mins before closing
Admission Free*

Museum- Glass

Broadfield House Glass Museum
Compton Drive Kingswinford West Midlands DY6
9NS (M5 J4 or J2 A491 Stourbridge /

Wolverhampton Road or A4101 Dudley /
Kingswinford Road)
Tel: 01384 812745 Fax: 01384 812746
This magnificent collection of 19th-and-20th centu-
ry glass focuses on the cut, etched, engraved and
coloured glass made in nearby Stourbridge during
the last century. Daily demonstrations of glass
blowing and engraving bring the skills of the past
to life.
*All year Tue-Fri & Sun 14.00-17.00, Sat 10.00-13.00
& 14.00-17.00, Bank Hol 10.00-17.00
Last Admission: 16.45
Admission Free*
*Discount Card Offer: 10% Discount Off Shop
Purchases*

Museum- Industrial

Bell Foundry Museum
Freehold Street Loughborough Leicestershire LE11
1AR *(brown sign posted from A6 and A60. BR:
Loughborough 0.5m)*
Tel: 01509 233414 Fax: 01509 263305
Located in the former fettling shop of the John
Taylor Bell Foundry, the museum is part of the
largest working bell foundry in the world. Exhibits
follow the evolution of the bell founder's craft,
showing techniques of molding, casting, turning
and fitting, including modern craft practices.
Evening tours by appointment.
*All year Tue-Sat 09.30-12.30 & 13.30-16.30. Special
Tours on Bank Hol Mon 11.00-14.15. Also 1st Sun in
the month*
*Museum only: A£1.00 C(6-15)£0.50 Tour and
Museum combined: A£3.00 C(6-15)£1.50. Group
Rates: School/Young peoples' organisations - 1
adult free to each group of 15 children*

Birmingham Museum of Science and Industry
Newhall Street Birmingham West Midlands B3 1RZ
(10mins walk from City centre)
Tel: 0121 235 1661 Fax: 0121 233 9210
Full of fascinating and fun exhibits covering all
aspects of science, engineering and industry, it's
packed with many working displays including the
world's oldest steam engine, a real moving steam
locomotive, plus World War II Spitfire and
Hurricane. You can really experience all the sights
and sounds of the industrial era.
*All year Mon-Thur 10.00-17.00, Fri 10.30-17.00, Sat
10.00-17.00, Sun 12.30-17.00
Admission Free*

🖐 *suitable for pushchairs* 🍼 *mother & baby facilities* ♿ *suitable for wheelchairs* 🎁 *gift shop*
🤝 *corporate facilities* 🐕 *no dogs: except guide dogs* 🅿️ *parking on site* 🅿️ *parking nearby*
£ *charged parking* ☕ *café-restaurant* 🍷 *licensed* 🎂 *special events* 🎒 *educational pack*

Broseley Pipeworks

King Street Broseley Shropshire *(4m S of Telford off A4169)*
Tel: 01952 433522 Fax: 01952 432204
Clay tobacco pipe museum opened in 1995 to interpret this ancient local industry.
Mar-Nov daily 10.00-17.00. Closed Nov-Mar
Last Admission: 16.00
A£2.00 not on Ironbridge Passport

Canal Museum

Canal Street Castle Boulevard Nottingham
Nottinghamshire NG1 7EH
Tel: 0115 915 6870
The history of the River Trent from the Ice Age to the present day is told in the ground and first floors and wharf of this 19th century warehouse. Life size diorama's, models and an audio-visual presentation add impact to the displays which include local canal and river navigation, boats, bridges and archeology.
All year Wed-Sun & Bank Hol 10.00-17.00. Closed Christmas Day & Boxing Day
Admission Free

Coalbrookdale and Museum of Iron and Furnace Site

Telford Shropshire
Tel: 01952 433522 Fax: 01952 432204
This museum is close to Abraham Darby's blast furnace and tells the story of iron and the history of Coalbrookdale. Three floors of an original warehouse.
All year daily 10.00-17.00. Closed 24-25 Dec
Last Admission: 16.15
A£3.50 or on a passport to all attractions A£9.00 C&Students£5.30 Family Ticket (A2+C5)£28.00 OAPs£8.00

Derby Industrial Museum

The Silk Mill Silk Mill Lane Derby Derbyshire DE1 3AR *(off Full Street)*
Tel: 01332 255308
Displays form an introduction of the industrial history of Derby and Derbyshire. They include railway engineering and power galleries, and a major collection of Rolls Royce aero-engines ranging from an Eagle of 1915 to an RB211 from the first Tristar airliner. Temporary exhibitions and events.
Mon 11.00-17.00, Tue-Sat 10.00-17.00, Sun and Bank Hol 14.00-17.00
Admission Free

Etruria Industrial Museum

Lower Bedford Street Etruria Stoke-On-Trent Staffordshire ST4 7AF *(J15 M6 onto A500 then B5045)*
Tel: 01782 287557 Fax: 01782 260192
NEW for '98 - Visitor Centre with tea-room and shop. The Industrial Museum includes the Etruscan Bone and Flint Mill which was built in 1857 to grind materials for the agricultural and pottery industries. It's Britain's sole surviving, steam-powered potters' mill and contains an 1820's steam-driven beam engine, 1903 coal fired boiler and original grinding machinery. Also a working blacksmiths forge on site and a restored canal warehouse.
All year Wed-Sun 10.00-16.00. Closed Christmas & New Year
Admission by voluntary donation. A£1.50 C£1.00

Flint Mill

Cheadle Road Cheddleton Leek Staffordshire ST13 7HL
Tel: 01782 372561
Two water mills with wheels are preserved here. The 17th century south mill was used to grind corn but the 18th century north mill was built to grind flint for the pottery industry. Displays include aspects of the pottery industry with exhibits of motive power and transport and a haystack boiler of around 1770.
All year Sat & Sun 14.00-17.00, Apr-Oct Mon-Fri 10.00-17.00
Please telephone for admission details

Ironbridge Gorge Museums

Ironbridge Telford Shropshire TF8 7AW *(J4 M54, signposted)*
Tel: 01952 433522/432166 Fax: 01952 432204
Web Site: www.vtel
Ironbridge became famous when the world's first iron bridge was cast and built here in 1779, to span a narrow gorge over the River Severn. Now it is the site of a series of museums covering some six square miles. There is the Blists Hill Victorian Town, the Museum of Iron, the Jackfield Tile Museum and Coalport China Museum. Also a Visitor Centre housed in the restored Severn Warehouse. It outlines the story of the Gorge in the words and pictures of people who have visited over 2 centuries.
All year Mon-Sat & some Sun 10.00-17.00. Closed 24-25 Dec
A£9.00 to all Museums except Broseley Pipeworks C&Students£5.30 Family Ticket (A2+C5)£28.00 OAPs£8.00

🦡 *National Trust* 🎗 *National Trust for Scotland* 🏛 *English Heritage* 🚩 *Historic Scotland* 🍀 *CADW*
🍴 *guided tours available* 🍴 *picnic areas* ☕ *refreshments* 📷 *photography allowed* 1998 *visitor discount card offer* 🏖 *beach/coastal area* 💳 *Visa accepted* 💳 *Mastercard accepted* [C] *All cards accepted*

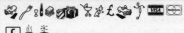

Nottingham Industrial Museum

Courtyard Buildings Wollaton Park Nottingham
Nottinghamshire NG8 2AE *(3m W off A609 Ilkeston Road)*

Tel: 0115 915 3910

In 18th century stable block displays of Nottingham Industrial history. Lace, hosiery and pharmaceutical industry, engineering, printing and tobacco. A beam engine and heavy agricultural machinery. Victorian street furniture displayed, also a horse gin from a local mine. New shop, visitor centre and gallery opening Easter 1997.

All year Apr-Sept Mon-Sat 10.00-17.00, Sun 13.00-17.00, Oct - Mar Thur-Sat 10.00-16.30, Sun 13.30-16.30
Mon-Fri Free Weekends & Bank Hol A£1.50
C&Concessions£0.75. Parking: £0.50 all day

The Lace Centre

Severns Building Castle Road Nottingham
Nottinghamshire NG1 6AA

Tel: 0115   941 3539

Exquisite Nottingham lace fills this small building to capacity there are even panels hanging from the beamed ceiling. There are demonstrations of lace-making on Thursdays from 14.00-16.00 between Easter and the end of October. Situated below the Castle wall opposite the Robin Hood statue.

All year Jan-Mar Mon-Sat 10.00-16.00, Sun 11.00-16.00, Apr-Dec Mon-Sat 10.00-17.00, Sun 11.00-16.00. Closed 25-26 Dec
Admission Free

The Lock Museum

54 New Road Willenhall West Midlands WV13 2DA
Tel: 01902 634542 Fax: 01902 634542

A museum of locks situated in a Victorian lock-smith's house and workshop.

All Year Tue Wed Thur Sat 11.00-17.00. Closed Christmas Period
Last Admission: 16.00
A£1.50 Concessions£0.70

Walsall Leather Museum

Wisemore Walsall West Midlands WS2 8EQ *(N at rear of Walsall College of Arts & Technology on ring road, Littleton Street)*

Tel: 01922 721153 Fax: 01922 725827

This museum is housed in a former leather goods factory dating from 1891. In the atmospheric workshops, rich with the aroma of leather, visitors can see how traditional leather goods have been made, and talk to leatherworkers about their craft.

All year Tue-Sat 10.00-17.00, Nov-Mar 16.00, Sun 12.00-17.00 also Bank Hol Mon. Closed 24-26 Dec & Easter Sun
Admission Free

Museum- Jewellery

Jewellery Quarter Discovery Centre

75-79 Vyse Street Hockley Birmingham West Midlands B18 6HA *(J6 M6 onto A38(M) or J1 M5 situated off A41, follow signs for Hockley & AA signs for Discovery Centre)*

Tel: 0121 554 3598 Fax: 0121 554 9700

Discover the skills of the jeweller's craft and enjoy a unique tour of an original jewellery factory frozen in time. For over eighty years the family-run firm and Smith and Pepper produced jewellery from the factory that is now the award-winning Jewellery Quarter Discovery Centre. This perfectly preserved 'time capsule' workshop has changed little since the beginning of the century. Enjoy a guided tour around the Smith and Pepper factory and meet skilled jewellers at work. Displays tell the story of this historic area - a centre for jewellery-making for over 200 years, it helped the city become known as 'the workshop of the world.' Most of the jewellery made in Britain today is produced in the workshops of Birmingham's Jewellery Quarter. The Discovery Centre showcases jewellery by some of the city's most exciting new designers. Visitor Centre with changing programme of exhibitions, workshops and events. Excellent selection of contemporary jewellery, gifts, books and souvenirs. A tea room, guided tours on tape in French, German, Spanish, Italian, Japanese and Hindi.

All year Mon-Fri 10.00-16.00, Sat 11.00-17.00
Last Admission: Allow 60mins for tour
A£2.00 C&Concessions£1.50 Family Ticket £5.00.
Discounts for pre-booked groups of 10+ 10%

Museum- Living History

Village Life Exhibition

The Old Mill Bourton-on-the-Water Gloucestershire GL54 2BY *(A429)*

Tel: 01451 821255

A complete Edwardian village shop is displayed with bathroom, kitchen and bedroom above. There is also a blacksmith's forge, a model of the old mill, photographs, toys and period advertising signs.

Feb-Nov daily 10.00-18.00
A£1.75 C£0.80 C(0-4)£Free

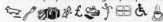

🐪 suitable for pushchairs   👶 mother & baby facilities   ♿ suitable for wheelchairs   🎁 gift shop
💼 corporate facilities   🐕 no dogs: except guide dogs   🚗 parking on site   🅿 parking nearby
£ charged parking   café-restaurant   🍷 licensed   🎂 special events   📚 educational pack

Museum- Local History

Abington Museum

Abington Park Northampton Northamptonshire NN1 5LW *(in Abington Park)*
Tel: 01604 31454
A 15th century manor house, once the home of Shakespeare's granddaughter Elizabeth Barnard, who is buried in the nearby church grounds. It is now a museum showing the social history of the house including Victorian Cabinet of Curiosities, a 19th-century fashion gallery too. Also here is the Northamptonshire Regiment museum and Northamptonshire Yeomanry.
All year Bank Hol Mon & Tue-Sun 13.00-17.00
Admission Free

Ashby-De-La-Zouch Museum

North Street Ashby-De-La-Zouch Leicestershire LE6 5HU *(J11 M42, J22 M1, on A444)*
Tel: 01530 560090
Small museum with local material; including model of Ashby Castle under attack, and early 20th century shop.
All year Easter-Sept Mon-Fri 10.00-12.00 & 14.00-16.00, Sat 10.00-16.00, Sun 14.00-16.00
A£0.30 C£0.20 OAPs£0.25. Pre-booked groups 20 max

Avoncroft Museum of Historic Buildings

Redditch Road Stoke Heath Bromsgrove Worcestershire B60 4JR *(2m S of Bromsgrove off the A38 Bromsgrove by-pass, 400 yards N of J with B4091, 3m N of J5 M5, 3.5m S of J1 M42)*
Tel: 01527 831363 Fax: 01527 876934
A visit to Avoncroft takes you through nearly 700 years of history. You can see 25 buildings rescued from destruction and authentically restored on a 15 acre rural site. The magnificent timbered roof of Worcester Cathedral's original Guest Hall dates from 1330, now crowns a modern hall in which a wide variety of functions, including civil weddings, are held.
June-Aug & Bank Hol Mon-Fri 10.30-17.00,Sat&Sun 17.30. Apr-May & Sept-Oct Mon-Fri 10.30-16.30, Sat&Sun 17.00. Closed Mon Mar & Nov 10.30-16.00. Closed Mon & Fri
Last Admission: 1 hour before closing
A£3.95 C£2.00 OAPs£3.25 Family Ticket £11.00

Bakewell Old House Museum

Cunningham Place Bakewell Derbyshire DE45 1DD

(0.25m town centre behind the church)
Tel: 01629 813165
An early Tudor house with original wattle and daub screen and open chamber. Costumes and Victorian kitchen, children's toys, craftsmen's tools and lacework.
Apr-Oct daily 13.30-16.00, July-Aug 11.00-16.00
A£2.00 C£1.00. Group bookings call for details

BEWDLEY MUSEUM

Bewdley Museum

The Shambles Load Street Bewdley Worcestershire DY12 2AE *(4M W of Kidderminster off A456 on B4190)*
Tel: 01299 403573 Fax: 01299 404740
The Shambles is an 18th-century row of butcher's shops, and makes an interesting setting for the attractive museum devoted to the crafts and industries of the Bewdley area, with displays of Bewdley pewter, agricultural implements and charcoal burning. There are also craft workshops within the museum, a sawyard area, and daily demonstrations including clay pipe making and rope making.
Easter-30 Sept Mon-Sun & Bank Hol 11.00-17.00
A£2.00 OAPs£1.00 C(unaccompained)£1.00 otherwise C£Free

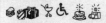

Brewhouse Yard Museum

Castle Boulevard Nottingham Nottinghamshire NG7 1FB
Tel: 0115 948 3600
17th century cottages on two acre site. Museum depicts everday life in Nottingham over 300 years. Period rooms with local objects displayed. Re-created shops, including between the wars shopping street. Displays of past and present life in Nottingham. A school room and toyshop of the thirties. Caves behind used as air raid shelters.
All year daily 10.00-17.00, Nov-Feb daily 13.00-17.00. Closed 25-26 Dec
Last Admission: 16.45
Mon-Fri £Free. Donations accepted Sat Sun & Bank Hol A£1.50 C&Concessions£0.75

Bromsgrove Museum

26 Birmingham Road Bromsgrove B61 0DD *(A38 Birmingham Rd)*
Tel: 01527 577983/831809
The Norton Collection of Social and Industrial History. Displays 19th-20th century shop windows including draper's, chemist, radio shop, photographer and cobbler. Local industries including nail making. Work and information on The Bromsgrove guild and A E Housman the author of a Shropshire lad.
Mon-Sat 09.30-17.00. Closed 25-26 Dec & 1 Jan A£1.20 C&OAPs£0.60. Pre-booked groups welcome

Buxton Museum and Art Gallery

Terrace Road Buxton SK17 6DU *(just off market place in centre of its town)*
Tel: 01298 24658 Fax: 01298 79394
Journey through time into the geology, archaeology and history of the Peak District in seven unusual settings ranging from a prehistoric Coal Forest to a Victorian Petrification shop. Complementing the Wonders of the Peak gallery is the period study of Sir William Boyd Dawkins and an extensive display of local history.
All year Tue-Fri 09.30-17.30, Sat 09.30-17.00. Sun in summer 10.30-17.00
A£1.00 C£0.50

Castle Museum

Castle Place Nottingham Nottinghamshire NG1 6EL
Tel: 0115 915 3700
17th century building with much restored 13th century gateway. Now a Museum and Art Gallery, guided tour of underground passages is conducted every afternoon. A 'Story of Nottingham' interactive display brings to life the history of the city. Collections of Silver, glass, ceramics, paintings and jewellery. Automated car for disabled.
All year daily 10.00-17.00, Nov-Feb Sat-Thur 12.00-17.00. Grounds: 08.00-dusk. Closed 25-26 Dec Mon-Fri £Free. Weekends & Bank Hol : A£1.50 C&Concessions£.75 includes admission to Brewhouse Yard Museum

Chesterfield Museum and Art Gallery

St Mary's Gate Chesterfield Derbyshire S41 7TY *(Town centre)*
Tel: 01246 345727
Museum depicting the story of chesterfield from Roman times until present day. Small Art Gallery.
All year Mon-Tue & Thur-Sat 10.00-16.00. Closed 25

& 26 Dec & 1 Jan
Admission Free

Cirencester Lock-Up

Trinity Road Cirencester Gloucestershire GL7 1PX *(Trinity Road adjoining the Council offices)*
Tel: 01285 655611 Fax: 01285 643286
Restored two-cell town lock-up dating from 1804 and incorporating interpretative displays on lock-up and workhouse history plus exhibition of architectural conservation in the Cotswolds.
All year daily, by arrangement
Admission Free key from Corinium Museum in park street or reception desk of the Council

Cotswold Countryside Collection

Fosseway Northleach Cheltenham Gloucestershire GL54 3JH *(12m E of Cheltenham on A429)*
Tel: 01451 860715 Fax: 01451 860091
The story of everyday rural life in the Cotswolds is told in this museum, housed in the remaining buildings of the Northleach House of correction.
1 Apr-Nov Mon-Sat 10.00-17.00 Bank Hol 10.00-17.30 Sun 14.00-17.00 . Nov-Christmas Sat only 10.00-16.00
A£1.50 C£0.75 OAPs£1.25 Students£1.00 Family Ticket£3.75

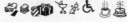

Erewash Museum

High Street Ilkeston Derbyshire DE7 5JA *(close to Ilkeston Market Place)*
Tel: 0115 944 0440 Ext 331
Eighteenth century town house, set in pleasant gardens, housing local history collections in room settings and galleries.
All year Tue Thur Fri and Sat 10.00-16.00 Bank Hol 10.00-16.00. Closed Jan, Christmas and New Year Admission Free

Eyam Museum

The Edge Eyam Sheffield South Yorkshire S30 1QP *(off A623 signed right to Eyam on B6521, follow white or brown signs)*
Tel: 01433 631371 Fax: 01433 630777
The newly enlarged museum presents a carefully researched account of the impact of bubonic plague on the small closely knit community which isolated itself in quarantine and suffered terribly. Unique painting vividly portrays the story, three dimensional life size models represent the first victim - the clergy and a victim dying in bed. A compelling story for young and adult.
Mar-3 Nov Tue-Sun 10.00-16.30

🏃 *suitable for pushchairs* 👶 *mother & baby facilities* ♿ *suitable for wheelchairs* 🎁 *gift shop*
🤝 *corporate facilities* 🐕 *no dogs: except guide dogs* 🚗 *parking on site* 🚙 *parking nearby*
£ *charged parking* 🍴 *café-restaurant* 🍷 *licensed* 🎂 *special events* 📦 *educational pack*

A£1.50 C&OAPs£1.00 Family Ticket £4.25. Group rates on application

Folk Museum

99-103 Westgate Street Gloucester Gloucestershire GL1 2PG

Tel: 01452 526467 Fax: 01452 330495

A group of Tudor and Jacobean houses illustrate the local history, domestic life and rural crafts of the city and county. The new extension houses a reconstructed Double Gloucester Dairy, wheelwright, carpenter's workshops and ironmonger's corner shop.

All year Mon-Sat 10.00-17.00 also Sun 10.00-16.00 July- Sept only
Admission Free

GRANTHAM MUSEUM

Grantham Museum

St Peter's Hill Grantham Lincolnshire NG31 6PY *(from A1 take B1174, A52 or A607 exits and follow signs for town centre)*

Tel: 01476 568783 Fax: 01476 592457

The Museum illustrates and interprets the history and heritage of Grantham and the surrounding area. Local personalities Sir Isaac Newton and Margaret Thatcher appear alongside Romans and RAF heroes, the Dambusters of 617 Squadron. Agriculture and industry, archaeology and ethnology - there's something for everyone at Grantham Museum.

All year Mon-Sat, Good Fri and all Bank Hol 10.00-17.00. Closed 25-26 Dec & 1 Jan
Admission Free

Harborough Museum

Council Offices Adam & Eve Street Market Harborough Leicestershire LE16 7AG *(A6)*

Tel: 01858 821085 Fax: 01530 813301

The Museum illustrates the history of the town and its surrounding area, from the medieval planned town to its role as a market, social, and hunting area and also as a stagecoach post. Displays include the Symington Collection of Corsetry and a reconstruction of a local bootmaker's workshop.

All year Mon-Sat 10.00-16.30, Sun 14.00-17.00. Closed Good Fri, 25-26 Dec
Admission Free

Hinckley and District Museum

Framework Knitters Cottages Lower Bond Street Hinckley Leicestershire *(BR: Hinckley .75m)*

Tel: 01455 251218

Restored 17th century thatched cottages. Displays illustrating aspects of the history of Hinckley and district. Hosiery exhibits include circa 1740 stacking frame. Garden and Tea Room.

Easter-end Oct Sat & Bank Hold Mon 10.00-16.00, Sun 14.00-17.00
A£0.50 C£0.25

Leicestershire Record Office

Long Street Wigston Magna Leicestershire LE18 2AH

Tel: 0116 257 1080 Fax: 0116 257 1120

Housed in a converted 19th century school in Wigston, the Record Office is the centre for the history of Leicestershire. It holds photographs, electoral registers and archive film, files of the local newspapers, history tapes and sound recordings, all of which can be studied. Records of the country's landed estates and families, and borough archives dating back to 1103.

All year Mon Tue & Thur 09.15-17.00, Wed 09.00-19.30, Fri 09.15-16.45, Sat 09.15-12.15. Closed Sun & Bank Hol weekends Sat-Tue
Admission Free

Ludlow Museum

Castle Street Ludlow Shropshire SY8 1AS *(on the A49)*

Tel: 01584 875384 Fax: 01584 872019

The Ludlow area is internationally renowned for its geology. Visit the fascinating museum and discover why the rocks of Ludlow gained this reputation and how they are contributing to important discoveries in the 1990s. Explore the displays and travel 400 million years through time. 'Reading the Rocks' - hands on opportunities. Use your visit as a starting point to explore this fine planned town. Holiday activities for children.

30 Mar-1 Nov Mon-Sat 10.30-13.00 & 14.00-17.00. Easter Sun, Sun 24 May & Sun in June, July, Aug
A£1.00 C£0.50

Lutterworth Museum

6 McCauley Road Lutterworth Leicestershire LE17 4XB

Tel: 01455 557635

Small friendly museum with a wealth of history from the Stone Age to World War II. Tucked away near the parish church of St Mary which is associated with John Wycliffe.

Feb-Nov Mon, Thur, Fri & Sat 10.00-16.00. Closed Dec and Jan

Admission Free but donations appreciated

Malvern Museum

Abbey Gateway Abbey Road Malvern Worcestershire WR14 3ES

Tel: 01684 567811

The local history exhibits range from the story of the Malvern Hills to the Water Cure and the lives of Sir Edward Elgar and Bernard Shaw, and from the first British motor car to radar and the silicone chip. The museum is housed in one of the two buildings that survive from the Benedictine monastery.

Easter-Oct daily 10.30-17.00. Closed Wed during term time

A£1.00 C£0.20

Manor House Museum

Sheep Street Kettering Northamptonshire NN16 0AN *(in the town centre)*

Tel: 01536 534219 Fax: 01536 534370

The Museum invites the historical re-enactment group, Time Travellers, to run educational weeks at the Museum for school visits. In addition the Museum runs activity days for children on every day during school holidays, including half terms. There are always based on the principal of making and taking home a museum-inspired object.

All year Mon-Sat 09.30-17.00 Closed Bank Hol

Last Admission: 16.45

Admission Free

MANSFIELD MUSEUM AND ART GALLERY

Mansfield Museum and Art Gallery

Leeming Street Mansfield Nottinghamshire NG18 1NG *(near Town Centre close to A60 to Mansfield Woodhouse)*
Tel: 01623 663088 Fax: 01623 663086
'Images of Mansfield past and present' uses objects and photographs to illustrate the history of the town, whilst 'Nature of Mansfield' looks at the natural history of the area. The museum's important display of William Bilingsley porcelain, Buxton watercolours show town and people in the early 19th century. Wide range of temporary exhibitions and activities.
All year Mon-Sat 10.00-17.00. Closed Sun & Bank Hol
Admission Free

Melton Carnegie Museum

Thorpe End Market Harborough Leicestershire LE13 1RB *(A607)*
Tel: 01664 69946 Fax: 01530 813301
The local museum of the history and environment of the Borough of Melton, including the famous Vale of Belvoir. The area is explored through a wonderful mixture of exhibits such as the fine collection of sporting paintings, local crafts and industries, archaeology, geology and a two-headed calf!
All year Mon-Sat 10.00-17.00. Easter-Sept also on Sun 14.00-17.00. Closed Good Fri 25 & 26 Dec
Admission Free

Millgate Museum

48 Mill Gate Newark Nottinghamshire NG24 4TS *(A1 signposted Newark A46 from Nottingham)*
Tel: 01636 679403 Fax: 10636 613279
Recreated streets, shops and houses in period settings. The museum displays illustrate the working and domestic life of local people, from Victorian times to 1950. The mezzanine gallery, houses temporary exhibitions of local artists work, artists,

🚼 suitable for pushchairs 👶 mother & baby facilities ♿ suitable for wheelchairs 🎁 gift shop
🤝 corporate facilities 🐕 no dogs: except guide dogs 🅿️ parking on site 🅿️ parking nearby
£ charged parking ☕ café-restaurant 🍸 licensed 🎂 special events 📋 educational pack

designers and photographers. Please note only guide dogs are allowed and there is wheelchair access only on the ground floor.
All year daily Mon-Fri 10.00-17.00 Sat & Sun 13.00-17.00
Last Admission: 16.30
Admission Free

Newark Museum

Appleton Gate Newark Nottinghamshire NG24 1JY
Tel: 01636 702358
The museum displays the archeology and local history of the area. There is some natural history too. Visitors can see an exhibition of 17th century Civil War items and a collection of militaria of the Sherwood Foresters.
All year Mon-Wed Fri 10.00-13.00 & 14.00-17.00 Sat 10.00-13.00 & 14.00-17.00. Apr-Sept Sun 14.00-17.00 Bank Hol 13.00-17.00
Admission Free

NEWARKE HOUSES MUSEUM

Newarke Houses Museum

The Newarke Leicester Leicestershire LE2 7BY
Tel: 0116 247 3222 Fax: 0116 247 3011
Shows the story of Leicestershire's social history to the present day throughout the county. Clocks, toys, Victorian toilets, instruments and furniture are among the many collections. A street scene gives glimpses of Victorian life and the fascinating life of Daniel Lambert, the famous 52-stone gaoler of the 18th century, is also told.
All year Mon-Sat 10.00-17.30 Sun 14.00-17.30. Closed 24-26 Dec
Admission Free

Nuneaton Museum and Art Gallery

Coton Road Riversley Park Nuneaton Warwickshire CV11 5TU (A444 S on Nuneaton-Bedworth / Coventry)
Tel: 01203 350 720 Fax: 01203 376 551
Features local history gallery focusing on the development of the borough including Nuneaton Priory, coal-mining, ribbon-weaving. Prehistoric flints. Also

George Eliot gallery including a reconstruction of her London drawing room. Permanent art gallery showing the museums's own collection and two temporary exhibition galleries.
All year Tue-Sat 10.30-16.30, Sun 14.00-16.30, Mon Tea-room only 10.30-16.30, Bank Hol Mon 10.30-16.30
Admission Free

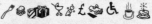

Pittville Pump Room Museum

Pittville Park East Approach Drive Cheltenham Gloucestershire GL52 3JE (at N end of town, close to Cheltenham racecourse)
Tel: 01242 523852 Fax: 01242 262334
Housed in an elegant spa building where you can taste the spa waters, original costumes bring to life the history of Cheltenham from its Regency heyday to the present day. Pre-booked Guide tours available
May-Sept Wed-Mon 11.00-16.30, Oct-Apr Wed-Mon 11.00-16.00.
A£1.50 Concessions£0.50

Rowley's House Museum

Barker Street Shrewsbury Shropshire SY1 1QH
(Shrewsbury town centre)
Tel: 01743 361196 Fax: 01743 358411
An impressive timber-framed building and attached 17th-century brick mansion. Major displays of the archaeology, geology, prehistory, ceramics and local history of the region, including much of the material excavated from Roman Wroxeter. There is also a costume gallery, an innovative Medieval Shrewsbury gallery and a varied programme of temporary and touring exhibitions.
All year Tue-Sat 10.00-17.00. Also Sun & Bank Hol Mon from end May-Sept 10.00-16.00
A£2.00 C£0.50 OAPs&Students£1.00. Joint admission to Rowley's House, Clive House, Shrewsbury Castle & Regimental Museum A£4.00 C£1.00 OAPs&Students£2.00

Rutland County Museum

Catmos Street Oakham Rutland LE15 6HW (near town centre on A6003 signposted)
Tel: 01572 723654 Fax: 01572 757576
Housing displays of farming equipment, machinery and wagons, rural tradesmen's tools, domestic collections and local archaeology, all in a splendid late 18th century cavalry riding school. There is a special gallery on the Volunteer Soldier in Leicestershire and Rutland.
All year Mon-Sat 10.00-17.00, Sun Apr-Oct 14.00-17.00, Nov-Mar 14.00-16.00. Closed Good Fri &

Christmas
Admission Free

Soho House

Soho Avenue off Soho Road Birmingham West Midlands B18 5LB *(City centre. Buses: 70 /74 /78 & 79)*

Tel: 0121 554 9122

The elegant home of industrial pioneer Matthew Boulton, who lived at Soho House from 1766 to 1809. Here, he met with some of the most important scientists, engineers and thinkers of his time - the Lunar Society. Possibly the first centrally heated English house since Roman times, Soho House has been carefully restored to its 18th Century appearance and contains some of Boulton's own furniture. Displays tell the story of this fascinating man and the interests he shared with his famous visitors. There's also the chance to see some of the products of Boulton's nearby factory where buttons and buckles, ormolu clocks and vases, and silver and Sheffield plate tableware were made - and where he developed the steam engine in partnership with James Watt. Meeting room for schools and community groups. Visitor centre with changing programme of exhibitions and activities.

All year Tue-Sat & Bank Hol Mon 10.00-17.00, Sun 12.00-17.00. Closed Mon
A£2.00 C&Concessions£1.50 Family Ticket £5.00.
Pre-booked groups of 10+ 10% discount

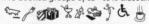

The Almonry Heritage Centre

Abbey Gate Evesham Worcestershire WR11 4BG
Tel: 01386 446944

The 14th century stone and timber building was the home of the Almoner of the Benedictine Abbey in Evesham. It now houses exhibitions relating to the history of Evesham Abbey, the battle of Evesham, and the culture and trade of Evesham. Evesham Tourist Information Centre is also located here.

All year Mon-Sat & Bank Hol Mon 10.00-17.00, Sun 14.00-17.00
A£2.00 C(0-16)£Free OAPs£1.00

The Bassetlaw Museum

Amcott House Grove Street Retford Nottingham DN22 6JU *(brown signposted)*
Tel: 01777 713749

Archaeology, local history, bygones, decorative arts. Percy Laws' gallery huoses a continuious programme of short term exhibitions and will in 1997 house the collection of Retford civic plate.

All year Mon-Sat 10.00-17.00 Closed Sun
Admission Free

The Museum

64 Barton Street Tewkesbury Gloucestershire GL20 5PX

Tel: 01684 295027

Old half-timbered building. Town history, heritage centre, fairground display, model of Battle of Tewkesbury.

Apr-mid Oct daily 10.00-16.30
Small fee. Special reductions for C&OAP's. Groups by arrangement all year

The Museum of Cannock Chase

The Valley Heritage Centre Valley Road Hednesford Cannock Staffordshire WS12 5TD *(off the A460, at the edge of Hednesford, signposted from Cannock and Ruseley)*

Tel: 01543 877666 Fax: 01543 462317

A delightful museum illustrating the history of Cannock Chase from mediaeval hunting forest to 19th century coalfield. Special events, exhibitions and activities.

Easter-Sept daily 11.00-17.00, Oct-Easter Mon-Fri 11.00-16.00
Last Admission: 30mins before closing
Museum: £Free. Half day tours, including refreshments: Mining Memories Tour £4.00, Heathland Habitats Tour £4.50

The Warwickshire Yeomanry Museum and Warwick Town Museum

The Court House Vaults Jury Street Warwick Warwickshire CV34 4EW *(centre of Warwick, within the TIC, follow signposts)*

Tel: 01926 492212 Fax: 01926 494837

The Warwickshire Yeomanry Museum has uniforms, arms, swords, sabres and selected silver. The Town museum has changing exhibitions each year. Very step staircase to museums not suitable for visually impaired or disabled.

Good Fri-end Sept Fri Sat Sun & Bank Hol 10.00-13.00 & 14.00-16.00
Admission Free

Warwickshire Museum

Market Place Warwick Warks CV34 4SA *(in the town centre)*
Tel: 01926 412500 Fax: 01926 419840
Web Site: www.warwickshire.gov.uk

Wildlife geology, archaeology and history of Warwickshire including the famous Sheldon tapestry map and giant fossil plesiosaur. Huge Brown Bear ancient jewelry, fantastic fossils bees and

---

🖼 *suitable for pushchairs* 🍼 *mother & baby facilities* ♿ *suitable for wheelchairs* 🏬 *gift shop* 🤝 *corporate facilities* 🐕 *no dogs: except guide dogs* 🚗 *parking on site* 🚗 *parking nearby* £ *charged parking* ☕ *café-restaurant* 🍷 *licensed* 🎪 *special events* ✏ *educational pack*

bugs.
All year Mon-Sat 10.00-17.00,May-Sept Sun 14.00-17.00
Admission Free

Museum- Mechanical

KEITH HARDING'S WORLD OF MECHANICAL MUSIC

Keith Harding's World of Mechanical Music
Oak House High Street Northleach Cheltenham
Gloucestershire GL54 3ET *(J9 or J11 M5 then at crossing of A40 and A429 Fosse Way)*
Tel: 01451 860181 Fax: 01451 861133
A fascinating collection of antique clocks, musical boxes, automats and mechanical musical instruments, restored and maintained in the world-famous workshops, displayed in period setting and played during regular tours.
All year daily 10.00-18.00 Closed 25 Dec
Last Admission: 17.00
A£5.00 C£2.50 Family Ticket £12.50
OAPs&Students £4.00
Discount Card Offer: Two For The Price Of One; Of Equal Or Higher Value Purchased

Museum- Mill

Arkwright's Cromford Mill
Mill Road Cromford Matlock Derbyshire DE4 3GL
(turn off A6 at Cromford follow brown tourist signs. BR: on Derby-Matlock branch line)
Tel: 01629 824297 Fax: 01629 823256
The world's first successful water powered cotton spinning mill. Guided tours, shops, restaurant. 1996 has seen massive a excavation uncovering exciting archaeological remains of the 1779 mill. There is an on going restoration programme and a guide will explain the history and plans for the future.
All year daily 09.00-17.00. Guided tours 09.00-17.00. Closed 25 Dec
Last Admission: 16.00

Guided tours & exhibitions: A£2.00 C&OAPs£1.50. Mill: Admission Free

Caudwell's Mill and Craft Centre
Bakewell Road Rowsley Matlock Derbyshire DE4 2EB *(off J28 or J29 M1, on A6 in village of Rowsley between Matlock and Bakewell)*
Tel: 01629 734374 Fax: 01332 880600
This 19th century water turbine powered flour mill with precision roller mills is still producing quality wholemeal flour for sale. See four floors of machinery and exhibitions. Crafts-people in the Stable Yard. Guided tours for pre-booked parties.
1 Mar-end Oct daily 10.00-18.00 Weekends only in winter 10.00-16.30
Last Admission: 30mins before closing
A£2.00 C(5-16)&OAPs£1.00

Forge Mill Needle Museum and Bordesley Abbey Visitor Centre
Needle Mill Lane Riverside Redditch Worcestershire B98 8HY *(N side of Redditch off A441 /J2 M42)*
Tel: 01527 62509
Displays about the Redditch needle-making industry and finds from extensive excavations at the adjacent mediaeval Bordesley Abbey are housed in attractive historic buildings. Working water-powered machinery; shop specialising in needles and gifts; picnic area; Abbey ruins; walks.
Easter-Sept Mon-Fri 11.00-16.30, Weekends 14.00-17.00. Feb-Easter & Oct-Nov Mon-Thur 11.00-16.00, Sun 14.00-17.00
A£1.80 C£0.55 OAPs£1.30. Free admission for persons with disabilities, their carers, unemployed & students. Groups by arrangement

Green's Mill
Windmill Lane Sneinton Nottingham Nottinghamshire NG2 4QB *(off A612)*
Tel: 0115 915 6878
Restored to working order, this wind mill can be seen in use when conditions allow. The adjacent Science Centre tells the story of George Green, one-time miller here and distinguished mathematician. Flour is on sale. Interactive displays exploring light, electricity and magnetism. Disabled access limited to Science centre and ground floor of windmill.
All year Wed-Sun 10.00-17.00 & Bank Hol. Closed 25-26 Dec
Admission Free

Industrial Museum
The Silk Mill Off Full Street Derbyshire DE1 3AR

(M1/A52)

Tel: 01332 255308 Fax: 01332 255804

The museum is set in an early 18th century silk mill and adjacent flour mill, displays cover local mining, quarrying and industries, and include a major collection of Roll Royce aero-engines from 1915- to the present. There is also a new railway section. Temporary exhibitions are held.

All year Mon 11.00-17.00 Tue-Sat 10.00-17.00 Sun & Bank Hol 14.00-17.00. Closed Christmas & New Year

Admission Free

Nether Alderley Mill

Congleton Road Nether Alderley Macclesfield Cheshire SK10 4TW *(1.5m S of Alderley Edge on E side of A34)*

Tel: 01625 523012

Correspondence & bookings 7 Oak Cottages, Styal Wilmslow SK9 4JQ 01625 523012. A fascinating National Trust overshot tandem-wheel watermill dating from 15th century with a stone tiled low-pitched roof. The machinery was derelict for 30 years, but has now been restored to full working order and grinds flour occasionally for demonstrations. School parties welcome by prior arrangement.

Apr-May & Oct Wed Sun & Bank Hol Mon 13.00-16.30, June-Sept Tue-Sun & Bank Hol Mon 13.00-17.00. Groups by arrangement

A£1.80 C£0.90

Sarehole Mill

Cole Bank Road Moseley Birmingham West Midlands B13 0BD *(on the A34 Stratford Road)*

Tel: 0121 777 6612

A fine display of Victorian rural life. This last water powered corn mill in the area was once the childhood haunt of 'Hobbit' author J R R Tolkien. Flour was made here, and the mill was also used to roll and smooth metal in the Industrial Revolution.

Apr-Oct daily 14.00-17.00

Admission Free

Museum- Mining

Peak District Mining Museum

The Pavilion Matlock Bath Matlock Derbyshire DE4 3NR *(Southern end of Matlock Bath off A6)*

Tel: 01629 583834

Museum explains the history of Derbyshire's lead industry from Roman times to present. Geology of area, mining, smelting processes, quarrying and people who lived and worked in area. Plenty of exhibits. An early 19th century water pressure pumping engine(only one in Britain). "Hazards of Mining" display.

All year Apr-Oct 10.00-17.00, Nov-Mar daily 11.00-16.00

Last Admission: 30mins before closing

Museum and Mine: A£3.00 Concessions£2.25 Family Ticket £7.00. Museum or Mine only: A£2.00 Concessions£1.50 Family Ticket £4.00

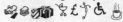

Tar Tunnel

Telford Shropshire *(close to Coalport China Museum)*

Tel: 01952 433522 Fax: 01952 432204

Web Site: www.vtel

An 18th century mining tunnel from which natural bitumen was extracted and where visitors may go underground wearing hard hats.

Mid Feb-31 Oct daily 10.00-17.00 & July-Aug 10.00-18.00. Closed Nov-mid Feb

Last Admission: 16.30

A£3.50 or on Passport ticket for all attractions: A£9.00 C&Students£5.30 Family Ticket (A2+C5)£28.00 OAPs£8.00

Museum- Motor

Donington Collection of Grand Prix Racing Cars

Exhibition Centre Donington Park Castle Donington Derbyshire DE74 2RP *(approx. 3m from J23a M1)*

Tel: 01332 811027 Fax: 01332 812829

Adjacent to the Motor Racing Circuit, the Museum houses the largest collection of single seater cars in the world, includes drivers' helmets, unique photographs and motorsport memorabilia, including life size bronze statues providing a permanent memorial to Senna and Fangio. Coach parties welcome. Guided tours available by prior arrangement. The museum remains open on all major circuit racing days. Conference facilities are available within the museum for functions/launches etc.

All year daily 10.00-17.00

Last Admission: 16.00

A£7.00 C(0-5)£Free C(5-15)£5.00 Family Ticket £14.00 OAPs&Students£5.00

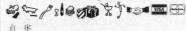

Heritage Motor Centre

Banbury Road Gaydon Warwickshire CV35 0BJ *(J12 M40, 2-3mins away on the B4100, follow signs)*

Tel: 01926 641188 Fax: 01926 641555

Heritage Motor Centre home of the Great British

Car Collection has around 200 vehicles on display. The Exhibition Hall features themed displays including the Time Road, 1930s garage and Corgi and Lucas Collections. Outside visitors can enjoy the 4x4 Off Road Circuit, children's roadway, adventure playground, small nature trail and picnic area. The Heritage Motor Centre is ideal for a family day out.

Apr-Oct daily 10.00-18.00, Nov-Mar daily 10.00-16.30. Closed 25-26 Dec
A£5.50 C(0-4)£Free C(5+)£3.50 Family Ticket (A2+C3)£15.00 OAPs£4.50

Midland Motor Museum

Stanmore Hall Stourbridge Road Bridgnorth Shropshire WV15 6DT *(2m E of Bridgnorth on A458 Stourbridge Road)*
Tel: 01746 762992 Fax: 01746 768104
A notable collection of over 90 well-restored sports and sports racing cars, and racing motor cycles dating from 1920 to 1980. They are housed in the converted stables of Stanmore Hall and surrounded by beautiful grounds.
All year daily 10.30-17.00
Last Admission: 16.30
A£3.50 C£1.75 OAPs£2.80 Family Ticket £9.95

Museum- Motorcycles

National Motorcycle Museum

Coventry Road Bickenhill Solihull West Midlands B92 0EJ *(Nr J6 of M42 off A45 nr NEC)*
Tel: 01675 443311 Fax: 01675 443310
Five exhibition halls showing British motorcycles built during the golden Age of motorcycling. Spanning 90 years, the immaculately restored machines are the products of around 150 different factories. Restoration work is carried out by enthusiasts, and new motorcycles are acquired from all over the world. Regular fairs most weekends
All year daily 10.00-18.00. Closed 24-26 Dec
Last Admission: 16.30
A£4.50 C&OAPs£3.25

Museum- Music

Elgar's Birthplace Museum

Crown East Lane Lower Broadheath Worcester Worcestershire WR2 6RH *(3m W off A44 to Leominster)*
Tel: 01905 333224
The cottage where Sir Edward Elgar the composer

was born in 1857 is now a museum. There is a comprehensive display of musical scores, photographs, letters and personal effects.
May-Sept Thur-Tue 10.30-16.00, Oct-15 Jan & 16 Feb-Apr 13.30-16.30
A£3.00 C£0.50 Students£1.00 OAPs£2.00

Museum- Natural History

Natural History Museum

Wollaton Hall Nottingham Nottinghamshire NG8 2AE *(3m W off A52 & A6514)*
Tel: 0115 915 3900 Fax: 0115 915 3932
A Robert Smythson Elizabethan manor House stands in a Deer Park, dates back to 1580. A wide variety of displays include birds, mammals, fossils and minerals. An interactive World of Wildlife gallery.
All year Apr-Sept Mon-Sat 10.00-17.00 Sun 13.00-17.00, Oct-Mar Mon-Sat 10.00-16.30 Sun 13.30-16.30, Nov-Feb Fri 13.00-16.30. Park open Mon-Fri 08.00-dusk Sat & Sun 09.00-dusk. Closed 25-26 Dec.
Weekends and Bank Hol A£1.50 C£0.75 Family Ticket £3.75. £Free weekdays. Joint ticket available with Wollaston Hall and Industrial Museum A£2.00 C£1.00

Wollaton Hall Natural History Museum

Wollaton Park Nottingham Nottinghamshire NG8 2AE *(2.5m W of City centre on A609 Ilkeston road)*
Tel: 0115 915 3900
A most spectacular, ornate Tudor building. Houses the city's Natural History Museum, high quality displays covering many aspects of the natural world can be enjoyed. 'World of Wildlife' gallery recreates an exciting African waterhole scene featuring many of the museums most popular large mammals. Interactive gallery exploring the world of nature.
All year Apr-Sept Mon-Sat 10.00-17.00 Sun 13.00-17.00, Oct-Mar Mon-Sat 10.00-16.30 Sun 13.30-16.30, Nov-Feb Fri 13.00-16.30. Park: Mon-Fri 08.00-dusk Sat & Sun 09.00-dusk. Closed 25-26 Dec.
Mon-Fri Free Weekends & Bank Hol A&OAPs£1.50 C£0.75 Parking £0.50 all day. Joint ticket available with Wollaston Hall and Industrial Museum A£2.00 C£1.00

Museum- Police

Winchcombe Folk and Police Museum

Old Town Hall Winchcombe Gloucestershire GL54

🦌 National Trust 🌳 National Trust for Scotland ✛ English Heritage ⚑ Historic Scotland ✚ CADW
🍃 guided tours available 🎪 picnic areas ☕ refreshments 📷 photography allowed [1998] visitor discount
card offer 🏖 beach/coastal area [VISA] Visa accepted 💳 Mastercard accepted [C] All cards accepted

5LJ *(B4632 M5 J9 not signposted)*
Tel: 01242 602925
A comprehensive display of artefacts illustrating the history of Winchcombe, together with a collection of British and international police uniforms.
1 Apr-end Oct Mon-Sat 10.00-17.00
A£0.80 C£0.40

Museum- Pottery

City Museum and Art Gallery

Bethesda Street Hanley Stoke-On-Trent Staffordshire ST1 3DE *(3m N of Stoke on Trent A50, A52, A53 all meet at Stoke on Trent)*
Tel: 01782 232323 Fax: 01782 232500
The story of the Potteries, including a dazzling display of more than 5,000 pieces of pottery. Other displays include natural history, archaeology and a Mark 16 Spitfire! Also a varied programme of exciting events and exhibitions.
All year Mon-Sat 10.00-17.00 Sun 14.00-17.00
Admission Free

THE MARK 16 SPITFIRE AT THE CITY MUSEUM AND ART GALLERY

Gladstone Pottery Museum

Uttoxeter Road Longton Stoke-On-Trent Staffordshire ST3 1PQ *(on A50 signposted from A5000 link with M6)*
Tel: 01782 319232 Fax: 01782 598640
Only remaining complete Victorian Pottery Factory from the era of coal-fired bottle kilns. Excellent restaurant and shop. Presenters show traditional skills of pottery making, have-a-go at throwing your own pot and making a china flower.
All year daily 10.00-17.00. Limited opening Christmas & New Year
Last Admission: 16.00
A£3.75 C£2.25 OAPs& Students£2.75

Museum- Regimental

Derby Museum and Art Gallery

The Strand Derby Derbyshire DE1 1BS *(M1 /A52 or M1 /A6)*
Tel: 01332 716659 Fax: 01332 716670
The museum has a wide range of displays, notably of Derby porcelain and of paintings by the local artist Joseph Wright (1734-97). Also antiquities, natural history and militaria, as well as many temporary exhibitions.
All year Mon 11.00-17.00, Tue-Sat 10.00-17.00, Sun and Bank Hol 14.00-17.00. Closed Christmas and New Year
Last Admission: 16.30
Admission Free

Soldiers of Gloucestershire Museum

Commercial Road Gloucester Gloucestershire GL1 2HE *(Gloucester docks)*
Tel: 01452 522682 Fax: 01452 522682
The story of the Glosters and the Royal Gloucestershire Hussars. Life-size displays with sound effects. Fascinating photographs from the last 100 years. Archive film of the Korean War.
All year Tue-Sun & Bank Hol Mon 10.00-17.00
A£3.50 C£1.90 Concessions£2.50

Staffordshire Regiment Museum

Whittington Barracks Lichfield Staffordshire WS14 9PY *(on A51 between Lichfield and Tamworth)*
Tel: 0121 311 3240/3229 Fax: 0121 311 3205
Adjacent to the barracks, the museum displays a collection of regimental militaria. The exhibits include the regiment's battle honours, captured trophies, a variety of weapons of different ages, medals and uniforms past and present.
All year Mon-Fri 09.00-16.30. Closed Bank Hol Christmas & New Year
Last Admission: 16.00
Admission Free

The Sherwood Foresters Museum (45th/95th Foot)

Castle Place Nottingham Nottinghamshire NG1 6EL *(M1 J26 - A610 City Centre, M1 J25 - A52 City Centre)*
Tel: 0115 946 5415 Fax: 0115 946 5712
The history of the Regiment from the formation of the 45th Regiment in 1741 to amalgamation with the Worcestershire Regiment in 1970. Many fine exhibits, including Regimental Colours, headdress, belt plates and badges dating from the 18th century to the present and a large medal collection.
Mar-Oct daily 10.00-17.00, Nov-end Feb Fri 13.00-

suitable for pushchairs mother & baby facilities suitable for wheelchairs gift shop corporate facilities no dogs: except guide dogs parking on site parking nearby £ charged parking café-restaurant & licensed special events educational pack

17.00. Closed 25-26 Dec
Mon-Fri: Admission Free. Weekends & Bank Hol:
A£1.50 C£0.80

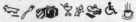

The Worcestershire Yeomanry Cavalry Regimental Museum

Foregate Street Worcester Worcestershire WR1 1DT
(in centre of Worcester, signposted Museum and
Art Gallery)
Tel: 01905 25371 Fax: 01905 616979
The City Museum and Art Gallery that houses the
Worcestershire Regiment Museum.
All year Mon, Tue, Wed, Fri 09.30-18.00 Sat 09.30-
17.00. Closed Christmas & New Year
Admission Free

Museum- Roman

Corinium Museum

Park Street Cirencester Gloucestershire GL7 2BX
(signposted from Market Sq)
Tel: 01285 655611 Fax: 01285 643286
Cirencester was the second largest town in Roman
Britain and the Corinium Museum displays use full-
scale reconstructions to bring alive the way of life
during this period in history. New Roman Military
Gallery and Medieval Gallery.
Apr-Oct Mon-Sat 10.00-17.00, Sun 14.00-17.00,
Bank Hol 10.00-17.00, Nov-Mar Tue-Sat 10.00-
17.00, Sun 14.00-17.00
Last Admission: 1hr before closing
A£2.50 C(5-16)£0.80 Students£1.00 OAPs£2.00

Museum- Science

Jenner Museum

Church Lane High Street Berkeley Gloucestershire
GL13 9BH (J13/14 M5, then A38 to Berkeley turn,
follow brown signs from A38)
Tel: 01453 810631 Fax: 01453 811690
Beautiful Georgian home of Edward Jenner, discov-
erer of vaccination against smallpox. The displays
record Jenner's life as an 18th century country doctor and his work on vaccination. Also his story of
the cuckoo and hibernation. New computerised
exhibition explaining immunology, the medical science founded by Jenner.
Apr-Sept Bank Hol Mon, Tue-Sat 12.30-17.30, Sun
13.00-17.30. Oct Sun only 13.00-17.30
Last Admission: 17.00
A£2.00 C£0.75 OAPs£1.50 Family Ticket £5.00

Museum- Teddy Bear

HENRY VIII BEAR AT THE TEDDY BEAR MUSEUM

The Teddy Bear Museum

19 Greenhill Street Stratford-Upon-Avon
Warwickshire CV37 6LF (off the M40 at
Longbridge roundabout, off the A46, in the centre
of Stratford)
Tel: 01789 293160
Ten settings in a house which dates from
Shakespeare's time, are devoted to bears of all
shapes and sizes. Many very old bears are dis-
played and there are also mechanical and musical
bears. Some of the bears belong to famous people,
for example, Jeffrey Archer and Barbara Cartland.
Pushchairs are required to be left at reception. Air
conditioned, call or write for a free mail order cata-
logue.
Mar-Dec daily 09.30-18.00, Jan & Feb 09.30-17.00.
Closed 25-26 Dec
A£2.25 C£1.00 Family Ticket (A2+C3)£5.95, Groups
rates of 20+ A£1.95 C£0.90
Discount Card Offer: One Child Free With One Full
Paying Adult

Museum- Textiles

Macclesfield Silk Museum

Heritage Centre Roe Street Macclesfield Cheshire
SK11 6UT (in town centre, signposted)
Tel: 01625 613210 Fax: 01625 617880
The silk museum presents the story of silk in
Macclesfield through a colourful audio-visual pro-
gramme, exhibitions, textiles, garments, models &
room settings.
All year Mon-Sat 11.00-17.00, Sun & Bank Hol
13.00-17.00
Last Admission: 16.00

A£2.40 C&OAPs&Disabled£1.60 Family Ticket £6.40. Joint Ticket with Paradise Mill A£4.20 C&OAPs&Disabled£2.40 Family Ticket £9.40. Evening visits by prior arrangement call to book

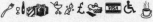

Museum of Costume and Textiles

43-51 Castle Gate Nottingham Nottinghshire NG1 6AF
Tel: 0115 915 3500
Costume from 1730 to 1960 is displayed in appropriate room settings. Other rooms contain 17th century costume and embroidery, dress accessories, the Lord Middleton collection and map tapestries. Knitted, woven and printed textiles are also on show, together with embroidery from Europe and Asia. Disabled access limited to ground floor.All year daily 10.00-17.00, Sun-Thur Nov-Feb 12.00-17.00. Closed 25-26 Dec
Admission Free

Paradise Mill

Old Park Lane Macclesfield Cheshire SK11 6TJ (off Mill Street in town centre, signposted)
Tel: 01625 618228
Award winning museum, former silk mill workers, illustrate the silk production process with the help of demonstrations from weavers. The museum was a working silk mill until 1981 when the last weaver retired. Exhibitions are on show.
All year Bank Hol Mon & Tue-Sun: Summer 13.00-17.00, Winter 13.00-16.00. Closed Good Fri, 24-26 Dec & 1 Jan
Last Admission: 60 mins before closing
A£2.40 C&OAPs&Disabled£1.60 Family Ticket £6.40. Joint Ticket withSilk Museum A£4.20 C&OAPs&Disabled£2.40 Family Ticket £9.40. Evening visits by prior arrangement call to book

Museum- Toy

Coventry Toy Museum

Much Park Street Coventry West Midlands CV1 2LT
Tel: 01203 227560
A collection of toys dating from 1740 to 1980, including trains, dolls, dolls' houses and games, housed in a 14th-century monastery gatehouse.
All year daily 12.00-18.00.
A£1.50 C&OAPs£1.00

Vina Cooke Museum of Dolls and Bygone Childhood

The Old Rectory Great North Road Cromwell Newark Nottinghamshire NG23 6JE (5m N of Newark off A1)
Tel: 01636 821364
Childhood memorabilia displayed in 17th century house, prams, toys, doll's houses, costumes and large collection of Victorian and Edwardian dolls including Vina Cooke hand-made character dolls.
All year Sun-Thur 10.30-12.00 & 14.00-17.00. Closed Fri. Other times by appointment
A£2.50 C£1.00 OAPs£2.00. Groups by arrangement

Museum- Transport

Museum of British Road Transport

St. Agnes Lane Hales Street Coventry West Midlands CV1 1PN (A45, A423, M6 meet at Coventry, Museum has a City centre location)
Tel: 01203 832425 Fax: 01203 832465
Web Site: www.mrbt.co.uk
You'll be fascinated by this display of British-made road transport. It spans over 100 years of history. From the first cycles to the very latest advances in technology like - Thrust 2, centre-piece of a thrilling audio visual display. At the birthplace of the British Motor Industry the Museum displays over 400 magnificent cars, motorcycles, cycles and commercial vehicles.
All year daily 10.00-17.00. Closed 24-26 Dec
Last Admission: 16.30
A£3.30 C&OAPs£2.30 Family Ticket £8.90
Discount Card Offer: £1.00 Off Admission

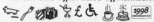

MUSEUM OF BRITISH ROAD TRANSPORT

National Tramway Museum

Matlock Road Crich Derbyshire DE4 5DP (off B5035)
Tel: 01773 852565 Fax: 01773 852326
Mile long scenic journey through a period street to open countryside with panoramic views. Unlimited tram rides. Exhibition hall holds largest national collection of vintage electric trams. Video theatre,

shops, cafe, playground and picnic area.
*All year daily 10.00-17.30 Sat Sun & Bank Hol
10.00-18.30. Closed some Fri's in Apr May Sep &
Oct*
Last Admission: 90mins before closing
A£5.40 C£2.70 Family Ticket £12.30 OAPs£4.20

Oswestry Transport Museum
Oswald Road Oswestry Shropshire SY11 1RE
Tel: 01691 671749
The Museum uses over 100 bicycles to display the
history of cycling through the ages. Displays
include bicycle parts, signs and Dunlop's development of the pneumatic tyre. There is also a large
exhibition of the Cambrian Railways where visitors
can see 12 railway engines and rolling stock. Short
steam rides are available from Easter.
*All year daily 10.00-16.00. Closed 25-26 Dec
A£1.50 C£0.60. Group rates 10+*

Shackerstone Railway Museum
Shackerstone Station Shackerstone Leicestershire
CV13 6NW *(A444 and A447, 3m N of Market
Bosworth)*
Tel: 01827 880754
Museum of Railwaymania, much of it 19th century
with special emphasis on railways of West
Leicestershire.
*Wed 14.00-17.00 Sun & Bank Hol Mon 11.00-18.00
A£0.50 Children £Free*

Museum- Victorian

Blists Hill Victorian Town
Legges Way Madeley Telford Shropshire TF8 7EF
(on the A442 from Telford, signposted)
Tel: 01952 433522 Fax: 01952 432204
Web Site: www.vtel
Recreated working Victorian town, staff in Victorian
costume, working exhibits, pub, restaurant, even
Victorian 'token' currency.
*Mar-Nov daily 10.00-17.00, Nov-Mar daily 10.00-
16.00. Closed 24-25 Dec*
Last Admission: 15.30
A£6.50 OAPs£5.50

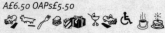

Kegworth Museum
52 High Street Kegworth Derbyshire DE74 2DR *(J24
M1 A6 to Kegworth. From Loughborough via A6 to
Kegworth High Street off village centre)*
Tel: 01509 672886 Fax: 01509 673801
The museum is housed in a restored mid 19th cen-
tury barn. Permanent displays include a Victorian

Parlour Scene; a history of Kegworth School from
Quill to Computer; Saddlers of Kegworth, a recon-
struction of Sutton's shop on the London Road,
using the original tools and furniture; Royal British
Legion memorabilia from both world wars.
*Easter-Eend Sept Sun, Wed, Bank Hol Mon 14.00-
17.00*
Last Admission: 16.45
A£0.50 Concessions£0.25. Call for Group rates

The Old House Museum
Cunningham Place Bakewell Derbyshire DE45 1AX
*(situated on A6, 12m S of Buxton and 8m N of
Matlock)*
Tel: 01629 813165
Bakewell Old House Museum is a Tudor house with
a collection of social life exhibits. It contains a
Victorian kitchen, costume displays on models, old
toys, artesan's craft workshops and tools, lace and
early cameras, etc
*Apr 1-Oct 31 daily 13.30-16.00, July & Aug 11.00-
16.00. Groups at other times*
Last Admission: 15.30
A£2.00 C£1.00

The Shambles
Church Street Newent Gloucestershire GL18 1PP
Tel: 01531 822144 Fax: 01531 821120
A museum of cobbled streets, alleyways, cottages
and houses. Shops, trades, cart sheds and even a
tin chapel and cottage garden all help to recreate
the feel and atmosphere of Victorian life.
Mar-Dec 10.00-18.00 ordusk if sooner
Last Admission: 17.00
A£3.25 C£1.95 OAPs£2.85. Group rates 15+ £2.75

Museum- Village

Hallaton Village Museum
The Post Office Hog Lane Hallaton Leicestershire
Tel: 01858 555216/555602
One of Leicestershire's most picturesque and his-
toric villages. Different aspects of past village life
recreated each year. A fascinating peep into the
past. Old and unusual agricultural and household
items. Photographic display.
*May-Oct Sat & Sun 14.30-17.00. Also Bank Hol Mon
Admission Free but donations appreciated*

Measham Museum
56 High Street Measham Leicestershire DE12 7HZ
Tel: 01530 273956
Small village museum with a fascinating collection

🐾 *National Trust* 🏴 *National Trust for Scotland* ⛪ *English Heritage* 🏛 *Historic Scotland* 🍀*CADW*
🌳 *guided tours available* 🧺 *picnic areas* 🍵*refreshments* 📷 *photography allowed* 1998 *visitor discount
card offer* 🏖 *beach/coastal area* VISA *Visa accepted* 💳 *Mastercard accepted* C *All cards accepted*

of artefacts, documents and illustrations preserved by a former village doctor and his father. Unique personal history of a community, covering almost 100 years.

All year Tue 10.00-12.00 & 14.00-17.00, Sat 10.00-12.00

Admission Free but donations appreciated

Museum- Waterways

NATIONAL WATERWAYS MUSEUM

National Waterways Museum
Llanthony Warehouse Gloucester Docks Gloucester Gloucestershire GL1 2EH *(Js 11, 12a & 12 M5, A38 & A40 then follow brown signs for Historic Docks)*
Tel: 01452 318054 Fax: 01452 318066
Award winning National Museum based within historic Gloucester Docks, is on three floors of a listed seven storey Victorian Warehouse. Entry is via a lock Chamber with running water, where a sense of adventure take you into the secret world of canals. Relive the 200 year story of Britain's first transport system, its tale of pioneering men, fortunes gained/lost. View the national collection of British Waterways. Working models/engines, archive film, hands-on exhibits and interactives brings all of this to life. Two sides of quay, where cargoes were once transferred, now sports boats of differing shapes and sizes including No 4 Steam Dredger and the newly renovated 'Northwich.' Explore Llanthony Yard, the Blacksmith's Workshop with its noises and smells, where on certain days Lawrence can be seen putting his skills in action. A staffed Activities Room in school holidays, gives all ages an opportunity to put their creative and constructive skills into practice. A flexible Museum ticket allows you freedom of entry on its day of purchase. With a tea room and specialist book/gift shop, add to the wide variety of things to do. Sit at the quayside and observe the water traffic negotiating Llanthony Bridge or take a boat trip along the Gloucester and Sharpness Canal.

All year daily Summer: 10.00-18.00. Winter: 10.00-17.00. Closed 25 Dec
Last Admission: 90mins before closing

A£4.50 C&OAPs£3.50 Family Tickets: (A2+C1)£10.00, (A2+C2)£11.00, (A2+C3)£12.00. Group rates call for details
Discount Card Offer: 20% Off Museum Entry

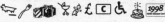

Stoke Bruerne Canal Museum
Bridge Road Stoke Bruerne Towcester Northamptonshire NN12 7SE *(4m S of J15 M1, off the A508 in the village of Stoke Bruerne, signposted)*
Tel: 01604 862229 Fax: 01604 862229
The three storeys of a former corn mill have been converted to hold a marvellous collection of bygones from over two centuries of the canals. The museum is near a flight of locks on the Grand Union Canal. Limited access for wheelchairs.
Nov-Easter Tue-Sun 10.00-16.00, Easter-Oct daily 10.00-18.00. Closed Christmas
A£2.70 C&OAPs£1.80 Family Ticket £6.30

Museum- Waterworks

ABBEY PUMPING STATION

Abbey Pumping Station
Corporation Road Leicester Leicestershire LE4 5PX *(3m N off A6)*
Tel: 0116 266 1330 Fax: 0116 261 2851
Built as a Pumping Station in 1891, this historic building and site have recently undergone refurbishment and restoration. Guides interpret the unique Victorian beam engines. The Exhibition Hall hosts a public health exhibition dedicated to 'Public Health Called Flushed With Pride.'
Apr-Dec Mon-Sat 10.00-17.30, Sun 14.00-17.30. Closed 24-26 Dec & Jan 1
Admission Free

🦖 suitable for pushchairs 🦖 mother & baby facilities ♿ suitable for wheelchairs 🎁 gift shop
🐾 corporate facilities 🐕 no dogs: except guide dogs 🅿️ parking on site 🅿️ parking nearby
£ charged parking ☕ café-restaurant ‽ licensed 🎂 special events 📬 educational pack

Museum- Yeomanry

Warwickshire Yeomanry Museum

The Court House Jury Street Warwick Warkickshire CV34 4EW *(in centre of Warwick off J15 M40)*
Tel: 01926 492212 Fax: 01926 494837
After a great fire in 1694, the court house was rebuilt between 1725 and 1728 in a style that befitted the wealthy merchants of the town. In the vaults there is now a museum displaying militaria from the county Yeomanry, dating from 1794 to 1945. It includes regimental silver, some very fine paintings, uniforms and weapons.
Good Fri-end Sept. Most Fri Sat & Sun & Bank Hol 10.00-13.00 & 14.00-16.00. Other times by prior arrangement
Last Admission: 15.30
Admission Free

Museums

Bantock House Museum in the Park

Finchfield Road Wolverhampton West Midlands WV3 9LQ *(Bus 513/543 from Wolverhampton town centre, 1.5m)*
Tel: 01902 312132 Fax: 01902 717775
Japanned ware and its history, fine collections of Staffordshire figures and Worcester ceramics, enamels, dolls and toys. Set in 43 acres of historic parkland. There is 'Pitch and Putt,' picnic facilities and a tea room. Grade II listed building retaining its Arts and Crafts flavour.
All year Tue-Sat 10.00-13.00 & 14.00-17.00. Closed Sun & Mon
Admission Free

Birmingham Museum And Art Gallery

Chamberlain Square Birmingham West Midlands B3 3DH *(Birmingham city centre)*
Tel: 0121 235 2834 Fax: 0121 236 6227
Home to the world's finest collection of Pre-Raphaelite paintings, and many other prestigious works from the renowned Old Masters. Historic interest comes in the prehistoric form of Tyrannosaurus Rex. Egyptian mummies and the elegant Edwardian Tea room complete your journey through time and art.
All year Mon-Thur 10.00-17.00, Fri 10.30-17.00, Sat 10.00-17.00, Sun 12.30-17.00
Admission Free. Exhibitions in Gas Hall charged

Clive House Museum

College Hill Shrewsbury Shropshire SY1 1LT *(Shrewsbury town centre)*

Tel: 01743 353811 Fax: 01743 358411
Town house with a long history, including a brief association in the 1760's with Robert, Lord Clive of India. New displays in 1997 feature Natural History and Natural Historians, including Charles Darwin. Also walled garden, children's room and old kitchen.
All year Tue-Sat 10.00-16.00 and Bank Hol Mon. Also Sun end May-end Sept. Closed Mid Dec-mid Jan
Last Admission: 15.30
A£2.00 C£0.50 OAPs & Student£1.00. Joint Admission to Clive House Rowley's House Shrewsbury Castle & Regimental Museum A£4.00 C£1.00 OAPs&Students£2.00

Coalport China Museum

Coalport Telford Shropshire *(M54 to Telford, then A4169)*
Tel: 01952 433522 Fax: 01952 432204
Web Site: www.vtel
Historic Coalport China made here from late 18th century until 1926. Marvellous displays and demonstrations and workshops. Tea room and YHA on site.
All year daily 10.00-17.00
Last Admission: 16.00
A£3.50 joint admission with the Tar Tunnel or buy a passport to all attractions for A£9.00 C&Students£5.30 Family Ticket (A2+C5)£28.00 OAPs£8.00

Cotswolds Motor Museum and Toy Collection

The Old Mill Bourton-on-the-Water Gloucestershire GL54 2BY *(A429)*
Tel: 01451 821255
Housed in a water mill on the River Windrush, the museum has cars and motorcycles from the vintage years up to the 1950's with a collection of 800 advertising signs and some 8000 pieces of automobilia. There is also the Childhood Toy Collection. Brum, the character from the children's BBC programme lives here.
Feb-Nov daily 10.00-18.00
A£1.75 C(0-2)£Free C(2-14)£0.80 Family Ticket £4.80

Dudley Museum and Art Gallery

St James's Road Dudley West Midlands DY1 1HU *(signposted within town centre)*
Tel: 01384 815 571 Fax: 01384 815 576
One of the Midland's most exciting exhibition venues, famous for its popular temporary shows.

Permanent displays include the acclaimed 'Time Trail' geology gallery featuring spectacular fossils from the local rocks. Also the Brooke Robinson collection of 17th-19th century paintings, furniture, ceramics and enamels.

All year Mon-Sat 10.00-17.00
Admission Free

Gloucester City Museum and Art Gallery

Brunswick Road Gloucester Gloucestershire GL1 1HP *(in centre of Gloucester close to shops and car parks)*
Tel: 01452 524131 Fax: 01452 410898
Fascinating displays show the early life of the City - with dinosaur bones, unique Roman remains and the amazing Birdlip mirror. There are special displays of furniture, the decorative arts, and paintings by well-known artists, including Turner. An exciting programme of activities and temporary exhibitions is available throughout the year. Disabled access - 100% for manual wheelchairs, 50% for electric wheelchairs. Toilets and a lift are available for the disabled.

All year Mon-Sat 10.00-17.00, July-Sept also Sun 10.00-16.00
Admission Free

Herbert Art Gallery and Museum

Jordan Well Coventry CV1 5QP *(close to the Cathedral and Tourist Information Centre)*
Tel: 01203 832381 Fax: 01203 832410
Coventry is associated with outstanding manufacturing skills, post war reconstruction and the legend of Lady Godiva. As a focus for the city's heritage and treasures, the Herbert Art Gallery and Museum offers a fascinating visit with international appeal.

All year Mon-Sat 10.00-17.30, Sun 14.00-17.00
Admission Free

Hereford and Worcester County Museum

Hartlebury Castle Hartlebury Kidderminster Worcestershire DY11 7XZ *(5m S of Kidderminster off A449)*
Tel: 01299 250416
Housed in the north wing of Hartlebury Castle, the County Museum contains a delightful display of crafts and industries. There are unique collections of toys, costume, domestic life, room settings and horse-drawn vehicles as well as a reconstructed forge, schoolroom, wheelwright's and tailor's shop. New for 1997 'Below Stairs' exhibition from Summer '97

Mar-Nov Mon-Thur & Bank Hol 10.00-17.00, Fri &

Sun 14.00-17.00
Last Admission: 16.30
A£1.90 C&OAPs£0.90 Family Ticket£5.00

Industrial Museum

Courtyard Buildings Wollaton Park Nottingham Nottinghamshire NG8 2AE *(off A609 Ilkeston Road from S J25 M1, from N J26. Wollaton Hall is signposted on Ring Road)*
Tel: 0115 915 3910 Fax: 0115 915 3941
A history of Nottingham industries from curtains to computers.

All year Apr-Sept Mon-Sat 10.00-17.00, Sun 13.00-17.00, Oct-Mar Mon-Sat 10.00-16.30, Sun 13.30-16.30, Nov-Feb Fri 13.00-16.30. Park: Mon-Fri 08.00-dusk Sat & Sun 09.00-dusk. Closed 25-26 Dec.
Last Admission: 16.30 Apr-Sept 16.00 Oct-Mar
A£1.50 C£0.75. Joint ticket available with Wollaston Hall and Natural History Museum A£2.00 C£1.00

Leicester Gas Museum - British Gas Services

195 Aylestone Road Leicester Leicestershire LE2 7QH
Tel: 0116 250 3190 Fax: 0116 250 3190
Housed in the Victorian gatehouse of one of Leicester's gasworks, this gem of a museum traces the story of gas from the early days of small gas works to the discovery of natural gas. Working gas lights from 1820, fires and cookers from 1880, washing machines / water heaters from 1890, even gas powered hairdryers and radio, and an all gas 1920s kitchen.

All year Tue-Fri 12.30-16.30. Closed Sat-Mon and Bank Hol
Admission Free

Much Wenlock Museum

Wilmore Street Much Wenlock Shropshire TF13 6HR *(A458)*
Tel: 01952 727773
Much Wenlock has kept its medieval flavour despite encroaching changes from the 20th century. Its museum, in the Old Market Hall, has an admirable collection illustrating the history of the town and its famous priory. There is also a display of memorabilia of the Much Wenlock Olympics. Hands on sessions being held at the museum, further information can be obtained from the museum.

Mar-Sept Mon-Sat 10.30-13.00 & 14.00-17.00.
A£0.50 C & OAPs & UB40's £Free

🖍 suitable for pushchairs   🍼 mother & baby facilities   ♿ suitable for wheelchairs   🎁 gift shop
🍬 corporate facilities   🐕 no dogs: except guide dogs   🚗 parking on site   🚗 parking nearby
£ charged parking   🍴 café-restaurant 🍷 licensed   🎂 special events   📕 educational pack

New Walk Museum

New Walk Leicester Leicestershire LE1 7EA

Tel: 0116 255 4100 Fax: 0116 247 3011

This major regional venue houses local and national collections. New galleries include 'Variety of Life' (natural history), Leicestershire's Rocks (geology), Ancient Egyptians and Discovering Art. Decorative arts cover ceramics, silver and glass. Lots of 'hands on' exhibits throughout the galleries, a newly opened 'Discovery Room' and a changing programme of temporary exhibitions.

All year Mon-Sat 10.00-17.30, Sun 14.00-17.30.
Closed 24-26 Dec & Jan 1
Admission Free

NEW WALK MUSEUM

Robert Opie Collection Museum of Advertising and Packaging

Albert Warehouse The Docks Gloucester Gloucestershire GL1 2EH *(J10,11 or 12 M5 head for the Docks)*

Tel: 01452 302309 Fax: 01452 308507

This museum is not only a feast of nostalgia, it is an exploration of the changes in advertising and packaging from 1870 to the present day. Based on the Robert Opie Collection the museum is the first of it's kind in the world. Project Sheets on History & Design & Technology for Schools. Old T.V. ads shown continuously in Tea Room.

All year Summer daily 10.00-18.00. Winter daily 10.00-17.00. Closed 25-26 Dec also Mon Nov-Feb inclusive
A£2.95 C£0.95 OAPs&Students£1.95 Family Ticket £6.95

Rosehill House and Dale House

Coalbrookdale Shropshire *(100yds walk uphill from Museum of Iron)*

Tel: 01952 433522/432551 Fax: 01952 432204
Web Site: www.vtel

Restored ironmaster's homes, set in the early 19th

century, typical of the Derby family house. Occasional Candlelit nights.

Mar-Nov daily 10.00-17.00. Closed Nov-Mar
Last Admission: 16.15
A£4.00 includes admission to Museum of Iron and Furnace Site, passport tickets to all attractions A£9.00 C&Students£5.30 Family Ticket (A2+C5)£28.00 OAPs£8.00

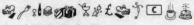

Royal Crown Derby Museum

194 Osmaston Road Derby Derbyshire DE23 8JZ

Tel: 01332 712800 Fax: 01332 712899

The only factory allowed to use the words 'Crown' and 'Royal', a double honour granted by George III and Queen Victoria. The museum, opened by the Duchess of Devonshire in 1969, traces the development of the company from 1748 to the present day. We regret that children under 10 years of age are not admitted.

Factory Tours & Shop: Weekdays 09.30-12.30 & 13.30-16.00. Closed factory holidays
Museum: £Free. Tours A£3.00 C(10+)&OAPs£2.75

Ruddington Framework Knitters' Museum

Chapel Street Ruddington Nottingham Nottinghamshire NG11 6HE *(A60 signposted)*

Tel: 0115 984 6914

Unique complex of frameshops - working handframes and allied machinery with cottages restored for 1850 and 1900. Communal wash house, privies, pump around courtyard. Shop. Video. Adjacent is a primitive Methodist Chapel.

Easter-mid Dec Wed-Sat and Bank Hol 11.00-16.30
Easter-end Sept also Sun 13.30-16.30 Pre-booked parties all year
Last Admission: 16.00A£2.00 C & Students & OAPs £1.25 Family Ticket £5.25

Samuel Johnson Birthplace Museum

Breadmarket Street Lichfield Staffordshire WS13 6LG

Tel: 01543 264972 Fax: 01543 258441

A statue of Dr Johnson sits at one end of Market Square facing his birthplace on the corner of Breadmarket Street. The house, where Samuel's father had a bookshop, is now a museum containing many of Johnson's personal relics. His favourite armchair and walking stick are among the collection.

All year daily 10.00-17.00. Closed Christmas & New Year

Selly Manor Museum

Maple Road Birmingham West Midlands B30 2AE *(off A38)*
Tel: 0121 472 0199 Fax: 0121 414 1348
This timber-framed house in delightful garden surroundings dates from the 14th century and is home to a fine collection of furniture and domestic objects. Guided tours are available around the house, for which booking is required. There are regular temporary exhibitions throughout the year.
All year Tue-Fri & Bank Hol Mon 10.00-17.00
A£1.00 C£0.50

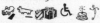

Stockport Museum

Vernon Park Turncroft Lane Stockport Cheshire SK1 4AR *(1m from town centre - follow signposts)*
Tel: 0161 474 4460 Fax: 0161 474 4449
Displays on the history of Stockport from Pre-historic times to the present, and the 'Green Gallery' - a display on the local environment. "Hidden Treasures" in the basement.
Apr-Oct daily 13.00-17.00, Nov-Mar Sat & Sun only 13.00-17.00
Admission Free

The Galleries of Justice

Shire Hall High Pavement Lace Market Nottingham Nottinghamshire NG1 1HN *(city centre, signposted both traffic and pedestrian, multi-story parking signposted, 5-10mins walk)*
Tel: 0115 952 0555 Fax: 0115 952 0557
This award-winning museum, which is located in the magnificent Shire Hall in the heart of Nottingham's historic Lace Market, is currently undergoing a £5.5million expansion programme. Phased over 2 years, the new development involves the acquisition, restoration and opening of an Edwardian police station, women's prison with bath house and laundry, 1833 goal, discovery centre, civil law gallery and temporary exhibition gallery. The Galleries of Justice currently offers a major crime and punishment exhibition Condemned! On arrival, you are issued with a prisoner identity number as the visit unfolds discover your fate, will it be a public flogging, transportation to a penal colony or ultimately, execution by hanging? A truly arresting experience awaits as past and present combine in our exciting new Police Galleries, opening 6 April 1998. Based in the original 1905 police station attached to the Shire Hall complex, Nicked! offers a unique insight into policing through time and includes objects from the museum's nationally important police collection and criminal evidence from past infamous crimes. Visitors to Nicked! will attend a crime scene and be invited to assess the evidence through the use of forensic, state of the art computers and eventually, they will discover for themselves, exactly what is involved in an arrest! A women's prison with bath house and laundry, 1833 goal and mediaeval cave system are being incorporated into the newly expanded and refurbished Condemned! Exhibition, which re-opens as the Crime and Punishment Galleries on 20 July 1998. Visitors will see the original lead lined bath, changing cubicles, drying racks and copper in the bath house and laundry, which largely remains untouched and they can also explore the man made mediaeval caves used for wool and food storage. Comprehensive educational programme for KS 2 and above. Wheelchair access limited to 60% of the building. Pushchairs may be left in the buggy store.
Apr-Aug Tue-Sun & Bank Hol Mon 10.00-18.00, Sept-Mar Tue-Sun & Bank Hol Mon 10.00-17.00
Last Admission: 60mins before closing
Condemned! Tour: 19 Apr 98: A£4.25 C&Concessions£2.95 Family Ticket (A2+C2)£11.95. Police Galleries: 6 Apr 98: A£3.95 C£3.50 Family Ticket (A2+C2)£11.95 Concessions£3.75. Crime & Punishment Galleries: 20 July 98: A£5.95 C£3.95 Family Ticket (A2+C2)£16.95 Concessions£4.75. Combination tickets for Police and Crime and Punishment Galleries available
Discount Card Offer: One Child Free When Accompanied By A Full Paying Adult

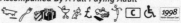

The Radbrook Culinary Museum

Radbrook College Radbrook Road Shrewsbury Shropshire SY3 9BL *(3m from Shrewsbury on the A488 Bishops Castle Road)*
Tel: 01743 232686 Fax: 01743 271563
A unique collection of domestic utensils and examples of household crafts covering the late Victorian and Edwardian era and tracing the early years in the formation of Shropshire Technical School for Girls.
Visitors welcome by appointment
Admission Free

West Park Museum

Prestbury Road Macclesfield Cheshire SK10 3BJ *(off A537)*
Tel: 01625 619831 Fax: 01625 617880
Collection of Egyptian antiquities can be seen at this museum together with fine and decorative arts. Paintings from 19th and early 20th century. Items relating to local history are also shown. The museum was established in 1898 by the Brocklehurst family.
All year Tue-Sun 13.00-16.30. Closed Bank Hol, Good Fri 25-26 Dec & 1 Jan

---

🛴 suitable for pushchairs 👶 mother & baby facilities ♿ suitable for wheelchairs 🎁 gift shop
🤝 corporate facilities 🐕 no dogs: except guide dogs 🚗 parking on site 🚙 parking nearby
£ charged parking 🍴 café-restaurant 🍸 licensed 🎂 special events 🎒 educational pack

Admission Free

National Parks

Longshaw Estate

Peak District National Park Sheffield S11 7TZ *(7.5m from Sheffield next to A625 Sheffield / Hathersage road Woodcroft car park is off B6055 200mtr S of J with A625. Car Park 200mtr from Visitor Centre, access difficult for coaches, no coaches at Weekends or Bank Hol)*
Tel: 01433 631708/631757
688 hectares of open moorland and farms in the Peak District National Park, with dramatic views and varied walking. Stone for the Derwent and Howden Dams was quarried from Bolehill, and mill-stones may be seen in quarries on the estate. There is a quarry winding house above Grindleford station. No dogs in Visitor Centre, on leads on walks only.
Estate: all year. Visitor Centre: all year Weekends & Bank Hol Mon 11.00-17.00 or sunset if sooner, Mar-Dec Wed & Thur 11.00-17.00, pre-booked Groups at other times, by arrangement

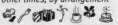

Peak District National Park

Aldern House Braslow Road Bakewell Derbyshire DE45 1AE *(High Peak Estate the Derwent Moors: on the county border in Yorkshire. South Peak on the Derbyshire / Staffordshire border)*
Tel: 01629 816200
A popular family destination with 22 million visitors a year, the Peak National Park covers 555 square miles at the southern end of the Pennines. Many visitors enjoy the softer, settled landscape of the White Peak area which is crisscrossed with 18th century limestone walls. This area is surrounded on three sides by the higher, bleaker and wilder moorlands known as the dark Peak. The Ranger Centre arranges a variety of events, guided walks and activity days. They have an environmental playscheme, nature fun days and woodland discovery trails. Children's playdays must be booked in advance. Contact the Ranger on 01629 815185 for further details.
All year during daylight hours
Admission Free

Nature Reserves

Birmingham Nature Centre

Pershore Road Edgbaston Birmingham West Midlands B5 7RL *(off A441 in Cannon Hill Park. Buses from City centre: 45/47 Bristol Road: 61, 62, 63)*
Tel: 0121 472 7775
Otters, foxes, lynxes, fallow deer, harvest mice and snowy owls are among 134 species of mainly British and European wildlife that can be found in the 6.5 acre site in leafy Edgbaston. The six and a half acre site in leafy Edgbaston is also home to creatures from elsewhere in the world, domestic animals such as goats and pigs, wild flowers and birds.
All year Apr-Oct daily 10.00-17.00, Nov-Mar Sun only 10.00-16.00
Last Admission: 16.00 15.00
A£1.50 C£Free Concessions£1.00

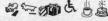

Brassey Nature Reserve

Upper Slaughter Naunton Gloucestershire
Tel: 01452 383333 Fax: 01452 383334
Brassey is a 2.1 hectare nature reserve on the north side of the Windrush Valley in the Cotswolds. Consisting of unimproved grassland with a fast moving tributary of the Windrush flowing through the site, it has one of the few remaining freshwater marshes in Gloucestershire. Local guide leaflet available.
Access by permit only in advance
Admission Free

Ulverscroft Nature Reserve

Nr Loughborough Leicestershire LE *(BR: Barrow Upon Soar & Loughborough)*
Tel: 01909 486411
Part of the ancient Charnwood forest, the area is especially fine in spring during bluebell time.
01162 553904

Parks

Cannon Hill Park

2 Russell Road Moseley Birmingham West Midlands B13 8RD *(J6 M6, A38, signposted)*
Tel: 0121 442 4226 Fax: 0121 449 0238
Formal park with conservation areas, tropical plant house, Nature Centre, Midland Art Centre, picnic areas, children's play areas, boating pools, fishing, tennis and bowls.
All year daily
Nature Centre: A£1.50 C£Free Concessions£1.00

Hawkstone Park

Weston Shrewsbury Shropshire SY4 5UY *(3m from Hodnet off A53)*
Tel: 01939 200611 Fax: 01939 200311

Created in the 18th century by the Hill family, Hawkstone was once one of the greatest historic parklands in history. After almost one hundred years of neglect it has been restored and designated a Grade I historic park. Visitors can experience this magical world of intricate pathways, arches and bridges, towering cliffs and follies, and an awesome grotto.

24 Mar-Oct daily 10.00-18.00. Dec weekends only for Father Christmas visits

£10.00 per car for 5 people Mon-Sat £12.00. Sun and Bank Hol: Early Bird 10.00-10.30 £5.00 per car

Norwood Park

Halam Road Southwell Nottinghamshire NG25 0PF *(1m from Southwell on the Halam road towards Mansfield)*

Tel: 01636 812 762/813 226 Fax: 01636 813 226

Glorious ancient parkland, trees, ponds, modern orchards with packing station. 18th century family house with history in every corner. Summer sports, cricket, lawn tennis etc.

Open by private arrangement

Picnic Areas

Alvecote Priory Picnic Area

Alvecote Tamworth Staffordshire *(J10 M42 between Polesworth / Shuttington)*

Tel: 01827 872660 Fax: 01827 875161

Web Site: www.warwickshire.gov.uk

The picnic area sits on a sharp bend of the Coventry Canal about 3 miles east of Tamworth. After some years of disuse the 3 acre site was reclaimed for recreation in 1978 by the County Council, with assistance from the countryside Commission. It is ideal for picnics and family games, amongst the mature shrubs and trees of what used to be the garden of a house built out of stone from an old Priory.

All year daily, hours according to season

Admission Free

Racecourses

Uttoxeter Racecourse

Wood Lane Uttoxeter Staffordshire ST14 8BD

Tel: 01889 562561 Fax: 01889 562786

With superb racing in beautiful surroundings, award winning Uttoxeter racecourse is famous for its warm and friendly welcome. Home of the Midlands Grand National, Uttoxeter guarantees a day to remember.

Open 20 Racedays throughout the year

A£4.00-£15.00 C(0-16)£Free

Railways

Battlefield Line

Shackerstone Station Shackerstone Nuneaton Warwickshire CV13 6NW *(3m NW of Market Bosworth on unclassified road at Shackerstone Station)*

Tel: 0116 291 7460 Fax: 0116 291 7460

Together with a regular railway service (mainly steam) from Shackerstone to Shenton, there is an extensive railway museum featuring a collection of rolling stock and a multitude of other relics from the age of steam rail travel. The return passenger trips are 9 miles in length.

Station & Museum all year Sat & Sun 11.30-17.30

Passenger steam train

Mar-Oct Sat, Sun & Bank Hol Mon Diesel trains: June-Aug Wed only

Return fare: A£4.70 C£2.30 Family Ticket £12.00

Birmingham Railway Museum

Warwick Road Tyseley Birmingham West Midlands B11 2HL *(3m S A41 Warwick Road)*

Tel: 0121 707 4696 Fax: 0121 764 4645

This is a working railway museum with a fully equipped workshop. There are numerous steam locomotives and historic carriages, wagons and other vehicles. Steam locomotive driving courses on either an Express Passenger Steam or Tank Loco are also available. Please telephone for details.

All year daily 10.00-17.00. Fully open at weekends. Closed 25-26 Dec & 1 Jan

A£2.50 Concessions£1.25 Family Ticket £6.25

DEAN FOREST RAILWAY

Dean Forest Railway

Norchard Centre Forest Road Lydney Gloucestershire GL15 4ET *(1m N of Lydney at New Mills on B4234)*

Tel: 01594 843423 info line

🏃 *suitable for pushchairs* 👶 *mother & baby facilities* ♿ *suitable for wheelchairs* 🎁 *gift shop*
🤝 *corporate facilities* 🚫🐕 *no dogs: except guide dogs* 🅿️ *parking on site* 🅿️ *parking nearby*
£ *charged parking* ☕ *café-restaurant* 🍷 *licensed* 🎂 *special events* 📚 *educational pack*

Steam standard gauge line from Norchard to Lydney Junction (2 miles). Museum, gift shop, riverside walk, forest trail, large car park.
Trains Run: Apr-Sept Sun. June-Aug Wed. Aug Tue Thur & Sat. All Bank Hol & Special Events. Call above info line for running times
Last Admission:
Standard Fares: A£3.50 C£2.00 OAPs£3.00
Discount Card Offer: One Child Free With Two Full Adult Paying Passengers

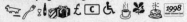

High Peak Junction Workshop
High Peak Junction Nr Cromford Derbyshire DE4 4LS *(signposted off A6, Cromford J28 M1 12m)*
Tel: 01629 822831 Fax: 01629 825336
Restored workshop of Cromford and High Peak Railway, one of Britain's earliest lines. Historic displays and artefacts tell the story of this unique line.
Easter-Sept daily 10.30-17.30 Winter weekends 10.30-16.00
A£0.40 C£0.30

Middleton Top Engine House
Middleton Top Visitor Centre Middleton by Wirksworth Derbyshire DE4 4LS *(0.5m S from B5036 signposted from A6, in Cromford J28 M1 12m)*
Tel: 01629 823204 Fax: 01629 825336
Set above the village of Middleton, site of one of Britain''s very few limestone mines, a beam engine built in 1829 for the Cronford and High Peak Railway can be seen in its octagonal engine house. The visitor centre tells the story of this historic railway.
Visitor Centre: Easter-Sept daily 10.00-18.00.
Winter: Weekends only 10.00-16.00
Last Admission: 16.30
Static engine: A£0.40 C£0.15. Working engine: A£0.70 C£0.40

Midland Railway Centre
Butterley Station Ripley Derbyshire DE5 3QZ *(J28 M1 then A38 to Derby, signposted from the A38)*
Tel: 01773 571140 info line Fax: 01773 570721
This centre not only operates a regular steam-train passenger service, but also provides the focal point for an industrial museum project. Amongst new inclusions are the fascinating museum; country park; farm park; narrow gauge, miniature & model railway and much more to provide an interesting and informative day out for the whole family.
Trains operate all year call for timetable
Last Admission: 16.15
A£6.95 OAPs£5.50 C£1.00. Groups 15+ call for details

Severn Valley Railway
The Railway Station Bewdley Worcestershire DY12 1BG *(Kidderminster town station is adjacent to BR station this in on Comberton Hill on the A448)*
Tel: 01299 403816 Fax: 01299 400839
The leading standard gauge steam railway, with one of the largest collections of locomotives and rolling stock in the country. Services operate from Kidderminster and Bewdley to Bridgnorth through 16 miles of picturesque scenery along the River Severn. Special steam galas and Friends of Thomas Weekends take place during the year.
Weekends throughout year, daily late May-end Sept plus school holidays
Prices depend on journey undertaken, call for details

Railways, Miniature

Brookside Miniature Railway
Brookside Garden Centre Macclesfield Road Poynton Cheshire SK12 1BY *(on A523 follow AA signposts)*
Tel: 01625 872919 Fax: 01625 859119
Extensive 7.25 inch gauge railway running through one of the country's premier garden centres. Steam and diesel locomotives, authentic GWR station, river bridges and tunnel. Museum of railway memorabilia.
All year Sat & Sun, Apr-Sept Wed, Sat & Sun, daily July & Aug
Train: all £0.50 C(0-2)£Free
Discount Card Offer: Two For One - Two People Can Ride For The Price Of One

Railways Steam/Light

Gloucestershire Warwickshire Railway
The Railway Station Toddington Winchcombe Gloucestershire GL54 5DT *(J between B4632 / B4077 on Stow Road, 8m from J9 M5)*
Tel: 01242 621405 Fax: 01242 233845
Web Site: www.gwsr.plc.uk/
A five mile long preserved steam railway operating through the scenic Cotswolds from the beautifully restored stations at Toddington and Winchcombe. There is a large collection of locomotives and rolling stock to view at Toddington. Various events throughout the year, talking Timetable 01242 621405
Mar-mid Oct Sat Sun & Bank Hol Mon. Dec weekends. Easter week. Spring Hol weeks and School Summer Hol Tue-Thur

Last Admission: 16.00
A£6.00 C(0-5)£Free C(5-15)£3.60 OAPs£4.00.
Groups rates 20+

Great Central Railway

Great Central Road Loughborough Leicestershire
LE11 1RW *(signposted from A6 and A60. BR: Loughborough 0.75m)*

Tel: 01509 230726 Fax: 01509 239791

This private steam railway runs over eight miles from Loughborough Central to Leicester, with all trains calling at Quorn & Woodhouse, Rothley and Leicester North. The locomotive depot and museum are at Loughborough Central. A buffet car runs on most trains. Features 'Footplate Experience' your chance to drive a steam train - please phone for further details.

Trains run daily throughout the Summer
Return fares: A£6.50 C&OAPs£4.50 Family Tickets also available Group Rates and suggested itinerary on request

Midland Railways Centre

Butterley Station Ripley Derbyshire DE5 3QZ *(M1 J28 signposted from A38 and A610 on B6179)*

Tel: 01773 747674/749788 Fax: 01773 570721

A unique attraction featuring preserved railway, farm park and country park. Narrow gauge, miniature and model railways. Museum with over 50 locomotives. Historic church and much more.

All year daily 11.00-17.00
Last Admission: 16.15
A£7.95 OAPs£6.50 Admission Free for 2 children with every paying adult

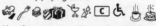

Northampton and Lamport Railway

Pitsford & Brampton Station Pitsford Road Chapel Brampton Northampton Northamptonshire NN6 8BA *(J15a /J15 M1, between A50 /A508)*

Tel: 01604 847318 Fax: 01604 670953
Web Site: www.nlr.org.uk

In 1981 a group was formed with the intention of reopening the branch from Northampton to Market Harborough which was designed by George Bidder and George R Stephenson and opened in 1859. In 1984 the Society started to rebuild the railway in the old goods yard at Pitsford and Brampton station. Phase 1 (now complete) consists of a station, two signal boxes, 3/4 mile of running lime and sidings. When completed to Lamport, the line will be approximately 6.5 miles long. The line was formally opened on 31st March 1996. Further work was started in early 1997. The current rolling stock consists of steam and diesel locomotives with further

stock in various stages of restoration. Other stock: carriages, guards vans and wagons are held, ready for use. The railway can offer private hire of trains for birthday parties, receptions or corporate entertainment. School parties, youth groups and society bookings are also welcome. For further information call our 24 hour line on 01604 820327 - manned on operating days.

2 Mar-26 May & 7 Sept-30 Nov Sun & Bank Hol 11.00-16.00, 15 June-31 Aug Sat & Sun & Bank Hol 10.30-17.00

Last Admission: 16.30

A£2.50 C(3-15)&OAPs£1.60 Family Ticket £7.00, special events rates may differ

Rutland Railway Museum

Cottesmore Iron Ore Mines Sidings, Ashwell Road Cottesmore Oakham Leicestershire LE15 7BX *(off B668)*

Tel: 01572 813203

Run by volunteers the museum has an extensive collection of industrial locomotives and rolling stock, many of which were used in local ironstone quarries operating around Cottesmore until the 1970s. Three-quarters of a mile of branch line in use for demonstrations. Annual Steam Gala August Bank Hol weekend. Also features a lakeside walkway leading to the remains of the Oakham Canal.

Sat-Sun for viewing 11.00-17.00. Specific steam operating days to be confirmed

A£2.50 C£1.50 OAPs£1.00 Family Ticket £6.50 including train rides

The Battlefield Line

Shackerstone Leicestershire *(3m NW of Market Bosworth, signposted from A444 and A447)*

Tel: 01827 880754

Join us for a steam hauled 9 mile round trip from Shackerstone to Shenton through the delightful scenery of south west Leicestershire. Impressive museum of railway memorabilia, locomotives and rolling stock at Shackerstone.

Sunday Service departures from Shackerstone Easter-Oct. Extra train on Bank Hol. Sat Diesel service May-Sept , also Wed and Fri in July and Aug. Museum: all year Sat & Sun 11.30-17.30

Return Fare: A£4.70 C&OAPs£2.30. Platform and Museum only: £0.50. Group discount 10%

🦯 suitable for pushchairs 👶 mother & baby facilities ♿ suitable for wheelchairs 🎁 gift shop
🤝 corporate facilities 🐕 no dogs: except guide dogs 🅿 parking on site 🅿 parking nearby
£ charged parking ☕ café-restaurant 🍷 licensed 🎂 special events 📖 educational pack

Reservoirs

Carsington Water Reservoir

Severn Trent Water Ashbourne Derbyshire DE6 1ST
*(off the B5035 between Ashbourne / Wirksworth,
follow Carsington Water signposts. 1hr from
Sheffield / Stoke, 75mins from Leicester and
90mins from Birmingham)*
Tel: 01629 540696

Seven Trent invite you to award-winning Carsington
Water, Britain's newest reservoir and an ideal place
for a day out in the beautiful Derbyshire countryside. There's something for everyone to enjoy,
whatever the weather! A fascinating exhibition
shows how we bring you a reliable and high quality
supply. The Kugel Stone, see how a thin film of
water supports this one-tonne granite ball!
Watersports: canoes, sailing and sailboards available for hire with tuition available. Cycling; adults
and children's mountain bikes for hire and sale. Fly
fishing; Bank and boat fishing for brown trout.
Children's playground; Wildlife centre and bird
hides, footpaths, cycle routes and events. The
Visitor Centre, Wildlife Centre and bird hides are
fully accessible for disabled visitors, while parts of
the playground are not suitable for children with
disabilities. There are surfaced footpaths around
the Visitor Centre, other tracks may be difficult for
wheelchairs users. Parking is free for cars displaying the orange badge.
*Visitor Centre: all year daily from 10.00 closing
times vary according to season. Watersports: from
10.00 or 09.30 on summer weekends. Playground
and car parks: all year daily 07.00-sunset. Trout
Fishing: mid Apr-mid Oct 07.00-1hr after sunset.
Restaurant: all year daily from 10.30. Closed
Christmas Day
Admission Free, daytime parking charged at the
main car park for cars and motorcycles, season
tickets available. All coach parties and large groups
must book in advance*

Edgbaston Reservoir

The Rangers Lodge 115 Reservoir Road Ladywood
Birmingham B16 9EE *(A456 Hagley road, B4126
Icknield Port rd)*
Tel: 0121 454 1908

Large expanse of water, lots of wildfowl.
Windsurfing lessons available. 1.5m path and a trim
trail around reservoir. Fishing, tickets available
from office.
*All year dawn till dusk. Rangers Office closed
Christmas day
Admission Free. Fishing: A£2.10, OAPs£1.05, pass-
ports to leisure*

Roman Remains

JEWRY WALL MUSEUM AND SITE

Jewry Wall Museum and Site

St. Nicholas Circle Leicester Leicestershire LE1 4LB
Tel: 0116 247 3021 Fax: 0116 247 3011

Behind the massive fragment of the Roman Jewry
wall and a Roman Baths site of the 2nd century AD
is the Museum of Leicestershire Archaeology, which
covers finds from the earliest times to the Middle
Ages.
*All year 10.00-17.30, Sun 14.00-17.30. Closed 24-26
Dec & Jan 1
Admission Free*

Wroxeter Roman City

Wroxeter Shrewsbury Shropshire SY5 6PH *(at
Wroxeter 5m E of Shrewsbury on B4380. Bus:
Williamsons X96 Birmingham / Shrewsbury. BR:
Shrewsbury 5.5m Wellington Telford West 6m)*
Tel: 01743 761330

The part-excavated centre of the fourth largest city
in Roman Britain, with impressive remains of the
second century municipal baths.
*22 Mar-31 Oct daily 10.00-1800 or dusk if sooner., 1
Nov-31 Mar Wed-Sun 10.00-16.00. Closed 13.00-
14.00. Closed 24-26 Dec
A£2.95 £2.20 OAPs£1.50*

Roman Sites

Chedworth Roman Villa

Yanworth Cheltenham Gloucestershire GL54 3LJ
*(3m NW of Fossebridge on Cirencester / Northleach
road A429 approach from A429 via Yanworth of
from Withington. BR: Cheltenham Spa)*
Tel: 01242 890256 Fax: 01242 890544

The remains of a Romano-British villa, excavated in
1864. Set in beautiful wooded combe. Includes fine
4th century mosaics, two bath houses, spring with
temple. A museum houses the smaller finds. There
is a 9min introductory film. Strong companions
needed for wheelchair users. Guide for pre-booked
groups only.
*3-27 Feb Tue-Fri 10.00-16.00 pre-booked groups
only. 28 Feb-24 Oct Tue-Sun & Bank Hol Mon 10.00-
17.00. 25 Oct-29 Nov Tue-Sun 10.00-16.00, 6-7 Dec*

10.00-16.00
A£3.20 C£1.70 Family Ticket £8.00. No reduction
for Groups. Guided tours and activity room available for pre-booked groups

Wall Roman Site (Letocetum)

Watling Street Wall Lichfield Staffordshire WS14
0AW *(off A5 at Wall Nr. Lichfield)*
Tel: 01543 480768
Originally the Roman fort of Letocetum situated at
the crossroads of Watling Street and Rykneild
Street. 19th century excavations revealed the most
complete bath house ever found in Britain. Three
baths: cold, tepid and hot as well as a furnace
room and an exercise hall. Museum of finds on site.
*1 Apr-31 Oct daily 10.00-18.00 or dusk. Closed
13.00-14.00*
A£1.75 C£0.90 Concessions£1.30

Roman Villas

Great Witcombe Roman Villa

Great Witcombe Gloucestershire *(5m SE of
Gloucester, off A417, 0.5m S of reservoir in
Wicombe Park. Bus: Stagecoach City of Gloucester
50. BR: Gloucester 6m. NO coach access)*
Tel: 0117 975 0700
The remains of a large villa. Built around three
sides of a courtyard. It had a luxurious bath-house
complex and several mosaic pavements have been
preserved and there is also evidence of underfloor
heating from a hypocaust.
*Any reasonable time for exterior. Guided tours:
please contact above number*
Admission Free

Safari Parks

West Midland Safari and Leisure Park

Spring Grove Bewdley Worcestershire DY12 1LF *(on
the A456 between Kidderminster and Bewdley)*
Tel: 01299 402114 Fax: 01299 404519
A drive-around wild animal safari park with over 40
species of exotic animals to see. Pets's corner,
Sealion show, Reptile House, Parrot Show, Goat
Walk and Deer Park. Other attractions include a
variety of rides in the leisure area.
Apr-Oct daily 10.00-17.00
Last Admission: 60mins before closing
*Safari Park: A£4.50 C(0-4)£Free C(5-16)£4.50. Ride
Tickets: 5-£3.50 10-£7.00 or 20-£12.50. Unlimited
ride wristband: £5.50*

Science Centres

Jodrell Bank Science Centre and Arboretum

Jodrell Bank Lower Withington Macclesfield
Cheshire SK11 9DL *(J18 M6 A535 Holmes Chapel-
Chelford road)*
Tel: 01477 571339 Fax: 01477 571695
Web Site:
**www.openworld.co.uk/britain/pages/J/JOD19D
La.htm1**
The Science Centre stands at the feet of one of the
largest radio telescopes in the world, the Lovell
telescope, a landmark in both Cheshire & in the
world of astronomy. There are exhibitions & half-
hour shows in the Planetarium. Children under 5
not permitted in Planetarium.
*Mar-Oct daily 10.30-17.30 Nov-Mar daily, weekends
and School Holidays 11.00-16.30*
Last Admission: Summer 16.30. Winter 15.30
A£4.00 C£2.00 OAPs£2.80 Family Ticket £11.50

Sea Life Centres

National Sea Life Centre

The Waters Edge Brindley Place Birmingham West
Midlands B1 2HL *(next to National Indoor Arena in
centre of Birmingham)*
Tel: 0121 643 6777 Fax: 0121 633 4787
The new National Sea Life Centre is Britain's first
inland Sea Life development. The Centre boasts the
world's first completely transparent underwater
tunnel allowing visitors to be surrounded on all
sides by sharks, rays and a host of other marine
marvels. Kingdom of the Seahorse - Seahorses
have amazed and enchanted human beings
throughout the centuries. Take a privileged peek
into their magical kingdom.
All year Mon-Sun daily 10.00-17.30
Last Admission: 17.00
A£6.50 C(0-4)£Free C(4+)£3.95 OAPs£5.50
Students£4.95

Showgrounds

Sandwell Showground

Salters Lane Sandwell West Midlands *(follow signs
for Sandwell Park Farm from West Bromwich ring-
way)*
Tel: 0121 569 3899 Fax: 0121 569 3899
Open on show days
Shows free car parking charged

 🏃 *suitable for pushchairs* 🍼 *mother & baby facilities* ♿ *suitable for wheelchairs* 🎁 *gift shop*
 🤝 *corporate facilities* 🐕 *no dogs: except guide dogs* 🚗 *parking on site* 🚗 *parking nearby*
 £ *charged parking* ☕ *café-restaurant* 🍴 *licensed* 🎂 *special events* 📖 *educational pack*

Shropshire and West Mid Show 1998

Agricultural Showground Berwick Road Shrewsbury Shropshire SY1 1ZZ *(on the B5067 AA signposted)*
Tel: 01743 362824 Fax: 01743 363779
Pedigree animals at our show set the seasons standards. Our champions go on to national and international honours. But it's not just a farmer's day out. It's something special for town and country to enjoy together. See how 21st century farming feeds the nation, interesting displays of National Cirriculum subjects to held childrens' studies, fashion, flowers, tasty bites and fun. 9 hours of entertainment.
Friday 15th & Saturday 16th May 1997, 08.30-19.00
Advance prices: A£5.50 C&OAPs£4.00 Family Ticket (A2+C3)£12.00. Gate Prices: All day A£7.00 C£4.00 Family Ticket (A2+C3)£15.00 OAPs£5.50. After 14.00: A£5.00 C£3.00 OAPs£4.00

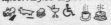

Ski Centres

Snowdome

Castle Grounds River Drive Tamworth Staffordshire B79 7ND
Tel: 01827 67905
Ski or snowboard on real snow in Europe's only - Snowdome. A truly alpine environment, ideal for beginners and experienced. Ski lessons. Free equipment. Tyrol and Aspen Bar and Restaurants. Ski shop.
All year daily 09.00-24.00, closed Christmas Day A£8.50-£14.50 C£5.50-£10.00, Family, corporate, student and group deals are always available

The Unusual

Daniel's Mill

Eardington Bridgnorth Shropshire WV16 5JL *(1m S of Bridgnorth on B4555 Highley road)*
Tel: 01746 762753
A picturesque working watermill with impressive 38ft waterwheel. Producing wholemeal flour with traditional mill stones. Exhibition of old country tools and domestic bygones. Experience the sights and sounds of yesteryear. Guided tours.
Apr-Sept Wed, Sat & Sun 14.00-18.00. Schools and Groups by prior arrangement all year
Last Admission: 17.30
A£2.00 C£1.00 OAPs£1.70. Group rates for 20+

Theatres

Buxton Opera House

Water Street Buxton Derbyshire SK17 6XN *(A6, in centre of Buxton behind Pavillion Gardens)*
Tel: 01298 72190 Fax: 01298 27563
Web Site: www.buxton-opera.co.uk
Various performances year through, please call for our literature.
Box Office: all year daily from 10.00. Guided tours on Sat, please phone for further details
Varies according to show

ROYAL SHAKESPEARE COMPANY

Royal Shakespeare Company

Waterside Stratford-Upon-Avon Warkwickshire CV37 6BB *(A3400 J15 M40. Theatre signposted within Stratford)*
Tel: 01789 296655 Fax: 01789 294810
At the Royal Shakespeare Theatre, the Swan Theatre and The Other Place, the Company performs plays by Shakespeare and other great playwrights including contemporary work. There are two restaurants. Tours of the RST are available enquiries by telephone 01789 412602. The RSC Swan Gallery is housed in the original Victorian building which opened in 1879. Comprising Theatre, Paintings and Sculpture Gallery, and Reading Room, the latter were not destroyed when the Theatre was burnt down in 1926.
Swan Gallery: All year Mon-Sat 09.15-end evening, Sun 12.00-16.30, Nov-Mar Sun 11.00-15.30. Closed 24 & 25 Dec. Dinner, theatre and overnight stay packages available all year round.Closed 24-25 Dec Exhibition: A£1.50 C&OAPs&Students £1.00.
Theatre Tours: A£4.00 C&OAPs&Students £3.00

Theme Parks

Alton Towers

Alton Stoke-On-Trent Staffordshire ST10 4DB *(from the S J23a M1 or J15 M6. From the N J28 M1 or J16 M6, clearly signposted)*
Tel: 0990 204060 24hr Fax: 01538 704097
Web Site: www.alton-towers.co.uk

Set in 500 acres of stunning countryside this magical experience offers attractions suitable for every member of the family. Rides include Nemesis, Toyland Tours, Haunted House and the Ripsaw Ride. The farm has been redeveloped and rides aimed at younger children introduced. New for 1998 is the £12 million white-knuckle ride 'Secret Weapon 4' which opens in March and promises to make Nemesis seem tame. Alternative telephone number 01538 703344.

Mar-Nov daily 09.00-17.30 yearly variations
A£19.00 C(4-14)£15.00 C(0-5)£Free Family Ticket £57.00

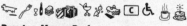

Drayton Manor Park
Nr Tamworth Staffordshire B78 3TW *(J9 or 10 M42 on A4091 near Tamworth. 10m N of Birmingham, signposted A5 /A38)*
Tel: 01827 287979 Fax: 01827 288916
250 acre theme park and zoo with over 50 rides and attractions to suit all ages. With extensive catering from fast food, bars, corporate banqueting and restaurants. Garden centre, shops, walks and a 15 acre zoo. Entertainment for all. Please ensure that you allow at least 6 hours to obtain maximum enjoyment from your visit.

End Mar-end Oct daily 10.30-19.00
A£3.00 C(4-15)£2.00 OAPs£2.00. Wheelchair visitor £2.00. Group rate £2.00. Wristbands: over 1.2m height £9.50, 800m to under 1.2m £6.50, wheelchair and helper £5.00 each. Ride Tickets 60p each (1,2 or 3 tickets for most rides). Special offer wristbands only £5.00 each Mon-Fri from beg Sept-mid Oct. Birthday Parties 10+: from £8.00 per child including admission, rides, food and special photograph. Organised coach groups of 20+ pay one price (admission and wristband): over 1.2m in height £8.50, 800mm to under 1.2mm £6.50, OAPs£6.50, wheelchair and helper £5.50 each. Schools groups of 20+ pay one price (admission and wristband): Mon-Fri term time only - low season (Apr, May, Jun, Sept, Oct) £5.50, high season (July) £6.50; teachers - 1 free per 10 pupils, group rates apply to extra adults, wheelchair and helper £5.50 each ; Admission only for coach groups (rides extra): A(16+)£2.50, C(4-15)£1.50, OAPs£1.50, Mother & Toddler Groups (2-4) £0.50

Gullivers Kingdom Theme Park
Temple Walk Matlock Derbyshire DE4 3PG
Tel: 01629 580540 Fax: 01629 57710
Plenty of attractions and rides to keep the whole family occupied, including cable car ride, Royal Cave Tour, Wild West Street, Ghost Hotel, and Alpine Log Flume.

22 Mar-6 Apr daily, 13 Apr-24 May Sat & Sun only, 25 May-7 Sept daily, call for times
A£5.25 C(under 90cm)£Free OAPs£4.45. Group rates 20+ £4.45.

Sundown Kiddies Adventureland
Sundown Pets Garden Treswell Road Rampton Nr Retford Nottinghamshire DN22 0HX *(3m off A57 at Dunham crossroads)*
Tel: 01777 248274 Fax: 01777 248967
'The children's story book theme park' Magical fairy tales come to life, nursery rhymes, castles wizards and dragons are just part of the attractions, with Smuggler's Cove and the Boozey Barrel Boat Ride. Indoors a jungle and musical pet shop, and a mini farm with live animals. Also a new story book village. Events throughout year to be advised. Special Christmas Weekends - Grand Opening 15 November.

All year daily from 10.00. Closed 25-26 Dec & weekdays during Jan, except for New Year Day.
Christmas opening times: Mon-Fri 10.00-16.00, Sat & Sun 10.00-19.00
All £4.00 C(0-2)£Free. Pre-booked School Parties and Playgroups 20+ £3.50 each

Tourist Information Centres

Ashbourne Tourist Information Centre
13 Market Place Ashbourne Derbyshire DE6 1EU
Tel: 01335 343666 Fax: 01335 300638

Ashby-de-la-Zouch Tourist Information Centre
North Street Ashby-De-La-Zouch Leicestershire LE65 1HU
Tel: 01530 411767

Bakewell Tourist Information Centre
Old Market Hall Bridge Street Bakewell Derbyshire DE45 1DS
Tel: 01629 813227 Fax: 01629 813227

Bewdley Tourist Information Centre
St George's Hall Load Street Bewdley Worcestershire DY12 2EQ
Tel: 01299 404740 Fax: 01299 404740

Birmingham Convention and Visitor Bureau
130 Colmore Row Victoria Square Birmingham West Midlands B3 3AP

🏃 *suitable for pushchairs* 👶 *mother & baby facilities* ♿ *suitable for wheelchairs* 🎁 *gift shop*
🤝 *corporate facilities* 🚫🐕 *no dogs: except guide dogs* 🚗 *parking on site* 🚙 *parking nearby*
£ *charged parking* ☕ *café-restaurant* 🍷 *licensed* 🎂 *special events* 📚 *educational pack*

Tel: 0121 693 6300 Fax: 0121 693 9600

Birmingham Tourist Information Centre

2 City Arcade Convention & Visitors Bureau Birmingham West Midlands B2 4TX *(city arcade)*
Tel: 0121 643 2514 Fax: 0121 616 1038
Tourist Information Centre supplies:
Accommodation Booking; National Express Agent; Theatre & Concert Ticket Agent; City Tours Booked During Summer Months.
All year Mon-Sat 09.30-17.30
Admission Free

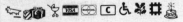

Borth Tourist Information Centre

High Street The Promenade Borth Dyfed SY24 5HY
Tel: 01970 871174

Bosworth Battlefield Tourist Information Centre

Ambion Lane Sutton Cheney Nuneaton Warwickshire CV13 0AD
Tel: 01455 292239

Brackley Tourist Information Centre

2 Bridge Street Brackley Northamptonshire NN13 5EP
Tel: 01280 700111 Fax: 01280 700157

Bridgnorth Tourist Information Centre

The Library Listley Street Bridgnorth Shropshire WV16 4AW
Tel: 01746 763358 Fax: 01746 766625

Broadway Tourist Information Centre

1 Cotswold Court Broadway Worcestershire WR12 7AA *(A44 Evesham to Moreton in Marsh)*
Tel: 01386 852937
Tourist Information Centre supplying: BABA Bookings; Local Bookings; Accommodation Lists; Eating Out Details; Walking Books and Maps.
Mon-Sat 10.00-13.00, 14.00-17.00
Admission Free

Bromsgrove Tourist Information Centre

26 Birmingham Road Bromsgrove Worcestershire B61 0DD
Tel: 01527 831809

Bromyard Tourist Information Centre

1 Rowberry Street Bromyard Herefordshire HR7 4DU
Tel: 01885 482038 Fax: 01885 488528

Burton upon Trent Tourist Information Centre

Unit 40 Octagon Centre New Street Burton-on-Trent Staffordshire DE14 3TN *(from S J11 M5, M42, A444, J22 M1, A511. From N J28 M1, A38, J15 M6, A50, A38)*
Tel: 01283 516609 Fax: 01283 517268
Tourist Information Centre supplying;
Accommodation and Book A Bed Ahead; Agents for Local Coach Companies - National Express; Purchase of Train Tickets; Places to Visit Locally and Throughout the Country; Box Office for Some Theatres and Events; Sells Maps; Guides, Local Books and Videos, Souvenirs, Postcards etc
All year Mon-Fri 10.00-17.30, Sat 10.00-16.00
Admission Free

Buxton Tourist Information Centre

Cavendish Arcade The Crescent Buxton Derbyshire SK17 6BQ
Tel: 01298 25106 Fax: 01298 73153

Cheltenham Tourist Information Centre

77 Promenade Cheltenham Gloucestershire GL50 1PP *(in the centre of Cheltenham which is on the A40)*
Tel: 01242 226554 Fax: 01242 255848
Tourist Information Centre supplying: Free Accommodation Boooking Service for Cheltenham & The Cotswolds; Book-A-Bed-Ahead; Travel Information; National Express Coach Tickets; Coach & Walking Tours; What's On; Information On Visitor Attractions; Wide Range Of Quality Gifts, Souvenirs, Maps & Guide Books; Independent Advice On Conference Venues; Tickets For Some Events.
July-Aug Mon-Fri 09.30-18.00, Sat 09.30-17.15, Sun 09.30-13.30. Sept-June Mon-Sat 09.30-17.15
Admission Free

Church Stretton Tourist Information Centre

Church Street Church Stretton Shropshire SY6 6DQ
Tel: 01694 723133 Fax: 01694 723045

Cirencester Tourist Information Centre

Corn Hall Market Place Cirencester Gloucestershire GL7 2NW
Tel: 01285 654180 Fax: 01285 641182
tourist Information Centre supplying:
Accommodation Booking Service; Theatre Bookings; National Trust; National Trust Membership.
All year Apr-Dec Mon-Sat 09.30-17.30. Jan-Mar

🐾 *National Trust* 🏴 *National Trust for Scotland* ✚ *English Heritage* ▌*Historic Scotland* 🌳*CADW*
🌳 *guided tours available* 🌲 *picnic areas* 🍴*refreshments* 📷 *photography allowed* 1998 *visitor discount card offer* 🏖 *beach/coastal area* VISA *Visa accepted* 💳 *Mastercard accepted* C *All cards accepted*

09.30-17.00
Admission Free

Coalville Tourist Information Centre

Snibston Discovery Park Ashby Road Coalville
Leicestershire LE67 3LN
Tel: 01530 813608 Fax: 01530 813301

Coleford Tourist Information Centre

High Street Royal Forest of Dean Coleford
Gloucestershire GL16 8HG
Tel: 01594 836307

Convention & Visitor Centre

National Exhibition Centre Birmingham West
Midlands B40 1NT
Tel: 0121 780 4321 Fax: 0121 780 4260

Corby Tourist Information Centre

Civic Centre George Street Corby Northamptonshire
NN17 1QB
Tel: 01536 407507 Fax: 01536 400200

Coventry Tourist Information Centre

Bayley Lane Coventry West Midlands CV1 5RN *(city centre, opposite cathedral)*
Tel: 01203 832303/4 Fax: 01203 832370
Tourist Information Centre supplying: Local
Accommodation Service and Book A Bed Ahead
Service; Gifts; Books; Maps; Tickets for Local
Events; UK Holiday Information Service.
All year daily Mon-Fri 09.30-16.30, Sat & Sun 10.00-16.30
Admission Free

Daventry Tourist Information Centre

Moot Hall Market Square Daventry
Northamptonshire NN11 4BH
Tel: 01327 300277

Derby Tourist Information Centre

Assembly Rooms Market Place Derby Derbyshire
DE1 3AH *(J25 M1, A52, follow signs for city centre.
A38 follow signs for city centre, A6)*
Tel: 01332 255802 Fax: 01332 256137
Staff at the centre will help you get the most from
your visit to Derby by offering advice on accommo-
dation and things to see and do during your stay.
Services include: Accommodation Bed Booking
Service; City Walking Tours; Theatre Tickets; Events
& National Express Coach Ticket Bookings.
*All year Mon-Fri 09.30-17.30, Sat 09.30-17.00, Sun
10.00-14.00. Summer closing 18.00*

Admission Free

Droitwich Spa Tourist Information Centre

St. Richard's House Victoria Square Droitwich
Worcestershire WR9 8DS
Tel: 01905 774312 Fax: 01905 794226

Dudley Tourist Information Centre

39 Churchill Shopping Centre Dudley West
Midlands DY2 7BL *(J2 M5, A4123, A461, left into
car park, walk over footbridge)*
Tel: 01384 812830 Fax: 01384 815580
Tourist Information Centre supplies: Holiday
Information Scheme; Tickets for Local Events; Sale
of Souvenirs, Postcards, Pictures and Local
Publications.
All year Mon-Sat 09.00-17.00, except Wed 09.00-13.00
Admission Free

Ellesmere Tourist Information Centre

The Meres's Visitor Centre The Mere Ellesmere
Shropshire SY12 0PA *(from A5 take A495, then
A528 towards Shrewsbury)*
Tel: 01691 622981
Tourist Information Centre supplying; Information
on Local Accommodation and Other Local Services;
Book A Bed Ahead Within the Area or the UK; Short
Break Information; Tourist Information for the
Whole of the UK; Information on Local and National
Events; Advice on Railway and National Express
Timetables; Booking Agency for Owen's Coaches;
CCTV Heron Watch in Spring; Wheely Boat for Hire
*All year daily Mar-31 Oct 10.30-17.00. July-Aug
10.30-18.00. Nov-Dec Sat&Sun only*
Admission Free

Evesham Tourist Information Centre

The Almonry Abbey Gate Evesham Worcestershire
WR11 4BG
Tel: 01386 446944

Glossop Tourist Information Centre

The Gatehouse Victoria Street Glossop Derbyshire
SK13 8HT
Tel: 01457 855920 Fax: 01457 855920

Gloucester Tourist Information Centre

28 Southgate Street Gloucester Gloucestershire
GL2 2DP *(city centre on main road opposite Bell
Walk entrance to shopping centre)*
Tel: 01452 421188 Fax: 01452 504273

🖈 *suitable for pushchairs* 🍼 *mother & baby facilities* ♿ *suitable for wheelchairs* 🎁 *gift shop*
🤝 *corporate facilities* 🐕 *no dogs: except guide dogs* 🅿 *parking on site* 🅿 *parking nearby*
£ *charged parking* 🍴 *café-restaurant* 🍷 *licensed* 🎂 *special events* 📚 *educational pack*

Tourist Information Centre supplies: Information on the historic city of Gloucester which includes the Cathedral, Victorian Docks, City and Folk Museums; Accommodation Bookings Service; Theatre Tickets; Tours at the TIC; Information about the surrounding areas of Gloucestershire, The Forest, Vale and Cotswolds.
All year Mon-Sat 10.00-17.00
Admission Free

Grantham Tourist Information Centre

Guildhall Arts Centre St Peter's Hill Grantham Lincolnshire NG31 6PZ *(off the A1, A607 or A52, into Grantham town centre)*
Tel: 01476 566444 Fax: 01476 591862
Tourist Information Centre supplies: Maps; Books; Accommodation Booking Service; Operated Holiday Information; Free Brochures and Leaflets about Town and Village Attractions around the UK.
All year Mon-Sat 09.30-17.00
Admission Free

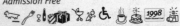

Hay-on-Wye Tourist Information Centre

Oxford Road Hay-on-Wye Herefordshire HR3 5DG *(turn off A438 Hereford / Brecon road for Hay. We are at top of main car park / corner of Craft Centre)*
Tel: 01497 820144 Fax: 01497 820015
Tourist Information Centre supplying: Accommodation Lists & Bookings; Tour Guides; Books, Maps, Postcards & Gifts.
Nov-Apr daily 11.00-13.00 & 14.00-16.00. Apr-Nov daily 10.00-13.00 & 14.00-17.00
Admission Free

Heart Of England Tourist Board

Woodside Lark Hill Road Worcester Worcs WR5 2EF
Tel: 01905 763436

Hereford Tourist Information Centre

1 King Street Hereford Herefordshire HR4 9BW
Tel: 01432 268430 Fax: 01432 342662

Hinckley Tourist Information Centre

Hinckley Library Lancaster Road Hinckley Leicestershire LE10 0AT
Tel: 01455 635106 Fax: 01455 251385

Kenilworth Tourist Information Centre

11 Smalley Place The Library Kenilworth Warwickshire CV8 1QG *(situated in Kenilworth town within the public library, opposite the De Montfort Hotel)*
Tel: 01926 852595 Fax: 01926 864503

Tourist Information Centre supplies: Free Accommodation Guide including Kenilworth, Warwick and Leamington.
All year Mon, Tue, Thur & Fri 09.30-19.00, Sat 09.30-16.00
Admission Free

Kettering Tourist Information Centre

The Coach House Sheep Street Kettering Northamptonshire NN16 0AN
Tel: 01536 410266

Kidderminster Tourist Information Centre

Severn Valley Railway Station Comberton Hill Kidderminster Worcestershire DY10 1QX
Tel: 01562 829400

Leamington Spa Tourist Information Centre

Jephson Lodge Jephson Gardens The Parade Leamington Spa Warwickshire CV32 4AB *(in the gatehouse entrance to Jephson Gardens)*
Tel: 01926 311470/884666 Fax: 01926 881639
Tourist Information Centre supplying: Accommodation Bookings; Maps; Souvenirs; Ticket Sales.
Easter-Nov Mon-Fri 09.30-17.00, Sat 10.00-16.00, Sun 10.00-13.00 & 14.00-16.00. Nov-Easter Mon-Fri 09.30-16.30

Ledbury Tourist Information Centre

3 The Homend Ledbury Herefordshire HR8 1BN
Tel: 01531 636147 Fax: 01531 634276

Leek Tourist Information Centre

1 Market Place Leek Staffordshire ST13 5HH *(J15/16 Mr, A53 from Stoke-On-Trent & Brandon. A523 from Macclesfield & Ashbourne)*
Tel: 01538 483741 Fax: 01538 483743
Tourist Information Centre supplying: Accommodation Booking; Theatre Tickets; National Express Tickets; YHA Membership; Rail Timetable Information; Attraction & Event Information; Walking & Cycling Guides, Maps, Stamps, Souvenirs & Local Crafts; UK Holiday Information Service.
All year Mon-Sat 10.00-17.00, Sat closing in Winter 16.00
Admission Free

Leicester Tourist Information Centre

St Margaret's Bus Station Leicester Leicestershire

LE1
Tel: 0116 251 1301 Fax: 0116 262 3199

Leicester Tourist Information Centre
7/9 Every Street Leicester Leicestershire LE1 6AG
Tel: 0116 265 0555 Fax: 0116 255 5726

Leominster Tourist Information Centre
1 Corn Square Leominster Herefordshire HR6 8LR
(on the crossroads between the A44 & A49)
Tel: 01568 616460 Fax: 01568 615546
Tourist Information Centre supplying: Local
Accommodation Booking; BABA Scheme;
*Mar-Oct Mon-Fri 09.30-17.30, Sat 09.00-17.00. Nov-
Feb Mon-Fri 09.30-16.00, Sat 09.00-16.00. Closed
Sun*
Admission Free

Lichfield Tourist Information Centre
Donegal House Bore Street Lichfield Staffordshire
WS13 6NE
Tel: 01543 252109 Fax: 01543 417308

Llanidloes Tourist Information Centre
Longbridge Street Llanidloes Powys SY18 6BN
Tel: 01686 412605

Loughborough Tourist Information Centre
John Storer House Wards End Loughborough
Leicestershire LE11 3HA
Tel: 01509 218113 Fax: 01509 218113

Ludlow Tourist Information Centre
Castle Street Ludlow Shropshire SY8 1AS
Tel: 01584 875053

Macclesfield Tourist Information Centre
Macclesfield Borough Council Council Offices Town
Hall Macclesfield Cheshire SK10 1DX *(town centre
location)*
Tel: 01625 504114 Fax: 01625 504116
Tourist Information Centre supplying: Hotel Guides;
Accommodation Booking; Walking Guides; Stamps;
Souvenirs; Local Theatre Tickets.
*All year Mon-Thur 08.45-17.00, Fri 08.45-16.30, Sat
09.00-16.00, Sun Apr-Sept 11.00-15.00*
Admission Free

Machynlleth Tourist Information Centre
Canolfan Owain Glyndwr Machynlleth Powys SY20
8EE

Tel: 01654 702401 Fax: 01654 703675

Malvern Tourist Information Centre
21 Church Street Malvern Worcestershire WR14 2AA
(J7 M5. A449 Malvern /Ledbury / Ross on Wye)
Tel: 01684 892289 Fax: 01684 892872
Tourist Information Centre supplying: BABA
Service, Local Accommodation Bookings.
*All year daily 10.00-17.00. Beg Dec-end Feb Sun
opening 10.15-16.15*
Admission Free

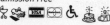

Market Drayton Tourist Information Centre
49 Cheshire Street Market Drayton Shropshire TF9
1PH
Tel: 01630 652139

Market Harborough Tourist Information Centre
Pen Lloyd Library Adam and Eve Street Market
Harborough Leicestershire LE16 7LT
Tel: 01858 468106 Fax: 01858 463168

Matlock Bath Tourist Information Centre
The Pavilion South Parade Matlock Bath Matlock
Derbyshire DE4 3NR
Tel: 01629 55082 Fax: 01629 56304

Melton Mowbray Tourist Information Centre
Melton Carnegie Museum Thorpe End Melton
Mowbray Leicestershire LE13 1RB
Tel: 01664 480992 Fax: 01664 480992

Merry Hill Tourist Information Centre
The Merry Hill Centre Brierley Hill West Midlands
DY5 1SY *(J2, 3 & 4 M5, on A4036)*
Tel: 01384 487911 Fax: 01384 487910
Tourist Information Centre supplies: BABA; Hiring
of: Wheelchairs (Manciel); Scooters (Electric); Baby
Buggies; Wrist Straps for Young Children; Baby
Bottle.
*All year daily Mon, Tue, Wed & Fri 10.00-20.00, Thur
10.00-21.00, Sat 10.00-19.00, Sun 11.00-17.00.
Closed Christmas Day, Boxing Day & Easter Sun*
Admission Free

Newark Tourist Information Centre
The Gilstrap Centre Castlegate Newark
Nottinghamshire NG24 1BG *(on A1 and A46, in cas-
tle grounds)*

🏃 *suitable for pushchairs* 🍼 *mother & baby facilities* ♿ *suitable for wheelchairs* 🎁 *gift shop*
🤝 *corporate facilities* 🐕 *no dogs: except guide dogs* 🚗 *parking on site* 🅿 *parking nearby*
£ *charged parking* ☕ *café-restaurant* 🍷 *licensed* 🎪 *special events* 📚 *educational pack*

Tel: 01636 678962 Fax: 01636 612274
Tourist Information Centre supplies: Local and
National Accommodation; Local and National
Information Bookings; Walk Books; Maps and
Guides; Local Theatre Tickets; Fax Service;
Photocopy Service; Gifts and Souvenirs; Induction
Loop Installed.
*All year daily Apr-Oct 09.00-18.00, Oct-Apr 09.00-
17.00*
Admission Free

Newcastle-under-Lyne Tourist Information Centre
Ironmarket Newcastle Staffordshire ST5 1AT
Tel: 01782 711964 Fax: 01782 717137

Newent Tourist Information Centre
The Library High Street Newent Gloucestershire
Tel: 01531 822145 Fax: 01531 822240

Newtown Tourist Information Centre
Central Car Park Newtown SY16 2PW
Tel: 01686 625580

Northampton Tourist Information Centre
Visitor Centre Mr Grant's House St Giles Square
Northampton Northamptonshire NN1 1DA *(oppo-
site town hall in town centre)*
Tel: 01604 22677 Fax: 01604 604180
Tourist Information Centre supplies: BABA; Free
and Saleable Literature for Residents and Tourists;
Local Box Office Facilities for Spinney Hill Hall, The
Stables at Wavendon, Roadmender, Guildhall
Guided Tours, Northampton Guided Walks, Castle
Theatre at Wellingborough, Yorks Travel Excursions,
Travel Tickets for London Theatres, Pop Concerts
and Sporting Events; Information on Events,
Leisure Activities, Where to Eat, Accommodation;
Bus and Train Information; Holiday Information;
Sales of Maps and Guides, Books, Videos, Stamps
and Souvenirs.
*All year Mon-Fri 09.30-17.00, Sat 09.30-16.00, Sun
in summer 12.00-16.00*
Admission Free

Northleach Tourist Information Centre
Cotswold Countryside Collection Cheltenham
Gloucestershire GL54 3JH
Tel: 01451 860715 Fax: 01451 860091

Nottingham (West Bridgford) Tourist Information Centre
County Hall Loughborough Road West Bridgford

Nottingham Nottinghamshire NG2 7QP *(on main
A60 Nottingham /Loughborough road on S side of
Trent Bridge)*
Tel: 0115 977 3558 Fax: 0115 977 3886
Tourist Information Centre supplies:
Accommodation Booking; Local Information;
National Information; Sales of Publications,
Nottingham Lace and other Gifts.
All year Mon-Thur 08.30-17.00, Fri 08.30-16.30
Admission Free

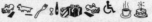

Nottingham Tourist Information Centre
1-4 Smithy Row Nottingham Nottinghamshire NG1
2BY
Tel: 0115 915 55330 Fax: 0115

Nuneaton Tourist Information Centre
Nuneaton Library Church Street Nuneaton
Warwickshire CV11 4DR
Tel: 01203 384027

Oakham Tourist Information Centre
Oakham Library Catmos Street Oakham
Leicestershire LE15 6HW
Tel: 01572 724329 Fax: 01572 724906

Ollerton Tourist Information Centre
Sherwood Heath Ollerton Roundabout Newark
Nottinghamshire NG22 9DR
Tel: 01623 824545 Fax: 01623 824545

Oswestry Mile End Tourist Information Centre
Oswestry Shropshire SY11 4JA *(Oswestry by-pass, J
of A5 & A483)*
Tel: 01691 662488 Fax: 01691 662883
Tourist Information Centre supplying:
Accommodation Booking; Books, Map, Local Crafts;
Ticket Sales.
All year Mon-Fri 09.00-17.00, Weekends 10.00-16.00
Admission Free

Oswestry Tourist Information Centre
2 Church Terrace The Heritage Centre Oswestry
Shropshire SY11 2TE
Tel: 01691 662753

Pershore Tourist Information Centre
19 High Street Pershore Worcestershire WR10 1AA
Tel: 01386 554262 Fax: 01386 561660

🦌 *National Trust* 🏴 *National Trust for Scotland* 🏛 *English Heritage* 🏰 *Historic Scotland* 🟢 *CADW*
🎵 *guided tours available* 🌳 *picnic areas* ☕ *refreshments* 📷 *photography allowed* 1998 *visitor discount
card offer* 🏖 *beach/coastal area* VISA *Visa accepted* 💳 *Mastercard accepted* © *All cards accepted*

Queenswood Tourist Information Centre
Queenswood Country Park Dinmore Hill Leominster Herefordshire HR6 0PY
Tel: 01568 797842

Redditch Tourist Information Centre
Civic Square Alcester Street Redditch Worcestershire B98 8AH
Tel: 01527 60806 Fax: 01527 65216

Retford Tourist Information Centre
40 Grove Street Retford Nottinghamshire DN22 6LD
Tel: 01777 860780

Ripley Tourist Information Centre
Town Hall Market Place Ripley Derbyshire DE5 3BT *(close to J28 M1, signposted from A38, A610 Ripley town centre)*
Tel: 01773 841488/6 Fax: 01773 841487
Tourist Information Centre supplying: Details on Attractions; Accommodation; Theatre Boookings, Travel Arrangements; Events in the Amber Valley; Maps and Local Souvenirs.
All year Mon-Fri 09.30-17.30, Sat 09.30-15.00
Admission Free

Ross on Wye Tourist Information Centre
Swan House Edde Cross Street Ross-On-Wye Herefordshire HR9 7BZ *(town centre of Ross-on-wye)*
Tel: 01989 562768 Fax: 01989 565057
Tourist Information Centre supplying: Accommodation Booking Services; Agents for National Express; Maps; Guides & Gifts for Sale
All year Mon-Sat 09.30-16.30
Admission Free

Rugby Tourist Information Centre
The Libary St. Matthews Street Rugby Warwickshire CV21 3BZ
Tel: 01788 535348 Fax: 01788 573289
All year Mon-Sat
Admission Free

Rutland Water Tourist Information Centre
Sykes Lane Empingham Nr Oakham Leicestershire LE15 8PX *(A1 N, A1 S, A606)*
Tel: 01572 653026 Fax: 01572 653027
Tourist Information Centre supplies: Accommodation Booking; Guided Visit Service.
Mar-15 Dec daily Mon-Fri 11.00-16.00, Sat & Sun 11.00-17.00. Open Feb Sat & Sun only. Closed 16 Dec-1 Feb.
Admission Free

Shrewsbury Tourist Information Centre
The Music Hall The Square Shrewsbury Shropshire SY1 1LH
Tel: 01743 350761 Fax: 01743 358780

Solihull Tourist Information Centre
Central Library Homer Road Solihull West Midlands B91 3RG
Tel: 0121 704 6130/4 Fax: 0121 704 6991

Stafford Tourist Information Centre
The Ancient High House Greengate Street Stafford Staffordshire ST16 2HS
Tel: 01785 240204 Fax: 01785 240204

Stockport Tourist Information Centre
Graylaw House Chestergate Stockport Cheshire SK1 1NG
Tel: 0161 474 3320/1

Stoke-on-Trent Tourist Information Centre
Potteries Shopping Centre Quadrant Road Stoke-On-Trent Staffordshire ST1 1RZ
Tel: 01782 284600 Fax: 01782 219276

Stow-on-the-Wold Tourist Information Centre
Hollis House The Square Stow on the Wold Cheltenham Gloucestershire GL54 1AF
Tel: 01451 831082 Fax: 01451 870083

Stratford-Upon-Avon Tourist Information Centre
Bridgefoot Stratford-Upon-Avon Warwickshire CV37 6GW *(J15 M40, A46, A439 into Stratford-Upon-Avon)*
Tel: 01789 293127 Fax: 01789 295262
Tourist Information Centre supplying: Accommodation Bookings; Book a Bed Ahead; Ticket Sales; Foreign Exchange; Gift Shop Selling Guide Books, Souvenirs; Phone Cards; Stamps; Films; Blue Badge Guide Service; Local and National Bus Information
Apr-Oct Mon-Sat 09.00-18.00, Sun 11.00-17.00. Oct-Mar Mon-Sat 09.00-17.00
Admission Free

Stroud Tourist Information Centre
Subscription Rooms George Street Stroud Gloucestershire GL5 1AE
Tel: 01453 765768 Fax: 01453 755658

🖈 suitable for pushchairs   👶 mother & baby facilities   ♿ suitable for wheelchairs   🎁 gift shop   🤝 corporate facilities   🐕 no dogs: except guide dogs   🚗 parking on site   🅿 parking nearby   £ charged parking   ☕ café-restaurant   ⚲ licensed   🎂 special events   educational pack

Tamworth Tourist Information Centre

Town Hall Market Street Tamworth Staffordshire
B79 7LY
Tel: 01827 59134 Fax: 01827 59134

Telford Tourist Information Centre

Telford Centre Management Suite Telford
Shropshire TF3 4BX
Tel: 01952 291370 Fax: 01952 291723

Tetbury Tourist Information Centre

33 Church Street Tetbury Gloucestershire GL8 8JG
*(from Market Hall take A433 to Bath, alongside
church in Church street)*
Tel: 01666 503552 Fax: 01666 503552
Tourist Information Centre Supplies: BABA Scheme;
Local Booking Scheme; Rail/Bus Timetables; Sale
of Maps, Books and Postcards.
*All year Mar-Oct Mon-Sat 09.30-16.30, Nov-Feb
Mon-Sat 11.00-14.00*

Tewkesbury Tourist Information Centre

64 Barton Street Tewkesbury Gloucestershire GL20
5PX
Tel: 01684 295027

Tregaron Tourist Information Centre

The Square Tregaron Dyfed SY25 6JN
Tel: 01974 298144 Fax: 01974 626566

Upton Upon Severn Tourist Information Centre

4 High Street Upton Upon Severn Worcestershire
WR8 0HB *(J1 M50, A38, A9104 to Upton)*
Tel: 01684 594200
Tourist Information Centre supplies: Local and
National Accommodation Bookings; Souvenirs;
Guides; Maps; Postcards; Events; Places to Visit;
National Express Coach Bookings; Local Coach
Company Bookings.
All year daily 10.00-17.00
Admission Free

Visitor Information Centre

130 Colmore Row Birmingham West Midlands B3
3AP
Tel: 0121 693 6300 Fax: 0121 693 9600

Warwick Tourist Information Centre

The Court House Jury Street Warwick Warwickshire
CV34 4EW
Tel: 01926 492212 Fax: 01926 494837

Wellingborough Tourist Information Centre

Wellingborough Library Pebble Lane
Wellingborough Northamptonshire NN8 1AS
Tel: 01933 228101

Welshpool Tourist Information Centre

Flash Centre Salop Road Welshpool Powys SY21
7DH
Tel: 01938 552043

Whitchurch Tourist Information Centre

The Civic Centre High Street Whitchurch Shropshire
SY13 1AX *(located in the centre of town, signed
from all approach roads into town)*
Tel: 01948 664577 Fax: 01948 665761
Tourist Information Centre supplying:
Accommodation Booking Service; AA Route
Planning; AA Membership; Theatre Ticket Sales;
Coach & Rail Information; Souvenirs; Postage
Stamps; Telephone Cards; Maps & Guides;
Postcards; Special Event Ticket Sales
*All year Summer: Mon, Tue, Thur, Fri 09.00-17.30,
Wed 09.00-17.00, Sat 10.00-17.00. Winter: Mon-
Thur 09.00-17.00, Fri 09.00-16.30*
Admission Free

Wolverhampton Tourist Information Centre

18 Queen Square Wolverhampton West Midlands
WV1 1TQ *(in the centre of Wolverhampton approxi-
mately 5m from J10 M6 & 4m from J2 M54)*
Tel: 01902 312051 Fax: 01902 556111
Tourist Inforamtion Centre supplying: Local accom-
modation information; Local/regional information;
National information; Local Theatre information;
Local Bus timetables; Souvenirs; postage stamps;
Special event information; UK holiday information;
Map and books; Council information.
All year Mon 10.00-17.00 Tue-Sat 09.00-17.00
Admission Free

Worcester Tourist Information Centre

The Guildhall High Street Worcester Worcestershire
WR1 2EY
Tel: 01905 726311

Worksop Tourist Information Centre

Worksop Library Memorial Avenue Worksop
Nottinghamshire S80 2BP
Tel: 01909 501148 Fax: 01909 501611

National Trust ☘ **National Trust for Scotland** ✠ **English Heritage** ▮ **Historic Scotland** ❀ **CADW**
🎵 **guided tours available** ☻ **picnic areas** ☕ **refreshments** 📷 **photography allowed** **1998** **visitor discount**
card offer **beach/coastal area** **VISA** **Visa accepted** **Mastercard accepted** **C All cards accepted**

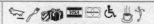

Town Shows

Northampton Town Show

Abington Park Northampton

Tel: 01604 238791 Fax: 01604 238796

Typical town show with the added attraction of live bands and fireworks in the evenings. A great day out for all the family.

17-19 July from 10.00, Fri & Sat: Evening concert with support act followed by a firework display 22.00. 19th 10.00-18.00

Car Park £3.00

Visitor Centres

Royal Doulton Visitor Centre

Nile Street Burslem Stoke-on-Trent Staffordshire ST6 2AJ

Tel: 01782 292434 Fax: 01782 292424

The home of the Royal Doulton figure; over 1,500 figures on display, live demonstrations, video theatre and museum. Factory tours available Mon-Fri. Factory shop on site.

All year Mon-Sat 09.30-17.00, Sun 10.00-16.00

Visitor Centre: A£2.50, Factory Tour: A£5.00

Spode Museum and Visitor Centre

Church Street Stoke-On-Trent Staffordshire ST4 1BX *(A50, A52, A53 all meet in Stoke on Trent)*

Tel: 01782 744011 Fax: 01782 744220

The Spode Museum and Visitor Centre is a truly unique experience to all those who appreciate the finest quality fine Bone China and Imperialware. The oldest pottery company operating on its original site. Spode is the original in every way. We are pleased to offer Factory Tours, Connoisseur Tours, Craft Demonstrations, 'Hands On' Experience and view the world renown Museum. Pick up a bargain in our Factory Shops and take time out for refreshments in our Blue Italian Restaurant. Full and half day packages plus special evening functions available.

Visitor Centre Museum & Site factory shop: all year Mon-Sat 09.00-17.00, Sun 10.00-16.00. Factory Tours by prior appointment weekdays only

Last Admission: 30mins before closing, shops as hours

Visitor Centre: A£2.50 Concessions£1.50. Group rates 20+ A£2.25 Concessions£1.25. Factory Tour: A£4.00 Concessions£2.50. Group rates 20+ A£3.25 Concessions£2.00. Connoisseur Tour: £6.50 Concessions£4.50. Group rates 20+ A£6.00 Concessions£4.50. Concessions apply to Students, C(0-14)&OAPs

Walks

Swannington Heritage Trail

Swannington Leicestershire

Tel: 01530 222330

Developing heritage trail through pleasant countryside featuring 1833 Leicester and Swannington Railway Incline, historic buildings including early Quaker settlement, horse-operated tramroads, ancient bell-pits and Swannington windmill. Trail booklet from village post office.

Access at all times

Admission Free but donations appreciated

Water Gardens

Sezincote House

Moreton-in-Marsh Sezincote Gloucestershire GL56 9AW *(1.5m on A44 Evesham road)*

Tel: 01386 700444

The Indian-style house at Sezincote was the inspiration for Brighton Pavilion. It's charming water garden adds to it's exotic aura and features trees of unusual size. Children not permitted in house.

Gardens: all year Thur, Fri & Bank Hol Mon 14.00-18.00 or dusk if earlier. Closed Dec. House: May, June, July & Sept Thur & Fri

House & Garden A£4.50. Garden only: A£3.00 C£1.00

Westbury Court Garden

Westbury-On-Severn Gloucestershire GL14 1PD *(9m SW of Gloucester on A48 BR: Gloucester)*

Tel: 01452 760461

A formal water garden with canals and yew hedges, laid out between 1696 and 1705. It is the earliest form of its kind remaining in England, restored in 1971 and planted with species dating from pre-1700, including apple, pear and plum trees. Guide dogs only. Braille guide.

Easter Sat-Oct Wed-Sun & Bank Hol Mon 11.00-18.00. Other months by appointment. Closed Good Fri

Last Admission: 17.30

A£2.50. Groups of 15+ by written arrangement

Water Parks

Bosworth Water Trust Leisure and Water Park

Far Caten Lane Wellsboroughq Nr Nuneaton

Warwickshire CV13 6PD *(B585 west of Market Bosworth)*
Tel: 01455 291876
50-acre leisure park with 20 acres of lakes for dinghy, boardsailing and fishing. Sailboards, canoes, dinghies, rowing boats, wetsuits for hire. Caravan and camping areas adjacent to the lake. Ideal venue for a family activity weekend, large enough to provide excellent sailing, compact enough for children to be watched. Site well grassed and gently sloping. Changing rooms, toilets, showers. Snack bar open during the main season. Courses on sailing, windsurfing and canoeing.
All year daily 10.00-dusk
£1.00 per car, please phone for hire charges

Rutland Water
Sykes Lane Empingham Oakham Leicestershire LE15 8PX *(A606 Oakham-Stamford)*
Tel: 01780 460321/276427 Fax: 01780
Largest man made lake in Western Europe, 3100 acres. Information Centre Sykes Lane. Water and land based recreational facilities. Pleasure Cruiser and Church Museum, Butterfly and Aquatic Centre.
Water park all year daily during daylight hours
Attractions Easter-Oct
Varies according to activity

Watermill

Brindley Water Mill And Museum
Daintry Street Leek Staffordshire ST13 5PG *(J Mill Street / Abbey Green Road, Leek)*
Tel: 01538 381446
Operational corn mill built by James Brindley.
All year Easter-end Oct weekends & Bank Hol 14.00-17.00 also from mid-July to end of August Mon Tue Wed 14.00-15.00
A£1.20 C&OAP£0.60

STAINSBY MILL

Stainsby Mill
Hardwick Estate Doe Lea Chesterfield Derbyshire S44 5QJ *(J29 M1, take A6175 signposted to Clay Cross then first left and left again to Stainsby Mill)*
Tel: 01246 850430 Fax: 01246 854200
There has been a water-powered flour mill at Stainsby since the 13th century. It passed to Bess of Hardwick with the purchase of the Manor of Stainsby in 1593. It is remarkably complete, with newly reconstructed 1849-50 machinery. Includes a kiln, drying floor, three pairs of millstones and an iron water wheel. In working order. Limited wheelchair access to ground floor only, braille guide. School parties Wed, Thur & Fri. Dogs on leads in park only, not in Mill.
Apr-Oct Wed-Thur Weekends & Bank Hol Mon 11.00-16.30, additionally Fri during June, July, Aug & Sept
Last Admission: 16.00
A£1.50 C£0.70 Family Ticket £3.70. Children under 15 must be accompanied by an adult. No reduction for pre-booked groups or OAPs

Wellesbourne Watermill
Kineton Road Wellesbourne Warwick Warwickshire CV35 9HG *(14m NW of Banbury)*
Tel: 01789 470237
An historic working watermill, rural craft demonstrations and tea rooms.
Easter-Sept Thur-Sun & Bank Hol Mon, Oct & Mar Sun 14.00-16.30

Wildlife Parks

Riber Castle Wildlife Park
Riber Matlock Derbyshire DE4 5JU *(off A615 via Alders Lane and Carr Lane)*
Tel: 01629 582073
Wildlife Park set in grounds of ruined 19th century Riber Castle. Magnificent views of the Derwent Valley and towards Crich Stand. The Park houses unique collection of animals, rare lynx, zebras, otters, plus Shetland ponies, goats, tortoises etc. Many breeding programmes in progress. Daily "Meet the Keeper" events.
All year daily from 10.00 closing times between 15.00 and 18.00
A£4.00 C£2.50 OAPs£3.50

Wildlife Reserves

Gloucestershire Wildlife Trust
Dulverton Building Robinswood Hill Country Park Reservoir Road Gloucester Gloucestershire GL4 6SX

(Various throughout Gloucestershire)
Tel: 01452 383333 Fax: 01452 383334
There are many NNR= National Nature Reserves and SSSI = Sites of Special Scientific Interests in Gloucestershire, those following are SSSI. (C1) Ashleworth Ham/Meerend Thicket SSSI Reserve in Hasfield Village featuring Over-wintering water-fowl. (C2) Badgeworth SSSI Reserve in cold Pool Lane featuring Adders-tongue Spearwort, May to September. (A) Betty Daw's Wood SSSI Reserve in Four Oaks, Oxenhall featuring Sessile Oak wood, wild daffodils March to April. (C) Breakheart Hill SSSI Reserve nr Woodchester featuring Limestone scree and mixed woodland. (C) Quarry Wood SSSI Reserve in St Briavels featuring Ancient Sessile Oak wood. (A) Stenders Quarry SSSI Reserve in Mitcheldean featuring Geological exposures and limestone flora. (B1) Stuart Fawkes SSSI Reserve in Box featuring Site of Meadow Clary and limestone grassland flowers. (A) Wetmoor SSSI Reserve in Wickwar Lower Woods featuring Ancient woodland; spring flowers and bird song. (A) Collin Park Wood SSSI Reserve featuring Ancient Small-leaved lime coppice. (A) Coombe Hill Canal SSSI Reserve featuring Aquatic and bankside plants. (D) Daneway Banks SSSI Reserve featuring Limestone grassland; flowers May-August. (A) Elliot (Swifts' Hill) SSSI Reserve in Slad featuring Typical limestone grassland. (A) Frith Wood - Moreley Penistan Memorial SSSI Reserve in Bulls Cross featuring Ancient Beech wood. (A) Hobbs Quarry SSSI Reserve featuring Geological exposures and woodland. (A) Lancaut SSSI Reserve in Chepstow featuring Cliffs, mixed woodland and salt marsh. (C) Lark Wood SSSI Reserve featuring Ancient coppice-with-standards, Oak woodland. (C) Old London Road SSSI Reserve featuring Limestone Woundwort. (C) Pasqueflower SSSI Reserve in Cirencester featuring Limestone grassland with Pasqueflowers in late April. (A) Popes' Wood SSSI Reserve in Prinknash Abbey featuring Ancient Beech Wood.

(A) Open to members at all times (B) Open at certain specified times (C) Access by permit only (D) Public footpaths and bridleways open: access to remainder of reserve by permit only (1) Birds can be viewed from observation hides near road (Meerend Thicket) (2) Secured by combination padlock; code number from the Trust on application (3) Key required

Wetlands Waterfowl Reserve and Exotic Bird Park
Sutton Retford Nottinghamshire DN22 8SB *(off Loundlow Road)*
Tel: 01777 818099
The collection of waterfowl includes ducks, geese

and swans, on two lagoons voering some 32 acres and many wild birds live here. There are also parrots, a variety of trees and plants and a children's farm.
All year daily 10.00-17.30 or dusk if sooner. Closed 25-26 Dec.
A£1.50 Concessions£1.00

WWT Slimbridge
Slimbridge Gloucester Gloucestershire GL2 7BT *(J13 & J14 M5 off A38 between Gloucester and Bristol signed from motorway)*
Tel: 01453 890333 ext. 223 Fax: 01453 890827
One of the finest collections of waterfowl in the world. Set in 800 acres of varied wetland habitat. Tropical House, hides, restaurant, shop, free parking. Enjoyable for all ages and abilities.
All year daily Summer: 09.30-17.00. Winter: 09.30-16.00
A£5.25 C£3.00 OAPs£4.25. Group rates available

Windmills

Greens Mill and Science Centre
Windmill Lane Sneinton Nottingham Nottinghamshire NG2 4QB *(1m E of city centre off A612, signposted from city centre)*
Tel: 0115 915 6878
A restored working windmill and interactive science centre with exhibits that explore all about light, magnetism and electricity.
All year Wed-Sun & Bank Hol Mon 10.00-17.00. Closed Dec 25-26
Last Admission: 16.45 Admission Free

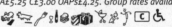
Woods

Burbage Common and Woods
c/o Hinckley and Bosworth Borough Council Argents Mead Hinckley Leicestershire LE10 1BZ *(B4668 E of Hinckley. BR: Hinckley 1.5m)*
Tel: 01455 633712
Burbage Woods - nationally important because of spectacular ground flora. Burbage Common - one of largest areas of natural grassland locally. Network of footpaths, wheelchair access, visitor centre, bird observation hide, picnic tables. Full colour brochure from Hinckley and Bosworth Borough Council, or from the visitor centre.

🏇 *suitable for pushchairs* 👶 *mother & baby facilities* ♿ *suitable for wheelchairs* 🎁 *gift shop*
🕴 *corporate facilities* 🦮 *no dogs: except guide dogs* 🚗 *parking on site* 🚗 *parking nearby*
£ *charged parking* ☕ *café-restaurant* 🍷 *licensed* 🎂 *special events* 📋 *educational pack*

Jubilee Wood

Woodhouse Lane Nanpantan Loughborough
Leicestershire LE *(off B5350)*
Tel: 01509 890048
Mixed woodland with rocky outcrops.
All year daily during daylight hours
Admission Free

🐾 £

Zoos

Dudley Zoo and Castle

The Broadway Dudley West Midlands DY1 4QB
Tel: 01384 215300 Fax: 01384 456048
The wooded grounds of Dudley Castle make a wonderful setting for the long-established, traditional
zoo, which has animals from every continent. The
castle ruins are impressive, and a chairlift and land
train take you to the top of Castle Hill.
*All year Easter-mid Sept daily 10.00-16.30. Mid
Sept-Easter daily 10.00-15.30. Closed 25 Dec
A£4.95 C&OAPs£2.95 Family Ticket £15.50. Group
rates 15+*

🛶 ⛵ 🎁 £ C ♿

Twycross Zoo Park

Atherstone Warwickshire CV9 3PX *(A444 near
Market Bosworth on the Burton to Nuneaton Road)*
Tel: 01827 880250 Fax: 01827 880700
Specialises in primates, and also includes gibbons,
gorillas, orang-utangs and chimpanzees. There is a
huge range of monkeys from the tiny tamarins and
spider monkeys to the large howler monkeys. Also
various other animals such as lions, tigers, ele-
phants and giraffes, with a pets' corner for younger
children.
*All year daily 10.00-18.00. Winter closing 16.00.
Closed 25 Dec
A£5.50 C(3-14)£3.50 OAPs£4.00. Group rates 25+
A£4.00 C(3-14)£3.00 C(1-3)£0.50. Special rates for
school, college, university parties and physically
handicapped/special needs*

🐾 🛶 🎁 ♿ ☕

🦌 *National Trust* 🏛 *National Trust for Scotland* ✠ *English Heritage* 🏴 *Historic Scotland* 🌳*CADW*
🎋 *guided tours available* 🍴 *picnic areas* ☕ *refreshments* 📷 *photography allowed* 1998 *visitor discount
card offer* 🏖 *beach/coastal area* VISA *Visa accepted* 🔲 *Mastercard accepted* C *All cards accepted*

Venom!

14/9/97	DUDLEY MUSEUM AND ART GALLERY
22/4/98	Tel: 01384 815571

Explore the perilous Indiana Jones world of Spiders, Snakes, Scorpions and other venomous creatures

Museums

The Rover Gas Turbine

1/1/98	HERITAGE MOTOR CENTRE
31/3/98	Tel: 01926 641188

An exhibition of this unique engine.

Museum- Motor

The Country Bus Special Exhibition

12/1/98	HARBOROUGH MUSEUM
17/4/98	Tel: 01858 821085

A Century of Rural Transport in Leicestershire and Rutland

Museum- Local History

Wildlife Photographer of the Year - Travelling Exhibition

7/2/98	CENTRAL MUSEUM AND ART GALLERY
15/3/98	Tel: 01604 39415

The British Gas Wildlife Photographer of the year competition is recognised as the largest most prestigious international competition of its kind showing the best of contemporary wildlife photography

Art Galleries

'Life and Soul' - An Exhibition of Excellence in British Men's Footwear Design

14/2/98	CENTRAL MUSEUM AND ART GALLERY
15/3/98	Tel: 01604 39415

An exhibition organised in collaboration with Jeffrey-West to show great British men's shoe design in the past and to demonstrate the excellence of contemporary design. The exhibition contains items from the museum's own collection as well as material from important current British manufacturers and designers such as Jeffrey-West, Church and Paul Smith. The opening of the exhibition coincides with a special shoe theme Valentines Day Ball at the Guildhall organised by Guy West

Art Galleries

The Dodeka Group

14/2/98	MANSFIELD MUSEUM AND ART GALLERY
28/3/98	Tel: 01623 663088

An Exhibition by the members of the Dodeka group of artists including textiles and ceramics

Museum- Local History

10th Anniversary Touring Exhibition: "Here & Now"

21/2/98	QUARRY BANK MILL AND STYAL COUNTRY PARK
22/3/98	Tel: 01625 527468

By the Cheshire Textile Group. Open daily from 11.00-15.30 (closed Mon), free entry, donations appreciated

Heritage Centres

Ancient Greeks

1/3/98	GRANTHAM MUSEUM
18/4/98	Tel: 01476 568783

A superb exhibition showing how mighty the ancient Greek civilisation was

Museum- Local History

Body Politics

1/3/98	DERBY MUSEUM AND ART GALLERY
26/4/98	Tel: 01332 716659

An exciting exhibition looking at the ways in which artists use the human body as a potent vehicle for expression in painting, sculpture and photography

Museum- Regimental

Bottle It Up

5/3/98	FORGE MILL NEEDLE MUSEUM AND BORDESLEY ABBEY VISITOR CENTRE
5/3/98	Tel: 01527 62509

Coffee morning in the New Town-New Start exhibition sitting room. Make your own herbal oils for the kitchen and the bath in the afternoon

Museum- Mill

Home Interior Design Exhibition

6/3/98	HANBURY HALL
8/3/98	Tel: 01527 821214

Over a hundred exhibitors selling their wares for the home. 10.00-18.00.

Historic Houses & Gardens

The Restoration of the Derby Canal: A Project in Progress

7/3/98	CANAL MUSEUM
7/3/98	Tel: 0115 915 6870

The restoration of the Derby Canal is one of the largest canal projects in the region. In this illustrated talk you can find out how the project got started, and how modern methods of reconstruction are being used to bring boats back to Derby, 14.30, £1.00. No need to book. Suitable for adults

Museum- Industrial

Workshop: Charcoal Drawing

7/3/98	DEAN HERITAGE CENTRE
7/3/98	Tel: 01594 822170

Advance booking necessary. Open to adults and children. Please telephone for further information

Heritage Centres

Down on the Farm
7/3/98 SHELDON COUNTRY PARK
7/3/98 Tel: 0121 742 0226
A guided tour of Old Rectory Farm, 14.00-15.00
Country Parks

BRDC Marshalls's Club Raceday
7/3/98 SILVERSTONE CIRCUIT
7/3/98 Tel: 01327 857271
Please call for further information.
Motor Racing Circuit

Tree Planting
7/3/98 SNIBSTON DISCOVERY PARK
7/3/98 Tel: 01530 510851/813256
Join the Rangers to identify species of trees growing on site and plant a tree yourself. Meet in the museum foyer at 13.00 wearing suitable clothing and footwear. Suitable for all ages
Industrial Heritage

Angels & Pigheads Workshops
7/3/98 NOTTINGHAM CASTLE MUSEUM AND ART GALLERY
21/3/98 Tel: 0115 915 3700
Saturdays 7,14 & 21 March only. Come along and meet the artists exhibiting in 'Angels & Pigheads' and make amazing artworks from old junk and scrap material, 14.00-16.00. No need to book. Admission Free. Suitable for all
Castles

Angels and Pigheads
7/3/98 NOTTINGHAM CASTLE MUSEUM AND ART GALLERY
22/3/98 Tel: 0115 915 3700
Now in its second year, 'A Big Hand For...' is a unique post-graduate training scheme aimed at helping artists develop their financial, business, artistic and organisational skills. Twelve artists from the scheme will be exhibiting new work including textiles, jewellery, metalwork, sculpture, paintings and mixed media
Castles

Pre-Raphaelite Women
7/3/98 BIRMINGHAM MUSEUM AND ART GALLERY
24/5/98 Tel: 0121 235 2834
While the work of the Pre-Raphaelite Brotherhood is well known and extremely popular, the contribution of women artists to the group has hitherto been neglected. This exhibition of around 75 works highlights the strength and diversity of each artist's work. Many of the paintings are being shown for the first time this century, having come from the private collections of the artists' descendants, and many retain their original frames which enhances their interest. Admission Free
Museums

Survivors
8/3/98 HARTSHILL HAYES COUNTRY PARK
8/3/98 Tel: 01203 395141
Winter takes its toll on the small bird population. Take a walk with a Countryside Ranger to find the survivors who have made it through the winter and will make up the breeding stock for the coming year. Meet at the Visitor Centre, 10.30-12.30
Country Parks

Spring Birdwatching
8/3/98 KINGSBURY WATER PARK
8/3/98 Tel: 01827 872660
Join a Ranger on a walk to spot birds, we may even have some early migrants returning. Binoculars useful. Meet at the Visitor Centre, 10.30-12.30
Country Parks

Motorcycle Racing
8/3/98 MALLORY PARK
8/3/98 Tel: 01455 842931
D/Phoenix Club. Please call for further information
Motor Racing Circuit

Wood and Fort
8/3/98 RYTON POOLS COUNTRY PARK
8/3/98 Tel: 01203 305592
A 7 mile walk to the fort at Wappenbury taking in ancient woodland. Meet at the Visitor Centre, Ryton Pool Country Park, 14.00-17.30
Country Parks

Dancing the Old Fashioned Way
12/3/98 NOTTINGHAM CASTLE MUSEUM AND ART GALLERY
12/3/98 Tel: 0115 915 3700
Fancy a dance down memory lane? Come along and let Vicky Roberts remind you of those popular easy sequence dances. Feel free to participate or watch, request your favourite tunes and finish off with a cup of tea and a piece of cake all for £1.50, 10.00-12.00. For bookings please telephone 0115 915 3692/3696
Castles

Sewing for Pleasure
12/3/98 NATIONAL EXHIBITION CENTRE
15/3/98 Tel: 0121 780 4141 x2604
Hall 12. Learn, buy and be inspired by over 200 stands covering a wide variety of fabrics, embroidery, quilting and other textile crafts. 09.30-17.30, 17.00 on Sun. A£8.00 C(0-16)£1.00 or Free if accompanied by an Adult OAPs£7.00
Exhibition Centres

Hobbycrafts

12/3/98
15/3/98

NATIONAL EXHIBITION CENTRE

Tel: 0121 780 4141 x2604

Hall 11. Whatever your craft come and see over 100 exhibitors demonstrating, teaching and selling supplies for over 30 different hobbies. 09.30-17.30 17.00 on Sun. A£6.50 C(0-16)£1.00 or Free if accompanied by an Adult OAPs£5.50

Exhibition Centres

Steambent Furniture Exhibition

13/3/98

THE FERRERS CENTRE FOR ARTS AND CRAFTS

10/5/98

Tel: 01332 865408

An exhibition showing contemporary steambent furniture both small and large

Craft Galleries

Bolinder Bash

14/3/98
14/3/98

CANAL MUSEUM

Tel: 0115 915 6870

The Bolinder is the most famous of the canal boat engines. Introduced in the 1920's, it became the first really successful canal boat engine. Today it's distinctive sound is all too rare but here is a chance to find out something of its history, explore its mechanisms and then get your hands-on literally as you start it up, get it running and finally take our narrowboat Ferret for a trip on the canal, 10.30-16.30, £30.00 (includes lunch). Please book in advance on 0115 915 6870. Suitable for adults

Museum- Industrial

Pleasure Learning

14/3/98
14/3/98

GLOUCESTER LEISURE CRUISE

Tel: 01452 318054

Basic Tug Driving Course

Boat Trips

Sir Issac Newton Returns

14/3/98

JODRELL BANK SCIENCE CENTRE AND ARBORETUM

14/3/98

Tel: 01477 571339

Lecture in the Planetarium regarding gravity & motion in today's world.

Science Centres

Guided Walk - High Peak Estate

14/3/98
14/3/98

PEAK DISTRICT NATIONAL PARK

Tel: 01629 816200

Snake path and Fairbrook. 10miles. Meet 10.00 at Birchin Clough lay-by (grid ref 109915) A£2.00 C£free. Packed lunch required. No dogs please, call 01433 670368

National Parks

SUNBACC Raceday

14/3/98
14/3/98

SILVERSTONE CIRCUIT

Tel: 01327 857271

Please call for further information.

Motor Racing Circuit

The Robin Hood Good Coin Quest

14/3/98

NOTTINGHAM CASTLE MUSEUM AND ART GALLERY

15/3/98

Tel: 0115 915 3700

Detective fun for all. Your mission, should you choose to accept it, is to find the number of coins in the Sheriff's purse stolen by Robin Hood. Solve the clues left by Robin and you could be the winner of the purse itself, 10.00-17.00, £0.20. Suitable for all

Castles

Science Alive!

15/3/98

GREEN'S MILL WINDMILL & SCIENCE MUSEUM

15/3/98

Tel: 0115 915 6878

Green's Mill comes to life for National Science Week with fun activities for the whole family. Meet George Green - the nineteenth century mathematical miller, choose which scientists will live or die in the Great Balloon debate and take part in fun and games with parachutes, giant dice and lots, lots more, 13.00-16.00, admission free. No need to book. Suitable for all

Museum- Mill

Spring Into Cycling

15/3/98
15/3/98

KINGSBURY WATER PARK

Tel: 01827 872660

A bike ride starting from Kingsbury Water Park with a stop for cakes at a local cafe (approximately 15 miles with 2 major junctions to negotiate, not suitable for young children). Meet at the Visitor Centre, 10.00-13.00

Country Parks

Nature Detective Ramble

15/3/98
15/3/98

LICKEY HILLS COUNTRY PARK

Tel: 0121 447 7106

The woods are just coming to life after the winter. Come along and look for clues and signs of life. 14.00-16.00

Country Parks

Motorcycle Racing

15/3/98
15/3/98

MALLORY PARK

Tel: 01455 842931

New Era Club. Please call for further information

Motor Racing Circuit

Snakes Alive!

15/3/98
15/3/98

WWT SLIMBRIDGE

Tel: 01453 890333 ext. 223

Get close to snakes, tarantulas, lizards and other marvellous creatures and hear about their fascinating lives. 11.00-17.00 in the Discovery Room

Wildlife Reserves

Lambing Days
16/3/98
12/4/98
CALKE ABBEY
Tel: 01332 863822
Sheep and lambs available to view during daylight hours. Vehicle charge applies
Historic Houses & Gardens

The March Ramble
17/3/98
17/3/98
SHELDON COUNTRY PARK
Tel: 0121 742 0226
A monthly ramble to discover the seasonal changes. March, the month of Frog Spawn, Bumble Bee Queens, and Violets, 14.00-16.00
Country Parks

Travels in India - with Keith Mortimer
20/3/98
20/3/98
WWT SLIMBRIDGE
Tel: 01453 890333 ext. 223
Stunning pictures and personal insights from our much travelled In Focus shop Manager. Time 19.30 in the lecture theatre, £4.70 (£3.20 WWT Members)
Wildlife Reserves

Peterborough Motor Club Raceday
21/3/98
21/3/98
SILVERSTONE CIRCUIT
Tel: 01327 857271
Please call for further information.
Motor Racing Circuit

Midlands Grand National
21/3/98
21/3/98
UTTOXETER RACECOURSE
Tel: 01889 562561
Please call for further information.
Racecourses

Naturally Scientific
21/3/98
21/3/98
WOLLATON HALL NATURAL HISTORY MUSEUM
Tel: 0115 915 3900
Celebrate National Science Week by exploring Wallaton's world of wildlife in a fun packed day of activities. Try your hand at pond dipping, be creative in our science experiments and investigate the tiny world of nature using microscopes, 10.30-16.00. Museum entrance fee applies. Suitable for all. Science week logos
Museum- Natural History

Mothers' Day Special
22/3/98
22/3/98
BLACK COUNTRY LIVING MUSEUM
Tel: 0121 557 9643
Please telephone for further information
Industrial Heritage

Mothering Sunday Lunches
22/3/98
22/3/98
CALKE ABBEY
Tel: 01332 863822
Bring your Mother along for a special lunch, pre-booking only, call to book
Historic Houses & Gardens

British F3 Championship
22/3/98
DONINGTON COLLECTION OF GRAND PRIX RACING CARS
22/3/98
Tel: 01332 811027
BRDC championship racing with a host of support races.
Museum- Motor

Lambstails and Pussy Willows
22/3/98
22/3/98
KINGSBURY WATER PARK
Tel: 01827 872660
A walk with Senior Countryside Ranger, Fred Hopkins, to discover a whole new world. Meet at the Visitor Centre. 10.00-12.00
Country Parks

750 Car Club Meeting
22/3/98
22/3/98
MALLORY PARK
Tel: 01455 842931
Please call for further information
Motor Racing Circuit

Mothering Sunday Stroll
22/3/98
22/3/98
RYTON POOLS COUNTRY PARK
Tel: 01203 305592
A short 2-mile walk in beautiful Ryton Wood on this special day. Meet at the Visitor Centre. 14.30-16.30
Country Parks

Mothers Day
22/3/98
22/3/98
THE BASS MUSEUM
Tel: 01283 511000
Treat Mum on this special day to a lovely Sunday lunch in this unique setting with a four course meal, entertainment and a gift for all mums
Breweries

Town to Country
22/3/98
22/3/98
THE GREENWAY
Tel: 01827 872660
A lovely 5-mile walk down the Avon Valley and back along The Greenway with Assistant Ranger, Bob McFall. Meet at the Gower Memorial (opposite the Stratford Tourist Information Centre), Bancroft Gardens, Stratford. 14.00-16.30
Country Parks

Plants and Medicines
23/3/98
WOLLATON HALL NATURAL HISTORY MUSEUM
24/3/98
Tel: 0115 915 3900
The earliest doctors need to be expert botanists. Come and see how we still depend on plants for many of our modern medicines as well as many traditional ones, 13.00-14.00, admission free, suitable for all. Please book in advance to avoid disappointment on 0115 915 3900
Museum- Natural History

The full information on the venues listed can be found in the main classified section under the classification shown under the entry. Please mention Best Guides when calling or visiting.

Friends of the Museum Evening Meeting

24/3/98 GLOUCESTER LEISURE CRUISE

24/3/98 Tel: 01452 318054

Please call for further information.

Boat Trips

Under 5s' Access Day

24/3/98 SNIBSTON DISCOVERY PARK

24/3/98 Tel: 01530 510851/813256

Clowns, storytelling, games, toys and fun activities for children under five. Free to under fives and their carers, 10.00-12.00

Industrial Heritage

Dear Diary

25/3/98 BREWHOUSE YARD MUSEUM

25/3/98 Tel: 0115 948 3600

Derrica Hodgson gives a peep into the life of Abigail Gawthorne, Georgian diarist of Nottingham

Museum- Local History

Surjit Simplay

25/3/98 NOTTINGHAM CASTLE MUSEUM AND ART GALLERY

31/5/98 Tel: 0115 915 3700

Simplay's digital images humorously reject the stereotypical portrayal of Indian Women in Western culture and replaces it with strong and powerful images celebrating women's sexuality. A small part of this exhibition will not be on show between 21 and 31 May

Castles

Birdwatch

28/3/98 SNIBSTON DISCOVERY PARK

28/3/98 Tel: 01530 510851/813256

Take a walk around the site and the Grange Nature Reserve with the Rangers and discover native British birds and other feathered visitors from afar. Meet in the museum foyer at 08.00 wearing suitable footwear and clothing. Suitable for all ages

Industrial Heritage

Pop Prints

28/3/98 ALFRED EAST ART GALLERY AND MANOR HOUSE MUSEUM

25/4/98 Tel: 01536 534381/534219

Famous prints from the pop-art period, on a national tour.

Art Galleries

Lambing

28/3/98 COTSWOLD FARM PARK

4/5/98 Tel: 0121 850307

Newborn lambs, maybe even watch one being born

Farm Parks

Birmingham Arts Lab

28/3/98 BIRMINGHAM MUSEUM AND ART GALLERY

31/5/98 Tel: 0121 235 2834

This exhibition celebrates the achievements of the Birmingham Art Lab which began in the late 1960s from one room in Tower street, and became one of the leading alternative centres for the Arts in the country during the 1970's. Its radical programme of cinema, performance, film, dance, poetry, music, graphic and comic book production is reflected in a series of posters, presented to Birmingham Museums and Art Gallery by Ernie Hudson, and an equally rare collection of associated archive, photographic and ephemeral material. Admission Free

Museums

Independent Thoughts: New Work by Permindar Kaur

28/3/98 NOTTINGHAM CASTLE MUSEUM AND ART GALLERY

31/5/98 Tel: 0115 915 3700

Born in Nottingham, Permindar Kaur has been commissioned to produce a new work for the Nottingham Castle Museum collection to mark the 50th anniversary of Indian and Pakistani Independence. Although inspired by the Sikh struggle for independence from India, Permindar's army of toy-like figures do not refer to any particular political event but suggest rather a continual struggle for an unnamed cause

Castles

Telling Tales: of Self, of Nation, of Art

28/3/98 NOTTINGHAM CASTLE MUSEUM AND ART GALLERY

31/5/98 Tel: 0115 915 3700

'Telling Tales' brings together the work of five contemporary Indian women artists each of whom explores in her work issues of self-identity and nationhood. The wide ranging media used by the artists reflects the richness and depth of Indian art and crafts and a keen awareness of international developments in contemporary art. 'Telling Tales' has been selected and curated by Indian art historian Rasna Bhushan in collaboration with the Bath Festivals Trust

Castles

Bugs, Beast and Butterflies: Nature at the Museum

28/3/98	CENTRAL MUSEUM AND ART GALLERY
14/6/98	Tel: 01604 39415

An exhibition designed by Northampton Museum's staff, displaying all aspects of the museum's natural history collections including fossils (our type specimens are of international importance), shells, the herbarium (which connects to Charles Darwin) and stuffed animals. The exhibition will include things for children to do, such as an animal maze and a foot print trail around the galleries

Art Galleries

Landscapes and Lives

28/3/98	THE HARLEY GALLERY
14/6/98	Tel: 01909 501700

Paintings, photographs & prints.

Art Galleries

Clubmans Motorcycle Meeting

29/3/98	DONINGTON COLLECTION OF GRAND PRIX RACING CARS
29/3/98	Tel: 01332 811027

All classes of national solo motorcycles and sidecars.

Museum- Motor

East Midlands Doll Fair

29/3/98	LEICESTER TOURIST INFORMATION CENTRE
29/3/98	Tel: 0116 251 1301

Venue: Aylestone Leisure Centre, Leicester. A wonderful Doll Fair with dolls houses and teddies - 'a miniature wonderland.' Top quality collectors, artists and craftspeople bring old and soft dolls, dollshouse dolls, miniatures, teddy bears, dollcraft materials, kits, magazines and juvenilia, 10.30-16.30, A£2.30 Student&OAPs£1.20 AccompaniedC£Free

Tourist Information Centres

BRSCC Club Meeting

29/3/98	MALLORY PARK
29/3/98	Tel: 01455 842931

Please call for further information

Motor Racing Circuit

Gloucester Boat and Watersports Jumble

29/3/98	NATIONAL WATERWAYS MUSEUM
29/3/98	Tel: 01452 318054

1000's of new and used bargains!! 200 stalls. Boats, dinghies, canoes, sailboards, engines, outboards, chandlery, fishing tackle, tools, electrics, clothing, diving equipment, trailers, accessories, rope, paint and miscellany. Everything the professional or beginner needs for offshore, river, canal or lake at prices and discounts that defy competition. Admission A£2.50 (including free admission to the museum), accompanied C£Free. Stalls: covered £26.00 uncovered £22.00

Museum- Waterways

Sounds Natural!

29/3/98	WOODGATE VALLEY COUNTRY PARK
29/3/98	Tel: 0121 421 7575

A fun afternoon for families to make music from natural materials found in Woodgate Valley. Please book in advance, starts 14.00

Country Parks

Early Opening

30/3/98	WWT SLIMBRIDGE
30/3/98	Tel: 01453 890333 ext. 223

To coincide with the Severn Bore; high tides bring birds closer to the Hides - enjoy the peace and quiet of an early opening as well as great birdwatching. Centre opens at 08.30 ready to be in the Holden Tower for the tide at around 09.00. Normal admission prices apply

Wildlife Reserves

Grantham Mid-Lent Fair

30/3/98	GRANTHAM TOURIST INFORMATION CENTRE
1/4/98	Tel: 01476 566444

Please call TIC for further information

Tourist Information Centres

Northleach - The Cotswold Experience

1/4/98	COTSWOLD COUNTRYSIDE COLLECTION
17/4/98	Tel: 01451 860715

This exhibition looks at the natural beauty of the Cotswolds and the work of the Area of Outstanding Natural Beauty Service, based at Shire Hall, Gloucester, in preserving it for visitors and residents to enjoy. To accompany the exhibition there will be children's workshops, drystone walling demonstrations and guided walks by wardens. The exhibition includes giant jigsaws, scale models of dry stone walls and stiles and other interactive activities

Museum- Local History

Memories

1/4/98
26/4/98
COTSWOLD COUNTRYSIDE COLLECTION
Tel: 01451 860715
In the Reception Gallery. Work reflecting memories, a response to things seen and experienced, remembered fragments of life, thoughts, nature, journeys and interests of artist and teacher Pam Harrison. Plus mixed media textiles inspired by travels in India by Christina Dreher

Museum- Local History

Ruinous Perfection: Byron and Newstead Abbey

1/4/98
3/10/98
NEWSTEAD ABBEY
Tel: 01623 793557
In the Manuscript Room. Byron was just ten years old when he inherited Newstead Abbey in 1798. He immediately succumbed to the romance of its "ruinous perfection" which his poetry was to make famous worldwide. First in a new series of temporary exhibitions exploring aspects of Byron's life and work, this bicentenary show celebrates the poet's great passion for his ancestral home. Pictures, manuscripts and letters portray the wonderfully eccentric household Byron established at Newstead - the Gothic mansion which inspired some of his best writing and remains a symbol of his own very dramatic fate

Historic Houses & Gardens

Behind The Scenes Days

4/4/98
4/4/98
CHATSWORTH
Tel: 01246 582204/565300
Spend a day backstage at Chatsworth and meet the people who look after the House and its collections, the Garden and Park. Book on 01246 582204 contact Mrs Sue Gregory

Historic Houses & Gardens

Guided Walks with the Cotswold Voluntary Wardens

4/4/98
4/4/98
COTSWOLD COUNTRYSIDE COLLECTION
Tel: 01451 860715
Join a guided walk in the countryside the Cotswold Countryside Collection. There will be an audio-visual presentation running in the museum to accompany the walks. Times to be arranged, please telephone for further information

Museum- Local History

Steaming Weekends

4/4/98
5/4/98
ETRURIA INDUSTRIAL MUSEUM
Tel: 01782 287557
Princess, an 1820s beam engine drives the original 1856 grinding machinery; a coal fired 1903 boiler supplies the steam. 13.00-16.30

Museum- Industrial

Silverstone Spring Trophy

4/4/98
5/4/98
SILVERSTONE CIRCUIT
Tel: 01327 857271
Please call for further information.

Motor Racing Circuit

Drawn to the Park

4/4/98
8/4/98
CLUMBER PARK
Tel: 01909 476592
The New English School of Drawing in association with the New English Art Club and National Trust Education presents a series of workshops led by Duncan Wood at Clumber Park. Book one or more days, £22.00 each. 10.00-16.30. To book call Lynn Mowbray 01909 486411

Historic Houses & Gardens

Easter Egg Hunt & Quiz

4/4/98
19/4/98
CANAL MUSEUM
Tel: 0115 915 6870
Back by popular demand - the Canal Museum Easter Egg Hunt. Find the eggs, answer the questions, finish with a drawing and you may win a prize! No need to book, £0.40, suitable for children

Museum- Industrial

Easter Eggsplorers

4/4/98
19/4/98
WWT SLIMBRIDGE
Tel: 01453 890333 ext. 223
Lots of Egg-citing activities and egg-speriments for children including the Great Egg Hunt. Activities 11.00-16.00 daily

Wildlife Reserves

The People's Show

4/4/98
4/5/98
CORINIUM MUSEUM
Tel: 01285 655611
An opportunity to see what people are collecting and why. In fact if you have an interesting collection which you would like to display why not contact Judy Mills at the Corinium Museum

Museum- Roman

Animal Days Exhibition

4/4/98
21/6/98
BROADFIELD HOUSE GLASS MUSEUM
Tel: 01384 812745
Animal Days: An exhibition of miniature glass animals to delight and amaze all ages

Museum- Glass

Exhibition: Aspects of the Forest

4/4/98
28/6/98
DEAN HERITAGE CENTRE
Tel: 01594 822170
John Belcher - mixed media art capturing the continuity of Forest life.

Heritage Centres

Cotswold Horse Driving Show

5/4/98
5/4/98
COTSWOLD FARM PARK
Tel: 01451 850307
A display of horse and carriage driving negotiating tricky obstacles

Farm Parks

All Day Round Trip to Tewkesbury
5/4/98 GLOUCESTER LEISURE CRUISE
5/4/98 Tel: 01452 318054
Cruise north on one of Britain's greatest water highways. Taking you through a quiet rural landscape it offers an enjoyable and relaxing trip with the added experience of going through two locks. You will be able to take a stroll around the old abbey town of Tewkesbury, 10.00-17.00

Boat Trips

Wagon Finance Race of the Year
5/4/98 MALLORY PARK
5/4/98 Tel: 01455 842931
Motorcycle Racing, call for further details

Motor Racing Circuit

Holy Week
5/4/98 LICHFIELD CATHEDRAL
12/4/98 Tel: 01543 306240
Special services throughout the week leading up to Easter Day

Cathedrals

Children's Easter Holiday Activity - Nature Collage
6/4/98 COTSWOLD COUNTRYSIDE COLLECTION
6/4/98 Tel: 01451 860715
Make a tactile framed collage using natural materials found in the surrounding countryside and recycled objects in everyday use. For children aged 5-10 years, 10.00-12.30, £6.00 (10% discount with Cotswold Museums Card)

Museum- Local History

Little Five Jelly Challenge
6/4/98 ALTON TOWERS
10/4/98 Tel: 0990 204060 24hr
Gives the younger thrill-seeker the chance to prove they're no jelly by taking on five of the smaller rides. With an overload of entertainment, giveaways and fun galore, this jellytastic week is not to be missed!

Theme Parks

Drystone Walling Demonstration
7/4/98 COTSWOLD COUNTRYSIDE COLLECTION
7/4/98 Tel: 01451 860715
Demonstrated by the Cotswold Voluntary Wardens, please telephone for further information

Museum- Local History

Wild & Wacky Flowers
7/4/98 COTSWOLD COUNTRYSIDE COLLECTION
7/4/98 Tel: 01451 860715
Use basic modelling skills with everyday waste materials to create and decorate a bold, man-eating or friendly flower! For children aged 5-10 years, 10.00-12.30, £6.00 (10% discount with Cotswold Museums Card)

Museum- Local History

Iron Age Mam Tor - High Peak Estate
7/4/98 PEAK DISTRICT NATIONAL PARK
7/4/98 Tel: 01629 816200
Guided walk exploring the history of this famous hill. Meet 10.00 at foot of Mam Tor steps. £0.50 per person. No dogs please call 01433 670368

National Parks

"Pole to Pole"
7/4/98 QUARRY BANK MILL AND STYAL COUNTRY PARK
14/4/98 Tel: 01625 527468
2nd in the series of Children's Workshops, 7th - Underwater monsters, masks, 8th - Skittles, soldiers, sailors, clowns and jugglers, 9th - The Great Bunny Hunt, 14th - Pom-poms and making Quarry Bank Mill mice. (NOT 10th/11th/12th)

Heritage Centres

Recycled Bugs & Animals
8/4/98 COTSWOLD COUNTRYSIDE COLLECTION
8/4/98 Tel: 01451 860715
Create ladybirds, spiders, owls, frogs, butterflies and other animals with tactile surfaces using plastic bottles, egg boxes, crisp packets and other household waste materials. For children aged 5-10 years, 10.00-12.30, £6.00 (10% discount with Cotswold Museums Card)

Museum- Local History

Beastly Easter Bonnets
8/4/98 GREEN'S MILL WINDMILL & SCIENCE MUSEUM
8/4/98 Tel: 0115 915 6878
Easter bonnets are traditional but here's your chance to make them in the shape of weird and wonderful animals using scrap materials, 11.30-13.00, £1.00. No need to book. Suitable for children of all ages

Museum- Mill

Working with Willow
9/4/98 COTSWOLD COUNTRYSIDE COLLECTION
9/4/98 Tel: 01451 860715
Traditional basketmaking techniques for children aged 8-12 years, 10.00-12.30, £7.00 including materials, (10% discount with Cotswold Museums Card)

Museum- Local History

Easter Egg Decorating
9/4/98 GREEN'S MILL WINDMILL & SCIENCE MUSEUM
9/4/98 Tel: 0115 915 6878
It's Spring again! Bring your own hard boiled egg ready for decorating in this traditional Easter activity, 13.00-14.30, £0.50. No need to book. Suitable for children of all ages

Museum- Mill

The full information on the venues listed can be found in the main classified section under the classification shown under the entry. Please mention Best Guides when calling or visiting.

25th Anniversary
NEWARK AIR MUSEUM
9/4/98
14/4/98
Tel: 01636 707170
Five days worth of events to celebrate 25 years on the Museum being open to the public, plenty to see and do for everyone, come along and join in the fun
Museum- Aviation

Ragrugmaking Demonstration
COTSWOLD COUNTRYSIDE COLLECTION
10/4/98
10/4/98
Tel: 01451 860715
Please telephone for further information
Museum- Local History

Felt Making Squares
COTSWOLD COUNTRYSIDE COLLECTION
10/4/98
10/4/98
Tel: 01451 860715
Make spring walks fun by looking out for bits of wool in the countryside and use them, with a bit of elbow grease, to make a felted square. For children aged 7-12 years, 10.00-12.30, £6.00 (10% discount with Cotswold Museums Card)
Museum- Local History

Easter Steamings
MUSEUM OF BRITISH ROAD TRANSPORT
10/4/98
13/4/98
Tel: 01203 832425
Travelling Post Office demonstrations Saturday to Monday. Easter Egg Hunt Sunday & Monday
Museum- Transport

17th Century Camp Battle
THE COMMANDERY
10/4/98
13/4/98
Tel: 01905 355071
The Commandery and Powick Bridge are hosts to a 17th century camp and a battle re-enactment
Historic Buildings

The King's Progress
WARWICK CASTLE
10/4/98
14/4/98
Tel: 01926 406600
See the Earl and his household prepare for the visit of Richard III, and join in their celebrations, watch the knights in combat or wonder at the large Birds of Prey as they swoop and fly above the Castle ramparts.
Castles

Guided Walks with the Cotswold Voluntary Wardens
COTSWOLD COUNTRYSIDE COLLECTION
11/4/98
11/4/98
Tel: 01451 860715
Please see 4 April entry for details
Museum- Local History

Easter Egg Hunt
ILAM PARK
11/4/98
11/4/98
Tel: 01335 350245/350503
Follow the Easter Egg Trail and find yourself a prize. Booking essential
Country Parks

Easter Egg Hunt - South Peak Estate
PEAK DISTRICT NATIONAL PARK
11/4/98
11/4/98
Tel: 01629 816200
Where are they? Can you find them. £1.50, booking essential call 01335 350503
National Parks

Easter Egg Hunt
SNOWSHILL MANOR
11/4/98
11/4/98
Tel: 01386 852410
Come along to try and find these craftily hidden eggs. 11.00 start. Normal admission charges apply
Historic Houses & Gardens

Easter Egg Hunt
CHEDWORTH ROMAN VILLA
11/4/98
13/4/98
Tel: 01242 890256
For children - site trail and quiz with seasonal prizes. £0.50 per entry (tickets on gate). Please telephone for further information and times
Roman Sites

FIM World Superbike Championship
DONINGTON COLLECTION OF GRAND PRIX RACING CARS
11/4/98
13/4/98
Tel: 01332 811027
Featuring two rounds of the World Superbike Championship and a host of support races.
Museum- Motor

Easter Egg Hunt
LOWER BROCKHAMPTON
11/4/98
13/4/98
Tel: 01885 488099
Come along and try to find these craftily hidden eggs. Normal admission charges apply (tickets on gate)
Historic Houses

Easter Festival
THE BASS MUSEUM
11/4/98
13/4/98
Tel: 01283 511000
A three day festival of nostalgia and steam with working engines from all over the country, with side stalls and demonstrations
Breweries

Easter Egg Hunt
BADDESLEY CLINTON HOUSE
12/4/98
12/4/98
Tel: 01564 783294
Children's Easter Egg Hunt with quiz around the grounds offering a chocolate reward. 12.00 onwards, £1.50 per child (tickets on gate)
Historic Houses & Gardens

Easter Egg Hunt
BERRINGTON HALL
12/4/98
12/4/98
Tel: 01568 615721
Supported by Barclays. 14.00, A£1.80 C£0.80 (tickets on gate)
Historic Houses & Gardens

Easter Egg Hunt

12/4/98 CASTLE BROMWICH HALL GARDENS

12/4/98 Tel: 0121 749 4100

Search the gardens for eggs or enter the Easter Bonnet Parade, call for times

Gardens

Rare & Unusual Plant Fair

12/4/98 FULBECK HALL

12/4/98 Tel: 01400 272205

Over 30 nurseries selling unusual perennials, shrubs, wild flowers etc. 10.00-16.00 A£2.00

Historic Houses & Gardens

Easter Egg Hunt

12/4/98 HANBURY HALL

12/4/98 Tel: 01527 821214

Come and hunt for these craftily hidden Easter Eggs, 14.30, £1.50 in addition to normal admission charges

Historic Houses & Gardens

Motorcycle Vintage Meeting

12/4/98 MALLORY PARK

12/4/98 Tel: 01455 842931

Please call for further information

Motor Racing Circuit

Easter Celebration

12/4/98 NEWSTEAD ABBEY

12/4/98 Tel: 01623 793557

Celebrate traditional Easter at Newstead Abbey with fun events for all the family, 12.00-17.00. Museum entrance fee applies

Historic Houses & Gardens

Easter Egg Hunt

12/4/98 SNIBSTON DISCOVERY PARK

12/4/98 Tel: 01530 510851/813256

Hunt for the clues hidden around the museum, solve the riddle and win a Cadbury's Creme Egg! Free gallery paying visitors. 11.00-17.00. Suitable for all ages

Industrial Heritage

Resisting the Invader - Regia Anglorum

12/4/98 ASHBY-DE-LA-ZOUCH CASTLE

13/4/98 Tel: 01530 413343

The early 12th century: The Saxons' simmering resentment of their Norman overlords explodes into action! Encampment warriors, weapons and a ferocious skirmish at 15.00. Inspired by Sir Walter Scott's 'Ivanhoe.' A£3.00 Concessions£2.30 C£1.50 EH Members Free. From 12.00

Castles

Arms and Armour and The History Man - Brian McNerney and David Rutherford-Edge

12/4/98 BOLSOVER CASTLE

13/4/98 Tel: 01246 823349

Fascinating 'hands on' talks about the history of arms and armour from the Romans to modern times, with unusual guided tours by the presenter of the BBC's ever popular History Man programme. But be warned, his enthusiasm is notoriously contagious and there is no antidote! Performing without costumes, props or even a safety net, he brings the past to life before your very eyes! From10.00-17.00. A£4.00 Concessions£3.00 C£2.00 EH Members Free. (House extra, subject to capacity)

Castles

Hunting for King Charles II, 1651

12/4/98 BOSCOBEL HOUSE

13/4/98 Tel: 01902 850244

17th century intrigues and living history as the victorious parliamentary search for Charles II after the Battle of Worcester. Cries of 'He's in the tree!' considered a bit unfair! From 12.00. Normal admission prices. EH Members Free

Historic Houses

Easter Bunny Hunt

12/4/98 BROADFIELD HOUSE GLASS MUSEUM

13/4/98 Tel: 01384 812745

Hunt the glass bunnies hidden around the museum, and join in on egg painting and glass engraving activities

Museum- Glass

Medieval Music - Misericordia

12/4/98 GOODRICH CASTLE

13/4/98 Tel: 01600 890538

Lively medieval music played by a costumed duo. From 12.00. A£3.00 C£1.50 Concessions£2.30. EH Members Free

Castles

This Costly Countess - English Renaissance

12/4/98 HARDWICK OLD HALL

13/4/98 Tel: 01246 850431

Episodes from the life of Bess of Hardwick, with music, dance and military displays. From 12.00. A£3.00 C£1.50 Concessions£2.30. EH Members Free

Historic Houses

The full information on the venues listed can be found in the main classified section under the classification shown under the entry. Please mention Best Guides when calling or visiting.

Victorian Easter Bank Holiday

12/4/98 HOLDENBY HOUSE, GARDENS AND
FALCONRY CENTRE

13/4/98 Tel: 01604 770074

Celebrate Easter the Victorian way with
Carriage rides; House tours (Monday
only), Victorian games; Teas in the
Victorian tearoom; Crafts; Easter Egg
Hunt; Easter Bunny and much more

Historic Houses & Gardens

Time-Travelling Players

12/4/98 LYDDINGTON BEDE HOUSE

13/4/98 Tel: 01572 822438

Mythical and magical stories. From 12.00.
Normal admission prices . EH Members
Free

Historic Houses

Mediaeval Festival

12/4/98 MIDDLETON HALL

13/4/98 Tel: 01827 283095

Knights and ladies in Mediaeval dress.
Knights in battle medieval dance
tableaux. Sun: 14.00-17.00, Mon: 11.00-
17.00

Historic Houses & Gardens

Easter Treasure Hunt

12/4/98 SHERWOOD FOREST FARM PARK

13/4/98 Tel: 01623 823558

Family fun looking for answers among the
many animal friends

Farm Parks

Time-Travelling Players

12/4/98 STOKESAY CASTLE

13/4/98 Tel: 01588 672544

Mythical and magical stories. From 12.00.
Normal admission price. EH Members
Free

Castles

Midlands Festival Of Transport

12/4/98 WESTON PARK

13/4/98 Tel: 01952 850207

A fine collection of vintage and classic
vehicles. Arena displays, good all round
Family Entertainment

Historic Houses & Gardens

Basketmaking Demonstration

13/4/98 COTSWOLD COUNTRYSIDE COLLECTION

13/4/98 Tel: 01451 860715

Please telephone for further information

Museum- Local History

Craft Demonstration

13/4/98 FORGE MILL NEEDLE MUSEUM AND
BORDESLEY ABBEY VISITOR CENTRE

13/4/98 Tel: 01527 62509

Tea-room open

Museum- Mill

BRSCC Club Meeting

13/4/98 MALLORY PARK

13/4/98 Tel: 01455 842931

Eurocar - Opening round. Please call for
further information

Motor Racing Circuit

Great Easter Egg Hunt

13/4/98 PACKWOOD HOUSE

13/4/98 Tel: 01564 782024

Come and find those craftily hidden eggs,
14.00-15.00. Normal admission rates plus
£1.50 per child taking part in Easter Egg
Hunt (tickets on the gate)

Historic Houses & Gardens

Annual Easter Monday Extravaganza

13/4/98 VINA COOKE MUSEUM OF DOLLS AND
BYGONE CHILDHOOD

13/4/98 Tel: 01636 821364

Morris Dancing, Puppets, Crafts, Working
Models, etc, 10.30-17.00

Museum- Toy

Drystone Walling Demonstration

14/4/98 COTSWOLD COUNTRYSIDE COLLECTION

14/4/98 Tel: 01451 860715

Demonstrated by the Cotswold Voluntary
Wardens, please telephone for further
information

Museum- Local History

Women of the Cut

15/4/98 CANAL MUSEUM

15/4/98 Tel: 0115 915 6870

Can you imagine bringing up four children
in a tiny, cramped cabin with no toilet, no
bathroom and no privacy? Wendy Freer
has researched the life of women working
on the canals and in this illustrated talk
will tell how, from the 1780's onwards,
thousands of women achieved this seem-
ingly impossible task, 19.00, A£1.50
Concessions£1.00. Please book in
advance on 0115 915 6870

Museum- Industrial

Marvellous Minibeasts

15/4/98 COTSWOLD COUNTRYSIDE COLLECTION

15/4/98 Tel: 01451 860715

Take part in the Caterpillar race, explore
the World through the eyes of a ladybird,
play the predator prey game and make
your own bug or beastie to take home!
For children aged 7-12 years, 10.00-12.30,
£3.00 (10% discount with Cotswold
Museums Card)

Museum- Local History

Marvellous Minibeasts

16/4/98 COTSWOLD COUNTRYSIDE COLLECTION

16/4/98 Tel: 01451 860715

Please see 15 April entry for details

Museum- Local History

Asian Cookery

16/4/98 NOTTINGHAM CASTLE MUSEUM AND ART
GALLERY

16/4/98 Tel: 0115 915 3700

Learn to make tasty Asian snacks with
teacher and cook Sushma Pazaz. By the
end of the afternoon you will have made
pakoras, namkeens (savoury shortbread)
and eaten them! A hands-on session,
14.00-16.00. Children to be accompanied
by adults. A£3.50 Concessions£2.50.
Suitable for all ages. Not accessible for
wheelchair users. Please book in advance
on 0115 915 3652 (ansaphone)

Castles

The NEC Antiques For Everyone Fair

16/4/98 NATIONAL EXHIBITION CENTRE

19/4/98 Tel: 0121 780 4141 x2604

A major event featuring 600 dealers
exhibiting in a two-section event based on
the highly successful NEC August Fair. 200
dealers offer antiques and fine art datelined to 1914 in plush, stand-fitted Section
One; 400 dealers occupy unit-displays in
Section Two, showing all things antique
and collectable made prior to 1940. An
enormous range of very fine quality
antiques and collectibles for every pocket
with prices from less than £10 to over
£100,000. 25,000 visitors anticipated.
Open Thur & Fri 11.00-20.00, Sat & Sun
11.00-18.00

Exhibition Centres

Bargain Weekend One

17/4/98 BILLING AQUADROME LIMITED

19/4/98 Tel: 01604 408181

Tel 01604 408181 for more details

Country Leisure Parks

Guided Walks with the Cotswold Voluntary Wardens

18/4/98 COTSWOLD COUNTRYSIDE COLLECTION

18/4/98 Tel: 01451 860715

Please see 4 April entry for details

Museum- Local History

Workshop: Plant Dyeing

18/4/98 DEAN HERITAGE CENTRE

18/4/98 Tel: 01594 822170

Making beautiful natural dyes. Advance
booking necessary. Open to adults and
children. Please telephone for further
information

Heritage Centres

All Day Round Trip to Sharpness

18/4/98 GLOUCESTER LEISURE CRUISE

18/4/98 Tel: 01452 318054

The Gloucester & Sharpness Canal was
the widest and deepest in the world when
it was opened in 1827. During your cruise
fourteen bridges will open on your journey south to Sharpness, passing through
Frampton on Severn with its beautiful village green and stopover at the unusual
boat graveyard at Purton, 10.00-17.00

Boat Trips

Vintage Raceday - VSCC

18/4/98 SILVERSTONE CIRCUIT

18/4/98 Tel: 01327 857271

Please call for further information.

Motor Racing Circuit

Belton Horse Trials

18/4/98 BELTON HOUSE

19/4/98 Tel: 01476 566116

The annual horse trials. Entry via Belton
Village entrance. £8.00 per car. Further
details on 01775 680333 - Charles
Harrison

Historic Houses

Spring Gardener's Weekend

18/4/98 RAGLEY HALL

19/4/98 Tel: 01789 762090

Call for further information

Historic Houses & Gardens

Gamekeepers Fair

18/4/98 SHUGBOROUGH ESTATE

19/4/98 Tel: 01889 881388

Official BASC Annual Country Fair.
Competitions, falcony, displays and clay
shoots. Over 100 stalls with something for
all the family

Country Estates

Writers at Wroxeter

18/4/98 WROXETER ROMAN CITY

19/4/98 Tel: 01743 761330

Readers in the ruins from the works of AE
Houseman, Wilfred Owen and Mary Webb,
together with guided tours. From 12.00.
A£3.50 C£1.75 Concessions£1.75. EH
Members Free

Roman Remains

Tudor Life

18/4/98 THE COMMANDERY

19/8/98 Tel: 01905 355071

Come and see how the Tudors made
music and how they danced to it

Historic Buildings

Plant Sale

19/4/98 CALKE ABBEY

19/4/98 Tel: 01332 863822

11.00-17.00. Property open as usual. Free
parking, entry to sale £1.00

Historic Houses & Gardens

---

*The full information on the venues listed can be found in the main classified section under the
classification shown under the entry. Please mention Best Guides when calling or visiting.*

East Midlands Doll Fair

19/4/98 ELVASTON CASTLE COUNTRY PARK
19/4/98 Tel: 01332 571342

A wonderful Doll Fair with dolls houses and teddies - 'a miniature wonderland.' Top quality collectors, artists and craftspeople bring old and soft dolls, dollshouse dolls, miniatures, teddy bears, dollcraft materials, kits, magazines and juvenilia, 10.30-16.30, A£2.50 Student&OAPs£1.50 AccompaniedC£Free, £0.50 refund on car park fee at fair. Wheelchair access downstairs only

Country Parks

Launch of Archaeological Activity

19/4/98 FORGE MILL NEEDLE MUSEUM AND BORDESLEY ABBEY VISITOR CENTRE
19/4/98 Tel: 01527 62509

Centre and Craft Demonstrations in Forge Mill. Tea-room open. Slide show about Tanzania by David Morgan

Museum- Mill

EMRA Club Meeting

19/4/98 MALLORY PARK
19/4/98 Tel: 01455 842931

Please call for further information

Motor Racing Circuit

Iron Age Mam Tor - High Peak Estate

19/4/98 PEAK DISTRICT NATIONAL PARK
19/4/98 Tel: 01629 816200

Guided walk exploring the history of this famous hill. Meet 10.00 at foot of Mam Tor steps. £0.50 per person. No dogs please call 01433 670368

National Parks

Lancia Giorno della Montecarlo

19/4/98 STANFORD HALL
19/4/98 Tel: 01788 860250

Lancia Giorno della Montecarlo (Provisional booking)

Historic Houses

Focus on Bats

20/4/98 WOLLATON HALL NATURAL HISTORY MUSEUM
20/4/98 Tel: 0115 915 3900

An illustrated talk by Sheila Wright on the natural history of bats from Britain and around the world. Come and find out about the life cycle and behaviour of these intriguing mammals. There will also be a chance to view bat specimens from the musuem's collections, 14.00-15.30, admission free. Please book in advance on 0115 915 3900

Museum- Natural History

Behind The Scenes Days

22/4/98 CHATSWORTH
22/4/98 Tel: 01246 582204/565300

Spend a day backstage at Chatsworth and meet the people who look after the House and its collections, the Garden and Park. Book on 01246 582204 contact Mrs Sue Gregory

Historic Houses & Gardens

Adult Dayschool - Basketmaking

22/4/98 COTSWOLD COUNTRYSIDE COLLECTION
22/4/98 Tel: 01451 860715

Make a basket in a day using traditional basketmaking techniques, 10.00-17.00, £22.00 (10% discount with Cotswold Museums Card)

Museum- Local History

St George's Day

23/4/98 WARWICK CASTLE
23/4/98 Tel: 01926 406600

See the St George's Knight, listen to his legends and find out about our St George-Guy of Warwick.

Castles

Spring Horse Trials

24/4/98 WESTON PARK
26/4/98 Tel: 01952 850207

Three day event of all classes, includes Dressage, Show Jumping and Cross Country

Historic Houses & Gardens

East Midlands Doll Fair

25/4/98 STRATFORD-UPON-AVON TOURIST INFORMATION CENTRE
25/4/98 Tel: 01789 293127

Venue: Civic Hall, Stratford-upon-Avon. A wonderful Doll Fair with dolls houses and teddies - 'a miniature wonderland.' Top quality collectors, artists and craftspeople bring old and soft dolls, dollshouse dolls, miniatures, teddy bears, dollcraft materials, kits, magazines and juvenilia, 10.30-16.30, A£2.50 Student&OAPs£1.50 AccompaniedC£Free, refreshments available

Tourist Information Centres

Pleasure Learning Weekend

25/4/98 GLOUCESTER LEISURE CRUISE
26/4/98 Tel: 01452 318054

Signwriting Course

Boat Trips

Staffordshire Spring Flower Show

25/4/98 SHUGBOROUGH ESTATE
26/4/98 Tel: 01889 881388

Gardening lovers and experts unite at this major two day floral extravaganza

Country Estates

Silverstone International Raceday
25/4/98 SILVERSTONE CIRCUIT
26/4/98 Tel: 01327 857271
Please call for further information.
Motor Racing Circuit

Focus on Birds Weekend - Ducks
25/4/98 WWT SLIMBRIDGE
26/4/98 Tel: 01453 890333 ext. 223
Fascinating, useful and beautiful, ducks
appeal to us in many ways. Find out more
about them through artifacts and a walk.
Meet at 11.00 or 14.00 in the Decoy Hide -
no need to book
Wildlife Reserves

An Exhibition of Underwear
25/4/98 COTSWOLD COUNTRYSIDE COLLECTION
17/5/98 Tel: 01451 860715
A tantalising glimpse into the history of
underwear!
Museum- Local History

Pets Progress - The Pussy Cat
25/4/98 GRANTHAM MUSEUM
8/8/98 Tel: 01476 568783
Meet the Pussy Cat, curious? call for
details!
Museum- Local History

Orchid Show
26/4/98 BIRMINGHAM BOTANICAL GARDENS AND
         GLASSHOUSES
26/4/98 Tel: 0121 454 1860
Hundreds of these beautiful exotic flowers
on display. Plant sales and advice
Gardens- Botanical

'Kill or Cure'
26/4/98 FORD GREEN HALL
26/4/98 Tel: 01782 233195
The ever popular Obadiah Ringwood, 17th
century soldier turned surgeon, returns
once again to demonstrate the tools and
techniques of his trade. Not for the squea-
mish! 13.00-16.30
Historic Houses

NCCPG (Lincolnshire)
26/4/98 HARLAXTON MANOR GARDENS
26/4/98 Tel: 01476 592101
Plant fair call for further details
Historic Houses & Gardens

Land Rover 50th Anniversary Day
26/4/98 HERITAGE MOTOR CENTRE
26/4/98 Tel: 01926 641188
Celebrate this milestone in motoring history.
Museum- Motor

BARC Club Meeting
26/4/98 MALLORY PARK
26/4/98 Tel: 01455 842931
Please call for further information
Motor Racing Circuit

Riders Association of Triumph Rally
26/4/98 STANFORD HALL
26/4/98 Tel: 01788 860250
Telephone 01788 860250 for more details
Historic Houses

Friends of the Museum Evening Meeting
28/4/98 GLOUCESTER LEISURE CRUISE
28/4/98 Tel: 01452 318054
Evening Meeting and AGM
Boat Trips

Female Victorian Emigration
29/4/98 BREWHOUSE YARD MUSEUM
29/4/98 Tel: 0115 948 3600
Carole Walker discusses the social conditions which encouraged female emigration, their often difficult passage and the
varied lives they found in the New World
Museum- Local History

Barnsley Village Festival
1/5/98 BARNSLEY HOUSE GARDEN
1/5/98 Tel: 01285 740281
10 gardens open and church, 10.00-17.00.
Need to confirm date
Gardens

Ragrugmaking Demonstration
1/5/98 COTSWOLD COUNTRYSIDE COLLECTION
1/5/98 Tel: 01451 860715
Please telephone for further information
Museum- Local History

Sprite Owners Club
1/5/98 BILLING AQUADROME LIMITED
4/5/98 Tel: 01604 408181
Tel 01604 408181 for more details
Country Leisure Parks

All Day Round Trip to Tewkesbury
2/5/98 GLOUCESTER LEISURE CRUISE
2/5/98 Tel: 01452 318054
Please see 5 April entry for details
Boat Trips

Albrighton Point to Point
2/5/98 WESTON PARK
2/5/98 Tel: 01952 850207
An enjoyable family day out with plenty of
action
Historic Houses & Gardens

Steaming Weekends
2/5/98 ETRURIA INDUSTRIAL MUSEUM
3/5/98 Tel: 01782 287557
Princess, an 1820s beam engine drives
the original 1856 grinding machinery; a
coal fired 1903 boiler supplies the steam.
13.00-16.30
Museum- Industrial

Historic Race Meeting - HSCC
2/5/98 SILVERSTONE CIRCUIT
3/5/98 Tel: 01327 857271
Please call for further information.
Motor Racing Circuit

---

*The full information on the venues listed can be found in the main classified section under the
classification shown under the entry. Please mention Best Guides when calling or visiting.*

Calke Abbey Craft Show
2/5/98
4/5/98
CALKE ABBEY
Tel: 01332 863822
Craft sale and demonstrations, entry
charge including National Trust members,
parking free, call for further details
Historic Houses & Gardens

May Day Mummers
2/5/98
4/5/98
WARWICK CASTLE
Tel: 01926 406600
Listen to the mediaeval storytellers as
they weave their tales of old and see the
13th century knight in combat. Watch the
large birds of prey swoop and fly above
the castle ramparts.
Castles

Bank Holiday Weekend
2/5/98
4/5/98
WEDGWOOD VISITOR CENTRE
Tel: 01782 204141/204218
Entertainment and fun for all the family.
Visit the centre and try your hand at the
various skills. For children there will be
entertainment throughout the day.
Normal admission charges apply
Factory Tours and Shopping

Paper, Felt & Fibre
2/5/98
26/5/98
COTSWOLD COUNTRYSIDE COLLECTION
Tel: 01451 860715
In the Reception Gallery, an exhibition of
work combining felts, paper and stitching
plus found materials inspired by travel.
Work by Lyn Giffiths
Museum- Local History

Hand to Mouth
2/5/98
7/6/98
DERBY MUSEUM AND ART GALLERY
Tel: 01332 716659
The Form and Culture of Eating
Implements. This explores the use of eat-
ing implements within an historical and
contemporary framework. Work by Susan
Vernon is shown alongside items curated
from Museum archives
Museum- Regimental

Rare Plant Fair
3/5/98
3/5/98
CASTLE BROMWICH HALL GARDENS
Tel: 0121 749 4100
Rare and specialist plants on sale
Gardens

Craft Workshop
3/5/98
3/5/98
FORGE MILL NEEDLE MUSEUM AND
BORDESLEY ABBEY VISITOR CENTRE
Tel: 01527 62509
Please call for further information
Museum- Mill

New Era Club Meeting
3/5/98
3/5/98
MALLORY PARK
Tel: 01455 842931
Please call for further information
Motor Racing Circuit

Volkswagen Owners Club Rally
3/5/98
3/5/98
STANFORD HALL
Tel: 01788 860250
Warwickshire & Leicestershire branch.
Telephone 01788 860250 for more details
Historic Houses

Civil War Living History
3/5/98
4/5/98
ASHBY-DE-LA-ZOUCH CASTLE
Tel: 01530 413343
The English Civil War Society. 17th century
living history weapons, drill and musket
firing set during the Naseby Campaign of
1645. From 12.00. A£3.00
Concessions£2.30 C£1.50 EH Members
Free
Castles

The Lion Rampant
3/5/98
4/5/98
BOLSOVER CASTLE
Tel: 01246 823349
Music, dance and archery from 12.00, with
drama and combat from 14.30. A£3.50
Concessions£2.50 C£1.80 EH Members
Free
Castles

Meet the Mad Hater!
3/5/98
4/5/98
BOSCOBEL HOUSE
Tel: 01902 850244
Join the Mad Hatter for tea, but watch out
for the Queen of Hearts! From 12.00.
Normal admission prices. EH Members
Free
Historic Houses

National Kit Car Motor Show
3/5/98
4/5/98
COVENTRY TOURIST INFORMATION CENTRE
Tel: 01203 832303/4
Motor show for kit car enthusiasts. Held
at N.A.C. Stoneleigh Park. Please call
01775 712100 for further information
Tourist Information Centres

British Touring Car Championship
3/5/98
4/5/98
DONINGTON COLLECTION OF GRAND PRIX
RACING CARS
Tel: 01332 811027
Two rounds of the Auto Trader RAC cham-
pionship.
Museum- Motor

**The Tudor Dynasty - english
Renaissance**
3/5/98
4/5/98
GOODRICH CASTLE
Tel: 01600 890538
Meet monarchs of the famous ruling
dynasty as they deal with the major
issues of their reigns. Features Henry VII,
Henry VIII, Edward VI, Mary I and
Elizabeth I, plus courtly music, dance and
military displays. From 13.30. A£3.50
C£1.80 Concessions£2.50. EH Members
Free
Castles

Alice in Wonderland - Labyrinth Productions

3/5/98
4/5/98

KENILWORTH CASTLE

Tel: 01926 852078

Follow Alice and White Rabbit as they go through Wonderland, meting all manner of weird, wonderful and totally made characters. From 14.30. A£4.00 C£2.00 Concessions£3.00. EH Members Free

Castles

Medieval Entertainment - The Company of the White Boar

3/5/98
4/5/98

KIRBY MUXLOE CASTLE

Tel: 01604 730320

Small military camp, period cooking and demonstrations of weapons and armour. From 12.00. A£2.50 C£1.30 Concessions£1.90. EH Members Free

Castles

May Day Entertainment

3/5/98
4/5/98

MIDDLETON HALL

Tel: 01827 283095

Continuous entertainment both days of singers, dancers and children's attrac-tions. May Day Pole. Sun: 14.00-17.00, Mon: 11.00-17.00

Historic Houses & Gardens

"Piggy Days"

3/5/98
4/5/98

SHERWOOD FOREST FARM PARK

Tel: 01623 823558

An in depth look at the many different rare breeds of pig who live at the farm park

Farm Parks

8th Staffordshire Classic Car and Transport Show

3/5/98
4/5/98

SHUGBOROUGH ESTATE

Tel: 01889 881388

Displays of over 750 cars, bikes, buses and agricultural vehicles from 1905 to the present day

Country Estates

The Bard's Best Bits - Oddsocks Theatre

3/5/98
4/5/98

STOKESAY CASTLE

Tel: 01588 672544

Once again this hugely entertaining group comprehensively demolish Shakespeare! See the best bits from Julius Caesar, Romeo and Juliet and A Midsummer Night's Dream. Don't miss it! From 14.30. A£3.50 C£1.80 Concessions£2.50. EH Members Free

Castles

Warriors!

3/5/98
4/5/98

WROXETER ROMAN CITY

Tel: 01743 761330

Meet ancient warriors from Shropshire. Contrast victorious Roman legionaries of the 1st century with embattled Imperial troops of 400 AD facing Pictish warriors, witness a savage battle between Vikings and Saxons and watch the deadly skills of 12th century Knights of the Welsh Marches. From 12.00. A£4.00 C£2.00 Concessions£3.00. EH Members Free.

Roman Remains

Victorian May Day

4/5/98
4/5/98

BREWHOUSE YARD MUSEUM

Tel: 0115 948 3600

Look out for details of this popular family event. Victorian sights, costumes and characters are the order of the day, with traditional English Folk dancing, brass band and of course Maypole dancing

Museum- Local History

Newborough Well Dressing

4/5/98

BURTON UPON TRENT TOURIST INFORMATION CENTRE

4/5/98

Tel: 01283 516609

In the village of Newborough, 10.00-16.00, blessing of wells at 11.00. Please call 01283 575430 for further information

Tourist Information Centres

Flower Fair:

4/5/98
4/5/98

HERGEST CROFT GARDENS

Tel: 01544 230160

With specialist plant and craft stalls, char-ity auction, garden walks and other attrac-tions, £5.00 entry, call for further details

Gardens

Brass Rubbing & Writing Experience

4/5/98
4/5/98

ILAM PARK

Tel: 01335 350245/350503

with Derek Hanley. Everyone welcome, small charge for materials. Ilam Stableblock at 11.00. Booking essential

Country Parks

BRSCC Club Meeting

4/5/98
4/5/98

MALLORY PARK

Tel: 01455 842931

Please call for further information

Motor Racing Circuit

May Day Celebrations

4/5/98
4/5/98

TAMWORTH CASTLE

Tel: 01827 63563

Craft displays and demonstrations inside the Castle

Castles

The full information on the venues listed can be found in the main classified section under the classification shown under the entry. Please mention Best Guides when calling or visiting.

Bretby Classic Car and Motorcycle Rally

4/5/98
4/5/98

THE BASS MUSEUM
Tel: 01283 511000
The third annual rally will take place again this year at the Museum. This very popular event attracts classic vehicles from all over the British Isles

Breweries

Indpendent Thoughts: Permindar Kaur in Conversation

6/5/98
6/5/98

NOTTINGHAM CASTLE MUSEUM AND ART GALLERY
Tel: 0115 915 3700
10.30-14.30. Suitable for adults. Admission Free

Castles

Malvern Spring Gardening Show

8/5/98
10/5/98

MALVERN TOURIST INFORMATION CENTRE
Tel: 01684 892289
Venue: Three Counties Showground, Malvern, Worcestershire. Organised jointly by the RHS and the Three Counties Agricultural Society, the Malvern Spring Gardening Show is the first of the season. Against the stunning backdrop of the Malvern Hills, the show is a joyful celebration of spring. New features for 1998 include a massive horticultural marquee and a specialist marquee with a different feature each day of the show. Combining the enthusiasm of amateur growers with the experience of Britain's top professionals, other highlights include floral art, around 500 sundries stands, courtyard gardens, a specialist society section and the RHS Advisory desk. 8-9/5 09.00-18.00, 10/5 09.00-17.00. Advance RHS Members £7.00, Advance Public £8.00, Tickets on day £10.00, C(0-16)£Free, groups 10+ £7.50 tel: 01684 584900, all advance booking orders must be made by 22 April latest, car parking free

Tourist Information Centres

Open Day

9/5/98
9/5/98

BELTON HOUSE
Tel: 01476 566116
Gardens are open today in aid of the National Gardens Scheme - proceeds will be given to the Scheme which helps to preserve and restore some of the finest gardens in the country

Historic Houses

Alice in Wonderland Questt

9/5/98
9/5/98

CALKE ABBEY
Tel: 01332 863822
An animated trails for children, with plenty of family fun. 11.00-16.00. Call for further details

Historic Houses & Gardens

Lichfield Cathedral Special Choir

9/5/98
9/5/98

LICHFIELD CATHEDRAL
Tel: 01543 306240
Beethoven Mass in C and Handel Coronation Anthems, Tickets: £10.00, £8.00, £6.00, unreserved £5.00, call to book

Cathedrals

Aeroboot

9/5/98
9/5/98

NEWARK AIR MUSEUM
Tel: 01636 707170
An aviation and avionic sale, great place to find those hard to find parts

Museum- Aviation

Angling Fair

9/5/98
10/5/98

CHATSWORTH
Tel: 01246 582204/565300
One of the only specialist Angling Fairs in the country catering for games, coarse and sea-fishing enthusiasts, with added attractions for families

Historic Houses & Gardens

Grand Prix Weekend - Competition Ballooning Event

9/5/98
10/5/98

STANFORD HALL
Tel: 01788 860250
Organised by the Competitions Club section of the British Balloon and Airship Club. For further details please contact Neil Gabriel Tel: 01773 531551

Historic Houses

Toy Tiger Taxonomy Trace

9/5/98
7/6/98

DERBY MUSEUM AND ART GALLERY
Tel: 01332 716659
An exhibition of work by Martyn Blundell who is now recognised as one of the region's most exciting artists and has works in many collections, both in the UK and USA

Museum- Regimental

Images 22

9/5/98
21/6/98

DERBY MUSEUM AND ART GALLERY
Tel: 01332 716659
This exhibition is one of the few ways the public can appreciate the very best of British illustration encountered in books, magazines, newspapers, greeting cards and advertising

Museum- Regimental

21st Sandwell Historic Vehicle Parade and Show

10/5/98
10/5/98

BIRMINGHAM TOURIST INFORMATION CENTRE
Tel: 0121 643 2514
A superb collection of historic vehicles will be on display at Sandwell Park, West Bromwich

Tourist Information Centres

National Mills Day
10/5/98 DANIEL'S MILL
10/5/98 Tel: 01746 762753
Please call for further information.
The Unusual

Period Garden Tour
10/5/98 FORD GREEN HALL
10/5/98 Tel: 01782 233195
Find out about the design uses, and plants of early 17th century gardens, as recreated in the grounds of the Hall, 14.30 & 15.30
Historic Houses

National Mills Day
10/5/98 FORGE MILL NEEDLE MUSEUM AND BORDESLEY ABBEY VISITOR CENTRE
10/5/98 Tel: 01527 62509
Free Open Day. Wheel working. Tea-room open
Museum- Mill

Spring Autotest
10/5/98 HERITAGE MOTOR CENTRE
10/5/98 Tel: 01926 641188
Call for more details.
Museum- Motor

EMRA Club Meeting
10/5/98 MALLORY PARK
10/5/98 Tel: 01455 842931
Please call for further information
Motor Racing Circuit

Stationary Engine Day
10/5/98 NATIONAL WATERWAYS MUSEUM
10/5/98 Tel: 01452 318054
All engines of different shapes and sizes humming and working with their proud owners
Museum- Waterways

Guided Walk - High Peak Estate
10/5/98 PEAK DISTRICT NATIONAL PARK
10/5/98 Tel: 01629 816200
Walk to Alport Valley 10 miles. Meet 10.00, A57 lay-by (grid ref 171 872) A£2.00 C£Free. Bring a packed lunch. No dogs please. Call 01433 670368
National Parks

Wolves and Tors - South Peak Estate
10/5/98 PEAK DISTRICT NATIONAL PARK
10/5/98 Tel: 01629 816200
Guided walk. Meet 10.00 at Hartington Car park (OS Outdoor Leisure 24 SK 127602). Moderate walk, no dogs please, packed lunch required. Call 01335 350503
National Parks

Technology Challenge Day
10/5/98 SNIBSTON DISCOVERY PARK
10/5/98 Tel: 01530 510851/813256
For all those techno-skilled enthusiasts a challenge awaits you! Please telephone for further information
Industrial Heritage

National Mills Day
10/5/98 STAINSBY MILL
10/5/98 Tel: 01246 850430
Get enthusiastic about your local Mill day! Call for more details.
Watermill

Suzuki Motorcycle Owners Club Rally
10/5/98 STANFORD HALL
10/5/98 Tel: 01788 860250
Telephone 01788 860250 for more details
Historic Houses

Rover P4 Drivers Guild National Rally
10/5/98 STANFORD HALL
10/5/98 Tel: 01788 860250
Telephone 01788 860250 for more details
Historic Houses

Dawn Chorus Walk
10/5/98 WWT SLIMBRIDGE
10/5/98 Tel: 01453 890333 ext. 223
Experience the joys of the dawn chorus with one of our expert wardens. Relax over a full English breakfast in our restaurant. Time: 04.30 prompt at the entrance. Cost: £12.50 (£10.50 WWT members)
Wildlife Reserves

2nd National Trust Spring Plant Fair
11/5/98 PACKWOOD HOUSE
11/5/98 Tel: 01564 782024
Buy specially grown plants at good prices for your own garden and raise funds for Packwood House Gardens. Trade stands, Nurseries, Jazz Band and Children's Entertainment provide something for everyone. Enjoy a full day out 11.00-16.00. Normal admission rates apply
Historic Houses & Gardens

Ragrugmaking Demonstration
15/5/98 COTSWOLD COUNTRYSIDE COLLECTION
15/5/98 Tel: 01451 860715
Please telephone for further information
Museum- Local History

Galloway Antiques Fair
15/5/98 FULBECK HALL
17/5/98 Tel: 01400 272205
High quality dateline fair. Refreshments available. Fri/Sat 10.30-18.00 Sun 10.30-17.00 A£3.00 C£Free
Historic Houses & Gardens

British Empire Trophy
15/5/98 SILVERSTONE CIRCUIT
17/5/98 Tel: 01327 857271
Please call for further information.
Motor Racing Circuit

Baroque Music
16/5/98 CALKE ABBEY
16/5/98 Tel: 01332 863822
An introduction to historical musical instruments, call for further details
Historic Houses & Gardens

The full information on the venues listed can be found in the main classified section under the classification shown under the entry. Please mention Best Guides when calling or visiting.

Workshop: Using Iron Ochres
16/5/98 DEAN HERITAGE CENTRE
16/5/98 Tel: 01594 822170
Using Forest ochres for painting and decoration. Advance booking necessary. Open to adults and children. Please telephone for further information
Heritage Centres

All Day Round Trip Sharpness to Gloucester
16/5/98 GLOUCESTER LEISURE CRUISE
16/5/98 Tel: 01452 318054
Please see 18 April entry for details
Boat Trips

Horses Weekend
16/5/98 NATIONAL WATERWAYS MUSEUM
17/5/98 Tel: 01452 318054
The Museum Shire shows his friends what he does behind the scenes. Parade daily around the docks
Museum- Waterways

Heavy Horse Weekend
16/5/98 SEVERN VALLEY RAILWAY
17/5/98 Tel: 01299 403816
See horses performing many tasks at stations and in fields en-route
Railways

Leicestershire & Rutland Museums Festival
16/5/98 SNIBSTON DISCOVERY PARK
17/5/98 Tel: 01530 510851/813256
Everything the budding historian wants to know is at this festival. Please telephone for further information
Industrial Heritage

Ballads and Bayonets - Hautbois and the 47th Foot
16/5/98 STOKESAY CASTLE
17/5/98 Tel: 01588 672544
Lively music, British redcoats, drill, musket firing, encampment and a fascinating comparison between a soldier of 1778 and 1998. From 12.00. A£3.00 C£1.50 Concessions£2.30. EH Members Free
Castles

Meet a Roman Soldier
16/5/98 WROXETER ROMAN CITY
17/5/98 Tel: 01743 761330
Find out about the life of a Roman soldier, his armour and his weaponry. From 12.00. Normal admission price.
Roman Remains

Museums Week
16/5/98 ABINGTON MUSEUM
24/5/98 Tel: 01604 31454
A national event to celebrate and highlight the work of museums. Special themes for 1998 include conservation and hidden treasures
Museum- Local History

Museums Week 1998
16/5/98 CORINIUM MUSEUM
24/5/98 Tel: 01285 655611
Please telephone for further information
Museum- Roman

Museums Week 1998
16/5/98 COTSWOLD COUNTRYSIDE COLLECTION
24/5/98 Tel: 01451 860715
Please telephone for further information
Museum- Local History

Dinosaurs
16/5/98 BIRMINGHAM MUSEUM AND ART GALLERY
6/9/98 Tel: 0121 235 2834
This will be one of the biggest exhibitions of dinosaurs ever seen in Britain. The show will feature a special display of baby dinosaurs and dinosaur eggs as well as large robotic creatures. The centrepiece (if museum workers can fit the creatures in!) promises to be a full-size robotic Tyrannosaurus Rex. Measuring 13 metres long and 6 metres high, the beast is the size of a double decker bus! Admission A£4.00 C£2.00 (in school parties) Family Ticket (A2+C2) £12.00
Museums

Plant Fair
17/5/98 BERRINGTON HALL
17/5/98 Tel: 01568 615721
A plant fair for all those budding garden enthusiasts. No entrance fee. Please telephone for further information and times
Historic Houses & Gardens

Plant Market
17/5/98 BIRMINGHAM BOTANICAL GARDENS AND GLASSHOUSES
17/5/98 Tel: 0121 454 1860
Thousands of plants from dozens of specialist growers
Gardens- Botanical

Kite Flying Day
17/5/98 CALKE ABBEY
17/5/98 Tel: 01332 863822
With kite making workshop from 10.00. Bring your won kite. Admission Free
Historic Houses & Gardens

Plant Fair
17/5/98 CANONS ASHBY HOUSE
17/5/98 Tel: 01327 860044
If you would like to contribute plants for re-sale at this Plant Fair please call. All proceeds from plants sold at National Trust Plant Fairs go towards helping NT gardens nationwide
Historic Houses

Castlemilk Moorit Sheep Show
17/5/98 COTSWOLD FARM PARK
17/5/98 Tel: 01451 850307
View this prolific and graceful primitive breed of Parkland sheep at the Society's annual show
Farm Parks

Gardens Open
17/5/98 DEENE PARK
17/5/98 Tel: 01780 450223/450278
National Gardens Scheme. Please call venue for further details
Historic Houses

Steam Fair with Fred Dibnah
17/5/98 EASTNOR CASTLE
17/5/98 Tel: 01531 633160
Come along a see all your favourite steam powered vehicles
Castles

All Day Round Trip to Sharpness
17/5/98 GLOUCESTER LEISURE CRUISE
17/5/98 Tel: 01452 318054
Please see 18 April entry for details
Boat Trips

Spring Plant Fair
17/5/98 HANBURY HALL
17/5/98 Tel: 01527 821214
National Trust home grown and professional plant sale. 11.00-16.00. Usual admission charges apply (tickets on the gate)
Historic Houses & Gardens

BARC Meeting
17/5/98 MALLORY PARK
17/5/98 Tel: 01455 842931
Please call for further information
Motor Racing Circuit

Medieval Archery
17/5/98 PEVERIL CASTLE
17/5/98 Tel: 01433 620613
15th century archery and combat-at-arms. From 12.00. A£2.75 C£1.25 Concessions£2.00
Castles

Dressage Festival
17/5/98 SHUGBOROUGH ESTATE
17/5/98 Tel: 01889 881388
Staffordshire's only national dressage competition, attracting horses and riders from all over the U.K.
Country Estates

Leicestershire Ford RS Owners Club Rally
17/5/98 STANFORD HALL
17/5/98 Tel: 01788 860250
Telephone 01788 860250 for more details
Historic Houses

Dawn Chorus Walk
17/5/98 WWT SLIMBRIDGE
17/5/98 Tel: 01453 890333 ext. 223
Experience the joys of the dawn chorus with one of our expert wardens. Relax over a full English breakfast in our restaurant. Time: 04.30 prompt at the entrance. Cost: £12.50 (£10.50 WWT members)
Wildlife Reserves

Adult Learners Week Event
18/5/98 CALKE ABBEY
18/5/98 Tel: 01332 863822
Demonstration of Trust joinery and brickwork skills. Visitor opportunities to try these traditional skills, call for details
Historic Houses & Gardens

Tudor Music
18/5/98 CANONS ASHBY HOUSE
18/5/98 Tel: 01327 860044
Tudor Music day planned for adults with learning difficulties. Call venues for further details
Historic Houses

River Dipping - South Peak Estate
18/5/98 PEAK DISTRICT NATIONAL PARK
18/5/98 Tel: 01629 816200
River dipping, mini beast hunting, landscape sketching and tree activities. Call for details 01335 350503
National Parks

Gloucestershire Society of Botanical Illustrator's Annual Exhibition
19/5/98 CORINIUM MUSEUM
7/6/98 Tel: 01285 655611
This exhibition features the work of amateur and professional botanical illustrators. The GSBI actively seeks to encourage people to take up the art of Botanical Illustration and members of the society will be present during the exhibition. This exhibition will have works for sale
Museum- Roman

Behind The Scenes Days
20/5/98 CHATSWORTH
20/5/98 Tel: 01246 582204/565300
Spend a day backstage at Chatsworth and meet the people who look after the House and its collections, the Garden and Park. Book on 01246 582204 contact Mrs Sue Gregory
Historic Houses & Gardens

The full information on the venues listed can be found in the main classified section under the classification shown under the entry. Please mention Best Guides when calling or visiting.

Telling Tales: Talk by Dr Nima Poovaya-Smith

20/5/98 NOTTINGHAM CASTLE MUSEUM AND ART GALLERY

20/5/98 Tel: 0115 915 3700

Dr Nima Poovaya-Smith, Senior Keeper of International Arts at Cartwright Hall, Bradford, gives a guided tour of 'Telling Tales,' 12.00-13.00. Booking required only for groups. Admission Free. Suitable for Adults

Castles

Exhibition

21/5/98 LICHFIELD CATHEDRAL

8/6/98 Tel: 01543 306240

Exhibition of paintings by Robert Bradbury

Cathedrals

Disco Cruise

22/5/98 GLOUCESTER LEISURE CRUISE

22/5/98 Tel: 01452 318054

Come and have a bop on the water, 20.00-24.00

Boat Trips

Go Wild with a Warden

22/5/98 WWT SLIMBRIDGE

22/5/98 Tel: 01453 890333 ext. 223

An early evening walk on the reserve with one of our expert wardens. A great opportunity to birdwatch and see other wildlife at Slimbridge. Time: 19.00 at the entrance. Cost: £5.50 (£3.50 WWT members) includes tea/coffee and biscuits

Wildlife Reserves

BBC Top Gear Live

22/5/98 SILVERSTONE CIRCUIT

25/5/98 Tel: 01327 857271

Performances feature stunts,thrills, and spills in an adrenaline-fuelled atmosphere.Hands on activities-Karting, Off-Roading, Skid Pan, Young Drivers, Rally Course, Helecopter Rides. Call for prices and advanced ticket booking.

Motor Racing Circuit

Charles II's Restoration

22/5/98 THE COMMANDERY

25/5/98 Tel: 01905 355071

The re-creation of Charles II's restoration to the throne being acted over the Bank Holiday

Historic Buildings

50th ARC Land Rover Celebrations

22/5/98 EASTNOR CASTLE

31/5/98 Tel: 01531 633160

To celebrate fifty years of the production of the Land Rover, the Association of Rover Clubs (ARC) in conjunction with the Land Rover Company, are holding a nine day International Rally. The event will open with a cavalcade of Land Rover vehicles, one from each year of manufacture from 1948 to the present day. The International Rally will also attract the biggest gathering of Land Rover enthusiasts ever. There will be competitions staged during the nine day extravaganza from a showroom vehicle trial to speed events where 2.0 - 4.6 litre powered Land Rovers will be competing against each other in the Competitive Safari, a gruelling drive over rough terrain where competitors will be driving in total more than 30 miles aiming to be the fiftieth anniversary champion in the twenty first ARC International Rally. For the non-competitors there will be several vehicles for them to admire including several entries in the Concours d'Elegance. There will also be many of the special vehicles on display that, over the years, the Land Rover company have been commissioned to make. Call 01772 716956/01472 398019 for more information.

Castles

Si-Fi Fair

23/5/98 CASTLE BROMWICH HALL GARDENS

24/5/98 Tel: 0121 749 4100

TV and film merchandise, exhibitions and a Surprise Guest!

Gardens

FIA Professional European Championships

23/5/98 SANTA POD RACEWAY

24/5/98 Tel: 01234 782828

Round 1 of the Drag Racing Championships. Top Fuel, Top Alcohol and Pro Stock Drag Racing extravaganza!

Motor Sports

Coalport Figurine Painting Event

23/5/98 WEDGWOOD VISITOR CENTRE

24/5/98 Tel: 01782 204141/204218

Watch one of our Coalport artists decorate the figure of the year and purchase a signed copy available only at demonstration events. Call our Visitor Centre Shop to pre-book your figurine on 01782 282373

Factory Tours and Shopping

Spring Craft Show
23/5/98 SHUGBOROUGH ESTATE
25/5/98 Tel: 01889 881388
A fascinating range of traditional craft stalls. See skilled craft people at work. Entertainment for all the family
Country Estates

Jousting Weekend
23/5/98 WARWICK CASTLE
25/5/98 Tel: 01926 406600
Let Battle commence! as the first of this year's jousting contests unfurl.
Castles

Bank Holiday Weekend
23/5/98 WEDGWOOD VISITOR CENTRE
25/5/98 Tel: 01782 204141/204218
Please see 2-4 May entry for details
Factory Tours and Shopping

Traditional Charcoal Burning
23/5/98 DEAN HERITAGE CENTRE
26/5/98 Tel: 01594 822170
A seldom seen craft not to be missed. Please telephone for further information
Heritage Centres

Half-Term Holiday Activities for Children
23/5/98 CORINIUM MUSEUM
31/5/98 Tel: 01285 655611
Please telephone for further information
Museum- Roman

Downy Duckling Days
23/5/98 WWT SLIMBRIDGE
31/5/98 Tel: 01453 890333 ext. 223
The time of the year to see ducklings, goslings and cygnets! Behind the scenes tours of the Duckery (numbers limited so please book places on arrival) plus Duckling Survival Trails and other activities, 11.00 - 16.00
Wildlife Reserves

Shearing
23/5/98 COTSWOLD FARM PARK
21/6/98 Tel: 01451 850307
We will shear the wool off our 950 sheep
Farm Parks

Harlaxton Manor Open
24/5/98 HARLAXTON MANOR GARDENS
24/5/98 Tel: 01476 592101
The first in two special open days where the general public may visit Harlaxton Manor which is normally closed to public visits
Historic Houses & Gardens

HSCC Club Meeting
24/5/98 MALLORY PARK
24/5/98 Tel: 01455 842931
Please call for further information
Motor Racing Circuit

Ancient Woodland and Archaeology
24/5/98 PEAK DISTRICT NATIONAL PARK
24/5/98 Tel: 01629 816200
Guided walk (4.5m/7km). Meet 11.00, Kings Tree (reached by shuttle bus from Fairholmes Visitor Centre). Return to Fairholmes by bus at end of walk. A£2.00 C£Free. Charge does not include bus fare. Bring a packed lunch. No dogs please. Booking essential. Call 01433 670368
National Parks

Capri Club International National Rally
24/5/98 STANFORD HALL
24/5/98 Tel: 01788 860250
Telephone 01788 860250 for more details
Historic Houses

Siege Group, Battle Re-enactment
24/5/98 BELVOIR CASTLE
25/5/98 Tel: 01476 870262
Using examples of early firearms and cannon, authentically reproduced costumes the group recreate the sights and sounds of the historical battlefield.
Castles

The Bard's Best Bits - Oddsocks Theatre
24/5/98 BOLSOVER CASTLE
25/5/98 Tel: 01246 823349
Once again this hugely entertaining group comprehensively demolish Shakespeare! See the best bits from Julius Caesar, Romeo and Juliet and A Midsummer Night's Dream. Don't miss it! From 12.00
Castles

Spring Bank Holiday Fun
24/5/98 BROADFIELD HOUSE GLASS MUSEUM
25/5/98 Tel: 01384 812745
A Treasure Hunt for the under 12's, plus craft workshops and demonstrations, call for further details
Museum- Glass

Sheep Shearing
24/5/98 CHILDRENS FARM
25/5/98 Tel: 0121 329 3240
Sheep Shearing and Wool Spinning Demonstration
Farms

Storytelling
24/5/98 GOODRICH CASTLE
25/5/98 Tel: 01600 890538
Traditional folk tales, myths and legends. Plus on Monday only there is mask-making. From 12.00. Normal admission price. EH Members Free
Castles

The full information on the venues listed can be found in the main classified section under the classification shown under the entry. Please mention Best Guides when calling or visiting.

12th Century Knights

24/5/98
25/5/98

KENILWORTH CASTLE

Tel: 01926 852078

Displays of skills-at-arms and combat by late Norman mounted knights, foot soldiers, plus shooting of a war engine. From 12.00. A£4.00 C£2.00 Concessions£3.00. EH Members Free

Castles

Ragley Hall Classic Car and Transport Show

24/5/98
25/5/98

RAGLEY HALL

Tel: 01789 762090

Displays of cars, bikes, buses and agricultural vehicles from 1905 to the present day

Historic Houses & Gardens

"Woolly Sheep" Days

24/5/98
25/5/98

SHERWOOD FOREST FARM PARK

Tel: 01623 823558

A lighthearted look at traditional shearing skills and sheep management, spinning and knitting

Farm Parks

Scenes from Medieval Life - The Plantagenet Society

24/5/98
25/5/98

STOKESAY CASTLE

Tel: 01588 672544

Archery display, medieval combat and dance. From 12.00. Normal admission price. EH Members Free.

Castles

Medieval Weekend

24/5/98
25/5/98

SUDELEY CASTLE AND GARDENS

Tel: 01242 602308

Come along to Sudeley and meet the roving Minstrels, Jugglers, Jester and see the magnificent Knights in Combat during our Medieval Weekend

Castles

Meet a Roman Soldier

24/5/98
25/5/98

WALL ROMAN SITE (LETOCETUM)

Tel: 01543 480768

A Roman Centurion talking about Roman armour and military skills. Plus guided tours. From 13.00. A£2.00 C£1.00 Concessions£1.50. EH Members Free

Roman Sites

Grand Spring Plant Sale

25/5/98
25/5/98

ACTON SCOTT HISTORIC WORKING FARM

Tel: 01694 781306/7

In its 5th year, leading plantsmen and nurseries with stalls. Farm & plant sale standard admission price. Plant sale only £0.50. 10.30-16.30

Farms

BRSCC Club Meeting

25/5/98
25/5/98

MALLORY PARK

Tel: 01455 842931

Eurocar event. Please call for further information

Motor Racing Circuit

Melton Mowbray Show

25/5/98

MELTON MOWBRAY TOURIST INFORMATION CENTRE

25/5/98

Tel: 01664 480992

Great entertainment from top military & civilian acts including circus and specialist performers. Admission free including the show programme. Call 01664 61704 for more information.

Tourist Information Centres

Dressing for Battle

25/5/98
25/5/98

TAMWORTH CASTLE

Tel: 01827 63563

Displays and demonstrations giving an insight into what those Knights of old had to wear to protect themselves when they dressed for battle

Castles

Bank Holiday Family Festival

25/5/98
25/5/98

THE BASS MUSEUM

Tel: 01283 511000

Bank holiday event for the whole family with live entertainment, side shows and children's entertainer

Breweries

Iron Age Mam Tor - High Peak Estate

26/5/98
26/5/98

PEAK DISTRICT NATIONAL PARK

Tel: 01629 816200

Guided walk exploring the history of this famous hill. Meet 10.00 at foot of Mam Tor steps. £0.50 per person. No dogs please call 01433 670368

National Parks

Friends of Thomas the Tank Engine

26/5/98
31/5/98

DEAN FOREST RAILWAY

Tel: 01594 843423 info line

Come along and meet Thomas and Wilbert the Forest Engine

Railways

Sunset Cruise

27/5/98
27/5/98

GLOUCESTER LEISURE CRUISE

Tel: 01452 318054

Sit back and relax with the beautiful view, 19.00-22.00

Boat Trips

Lead Mining at Odin Mine - High Peak Estate

27/5/98
27/5/98

PEAK DISTRICT NATIONAL PARK

Tel: 01629 816200

Event for families exploring the history of lead mining in the area. Meet 10.30 at roadside by Odin Mine on old A625. £0.50 each, no dogs please. Call 01433 670368

National Parks

"Into the Garden"
27/5/98 COTSWOLD COUNTRYSIDE COLLECTION
21/6/98 Tel: 01451 860715
Embroidered pictures and textiles by
Esther Barrett
Museum- Local History

"Into the Garden"
28/5/98 COTSWOLD COUNTRYSIDE COLLECTION
21/6/98 Tel: 01451 860715
Embroidered pictures and textiles by
Esther Barrett. There will be items for sale
Museum- Local History

BARC Raceday
30/5/98 SILVERSTONE CIRCUIT
30/5/98 Tel: 01327 857271
Please call for further information.
Motor Racing Circuit

Bat Evening
30/5/98 SNIBSTON DISCOVERY PARK
30/5/98 Tel: 01530 510851/813256
Join the Rangers and the Leicestershire
Bat Group to learn about the fascinating
life of bats. There will be a talk and a slide
show followed by a walk in the Grange
Nature Reserve. Please meet in the museum foyer at 20.00 wearing suitable clothing and footwear. Suitable for all ages.
£1.00 per person
Industrial Heritage

National Street Rod Association
30/5/98 BILLING AQUADROME LIMITED
31/5/98 Tel: 01604 408181
Hundreds of 'Rods,' advice, displays,
trade hall, entertainment. Tel 01604
408181 for more details
Country Leisure Parks

17th Century Cannon Displays
30/5/98 BOSCOBEL HOUSE
31/5/98 Tel: 01902 850244
The firing of various artillery pieces, with
living history, to mark Oak Apple Day.
From 12.00. Normal admission prices. EH
Members Free
Historic Houses

Music from the Age of Richard III
30/5/98 BUILDWAS ABBEY
31/5/98 Tel: 01952 433274
15th century music and song, plus (safe)
archery for children. At 14.00 and 15.30.
A£3.00 C£1.50 Concessions£2.30. EH
Members Free
Historical Remains

Craft Fair
30/5/98 CASTLE BROMWICH HALL GARDENS
31/5/98 Tel: 0121 749 4100
Unique crafts and artwork on sale
Gardens

Archaeology Activity Weekend
30/5/98 CHEDWORTH ROMAN VILLA
31/5/98 Tel: 01242 890256
Mosaic maker, living history, meet the
archaeologists, activities, etc. A family
day out. £0.50 surcharge over entry
including members (tickets on gate)
Roman Sites

Patchwork Demonstration
30/5/98 COTSWOLD COUNTRYSIDE COLLECTION
31/5/98 Tel: 01451 860715
Please telephone for further information
Museum- Local History

Tender Mercies?
30/5/98 LYDDINGTON BEDE HOUSE
31/5/98 Tel: 01572 822438
A Tudor hospital in 1598. Are the cures
helping the sick or actually hindering
recovery? Part of Lyddington's fete weekend. From 12.00. A£3.00 C£1.50
Concessions£2.30 EH Members Free
Historic Houses

Friends of Thomas the Tank Engine
30/5/98 SEVERN VALLEY RAILWAY
31/5/98 Tel: 01299 403816
Thomas and his many friends are up to all
sorts of tricks on the railway. The Fat
Controller is in charge
Railways

Shearing Shropshire Sheep
31/5/98 ACTON SCOTT HISTORIC WORKING FARM
31/5/98 Tel: 01694 781306/7
Demonstration of sheep shearing with
man powered clippers and hand shears.
Usual admission prices. 10.30-16.30
Farms

Victorian Day
31/5/98 DEAN HERITAGE CENTRE
31/5/98 Tel: 01594 822170
Clog dancing, morris dancing, cooking in
the Forester's Cottage, children's games,
Silver Band and much more
Heritage Centres

**Richard Seaman Memorial Vintage
Trophy**
31/5/98 DONINGTON COLLECTION OF GRAND PRIX
RACING CARS
31/5/98 Tel: 01332 811027
Historic racing at it's best.
Museum- Motor

Period Garden Plant Sale
31/5/98 FORD GREEN HALL
31/5/98 Tel: 01782 233195
Lots of plants and herbs for sale, including some unusual varieties, many at bargain prices. All proceeds go to the Hall's
17th century style period garden, 13.00-
16.30
Historic Houses

---

*The full information on the venues listed can be found in the main classified section under the
classification shown under the entry. Please mention Best Guides when calling or visiting.*

Triumph 75th Anniversary
31/5/98 HERITAGE MOTOR CENTRE
31/5/98 Tel: 01926 641188
More celebrations of another great British car marque.
Museum- Motor

750 Car Meeting
31/5/98 MALLORY PARK
31/5/98 Tel: 01455 842931
Please call for further information
Motor Racing Circuit

RAC Classic Car Run
31/5/98 SILVERSTONE CIRCUIT
31/5/98 Tel: 01327 857271
Please call for further information.
Motor Racing Circuit

Silverstone Rally Sprint
31/5/98 SILVERSTONE CIRCUIT
31/5/98 Tel: 01327 857271
Please call for further information.
Motor Racing Circuit

RAC Classic Car Run
31/5/98 STANFORD HALL
31/5/98 Tel: 01788 860250
Telephone 01788 860250 for more details
Historic Houses

Weekday Entertainment
1/6/98 WARWICK CASTLE
31/8/98 Tel: 01926 406600
Each weekday come and watch the medieval craftsmen demonstrate their skills. Meet the fletcher, the woodturner, the blacksmith to the potter at his wheel.
Castles

Go Wild with a Warden
5/6/98 WWT SLIMBRIDGE
5/6/98 Tel: 01453 890333 ext. 223
An early evening walk on the reserve with one of our expert wardens. A great opportunity to birdwatch and see other wildlife at Slimbridge. Time: 19.00 at the entrance. Cost: £5.50 (£3.50 WWT members) includes tea/coffee and biscuits
Wildlife Reserves

Bargain Weekend Two and Fireworks
5/6/98 BILLING AQUADROME LIMITED
7/6/98 Tel: 01604 408181
Tel 01604 408181 for more details
Country Leisure Parks

Landrover Workers C.C.
5/6/98 BILLING AQUADROME LIMITED
7/6/98 Tel: 01604 408181
Tel 01604 408181 for more details
Country Leisure Parks

Peugeot Talbot C.C.
5/6/98 BILLING AQUADROME LIMITED
7/6/98 Tel: 01604 408181
Tel 01604 408181 for more details
Country Leisure Parks

The C.C. Club Heron Way
5/6/98 BILLING AQUADROME LIMITED
7/6/98 Tel: 01604 408181
Tel 01604 408181 for more details
Country Leisure Parks

Music from the Movies
6/6/98 SHUGBOROUGH ESTATE
6/6/98 Tel: 01889 881388
Classic film music from 'Dr Zhivago' to 'James Bond,' 'Out of Africa' to 'Star Wars,' 'Pink Panther' to 'The Dam Busters.' Here is a chance to re-live treasured moments from films past and present: to be transported from the sandy, hoof-thundering plains of the wild west to the swashbuckling, romantic world do the secret agent; from the innovation of a hi-tech future back into the jaunty, carefree humour of the present. The evening is a magical mix of passion, fantasy and misty-eyed nostalgia with glorious technicoloured fireworks as the grand climax. Tickets A£16.50 C(5-18)£9.00. Ticket Hotline: 01625 56 00 00
Country Estates

Woodford Air Show
6/6/98 STOCKPORT TOURIST INFORMATION CENTRE
6/6/98 Tel: 0161 474 3320/1
British Aerospace Airfield, Woodford, nr Stockport, Cheshire. Organised by the Royal Air Forces Association and local charities. Gates open 09.00, with main flying programme from 13.00. Ground displays, trade stands and children's entertainment throughout the day. Further details on 01772 555862
Tourist Information Centres

Medieval Skirmish and Living History
6/6/98 ASHBY-DE-LA-ZOUCH CASTLE
7/6/98 Tel: 01530 413343
Visit a 15th century encampment, with men-at-arms, music and archery. From Noon. A£3.00 Concessions£2.30 C£1.50. EH Members Free
Castles

Steaming Weekend
6/6/98 ETRURIA INDUSTRIAL MUSEUM
7/6/98 Tel: 01782 287557
The 6th Etruria Canal Festival: Princess, an 1820s beam engine drives the original 1856 grinding machinery; a coal fired 1903 boiler supplies the steam. 13.00-16.30
Museum- Industrial

Famous Foes - Various Performers
KENILWORTH CASTLE
6/6/98
7/6/98
Tel: 01926 852078
Accompanied by their advisors and courtiers, antagonists from history come face to face to argue their claims to power and glory for posterity. Includes Richard III versus Henry VII and Elizabeth I and Mary with Queen of Scots. From 12.00. A£4.00 C£2.00 Concessions£3.00. EH Members Free
Castles

Grand Prix Weekend - Competition Ballooning Event
LUDLOW TOURIST INFORMATION CENTRE
6/6/98
7/6/98
Tel: 01584 875053
Venue: Ludlow C of E School, Brimfield Road, Ludlow, Shropshire. Organised by the Competitions Club section of the British Balloon and Airship Club. For further details please contact Neil Gabriel Tel: 01773 531551
Tourist Information Centres

Tudor Mercenaries
WARWICK CASTLE
6/6/98
7/6/98
Tel: 01926 406600
Let the Castle echo to the sounds of battle as you witness the clash of Tudor Mercenaries. See the colour and splendor of a 16th century mercenary camp from this unique chapter in history.
Castles

Midsummer Music
CLUMBER PARK
6/6/98
27/6/98
Tel: 01909 476592
Brass Bands and Concert Bands will perform in Clumber Turning Yard (near the shop) on most Saturday afternoons midsummer, call 10909 476592 for further details
Historic Houses & Gardens

Arbury Hall Transport Spectacular
ARBURY HALL
7/6/98
7/6/98
Tel: 01203 382804
Displays of cars, bikes, buses and agricultural vehicles
Historic Houses

Garden and Craft Fair
BOLSOVER CASTLE
7/6/98
7/6/98
Tel: 01246 823349
Enjoy demonstrations of traditional country crafts and visit a garden fair. From 11.00-17.00. A£3.00 Concessions£2.50 C£2.00 EH Members Free
Castles

Craft workshop and Concert
FORGE MILL NEEDLE MUSEUM
7/6/98
7/6/98
Tel: 01527 62509
Please call for further information
Museum- Mill

All Day Round Trip To Tewkesbury
GLOUCESTER LEISURE CRUISE
7/6/98
7/6/98
Tel: 01452 318054
Please see 5 April entry for details
Boat Trips

BRDC Club Meeting
MALLORY PARK
7/6/98
7/6/98
Tel: 01455 842931
Please call for further information.
Motor Racing Circuit

4th Teddy Bears' Picnic
PACKWOOD HOUSE
7/6/98
7/6/98
Tel: 01564 782024
Welcome children to Packwood for another special day of your very own; bring along your favourite Teddy Bear and join in the fun. Children's rides, entertainers - join the fourth Great Bear Hunt in the woods or follow the clues and hunt for tasty treasure. Why not make a funny mask and join in the parade (you may win a prize!), 13.00. Picnic in the Ladeside Meadow. Normal grounds admission. Free to children accompanied by Teddy Bears
Historic Houses & Gardens

Dovedale Top & Bottom
PEAK DISTRICT NATIONAL PARK
7/6/98
7/6/98
Tel: 01629 816200
Guided walk. Meet 09.30 at the footbridge above Dovedale main car park (OS Outdoor Leisure 24 SK146509). Strenuous walk, no dogs please. Call 01335 350503
National Parks

Donkey Day
SHUGBOROUGH ESTATE
7/6/98
7/6/98
Tel: 01889 881388
Venue: Shugborough Park Farm, see themed activities
Country Estates

Lea-Francis Owners Club Rally & Jaguar Enthusiasts Club - Midlands Day
STANFORD HALL
7/6/98
7/6/98
Tel: 01788 860250
Telephone 01788 860250 for more details
Historic Houses

Capri Car Club rally
THE BASS MUSEUM
7/6/98
7/6/98
Tel: 01283 511000
Please call for further details
Breweries

Estuary Walk - to celebrate World Oceans Day
WWT SLIMBRIDGE
7/6/98
7/6/98
Tel: 01453 890333 ext. 223
Explore our section of the Severn Estuary with a Warden. Find out why they are such valuable habitats - see some of the birds and other wildlife. Time: 19.00 at the entrance, £5.50 (£3.50 WWT members)
Wildlife Reserves

The full information on the venues listed can be found in the main classified section under the classification shown under the entry. Please mention Best Guides when calling or visiting.

Sunset Cruise
10/6/98 GLOUCESTER LEISURE CRUISE
10/6/98 Tel: 01452 318054
Sit back and relax with the beautiful view, 19.00-22.00
Boat Trips

'A Midsummer's Night Dream'
10/6/98 PAINSWICK ROCOCO GARDEN
10/6/98 Tel: 01452 813204
Performed to a limited audience of 100 - picnic first in the gardens. Please telephone for further information
Gardens

BBC Gardeners' World Live
10/6/98 NATIONAL EXHIBITION CENTRE
14/6/98 Tel: 0121 780 4141 x2604
Gardening showbiz meets the very best in horticulture at this fun and energetic show. As well as enjoying the imaginative Show Gardens, beautiful displays in the RHS Floral Marquee, and countless garden accessory stands, visitors have the opportunity to learn from their favourite gardening celebrities at BBC Gardeners' World Live. The BBC Gardeners' World Magazine Theatre is an exceptionally popular feature giving visitors a rare opportunity to hear from gardeners such as Alan Titchmarsh and Pippa Greenwood at first hand. Plants and gardening sundries are for sale and RHS members can relax in a exclusive refreshment area. Ticket booking: 0121 767 4505. Public: Advance 09.00-18.00 £11.50, on the gate £12.50, C(5-15)£5.00 C(0-5)£Free, Group tickets £10.00 must be booked in advance, one companion for blind visitors or wheelchair users admitted free, guide dogs only.
Exhibition Centres

American Auto Club
11/6/98 BILLING AQUADROME LIMITED
14/6/98 Tel: 01604 408181
Thousands of American Cars and lots of American entertainment. You will not believe your eyes - guaranteed!!
Country Leisure Parks

Alice Through the Looking Glass
11/6/98 CLUMBER PARK
14/6/98 Tel: 01909 476592
Dramatisation by English Playtour Theatre, call for further details
Historic Houses & Gardens

Art of Living - Decorative Arts Fair
11/6/98 EASTNOR CASTLE
14/6/98 Tel: 01531 633160
Plenty for all enthusiasts, call venue for further details
Castles

Glass Exhibition
12/6/98 THE FERRERS CENTRE FOR ARTS AND CRAFTS
9/8/98 Tel: 01332 865408
A contemporary glass exhibition with both blown and kiln formed pieces
Craft Galleries

Workshop: Plant Papers
13/6/98 DEAN HERITAGE CENTRE
13/6/98 Tel: 01594 822170
Make your own hand-made papers using local plants. Advance booking necessary. Open to adults and children. Please telephone for further information
Heritage Centres

Woodturning Spectacular
13/6/98 FULBECK HALL
13/6/98 Tel: 01400 272205
Woodturner demonstrations and trade stands 10.00-17.00 A£3.00
Historic Houses & Gardens

La Traviata
13/6/98 HOW CAPLE COURT GARDENS
13/6/98 Tel: 01989 740612
An evening performance of open air opera by 'Opera Box'
Gardens

Macbeth (Heartbreak Theatre)
13/6/98 ILAM PARK
13/6/98 Tel: 01335 350245/350503
Outdoor theatre performance in 'The Oaks' at Ilam Park. Booking essential
Country Parks

Macbeth
13/6/98 PEAK DISTRICT NATIONAL PARK
13/6/98 Tel: 01629 816200
Please call for further information.
National Parks

Wild Flowers - South Peak Estate
13/6/98 PEAK DISTRICT NATIONAL PARK
13/6/98 Tel: 01629 816200
Guided walk. Meet at 13.45 Hulme End Visitor Centre (OS Outdoor Leisure 24 SK104593). Easy walk, suitable for families and wheelchair users. No dogs please
National Parks

Afternoon of Scottish Country Dance
13/6/98 SHUGBOROUGH ESTATE
13/6/98 Tel: 01889 881388
A flavour of Scotland performed by the Royal Scottish Country Dance Society
Country Estates

Vintage Raceday - VSCC
13/6/98 SILVERSTONE CIRCUIT
13/6/98 Tel: 01327 857271
Please call for further information.
Motor Racing Circuit

The Association of Crown Forces and Hautbois - Ballads and Bayonets

13/6/98 BOSCOBEL HOUSE

14/6/98 Tel: 01902 850244

Music, Redcoat drill plus musket and cannon firing of the year 1776. From 12.00. Normal admission prices. EH Members Free

Historic Houses

British Touring Car Championship

13/6/98 DONINGTON COLLECTION OF GRAND PRIX RACING CARS

14/6/98 Tel: 01332 811027

Two rounds of the Auto Trader RAC championship.

Museum- Motor

The Castle Garrison

13/6/98 WARWICK CASTLE

14/6/98 Tel: 01926 406600

Witness the 15th century Knights, sworn to protect their Earl, in hand to hand combat, young masters and mistresses can join the knights as they train and drill.

Castles

The People's Show

13/6/98 ALFRED EAST ART GALLERY AND MANOR HOUSE MUSEUM

18/7/98 Tel: 01536 534381/534219

An exhibition of collections made by local people - ties, frogs, carrier bags, etc.

Art Galleries

Jim Malone: Artist Potter

13/6/98 BIRMINGHAM MUSEUM AND ART GALLERY

30/8/98 Tel: 0121 235 2834

This is the first major retrospective exhibition of work by Jim Malone, one of Britain's leading artist potters. His substantial body of work makes an important and innovative contribution to the ceramic and literary tradition associated with Bernard Leach. Acknowledging the influence of Korean, early Chinese and mediaeval English pots, Malone's work is centered on the production of high-fired stoneware, and unrefined raw materials

Museums

Children's Festival

14/6/98 ASHBY-DE-LA-ZOUCH CASTLE

14/6/98 Tel: 01530 413343

A great day out for children of all ages. From Noon. A£3.00 Concessions£2.50 C & EH Members Free

Castles

Bonsai Show

14/6/98 BIRMINGHAM BOTANICAL GARDENS AND GLASSHOUSES

14/6/98 Tel: 0121 454 1860

Exhibition, demonstrations and advice on this fascinating eastern art

Gardens- Botanical

Period Garden Tour

14/6/98 FORD GREEN HALL

14/6/98 Tel: 01782 233195

Please see 10 May entry for details

Historic House

Concert

14/6/98 FORGE MILL NEEDLE MUSEUM AND BORDESLEY ABBEY VISITOR CENTRE

14/6/98 Tel: 01527 62509

The Arrowvale Singers. Please call for further information

Museum- M

East Midlands Doll Fair

14/6/98 LAMPORT HALL AND GARDENS

14/6/98 Tel: 01604 686272

A wonderful Doll Fair with dolls houses and teddies - 'a miniature wonderland.' Top quality collectors, artists and craftspeople bring old and soft dolls, dollshouse dolls, miniatures, teddy bears, dollcraft materials, kits, magazines and juvenilia, 10.30-16.30, A£2.70 Student&OAPs£1.50 AccompaniedC£Free, refreshments and free parking

Historic Houses & Garden

Music Day

14/6/98 LEA GARDENS

14/6/98 Tel: 01629 534380

From 12.00 onwards a selection of acoustic music performed round the garden

Gardens

Post TT Classic:

14/6/98 MALLORY PARK

14/6/98 Tel: 01455 842931

Motorcycle Racing, call for details

Motor Racing Circuit

Aston Martin Owners Club Raceday

14/6/98 SILVERSTONE CIRCUIT

14/6/98 Tel: 01327 857271

Please call for further information.

Motor Racing Circuit

Alfa-Romeo Owners Club National Rally

14/6/98 STANFORD HALL

14/6/98 Tel: 01788 860250

Telephone 01788 860250 for more details

Historic Houses

RAF Cosford Open Day

14/6/98 THE AEROSPACE MUSEUM

14/6/98 Tel: 01902 374872/374112

Royal Airforce Cosford Air Show 1998: Call for further information

Museum- Aerospace

The full information on the venues listed can be found in the main classified section under the classification shown under the entry. Please mention Best Guides when calling or visiting.

A One Man Show with Eric Knowles

5/6/98
5/6/98
WEDGWOOD VISITOR CENTRE
Tel: 01782 204141/204218

As our "Friends of Blue" exhibition comes to a close, Eric Knowles, from the BBC Antiques Roadshow will hold a one-man show. There will also be valuation and book signing opportunities. Eric will be holding one hour sessions at 11.00 & 14.30 in the cinema. Ticket for the joint demonstration plus access to all the Visitor Centre facilities £4.50

Factory Tours and Shopping

Well Dressing

15/6/98
25/6/98
RIPLEY TOURIST INFORMATION CENTRE
Tel: 01773 841488/6

The traditional Derbyshire Custom of Well Dressing takes place with everyone welcome to come along and join the race against time to complete the work or watch how this dressing is created. 15-18 June: 10.00-12.00, 14.00-16.00. Blessing Ceremony is on 19 June at 14.30. Display remains until 25 June

Tourist Information Centres

Brunel Broderers present 'Stretching the Boundaries'

15/6/98
5/7/98
CORINIUM MUSEUM
Tel: 01285 655611

An exhibition of contemporary Textile Art. The Brunel Broderers was formed in 1990 by a group of nine local artists. Members work in a variety of textile media, exploring the bounds a craft traditionally called 'embroidery.' This promises to be a richly coloured exhibition. There will be demonstrations by the artists to accompany the exhibition. This exhibition will have works for sale

Museum- Roman

Ecumenical Church Service

17/6/98
FORGE MILL NEEDLE MUSEUM AND BORDESLEY ABBEY VISITOR CENTRE

17/6/98
Tel: 01527 62509

Please call for further information

Museum- Mill

Sunset Cruise

17/6/98
17/6/98
GLOUCESTER LEISURE CRUISE
Tel: 01452 318054

Sit back and relax with the beautiful view, 19.00-22.00

Boat Trips

All Day Round Trip To Tewkesbury

19/6/98
19/6/98
GLOUCESTER LEISURE CRUISE
Tel: 01452 318054

Please see 5 April entry for details

Boat Trips

MCN British Superbike Championship

19/6/98
21/6/98
DONINGTON COLLECTION OF GRAND PRIX RACING CARS
Tel: 01332 811027

Two rounds of this series with a full support programme.

Museum- Motor

Toad of Toad Hall

20/6/98
20/6/98
CALKE ABBEY
Tel: 01332 863822

Troubadour Theatre open-air performance from Kenneth Grahame's Wind in the Willows. Commences 18.30. Bring rugs and picnics, call for further details

Historic Houses & Gardens

All Day Round Trip To Sharpness

20/6/98
20/6/98
GLOUCESTER LEISURE CRUISE
Tel: 01452 318054

Please see 18 April entry for details

Boat Trips

Antony & Cleopatra

20/6/98
20/6/98
KENILWORTH CASTLE
Tel: 01926 852078

Shakespeare's classic presented by Theatre Set Up. Please bring a picnic rug or folding chair. From May advance booking available, call 01926 855784 £7.50/£6.50 including EH members/£5.50. Tickets also available on the night. Starts at 19.30

Castles

Guided Walk

20/6/98
20/6/98
PEAK DISTRICT NATIONAL PARK
Tel: 01629 816200

Ilam to Wetton. Meet 10.00 in front of Ilam Hall. (OS Outdoor Leisure 24 SK132507). Strenuous 10 miles walk. Bring a packed lunch, no dogs please

National Parks

Rolls Royce Car Rally

20/6/98
20/6/98
THE BASS MUSEUM
Tel: 01283 511000

Please call for further details

Breweries

Have-a-go-Archery

20/6/98
21/6/98
ASHBY-DE-LA-ZOUCH CASTLE
Tel: 01530 413343

14th century archers introduce visitors to the art of archery. From Noon. A£2.50 Concessions£1.90 C£1.30. EH Members Free

Castles

American Motorhome

20/6/98
21/6/98
BILLING AQUADROME LIMITED
Tel: 01604 408181

Tel 01604 408181 for more details

Country Leisure Parks

Chatsworth Flower And Garden Show
20/6/98 CHATSWORTH
21/6/98 Tel: 01246 582204/565300
A truly fabulous two day event, the colour, the scents and the family enjoyment, not to be missed
Historic Houses & Gardens

Patchwork Demonstration
20/6/98 COTSWOLD COUNTRYSIDE COLLECTION
21/6/98 Tel: 01451 860715
Please telephone for further information
Museum- Local History

Fibrecraft Demonstration and Fleece Sale
20/6/98 COTSWOLD FARM PARK
21/6/98 Tel: 01451 850307
All our rare breeds and coloured fleeces will be available for sale. Find out about spinning, weaving, felting and dying
Farm Parks

The Lion Rampant
20/6/98 KENILWORTH CASTLE
21/6/98 Tel: 01926 852078
Music, dance and archery from 12.00 with drama and combat from 14.30. A£4.00 C£2.00 Concessions£3.00
Castles

Craft Fair
20/6/98 ROCKINGHAM CASTLE
21/6/98 Tel: 01536 770240
Please call for further information.
Castles

Tresham Trail Guided Tours
20/6/98 RUSHTON TRIANGULAR LODGE
21/6/98 Tel: 01536 710761
Guided tours around the most unusual building in the country. Normal admission price, EH Members Free
Historic Houses

Organic Gardening Weekend
20/6/98 RYTON ORGANIC GARDENS
21/6/98 Tel: 01203 303517
Over 70 organic gardens open to the public nationwide call for further details
Gardens

MG Car Club Race Meeting
20/6/98 SILVERSTONE CIRCUIT
21/6/98 Tel: 01327 857271
Please call for further information.
Motor Racing Circuit

Medieval Living History
20/6/98 STOKESAY CASTLE
21/6/98 Tel: 01588 672544
15th century life recreated with household duties and crafts by this highly authentic group. From 12.00. A£3.50 C£1.80 Concessions£2.50. EH Members Free
Castles

A Royal Victorian Weekend
20/6/98 WARWICK CASTLE
21/6/98 Tel: 01926 406600
Relive life at the Castle during its most elegant period. Be entertained by Victorian musicians and soldiers on parade. Meet the Victorian policeman and surgeon and discover the elegance and diversity of the Victorian era.
Castles

Telford Model Air Show
20/6/98 WESTON PARK
21/6/98 Tel: 01952 850207
Model aircraft displays at their best plus family and children's entertainment
Historic Houses & Gardens

D-Day Battles
20/6/98 WITLEY COURT
21/6/98 Tel: 01299 896636
Starting at 12.00 presented by the WWII Living History Association. Allied and axis troops from D-Day 1944, living history encampments, military vehicles, uniforms, weapons displays, with battle at 15.00. The Longest Day on the longest day! A£3.50 C£1.80 Concessions£2.50. EH Members Free
Historic Houses & Gardens

Fathers Day Special
21/6/98 BLACK COUNTRY LIVING MUSEUM
21/6/98 Tel: 0121 557 9643
Please telephone for further information
Industrial Heritage

'Playthings Past'
21/6/98 FORD GREEN HALL
21/6/98 Tel: 01782 233195
From 'Devil Among the Tailors' to Shovelboard and Tipcat, this is an opportunity for adults and children alike to try out a range of 17th century style toys and games, 13.00-16.30
Historic Houses

'An Elizabethan Enchantment'
21/6/98 FORD GREEN HALL
21/6/98 Tel: 01782 233195
An afternoon of outdoor theatre, music and food, on a Tudor theme. The Shakespeare in Education Theatre Company will perform a selected series of scenes from 'A Midsummer Night's Dream.' In the intervals between, period refreshments will be available, accompanied by live music from the Tudor age, 13.00-16.30. Please note that there is no cover in the event of rain, and seating is not provided. However, visitors are welcome to bring their own blanket or chairs
Historic Houses

Concert and Celebration Day
21/6/98 FORGE MILL NEEDLE MUSEUM AND
BORDESLEY ABBEY VISITOR CENTRE
21/6/98 Tel: 01527 62509
Folk Group Concert

Museum- Mill

BMC Marque Day
21/6/98 HERITAGE MOTOR CENTRE
21/6/98 Tel: 01926 641188
Call for more information.

Museum- Motor

BRSCC Club Meeting
21/6/98 MALLORY PARK
21/6/98 Tel: 01455 842931
Please call for further information

Motor Racing Circuit

Ashes Farm Family Day - High Peak Estate
21/6/98 PEAK DISTRICT NATIONAL PARK
21/6/98 Tel: 01629 816200
11.00-16.00. Children's activities, displays, demonstrations, hill farming, hay meadows, animals. Refreshments. Transport provided to and from Ashes Farm from Fairholmes visitor centre. Free admission and transport. Call 01433 670368

National Parks

Medieval Archery
21/6/98 PEVERIL CASTLE
21/6/98 Tel: 01433 620613
See May 17 for details

Castles

Music from the Movies with Fireworks
21/6/98 RAGLEY HALL
21/6/98 Tel: 01789 762090
Classic film music from 'Dr. Zhivago' to 'James Bond,' 'Out of Africa' to 'Star Wars,' 'Pink Panther' to 'The Dam Busters.' Here is a chance to re-live treasured moments from films past and present: to be transported from the sandy, hoof-thundering plains of the wild west to the swashbuckling, romantic world do the secret agent; from the innovation of a hi-tech future back into the jaunty, carefree humour of the present. The evening is a magical mix of passion, fantasy and misty-eyed nostalgia with glorious techni-coloured fireworks as the grand climax. Tickets A£16.50 C(5-18)£9.00. Ticket Hotline: 01625 56 00 00

Historic Houses & Gardens

All About Pigs
21/6/98 SHUGBOROUGH ESTATE
21/6/98 Tel: 01889 881388
at Shugborough Park Farm, see themed activities

Country Estates

Children's Literary Day
21/6/98 SHUGBOROUGH ESTATE
21/6/98 Tel: 01889 881388
A fun-filled day incorporating storybook characters, theatre, poetry and prose. Enjoy themed competitions and children's entertainment in the County Museum

Country Estates

Ford AVO Owners Club Rally
21/6/98 STANFORD HALL
21/6/98 Tel: 01788 860250
Telephone 01788 860250 for more details

Historic Houses

Fathers Day
21/6/98 THE BASS MUSEUM
21/6/98 Tel: 01283 511000
This time treat Dad to Sunday lunch in the Museum, as well as a superb meal there will be entertainment and a gift for Dad

Breweries

Alvis Register Club Rally
21/6/98 THE BASS MUSEUM
21/6/98 Tel: 01283 511000
Between 40-50 cars on show

Breweries

Tea Cruise
22/6/98 GLOUCESTER LEISURE CRUISE
22/6/98 Tel: 01452 318054
Enjoy tea on the river, 15.00-17.00

Boat Trips

Big Five Jelly Challenge
22/6/98 ALTON TOWERS
26/6/98 Tel: 0990 204060 24hr
A celebration of Alton Towers' biggest, most terrifying white knuckle rides - including the worlds most eagerly-anticipated ride, code named SW4. And if you can ride all five without turning to jelly, you can walk off with a special commemorative Alton Towers T-shirt - if your legs will let you! (Height restrictions apply)

Theme Parks

William Blake and His Circle
22/6/98 BIRMINGHAM MUSEUM AND ART GALLERY
6/9/98 Tel: 0121 235 2834
Better known as a poet, William Blake made a major contribution to early 19th century British art, particularly in the interpretation of poetry. Paintings like 'The Circle of the Lustful' moved away from mere illustration to a more symbolic interpretation of the subject matter. This exhibition investigates the artistic relationships between Blake and his contemporaries, most notably Henry Fusell and Samuel Palmer

Museums

For regular special events updates throughout the year and to leave your comments and suggestions dial into our on-line Internet site on www.thisislondon.com

Sunset Cruise

24/6/98 GLOUCESTER LEISURE CRUISE
24/6/98 Tel: 01452 318054

Sit back and relax with the beautiful view, 19.00-22.00

Boat Trips

Spectacular Music Festival

24/6/98 QUARRY BANK MILL AND STYAL COUNTRY PARK
28/6/98 Tel: 01625 527468

Evenings: 24th - Opera, 25th - Big Band Concert, 26th - MacKenzie concert with The Northern Chamber Orchestra followed by dinner, 27th - Jazz Concert. Afternoons: 27th - "Phil's Big top" Children's entertainment day with the BBC Philharmonic, circus tent musical shows throughout the day, facepainting and other family fun activities, 28th - Brass Band Concert. Please telephone for further information

Heritage Centres

Dusk Wildlife Walk - High Peak Estate

25/6/98 PEAK DISTRICT NATIONAL PARK
25/6/98 Tel: 01629 816200

Through Blackley Hay Wood. Meet 19.00 at Hagg Water Bridge, River Ashop (grid ref 163885). A£1.00 C£Free. No dogs please. Call 01433 670368

National Parks

Creda Cooking with Wedgwood

25/6/98 WEDGWOOD VISITOR CENTRE
25/6/98 Tel: 01782 204141/204218

11.00 - Summer Delights Cookery demonstration with Creda and at 14.00 - Flower arranging demonstration. Admission to both demonstrations and access to the Visitor Centre £4.50

Factory Tours and Shopping

Opera Brava: Gala

26/6/98 BADDESLEY CLINTON HOUSE
26/6/98 Tel: 01564 783294

Popular pieces al fresco including Gilbert and Sullivan highlights. Gates open 18.00, performance 19.30, £13.00 in advance, £15.00 at the door (for tickets please send a cheque payable to 'National Trust (Enterprises)' and s.a.e. to the property

Historic Houses & Gardens

Disco Cruise

26/6/98 GLOUCESTER LEISURE CRUISE
26/6/98 Tel: 01452 318054

Come and have a bop on the water, 20.00-24.00

Boat Trips

Opera Brava: Barber of Seville

27/6/98 BADDESLEY CLINTON HOUSE
27/6/98 Tel: 01564 783294

Rossini's best-loved comic opera performed al fresco. Gates open 18.00, performance 19.30, £13.00 in advance, £15.00 at the door (for tickets please send a cheque payable to 'National Trust (Enterprises)' and s.a.e. to the property

Historic Houses & Gardens

Alice in Wonderland Quest

27/6/98 CALKE ABBEY
27/6/98 Tel: 01332 863822

An animated trails for children, with plenty of family fun. 11.00-16.00. Call for further details

Historic Houses & Gardens

Concert with Bromyard Windband

27/6/98 LOWER BROCKHAMPTON
27/6/98 Tel: 01885 488099

With bonne mouche of glass of wine / real lemonade and dish of summer fruits and cream during interval. Gates open 18.00, performance 19.30. Tickets £6.00, for tickets please send a cheque payable to 'National Trust (Enterprises)' and s.a.e. to the property

Historic Houses

Evening of Entertainment

27/6/98 PAINSWICK ROCOCO GARDEN
27/6/98 Tel: 01452 813204

An evening of entertainment arranged for the whole family whilst picnicking in the gardens

Gardens

Battle

27/6/98 SNIBSTON DISCOVERY PARK
27/6/98 Tel: 01530 510851/813256

Pavanne bring your a spectacular traditional Irish dance musical starring Kelly May Grew, champion Irish dancer (formerly of Riverdance). A gripping storyline and fabulous dancing tell the tale of a young Irish dancer and her battle through life. The performance will be held in the Centry Theatre. Doors open 19.00, performance 19.30-22.00. Ticket prices A£6.50 Concessions£5.50 available from Coalville Tourist Information Centre 01530 813608 from May '98

Industrial Heritage

Rushden Mini Steam Enthusiasts

27/6/98 BILLING AQUADROME LIMITED
28/6/98 Tel: 01604 408181

Tel 01604 408181 for more details

Country Leisure Parks

The full information on the venues listed can be found in the main classified section under the classification shown under the entry. Please mention Best Guides when calling or visiting.

Medieval Music, Calligraphy and Spinning

27/6/98
28/6/98
BUILDWAS ABBEY
Tel: 01952 433274
Fascinating medieval crafts and lively medieval music, as part of Cistercian 900. From 12.00. A£3.00 C£1.50 Concessions£2.30 EH Members Free

Historical Remains

Jaguar XK 50th Anniversary

27/6/98
DONINGTON COLLECTION OF GRAND PRIX RACING CARS
28/6/98
Tel: 01332 811027
Two days of nostalgia, call for full information.

Museum- Motor

Tudor Dance - Twelfth Night of Ottawa

27/6/98
28/6/98
KENILWORTH CASTLE
Tel: 01926 852078
Dancers in colourful 16th century costumes perform dances from the Elizabethan Court, in a special appearance by this group from Canada. From 12.00. A£3.50 C£1.80 Concessions£2.50. EH Members Free

Castles

Large Birds of Prey

27/6/98
28/6/98
WARWICK CASTLE
Tel: 01926 406600
Witness the magnificent large birds of prey including Eagles and Vultures, as they swoop and fly around the Castle ramparts.

Castles

The National Hovercraft Championships

27/6/98
28/6/98
WESTON PARK
Tel: 01952 850207
A spectator sport event with plenty of action for the whole family to enjoy

Historic Houses & Gardens

Focus on Birds Weekend - Flamingos

27/6/98
28/6/98
WWT SLIMBRIDGE
Tel: 01453 890333 ext. 223
How do we keep them pink? What bit of them did the Romans eat? How do their bills work? Find out this weekend. Meet at 11.00 or 14.00 at the Andean and James' Flamingo House - no need to book

Wildlife Reserves

Justin Capp and Carry Akroyd - 'Feared and Revered'

27/6/98
26/7/98
CENTRAL MUSEUM AND ART GALLERY
Tel: 01604 39415
The exhibition will mix art and craft, leather masks and sculptures by Justin Capp, paintings and artist's prints by Carry Akroyd. Both are established artists

Art Galleries

"The Cotswolds in Watercolours"

27/6/98
26/7/98
COTSWOLD COUNTRYSIDE COLLECTION
Tel: 01451 860715
In the Reception Gallery a selection of original watercolour paintings and prints by Cheltenham artist Frederick Lea. There will be items for sale

Museum- Local History

British Tapestry

27/6/98
31/8/98
THE HARLEY GALLERY
Tel: 01909 501700
Call the gallery for more information.

Art Galleries

Open Air Concert

28/6/98
28/6/98
BELTON HOUSE
Tel: 01476 566116
East of England Orchestra play for your pleasure. Look forward to an evening of beautiful music. Gates open 17.00 for picnics, concert commences 20.00. Advance tickets A£15.00 C(5-16)£7.50. On the night A£17.00 C(5-16)£8.50. Call to book

Historic Houses

Medieval Jousting

28/6/98
28/6/98
BELVOIR CASTLE
Tel: 01476 870262
The Nottingham Jousting Association present their combination of timing, engaging humour and authentic action.

Castles

Children's Festival

28/6/98
28/6/98
BOLSOVER CASTLE
Tel: 01246 823349
A wonderful and unique day out for children of all ages. Theatre and puppet shows, storytelling, arts and crafts workshops and themed activities. Under 5's area. From 12.00. Free to children accompanied by an adult (one adult, max 5 children). A£3.00 Concessions£2.50

Castles

Sheep Dog Demonstrations

28/6/98
28/6/98
COTSWOLD FARM PARK
Tel: 01451 850307
One man and his dog

Farm Parks

Concert

28/6/98
FORGE MILL NEEDLE MUSEUM AND BORDESLEY ABBEY VISITOR CENTRE
Tel: 01527 62509
Please call for further information

Museum- Mill

Harlaxton Manor Open

28/6/98
28/6/98
HARLAXTON MANOR GARDENS
Tel: 01476 592101
The second of two special open days where the general public may visit Harlaxton Manor which is normally closed to public visits

Historic Houses & Gardens

Motorcycle - EMRA Club
28/6/98 MALLORY PARK
28/6/98 Tel: 01455 842931
ACU Road Race Championship
Motor Racing Circuit

Great Nottinghamshire Bike Ride
28/6/98 NOTTINGHAM TOURIST INFORMATION
CENTRE
28/6/98 Tel: 0115 915 55330
Annual fun cycle ride around
Nottinghamshire's prettiest countryside
with a choice of two routes. Call 0115 977
4374 for details.
Tourist Information Centres

Birds of Prey
28/6/98 PEVERIL CASTLE
28/6/98 Tel: 01433 620613
Birds of Prey on display and in flight. From
12.00. A£2.75 C£1.75 Concessions£2.00
EH Members Free
Castles

**Sandon Hall Classic Car and Transport
Show**
28/6/98 SANDON HALL
28/6/98 Tel: 01889 508004
Displays of cars, bikes, buses and agricultural vehicles from 1905 to the present
day
Historic Houses & Gardens

**American Civil War Society & Rover SDI
Club Rally**
28/6/98 STANFORD HALL
28/6/98 Tel: 01788 860250
Battle 15.00. Telephone 01788 860250 for
more details
Historic Houses

Folk Concert
30/6/98 SNOWSHILL MANOR
30/6/98 Tel: 01386 852410
An evening of folk music at 19.30. Please
telephone for further information and
prices
Historic Houses & Gardens

Sunset Cruise
1/7/98 GLOUCESTER LEISURE CRUISE
1/7/98 Tel: 01452 318054
Sit back and relax with the beautiful view,
19.00-22.00
Boat Trips

King Lear
1/7/98 CLUMBER PARK
4/7/98 Tel: 01909 476592
By William Shakespeare. Open-air theatre
from the Clumber Players, call for details
Historic Houses & Gardens

Liz and Rowan Yorath
1/7/98 ASHBY-DE-LA-ZOUCH CASTLE
31/7/98 Tel: 01530 413343
An exhibition
Castles

Diana's Final Resting Place
1/7/98 ALTHORP HOUSE AND PARK
30/8/98 Tel: 01604 592020 tickets
Open only from Diana, Princess of Wales'
birthday to the eve of the anniversary of
her death for those wishing to pay their
respects and view the £2 million project
by the Earl Spencer to commemorate his
sister's life
Historic Houses & Gardens

The Lichfield International Festival
2/7/98 LICHFIELD CATHEDRAL
12/7/98 Tel: 01543 306240
A simply superb Festival of Music and the
Arts - held in the Cathedral, catering for
all, from classical to jazz, from Mediaeval
Market to films, call for further details
Cathedrals

Ragrugmaking Demonstration
3/7/98 COTSWOLD COUNTRYSIDE COLLECTION
3/7/98 Tel: 01451 860715
Please telephone for further information
Museum- Local History

Johnny Coppin: "From Cotswold Edge"
3/7/98 SNOWSHILL MANOR
3/7/98 Tel: 01386 852410
Entertainment from 19.30. Please telephone for further information and prices
Historic Houses & Gardens

West Midlands C.C.C.
3/7/98 BILLING AQUADROME LIMITED
5/7/98 Tel: 01604 408181
Tel 01604 408181 for more details
Country Leisure Parks

Ford Cortina 1600E O.C.
3/7/98 BILLING AQUADROME LIMITED
5/7/98 Tel: 01604 408181
Tel 01604 408181 for more details
Country Leisure Parks

Ford Corsair O.C.
3/7/98 BILLING AQUADROME LIMITED
5/7/98 Tel: 01604 408181
Tel 01604 408181 for more details
Country Leisure Parks

British Motorcycle Grand Prix
3/7/98 DONINGTON COLLECTION OF GRAND PRIX
RACING CARS
5/7/98 Tel: 01332 811027
The biggest meeting of the year, fantastic
racing from a host of top international
stars.
Museum- Motor

Melrose Place Party
4/7/98 CASTLE BROMWICH HALL GARDENS
4/7/98 Tel: 0121 749 4100
The second event features more episode
screenings and exclusive merchandise
from the hit TV series
Gardens

---

*The full information on the venues listed can be found in the main classified section under the
classification shown under the entry. Please mention Best Guides when calling or visiting.*

All Day Round Trip To Tewkesbury
4/7/98
4/7/98
GLOUCESTER LEISURE CRUISE
Tel: 01452 318054
Please see 5 April entry for details
Boat Trips

Steaming Weekends
4/7/98
5/7/98
ETRURIA INDUSTRIAL MUSEUM
Tel: 01782 287557
Princess, an 1820s beam engine drives
the original 1856 grinding machinery; a
coal fired 1903 boiler supplies the steam.
13.00-16.30
Museum- Industrial

Garden Fair
4/7/98
5/7/98
FULBECK HALL
Tel: 01400 272205
Weekend Gala with plants for sale, accessories and demonstrations.
Historic Houses & Gardens

"The Cannonball"
4/7/98
5/7/98
SANTA POD RACEWAY
Tel: 01234 782828
Europe's largest funny Drag Car Racing
Festival
Motor Sports

1940's Weekend
4/7/98
5/7/98
SEVERN VALLEY RAILWAY
Tel: 01299 403816
The railway is dressed in wartime guise -
come in period costume!
Railways

Gardeners Weekend
4/7/98
5/7/98
SHUGBOROUGH ESTATE
Tel: 01889 881388
Shugborough hosts this fascinating
insight into the gardening world. Floral
displays, gardening exhibits, over 60 supportive craft stalls and experts on hand to
answer any horticultural queries
Country Estates

Grand Fireworks Concert
4/7/98
5/7/98
WARWICK CASTLE
Tel: 01926 406600
An evening of Anglo-American music performed by the world famous City of
Birmingham Symphony Orchestra, set in
grounds with a spectacular fireworks
finale. Evenings only and tickets must be
purchased in advance.
Castles

Knights Errant
4/7/98
5/7/98
WARWICK CASTLE
Tel: 01926 406600
Listen to the mediaeval storytellers as
they weave their tales of old and see the
13th century knight in combat. Watch the
large birds of prey swoop and fly above
the castle ramparts.
Castles

American Independence Weekend
4/7/98
5/7/98
WEDGWOOD VISITOR CENTRE
Tel: 01782 204141/204218
Entertainment for all the family with children's entertainers and live music. Try
your hand at the various skills on demonstration in the Visitor Centre. Normal
admission charges apply
Factory Tours and Shopping

English Civil War Re-enactment
4/7/98
5/7/98
WESTON PARK
Tel: 01952 850207
A battle re-enactment authentically performed in the woodland grounds
Historic Houses & Gardens

Young Images
4/7/98
2/8/98
CENTRAL MUSEUM AND ART GALLERY
Tel: 01604 39415
A visual arts exhibition by the
Northamptonshire Youth and Residential
Services
Art Galleries

Exhibition: The Only Way Is Up
4/7/98
27/9/98
DEAN HERITAGE CENTRE
Tel: 01594 822170
Exhibition exploring the life cycle of trees
in the Forest of Dean. Please telephone
for further information
Heritage Centres

Walsall Classic Car Show
5/7/98
5/7/98
BIRMINGHAM TOURIST INFORMATION
CENTRE
Tel: 0121 643 2514
Large display of classic cars at Walsall
Arboretum Extension, Walsall
Tourist Information Centres

Sheep Dog Demonstrations
5/7/98
5/7/98
COTSWOLD FARM PARK
Tel: 01451 850307
One man and his dog
Farm Parks

Craft Demonstration
5/7/98
5/7/98
FORGE MILL NEEDLE MUSEUM AND
BORDESLEY ABBEY VISITOR CENTRE
Tel: 01527 62509
Demonstration by Kingfisher Quilters
Museum- Mill

Aston Martin Club Meeting
5/7/98
5/7/98
MALLORY PARK
Tel: 01455 842931
Please call for further details
Motor Racing Circuit

Dovedale Skyline - South Peak Estate
5/7/98
5/7/98
PEAK DISTRICT NATIONAL PARK
Tel: 01629 816200
Guided Walk. Meet at 09.30 at the footbridge above Dovedale main car park. (OS
Outdoor Leisure 24 SK146509). Strenuous
walk, no dogs please. Call 01335 350503
National Parks

---

*For regular special events updates throughout the year and to leave your comments and
suggestions dial into our on-line Internet site on* **www.thisislondon.com**

Medieval Archery

5/7/98 PEVERIL CASTLE
5/7/98 Tel: 01433 620613
Please see May 17 for further details
Castles

Velocette Motorcycle Owners Club Rally

5/7/98 STANFORD HALL
5/7/98 Tel: 01788 860250
Telephone 01788 860250 for more details
Historic Houses

AC Owners Club Rally

5/7/98 STANFORD HALL
5/7/98 Tel: 01788 860250
Telephone 01788 860250 for more details
Historic Houses

Alvis Owners Club Rally

5/7/98 STANFORD HALL
5/7/98 Tel: 01788 860250
Telephone 01788 860250 for more details
Historic Houses

Noon Cruise

8/7/98 GLOUCESTER LEISURE CRUISE
8/7/98 Tel: 01452 318054
This longer cruise will take you north
towards Tewkesbury on the majestic River
Severn, past the old village of Ashleworth
and Wainlodes Hill, 11.30-14.30
Boat Trips

Sunset Cruise

8/7/98 GLOUCESTER LEISURE CRUISE
8/7/98 Tel: 01452 318054
Sit back and relax with the beautiful view,
19.00-22.00
Boat Trips

RAC British Grand Prix

9/7/98 SILVERSTONE CIRCUIT
12/7/98 Tel: 01327 857271
Please call for further information.
Motor Racing Circuit

Gamebore White Gold Cup

9/7/98 WESTON PARK
12/7/98 Tel: 01952 850207
Clay shooting annual International competition with very high standards of competitors
Historic Houses & Gardens

Shakespeare and Elizabethan Weekend

10/7/98 FULBECK HALL
12/7/98 Tel: 01400 272205
Performances of 'The Merry Wives of
Windsor' on Fri/Sat evenings and 'A
Midsummer Nights Dream' on Sun. Call
01400 272205 for details.
Historic Houses & Gardens

Folk and Food, Drink and Dance Festival

10/7/98 GRANTHAM TOURIST INFORMATION CENTRE
19/7/98 Tel: 01476 566444
Various locations, call the TIC for further
information
Tourist Information Centres

1970s Glam Rock

11/7/98 CLUMBER PARK
11/7/98 Tel: 01909 476592
An open-air concert with firework finale.
Featuring Showaddywaddy, The Glitter
Band and Bootleg Beach Boys. Gates
open 16.00 for 19.00 start. £15.00 in
advance, £17.00 on the day. Call Box
Office on 01909 511061 Mar-Apr Mon-Fri
09.00-17.00, May-end Aug Mon Fir 09.00-
17.30 Sat 09.00-15.00
Historic Houses & Gardens

20's Summer Follies

11/7/98 PACKWOOD HOUSE
11/7/98 Tel: 01564 782024
Sponsored by Ettington Park Hotel, a part
of Arcadian Hotels. An extravagant recreation of a dazzling 20's garden party as
once held by Graham Ash, Packwood's
last owner. Palm Court Theatre Orchestra,
Military Band, clowns, escapologist,
actors, jugglers, fire eater and Laurel and
Hardy will entertain you. Steam train
rides, vintage cars and cocktails available.
Fabulous fireworks across the lake and
dancing by candle light under the moon
and stars. Organise your Twenties costume, bring along your picnic hamper and
sufficient liquid refreshment, £20.00, for
tickets please send a cheque payable to
'National Trust (Enterprises)' and s.a.e. to
the property
Historic Houses & Gardens

Medieval Monastic Entertainers

11/7/98 BUILDWAS ABBEY
12/7/98 Tel: 01952 433274
Try your hand at calligraphy or authentic
period games as this popular duo take a
light-hearted look at monastic customs,
crafts and lifestyles. Learn about food
preparation, herbs and spice in cooking
and medicine, the mechanics of building
and lifting and may other skills. From
12.00. A£3.00 c£1.50 Concessions£2.30
EH Members Free
Historical Remains

Burton Regatta and Riverside Show

11/7/98 BURTON UPON TRENT TOURIST
INFORMATION CENTRE
12/7/98 Tel: 01283 516609
At Regatta Meadows off Watson Street.
Please call 01283 221333 for further infor-
mation
Tourist Information Centres

Gardeners Weekend

11/7/98 CASTLE BROMWICH HALL GARDENS
12/7/98 Tel: 0121 749 4100
Top nurseries from all over the Midlands
together for two days
Gardens

The full information on the venues listed can be found in the main classified section under the classification shown under the entry. Please mention Best Guides when calling or visiting.

Foxton Festival

11/7/98 FOXTON LOCKS CANAL MUSEUM
12/7/98 Tel: 0116 279 2285
Boat Trips, Stalls, Folk Singers, Morris Dancers, Boat Gathering etc.

Museum- Canal

Centenary of the Riley Car

11/7/98 HERITAGE MOTOR CENTRE
12/7/98 Tel: 01926 641188
Two days of Riley good fun!

Museum- Motor

Large Birds of Prey

11/7/98 WARWICK CASTLE
12/7/98 Tel: 01926 406600
Witness the magnificent large birds of prey including Eagles and Vultures, as they swoop and fly around the Castle ramparts.

Castles

Glevum Scribes Exhibition

11/7/98 CORINIUM MUSEUM
9/8/98 Tel: 01285 655611
A chance to see the work of the local calligraphy group, Glevum Scribes

Museum- Roman

The Open Air Art Exhibition

11/7/98 ABINGTON MUSEUM
16/8/98 Tel: 01604 31454
An annual event at the museum. The exhibition features paintings by local people, both amateur and professional. Free entry for all residents of Northamptonshire

Museum- Local History

One Man and His Dogs

12/7/98 ACTON SCOTT HISTORIC WORKING FARM
12/7/98 Tel: 01694 781306/7
Demonstration by local shepherd and his dogs. Usual admission prices. 11.00-16.00

Farms

Pygmy Goat Show

12/7/98 COTSWOLD FARM PARK
12/7/98 Tel: 01451 850307
Goats Galore!

Farm Parks

Period Garden Tour

12/7/98 FORD GREEN HALL
12/7/98 Tel: 01782 233195
Please see 10 May entry for details

Historic Houses

Country Fair

12/7/98 FORGE MILL NEEDLE MUSEUM AND BORDESLEY ABBEY VISITOR CENTRE
12/7/98 Tel: 01527 62509
Tea-room open

Museum- Mill

BBQ Cruise

12/7/98 GLOUCESTER LEISURE CRUISE
12/7/98 Tel: 01452 318054
Why not get a group together for an enjoyable trip with a difference. Take in the local scenery and view this historic part of Gloucester from the water, 17.30-21.30, £12.50 per head

Boat Trips

New Era Club Event

12/7/98 MALLORY PARK
12/7/98 Tel: 01455 842931
Please call for further information

Motor Racing Circuit

Vintage Vehicle Day

12/7/98 MIDDLETON HALL
12/7/98 Tel: 01827 283095
Vintage and classic vehicles and motor cycles. Live music from "Accord" singers and George Huxley Jazz Band. Time: 11.00-17.00

Historic Houses & Gardens

East Midlands Doll Fair

12/7/98 NOTTINGHAM TOURIST INFORMATION CENTRE
12/7/98 Tel: 0115 915 55330
Venue: The Dome Exhibition Hall & Conference Rooms, Kelham Hall, Nottinghamshire. A wonderful Doll Fair with dolls houses and teddies - 'a miniature wonderland.' Top quality collectors, artists and craftspeople bring old and soft dolls, dollshouse dolls, miniatures, teddy bears, dollcraft materials, kits, magazines and juvenilia, 10.30-16.30, A£2.90 Student&OAPs£1.50 AccompaniedC£Free

Tourist Information Centres

Sporting Escort Owners Club National Rally

12/7/98 STANFORD HALL
12/7/98 Tel: 01788 860250
Telephone 01788 860250 for more details

Historic Houses

Norton Rotary Enthusiasts Club Rally

12/7/98 STANFORD HALL
12/7/98 Tel: 01788 860250
Telephone 01788 860250 for more details

Historic Houses

Sunset Cruise

15/7/98 GLOUCESTER LEISURE CRUISE
15/7/98 Tel: 01452 318054
Sit back and relax with the beautiful view, 19.00-22.00

Boat Trips

Daily History

15/7/98	ALFRED EAST ART GALLERY AND MANOR HOUSE MUSEUM
1/9/98	Tel: 01536 534381/534219

From the 1st to the last day of the school summer holidays. History-based activities for visiting children. All events free, children must be accompanied by an adult.

Art Galleries

Land Rover Off Road Events

16/7/98	BILLING AQUADROME LIMITED
19/7/98	Tel: 01604 408181

Largest 4 x 4 show in Great Britain. Everything for the 4 x 4'er and his family. Tel 01604 408181 for more details

Country Leisure Parks

All Day Round Trip To Tewkesbury

17/7/98	GLOUCESTER LEISURE CRUISE
17/7/98	Tel: 01452 318054

Please see 5 April entry for details

Boat Trips

Hogarth's China Exhibition

17/7/98	WEDGWOOD VISITOR CENTRE
19/7/98	Tel: 01782 204141/204218

Official opening of the Hogarth's China exhibition with talks and book signing opportunities by Lars Tharp

Factory Tours and Shopping

Open Day

18/7/98	BELTON HOUSE
18/7/98	Tel: 01476 566116

Gardens are open today in aid of the National Gardens Scheme - proceeds will be given to the Scheme which helps to preserve and restore some of the finest gardens in the country

Historic Houses

Paint the Garden

18/7/98	CALKE ABBEY
18/7/98	Tel: 01332 863822

Small charge for materials. 11.00-17.30. Usual garden admission applies

Historic Houses & Gardens

Concert & Fireworks

18/7/98	KEDLESTON HALL AND PARK
18/7/98	Tel: 01332 842191

Spectacular outdoor Classical Concert with a splendid fireworks finale, call for times and prices

Historic Houses

Concert of Renaissance Music with Arden Consort

18/7/98	LOWER BROCKHAMPTON
18/7/98	Tel: 01885 488099

With bonne mouche of glass of wine / real lemonade and dish of summer fruits and cream during interval. Gates open 18.00, performance 19.30. Tickets £6.00, for tickets please send a cheque payable to 'National Trust (Enterprises)' and s.a.e. to the property

Historic Houses

Fireworks and Laser Symphony Concert

18/7/98	SHUGBOROUGH ESTATE
18/7/98	Tel: 01889 881388

Fireworks & Laser concerts are an irresistible summer cocktail. The piquant mixture is a blend of some of the best classical music ever written spiced with your mouth-watering picnics in the park and the whole topped by a liberal sprinkling of spectacle. It is delectable, exciting, satisfying and fun. Included in the programme this year are 'Light Cavalry Overtures' 'Skaters' Waltz' and Borodin's breathtaking 'Polovtsian Dances'...all with magnificent fireworks, brilliant lasers and whirling water fountains. Book early. Group bookings, with a discount of up to 20% for all concerts, can be made by reserving now and confirming final numbers at a later date. Tickets A£18.00 C(5-18)£9.00, Ticket Hotline: 01625 56 00 00

Country Estates

Balloon Nightfire Spectacular

18/7/98	WESTON PARK
18/7/98	Tel: 01952 850207

A wonderful display of glowing hot air balloons set to music with a firework finale

Historic Houses & Gardens

FIA International Sports Racing Series

18/7/98	DONINGTON COLLECTION OF GRAND PRIX RACING CARS
19/7/98	Tel: 01332 811027

The only chance to see these cars this year.

Museum- Motor

Medieval Living History

18/7/98	GOODRICH CASTLE
19/7/98	Tel: 01600 890538

15th century military and domestic life, with crafts, men-at-arms and period games. From 12.00. A£3.00 C£1.50 Concessions£2.30. EH Members Free

Castles

The full information on the venues listed can be found in the main classified section under the classification shown under the entry. Please mention Best Guides when calling or visiting.

Medieval Entertainers
18/7/98
19/7/98
HARDWICK OLD HALL
Tel: 01246 850431
Games, squire-training and talks on weaponry and armour. Also, try your hand at spinning, weaving and calligraphy and learn about herbal medicine. From 12.00. A£3.00 C£1.50 Concessions£2.30. EH Members Free

Historic Houses

Medieval Calligraphy and Spinning
18/7/98
19/7/98
HAUGHMOND ABBEY
Tel: 01743 709661
Step back in time to the 15th century and see how a clerk of minor orders went about his business! Authentic calligraphy, illuminating and book making skills are demonstrated, plus the use of an unusual spindle wheel. From 12.00. A£2.00 C£1.00 Concessions£1.50. EH Members Free

Historic Buildings

Have-A-Go-Archery
18/7/98
19/7/98
KENILWORTH CASTLE
Tel: 01926 852078
14th century archers introduce visitors to the art of archery. From 12.00. Normal admission price. EH Members Free

Castles

Tresham Trail Guided Tours
18/7/98
19/7/98
RUSHTON TRIANGULAR LODGE
Tel: 01536 710761
See 20-21 June for details

Historic Houses

Grand Prix Weekend - Competition Ballooning Event
18/7/98
19/7/98
STANFORD HALL
Tel: 01788 860250
Organised by the Competitions Club section of the British Balloon and Airship Club. For further details please contact Neil Gabriel Tel: 01773 531551

Historic Houses

Stories and Mask-Making
18/7/98
19/7/98
STOKESAY CASTLE
Tel: 01588 672544
Traditional folk tales, myths and legends, plus mask-making. From 12.00. Normal admission price. EH Members Free

Castles

Jousting Weekend
18/7/98
19/7/98
WARWICK CASTLE
Tel: 01926 406600
Discover the secrets of the tourney, as the jousting area resounds to the sounds of the battle, clash of steel and thunder of horses hooves as the mighty knights charge at full tilt.

Castles

Family Fun Day
19/7/98
19/7/98
BELTON HOUSE
Tel: 01476 566116
It's all planned and ready, all you have to do is turn up. Plenty for the whole family. Usual opening times and NO additional charges

Historic Houses

Gloucestershire Donkey Show
19/7/98
19/7/98
COTSWOLD FARM PARK
Tel: 01451 850307
Delightful donkeys of all shapes and sizes

Farm Parks

All Day Round Trip To Sharpness
19/7/98
19/7/98
GLOUCESTER LEISURE CRUISE
Tel: 01452 318054
Please see 18 April entry for details

Boat Trips

Supercar Sunday
19/7/98
19/7/98
HERITAGE MOTOR CENTRE
Tel: 01926 641188
Please call for more details.

Museum- Motor

VSCC Car Club Event
19/7/98
19/7/98
MALLORY PARK
Tel: 01455 842931
Please call for further information

Motor Racing Circuit

Mam Tour & the Winnats - High Peak Estate
19/7/98
19/7/98
PEAK DISTRICT NATIONAL PARK
Tel: 01629 816200
Guided Walk. Meet 10.00 in the main car park Castleton. 5 miles. A£2.00 C£Free. No dogs please. Call 01433 670368

National Parks

Early Birds - then Breakfast - High Peak Estate
19/7/98
19/7/98
PEAK DISTRICT NATIONAL PARK
Tel: 01629 816200
Early morning guided walk (2 hours) looking at the summer visitors to the High Peak. Meet 06.00 at Bowden Bridge car park (grid ref 048869). A£1.00 C£Free. Breakfast available from car park at end of walk. No dogs please. Call 01433 670368

National Parks

Macbeth
19/7/98
19/7/98
ROCKINGHAM CASTLE
Tel: 01536 770240
Please call for further information.

Castles

Goose Fair
19/7/98 SHUGBOROUGH ESTATE
19/7/98 Tel: 01889 881388
Witness a haphazard medley of riotous characters, entertainers and colourful market sellers, all the fun of the 1820 village fair at Shugborough Park Farm. Licensed bar and market stalls
Country Estates

Conservation Day
19/7/98 SNIBSTON DISCOVERY PARK
19/7/98 Tel: 01530 510851/813256
Join the Rangers for an informative and entertaining day which focuses on nature and rural crafts. There will be a large variety of displays by nature and conservation groups and demonstrations by crafts people. Attractions include falconry, Shire horses and ferret racing - a great day out for all the family. 10.00-16.00 in the Grange Nature Reserve
Industrial Heritage

Honda Motorcycle Classic Gathering
19/7/98 STANFORD HALL
19/7/98 Tel: 01788 860250
Telephone 01788 860250 for more details
Historic Houses

Balloon Festival
19/7/98 WESTON PARK
19/7/98 Tel: 01952 850207
Skydiving arena displays, aerobatics, hot air balloon displays. A full day of superb entertainment
Historic Houses & Gardens

Tea Cruise
20/7/98 GLOUCESTER LEISURE CRUISE
20/7/98 Tel: 01452 318054
Enjoy tea on the river, 15.00-17.00
Boat Trips

Summer Holiday Activities
20/7/98 FORGE MILL NEEDLE MUSEUM AND BORDESLEY ABBEY VISITOR CENTRE
6/8/98 Tel: 01527 62509
Please call for further information
Museum- Mill

'Taming of the Shrew'
21/7/98 PAINSWICK ROCOCO GARDEN
25/7/98 Tel: 01452 813204
Performed by the Gloucestershire Drama Association - covered seating, please telephone for further information
Gardens

Noon Cruise
22/7/98 GLOUCESTER LEISURE CRUISE
22/7/98 Tel: 01452 318054
Please see 8 July entry for details
Boat Trips

Sunset Cruise
22/7/98 GLOUCESTER LEISURE CRUISE
22/7/98 Tel: 01452 318054
Sit back and relax with the beautiful view, 19.00-22.00
Boat Trips

Macbeth
24/7/98 CALKE ABBEY
24/7/98 Tel: 01332 863822
An open-air performance given by Heartbreak Productions. Commences 19.30. Call for further details
Historic Houses & Gardens

Disco Cruise
24/7/98 GLOUCESTER LEISURE CRUISE
24/7/98 Tel: 01452 318054
Come and have a bop on the water, 20.00-24.00
Boat Trips

"Bug Jam '98"
24/7/98 SANTA POD RACEWAY
26/7/98 Tel: 01234 782828
Europe's biggest VW Beetle drag racing festival with hundreds of cars, side shows and four large music arenas with live bands and guest DJ's
Motor Sports

Coys International Historic Festival
24/7/98 SILVERSTONE CIRCUIT
26/7/98 Tel: 01327 857271
Please call for further information.
Motor Racing Circuit

Fireworks Concert 20.00
25/7/98 COUGHTON COURT
25/7/98 Tel: 01789 762435
Gates open at 17.30 for picnics, top class fireworks display, call for further details
Historic Houses & Gardens

An Evening with Col Lilburn's Dragoones
25/7/98 LOWER BROCKHAMPTON
25/7/98 Tel: 01885 488099
The Dragoones will demonstrate life for a small garrison. Bring a picnic to enjoy under the damson trees, 18.00. Tickets A£5.00 (up to 2 children with adults free)
Historic Houses

Herb Weekend
25/7/98 ACTON SCOTT HISTORIC WORKING FARM
26/7/98 Tel: 01694 781306/7
The Acton Scott Herb Garden, talks, herbs for sale, uses of herbs for medicinal and culinary purposes
Farms

The full information on the venues listed can be found in the main classified section under the classification shown under the entry. Please mention Best Guides when calling or visiting.

The Queen's Shilling
BOLSOVER CASTLE
25/7/98
26/7/98 Tel: 01246 823349
A colourful Recruiting Sergeant from 1897 will try to persuade you to join Queen Victoria's army. With rifle drill for children and adults and prizes for the best recruit! From Noon. A£3.00 Concessions£2.30 C£1.50. EH Members Free
Castles

National Archaeology Days
CHEDWORTH ROMAN VILLA
25/7/98
26/7/98 Tel: 01242 890256
Meet the Romans of LEGIO II living history society. Soldiers, ladies, servants, slaves reveal the details of life in Roman Britain. 3 "shows" daily. Plus mosaic workshop. £0.50 surcharge over entry including members (tickets on gate)
Roman Sites

Royal International Air Tattoo
25/7/98 CIRENCESTER TOURIST INFORMATION CENTRE
26/7/98 Tel: 01285 654180
Being held at RAF Fairford, The 1998 Theme is 80 years of the RAF. Tickets in advance A£19.50 on the day £24.00 C(0-15) £Free.
Tourist Information Centres

Model Wheelwrights Display
COTSWOLD COUNTRYSIDE COLLECTION
25/7/98
26/7/98 Tel: 01451 860715
Another chance to see the work of the Guild of Model Wheelwrights, making wagons in miniature
Museum- Local History

Medieval Music
GOODRICH CASTLE
25/7/98
26/7/98 Tel: 01600 890538
Enjoy melodies and dance tunes dating back to the 12th century. From 12.00
Castles

Open Air Plays - 'Twelfth Night'
25/7/98 HANBURY HALL
26/7/98 Tel: 01527 821214
Performance in the garden by the New Pilgrim Players. Bring picnics, rugs and chairs, 19.00. Tickets A£5.00 (A£6.00 on the gate), C£Free, for tickets please send a cheque payable to 'National Trust (Enterprises)' and s.a.e. to the property
Historic Houses & Gardens

The Bard and the Blade
25/7/98 KENILWORTH CASTLE
26/7/98 Tel: 01926 852078
Dramatic duels and dialogue from some of Shakespeare's most famous plays by Running Wolf Productions. From 12.00. A£3.50 C£1.80 Concessions£2.50.
Castles

Music from the Age of Elizabeth 1
LYDDINGTON BEDE HOUSE
25/7/98
26/7/98 Tel: 01572 822438
Lively 16th century music and song plus (safe) cannon game for children. At 14.30 and 15.30. A£3.00 C£1.50 Concessions£2.30. EH Members Free
Historic Houses

Tudor Players - Melford Hys Companie
STOKESAY CASTLE
25/7/98
26/7/98 Tel: 01588 672544
Elizabethan travelling players, period plays, juggling, archery practice and crafts. From 12.00. A£3.00 C£1.50 Concessions£2.30. EH Members Free
Castles

The Castle Garrison
WARWICK CASTLE
25/7/98
26/7/98 Tel: 01926 406600
Witness the 15th century Knights, sworn to protect their Earl, in hand to hand combat, young masters and mistresses can join the knights as they train and drill.
Castles

German Shepherd Dog Show
WESTON PARK
25/7/98
26/7/98 Tel: 01952 850207
Obedience, working dog trials, judged in classes. An interesting day out for the dog lover
Historic Houses & Gardens

Focus on Birds Weekend - Swans
WWT SLIMBRIDGE
25/7/98
26/7/98 Tel: 01453 890333 ext. 223
Meet some of the world's different kinds of swans today and hear some of the strange stories associated with them. Meet in the Peng Observatory at 11.00 or 14.00 - no need to book
Wildlife Reserves

Goose Games
WWT SLIMBRIDGE
25/7/98
30/8/98 Tel: 01453 890333 ext. 223
A selection of Summer Holiday Activities for all the family
Wildlife Reserves

Jousting
BELVOIR CASTLE
26/7/98
26/7/98 Tel: 01476 870262
The Nottingham Jousting Association present their combination of immaculate timing, engaging humour and authentic action.
Castles

Paint the Garden
CALKE ABBEY
26/7/98
26/7/98 Tel: 01332 863822
Small charge for materials. 11.00-17.30. Usual garden admission applies
Historic Houses & Gardens

26/7/98 26/7/98	**Harness Goat Driving and Workshop** COTSWOLD FARM PARK Tel: 01451 850307 A parade of harness goats pulling their purpose built vehicles *Farm Parks*

26/7/98 26/7/98	**Beaumanor Hall Classic Car and Transport Show** LEICESTER TOURIST INFORMATION CENTRE Tel: 0116 251 1301 Displays of cars, bikes, buses and agricultural vehicles from 1905 to the present day. Held at Beaumanor Hall, Woodhouse *Tourist Information Centres*

26/7/98 26/7/98	**Classic MCC Car Event** MALLORY PARK Tel: 01455 842931 Please call for further information *Motor Racing Circuit*

26/7/98 26/7/98	**Medieval Entertainments** PEVERIL CASTLE Tel: 01433 620613 Archery, dance and children's activities from 12.00 with mini 13th century tournament at 15.00. A£2.75 C£1.25 Concessions£2.00. EH Members Free *Castles*

26/7/98 26/7/98	**Vintage Motorcycle Club Founders Day Rally** STANFORD HALL Tel: 01788 860250 Telephone 01788 860250 for more details *Historic Houses*

27/7/98 27/7/98	**Teddy Bear's Picnic** SNOWSHILL MANOR Tel: 01386 852410 Bring your favourite Teddy Bear and your picnic hamper for a great afternoon out, 12.30-16.30. Ring Property Manager for details or see press *Historic Houses & Gardens*

28/7/98 28/7/98	**Children's Summer Holiday Activities Victorian Prison Day** COTSWOLD COUNTRYSIDE COLLECTION Tel: 01451 860715 Come and experience a day in the life of a prisoner in the museum formerly the Northleach House of Correction. Children get to dress up, make and eat gruel and take part in a courtroom play. For children aged 8-12 years, 10.30-14.30, £8.00 (10% discount with a Cotswold Museums Card) *Museum- Local History*

29/7/98 29/7/98	**National Gardens Scheme** CALKE ABBEY Tel: 01332 863822 Open day 11.00-17.00 *Historic Houses & Gardens*

29/7/98 29/7/98	**Paint the Garden** CALKE ABBEY Tel: 01332 863822 Small charge for materials. 11.00-17.30. Usual garden admission applies *Historic Houses & Gardens*

29/7/98 29/7/98	**Children's Summer Holiday Activities Victorian Day** COTSWOLD COUNTRYSIDE COLLECTION Tel: 01451 860715 Come and pretend to be a Victorian child for a day. Dress up as a Victorian child and have a go at some of the domestic duties such as buttermaking, washing and blackleading grates. For children aged 8-12 years, 10.30-14.30, £8.00 (10% discount with a Cotswold Museums Card) *Museum- Local History*

29/7/98 29/7/98	**Noon and Sunset Cruises** GLOUCESTER LEISURE CRUISE Tel: 01452 318054 11.30-14.30 & 19.00-22.00 *Boat Trips*

29/7/98 31/8/98	**Lift Off and Drag** JODRELL BANK SCIENCE CENTRE AND ARBORETUM Tel: 01477 571339 Space activities with Peter Williams. *Science Centres*

30/7/98 5/7/98	**Jabberwocky with Alice Through the Looking Glass** CALKE ABBEY Tel: 01332 863822 Playtour Theatre, open-air evening performance. Call 01302 751169 for further details *Historic Houses & Gardens*

30/7/98 30/7/98	**Children's Activity Day (ages 5-10)** ILAM PARK Tel: 01335 350245/350503 Various activities to suit children, £1.50 per child, booking essential *Country Parks*

30/7/98 30/7/98	**Children's Activity Day (5-10 years) - South Peak Estate** PEAK DISTRICT NATIONAL PARK Tel: 01629 816200 Various nature activities. C£1.50. Booking and details on 01335 350503 *National Parks*

31/7/98 2/8/98	**14th Annual Robin Hood Festival** SHERWOOD FOREST COUNTRY PARK AND VISITOR CENTRE Tel: 01623 823202 A weekend of medieval merriment in the home of the world's most famous outlaw. *Forest Visitor Centres*

The full information on the venues listed can be found in the main classified section under the classification shown under the entry. Please mention Best Guides when calling or visiting.

Granada MKI & MKII Drivers
BILLING AQUADROME LIMITED
31/7/98
3/8/98
Tel: 01604 408181
Tel 01604 408181 for more details
Country Leisure Parks

Summer Jazz Picnic
CHEDWORTH ROMAN VILLA
1/8/98
1/8/98
Tel: 01242 890256
You provide the picnic - we provide the music, with the mellow sounds of "Le Sept Tete." Picnics from 18.30, Band 19.30, Tickets A£6.00 C(0-14)£3.00, for tickets please send a cheque payable to 'National Trust (Enterprises)' and s.a.e. to the property
Roman Sites

Troubadour Theatre presents 'Toad of Toad Hall'
LOWER BROCKHAMPTON
1/8/98
1/8/98
Tel: 01885 488099
Gates open 17.30, performance 18.00. Tickets A£6.00 (up to 2 children with adults free) includes glass of wine / real lemonade
Historic Houses

Fireworks & Laser Symphony Concert
RAGLEY HALL
1/8/98
1/8/98
Tel: 01789 762090
Fireworks & Laser concerts are an irresistible summer cocktail. The piquant mixture is a blend of the best classical music spiced with your mouth-watering picnics in the park and topped by a liberal sprinkling of spectacle. It is delectable, exciting, satisfying and fun. Included in the programme this year are 'Light Cavalry Overtures' 'Skaters' Waltz' and Borodin's breathtaking 'Polovtsian Dances'...all with magnificent fireworks, brilliant lasers and whirling water fountains. Book early. Group bookings, with a discount of up to 20% for all concerts, can be made by reserving now and confirming final numbers at a later date. Tickets A£18.00 C(5-18)£9.00, Ticket Hotline: 01625 56 00 00
Historic Houses & Gardens

Murder at the Museum
SNIBSTON DISCOVERY PARK
1/8/98
1/8/98
Tel: 01530 510851/813256
Cynthia Starr, a top model in the 60s is murdered on New Year's Eve. But why? Was she killed for revenge, greed or love - or was it for more sinister reasons? Suspense, intrigue, comedy and acting of the highest order. Pavanne's 'Hint of Murder' Night challenges you to solve the mystery...A meal will be included in the ticket price. Telephone 01530 813608 for further details and tickets after May '98
Industrial Heritage

Toyota Enthusiasts Club
BILLING AQUADROME LIMITED
1/8/98
2/8/98
Tel: 01604 408181
Tel 01604 408181 for more details
Country Leisure Parks

Militaria Fair and Napoleonic Redcoats
BOLSOVER CASTLE
1/8/98
2/8/98
Tel: 01246 823349
Uniforms, medals and other original military items on sale. Plus Napoleonic redcoat drill and musket firing by the 45th Foot. From 12.00. A£4.00 Concessions£3.00 C£2.00. EH Members Free
Castles

Steaming Weekends
ETRURIA INDUSTRIAL MUSEUM
1/8/98
2/8/98
Tel: 01782 287557
Princess, an 1820s beam engine drives the original 1856 grinding machinery; a coal fired 1903 boiler supplies the steam. 13.00-16.30
Museum- Industrial

A Medieval Surgeon
GOODRICH CASTLE
1/8/98
2/8/98
Tel: 01600 890538
A fascinating and gruesome insight into 13th century medical care with presentations about cause, effect and treatment of wounds and everyday ailments. From 12.00. A£3.00 C£1.50 Concessions£2.30. EH Members Free
Castles

History in Action III
KIRBY HALL
1/8/98
2/8/98
Tel: 01536 203230
Enjoy the world's largest and best festival of multi-period living history and re-enactment. Bigger and better than ever, with an action-packed two-day programme featuring around 2000 participants from over 50 top societies including from Europe. Gates open 09.30, with major displays from 10.30-17.30. Includes historical craft market with over 50 stalls, children's activities, catering areas and ample free parking. 1 Day Ticket: A£8.00 C£4.00 Family Ticket £20.00 (A2+C2) Concessions£6.00 . 2 Day Ticket: A£14.00 C£7.00 Family Ticket £35.00 Concessions£10.50. EH Members Free
Historic Houses

Organic Gardening Weekend
RYTON ORGANIC GARDENS
1/8/98
2/8/98
Tel: 01203 303517
Over 70 organic gardens open to the public nationwide call for further details
Gardens

Medieval Entertainment - Merrie England
1/8/98
2/8/98
STOKESAY CASTLE
Tel: 01588 672544
Fighting knights, dancing, stories, children's games and juggling. From 12.00.
A£3.00 C£1.50 Concessions£2.30. EH Members Free

Castles

Jousting Weekend
1/8/98
2/8/98
WARWICK CASTLE
Tel: 01926 406600
Discover the secrets of the tourney, as the jousting area resounds to the sounds of the battle, the clash of steel and the thunder of horses hooves.

Castles

Exhibition
1/8/98
10/8/98
LICHFIELD CATHEDRAL
Tel: 01543 306240
Exhibition of work by Anne Crews

Cathedrals

Sculpture Show
1/8/98
31/8/98
CORINIUM MUSEUM
Tel: 01285 655611
In conjunction with Brewery Arts, please telephone for further information

Museum- Roman

"Pairs"
1/8/98
31/8/98
COTSWOLD COUNTRYSIDE COLLECTION
Tel: 01451 860715
In the Reception Gallery clay relief plaques hang on the wall inside, or in the garden. Pairs of people, animals and fish - entwined together! Work by Juliet Dyer. There will be items for sale

Museum- Local History

Dog Agility Finals
2/8/98
2/8/98
BILLING AQUADROME LIMITED
Tel: 01604 408181
Top 60 dogs and handlers compete for the ultimate championship

Country Leisure Parks

Craft Demonstration
2/8/98
FORGE MILL NEEDLE MUSEUM AND
BORDESLEY ABBEY VISITOR CENTRE
2/8/98
Tel: 01527 62509
Bobbin lace-making

Museum- Mill

All Day Round Trip To Tewkesbury & Sunset Cruises
2/8/98
2/8/98
GLOUCESTER LEISURE CRUISE
Tel: 01452 318054
10.00-17.00 & 19.00-22.00

Boat Trips

EMRA Motorcycle Club Event
2/8/98
2/8/98
MALLORY PARK
Tel: 01455 842931
Please call for further information

Motor Racing Circuit

Why do they burn heather? - High Peak Estate
2/8/98
2/8/98
PEAK DISTRICT NATIONAL PARK
Tel: 01629 816200
Guided Walk. Meet 13.00 at Fairholmes Visitor Centre, Derwent Valley. Finish at Strines Inn - transport back to Fairholmes. A£1.00 C£Free. Booking essential. No dogs please. Call 01433 670368

National Parks

Victorian Street Market
2/8/98
2/8/98
SHUGBOROUGH ESTATE
Tel: 01889 881388
All the colour and bustle of a traditional market as costumed merchants and street entertainers invite visitors to enjoy this most Victorian spectacle

Country Estates

Tea Cruise
3/8/98
3/8/98
GLOUCESTER LEISURE CRUISE
Tel: 01452 318054
Enjoy tea on the river, 15.00-17.00

Boat Trips

Basketmaking Demonstration
4/8/98
4/8/98
COTSWOLD COUNTRYSIDE COLLECTION
Tel: 01451 860715
Please telephone for further information

Museum- Local History

Children's Activity Afternoon
5/8/98
5/8/98
FORD GREEN HALL
Tel: 01782 233195
Creative 'drop-in' activities for children, 13.00-16.30. Please contact the Hall for further details

Historic Houses

Noon and Sunset Cruises
5/8/98
5/8/98
GLOUCESTER LEISURE CRUISE
Tel: 01452 318054
11.30-14.30 & 19.00-22.00

Boat Trips

Bakewell Show
5/8/98
6/8/98
DERBY TOURIST INFORMATION CENTRE
Tel: 01332 255802
Held at the Bakewell Showground this is a traditional agricultural show. Tel 01629 812736 for details.

Tourist Information Centres

Land Rover Safaris - South Peak Estate
6/8/98
6/8/98
PEAK DISTRICT NATIONAL PARK
Tel: 01629 816200
Accompany a National Trust warden patrolling Dovedale. 09.30 at Ilam Hall. A£2.00. Booking essential. Call 01335 350503

National Parks

The full information on the venues listed can be found in the main classified section under the classification shown under the entry. Please mention Best Guides when calling or visiting.

Creda Cooking With Wedgwood

6/8/98
6/8/98
WEDGWOOD VISITOR CENTRE
Tel: 01782 204141/204218
11.00 - Into Autumn Cookery demonstration with Creda and at 14.30 - Sugar Paste Cake Decorating. Admission to both demonstrations and access to the Visitor Centre £4.50

Factory Tours and Shopping

The NEC Antiques For Everyone Fair

6/8/98
9/8/98
NATIONAL EXHIBITION CENTRE
Tel: 0121 780 4141 x2604
A major event featuring 600 dealers exhibiting in a two-section event. 200 dealers offer antiques and fine art datelined to 1914 in plush, stand-fitted Section One; 400 dealers occupy unit-displays in Section Two, showing all things antique and collectable made prior to 1940. An enormous range of very fine quality antiques and collectibles for every pocket with prices from less than £10 to over £100,000. 25,000 visitors anticipated. Open Thur & Fri 11.00-20.00, Sat & Sun 11.00-18.00

Exhibition Centres

Mothing by Moonlight

7/8/98
7/8/98
WWT SLIMBRIDGE
Tel: 01453 890333 ext. 223
Join our moth expert to see what our (non-lethal) trap catches for you tonight. Slimbridge is home to an impressive variety of species so you could be in for a surprise. Includes tea/coffee and biscuits. Time: 21.30, £5.50 (£3.50 WWT members) at the entrance

Wildlife Reserves

Shakespeare in the Garden

8/8/98
8/8/98
BERRINGTON HALL
Tel: 01568 615721
Culture in the garden, A£7.00 C£4.00 (for tickets please send a cheque payable to 'National Trust (Enterprises)' and s.a.e. to the property. Please telephone for further information and times

Historic Houses & Gardens

Sharpness to Gloucester All Day Cruise

8/8/98
8/8/98
GLOUCESTER LEISURE CRUISE
Tel: 01452 318054
Please see 18 April entry for details

Boat Trips

Snake Path and Fairbrook - High Peak Estate

8/8/98
8/8/98
PEAK DISTRICT NATIONAL PARK
Tel: 01629 816200
Guided Walk. 10 miles. Meet 10.00 at Birchin Clough lay-by, A57 (grid ref 109915) A£2.00 C£Free. Bring a packed lunch, no dogs please. Call 01433 670368

National Parks

Bentley Drivers Club Raceday

8/8/98
8/8/98
SILVERSTONE CIRCUIT
Tel: 01327 857271
Please call for further information.

Motor Racing Circuit

The 1998 Music & Fireworks Spectacular

8/8/98
8/8/98
STANFORD HALL
Tel: 01788 860250
Telephone 01788 860250 for more details

Historic Houses

The Bard and the Blade

8/8/98
9/8/98
BOLSOVER CASTLE
Tel: 01246 823349
Dramatic duels and dialogue from some of Shakespeare's most famous plays

Castles

Fantastical Tales - Ancient Wisdom

8/8/98
9/8/98
GOODRICH CASTLE
Tel: 01600 890538
'The Cheese Wright of Cheltenham' is back and this time he's brought his friends! Prepare to be bedazzled as English Civil War era actors perform their very amusing play about 17th century space travel, savage duellists, love, hate, and of course cheese! Plus games and entertainments. A£3.50 C£1.80 Concessions£2.50. EH Members Free

Castles

Country Craft Festival

8/8/98
9/8/98
KENILWORTH CASTLE
Tel: 01926 852078
A country themed show with animal displays, including sheepdogs, sheep and geese, plus country craft stalls and demonstrations of crafts. From 12.00. A£3.50 C£1.80 Concessions£2.50. EH Members Free

Castles

Traditional Song

8/8/98
9/8/98
STOKESAY CASTLE
Tel: 01588 672544
A family of musicians performing delightful unaccompanied song. From 12.00. A£3.00 C£2.30 Concessions£1.50. EH Members Free

Castles

Large Birds of Prey

8/8/98
9/8/98
WARWICK CASTLE
Tel: 01926 406600
Witness the magnificent large birds of prey including Eagles and Vultures, as they swoop and fly around the Castle ramparts.

Castles

Philip Cox - 'My Best Friend'
ABINGTON MUSEUM
8/8/98
13/9/98
Tel: 01604 31454
An exhibition of life size, life like papier maché sculptures of people and animals
Museum- Local History

Summer Fayre
CANONS ASHBY HOUSE
9/8/98
9/8/98
Tel: 01327 860044
Enjoy the entertainment for the whole family at Canons Ashby Summer Fayre. Call for further details
Historic Houses

Fireworks & Laser Symphony Concert
CAPESTHORNE HALL
9/8/98
9/8/98
Tel: 01625 861221
Fireworks & Laser concerts are an irresistible summer cocktail. The piquant mixture is a blend of some of the best classical music ever written spiced with your mouth-watering picnics in the park and the whole topped by a liberal sprinkling of spectacle. It is delectable, exciting, satisfying and fun. Included in the programme this year are 'Light Cavalry Overtures' 'Skaters' Waltz' and Borodin's breathtaking 'Polovtsian Dances'...all with magnificent fireworks, brilliant lasers and whirling water fountains. Book early. Group bookings, with a discount of up to 20% for all concerts, can be made by reserving now and confirming final numbers at a later date. Tickets A£18.00 C(5-18)£9.00, Ticket Hotline: 01625 56 00 00
Historic Houses

Period Garden Tour
FORD GREEN HALL
9/8/98
9/8/98
Tel: 01782 233195
Please see 10 May entry for details
Historic Houses

Sunset Cruise
GLOUCESTER LEISURE CRUISE
9/8/98
9/8/98
Tel: 01452 318054
Sit back and relax with the beautiful view, 19.00-22.00
Boat Trips

MG Marque Day
HERITAGE MOTOR CENTRE
9/8/98
9/8/98
Tel: 01926 641188
Bring your real MG and join in the fun.
Museum- Motor

BARC Car Club Event
MALLORY PARK
9/8/98
9/8/98
Tel: 01455 842931
Please call for further information
Motor Racing Circuit

The Work of the National Trust
PEAK DISTRICT NATIONAL PARK
9/8/98
9/8/98
Tel: 01629 816200
In the Manifold Valley. Guided Walk. Meet 13.45 at trackside car park, Wetton Mill. (OS Outdoor Leisure 24 SK096561). Strenuous walk.
National Parks

Birds of Prey
PEVERIL CASTLE
9/8/98
9/8/98
Tel: 01433 620613
Please see 28 June for further details
Castles

Francis Barnett Motorcycle Owners Club Rally.
SHUGBOROUGH ESTATE
9/8/98
9/8/98
Tel: 01889 881388
Francis Barnett Motorcycle Owners Club Rally.
Country Estates

Francis Barnett Motorcycle Owners Club Rally
STANFORD HALL
9/8/98
9/8/98
Tel: 01788 860250
Telephone 01788 860250 for more details
Historic Houses

Triumph Sports 6 Owners Club Rally
STANFORD HALL
9/8/98
9/8/98
Tel: 01788 860250
Telephone 01788 860250 for more details
Historic Houses

Children's Activity Afternoon
FORD GREEN HALL
12/8/98
12/8/98
Tel: 01782 233195
Creative 'drop-in' activities for children, 13.00-16.30. Please contact the Hall for further details
Historic Houses

Noon and Sunset Cruises
GLOUCESTER LEISURE CRUISE
12/8/98
12/8/98
Tel: 01452 318054
11.30-14.30 & 19.00-22.00
Boat Trips

Teddy Bears Picnic
HANBURY HALL
12/8/98
12/8/98
Tel: 01527 821214
Bring your teddy and your picnic for an afternoon of fun, 14.00. Usual admission charges apply
Historic Houses & Gardens

Land Rover Safaris - South Peak Estate
PEAK DISTRICT NATIONAL PARK
13/8/98
13/8/98
Tel: 01629 816200
Accompany a National Trust warden patrolling Dovedale. 09.30 at Ilam Hall. A£2.00. Booking essential. Call 01335 350503
National Parks

The full information on the venues listed can be found in the main classified section under the classification shown under the entry. Please mention Best Guides when calling or visiting.

Classics in the House

13/8/98 WESTON PARK
14/8/98 Tel: 01952 850207

A selection of classical musical evenings performed in the magnificent house with Gourmet Dinner, call for times and prices

Historic Houses & Gardens

The Best of the West End

14/8/98 CALKE ABBEY
14/8/98 Tel: 01332 863822

Open air concert with a performance of songs form the most popular West End Musicals and a brilliant firework finale. Gates open 17.45. Performance starts 20.00. Tickets £15.00 in advance, £17.00 on the gate, £22.20 if both concerts booked together. Booking office 01909 511061

Historic Houses & Gardens

Noon Cruise

14/8/98 GLOUCESTER LEISURE CRUISE
14/8/98 Tel: 01452 318054

Please see 8 July entry for details

Boat Trips

Kids End of Summer Party

14/8/98 BILLING AQUADROME LIMITED
16/8/98 Tel: 01604 408181

Adult Entertainment in Marquee in evenings. Tel 01604 408181 for more details

Country Leisure Parks

Northampton Balloon Festival

14/8/98 NORTHAMPTON BALLOON FESTIVAL
16/8/98 Tel: 01604 238791

Over 200,000 people visited the 1997 festival making it one of the most successful ever held. Three days of Balloon glows, flights, fireworks and festival fun.

Balloon Festivals

Classical Spectacular

15/8/98 CALKE ABBEY
15/8/98 Tel: 01332 863822

Open air concert featuring The English National Orchestra with a grand firework finale. Gates open 17.45. Performance starts 20.00. Tickets £15.00 in advance, £17.00 on the gate, £22.50 if both concerts booked together. Booking office 01909 511061. House and gardens closed all day

Historic Houses & Gardens

All Day Round Trip to Sharpness

15/8/98 GLOUCESTER LEISURE CRUISE
15/8/98 Tel: 01452 318054

Please see 18 April entry for details

Boat Trips

Children's Nature Walk (ages 5-10)

15/8/98 ILAM PARK
15/8/98 Tel: 01335 350245/350503

A walk around the park on the look out for wildlife, and more. Booking essential, 50p per child

Country Parks

Children's Nature Walk (5-10 years) - South Peak Estate

15/8/98 PEAK DISTRICT NATIONAL PARK
15/8/98 Tel: 01629 816200

Lookout for wildlife. 14.00, £0.50 per child. Booking and details on 01335 350503

National Parks

Last Night Of The Proms

15/8/98 WESTON PARK
15/8/98 Tel: 01952 850207

An outdoor 'Proms' concert in traditional style with a spectacular firework finale

Historic Houses & Gardens

Horse Trials

15/8/98 BERRINGTON HALL
16/8/98 Tel: 01568 615721

£5.00 per car (tickets on gate). Please telephone for further information and times

Historic Houses & Gardens

Skulduggery!

15/8/98 BOLSOVER CASTLE
16/8/98 Tel: 01246 823349

Silly tales of secret maps, buried treasure and famous pirates. From 12.00. Normal admission price. EH Members Free

Castles

Time-Travelling Players

15/8/98 GOODRICH CASTLE
16/8/98 Tel: 01600 890538

Mythical and magical stories

Castles

Tudor Arms and Armour, Tunes and Toys

15/8/98 KENILWORTH CASTLE
16/8/98 Tel: 01926 852078

Fascinating arms and armour, with items to handle, music and traditional toy making. From 12.00. Normal admission price. EH Members Free

Castles

MCRCB Event

15/8/98 MALLORY PARK
16/8/98 Tel: 01455 842931

MCN British Superbike. Please call for further information

Motor Racing Circuit

Medieval Family Entertainers - Herce Ewe

15/8/98	STOKESAY CASTLE
16/8/98	Tel: 01588 672544

Games, have-a-go archery, costumes for children to try on and talks on weaponry. From 12.00. A£3.00 C£1.50 Concessions£2.30. EH Members Free

Castles

The History Man - Brian McNerney

15/8/98	WROXETER ROMAN CITY
16/8/98	Tel: 01743 761330

Enjoy unusual guided tours by the presenter of the BBC's ever popular History Man programmes. But be warned, his enthusiasm is notoriously contagious and there is no antidote! Performing without costumes, props or even a safety net, he brings the past to life before your very eyes! From 12.00. A£3.00 C£1.50 Concessions£2.30 EH Members Free

Roman Remains

Focus on Birds Weekend - Geese

15/8/98	WWT SLIMBRIDGE
16/8/98	Tel: 01453 890333 ext. 223

Which is a high altitude flyer? The ancestor of domesticated geese? The rarest or the smallest? Find out the answers to these and many more questions. Meet at 11.00 or 14.00 in the South Lake Observatory, no need to book

Wildlife Reserves

Rare Breeds Day

16/8/98	COTSWOLD COUNTRYSIDE COLLECTION
16/8/98	Tel: 01451 860715

An opportunity to see the work of the Rare Breeds Society and to meet some of the rare breeds in person

Museum- Local History

Ragrugmaking Demonstration

16/8/98	COTSWOLD COUNTRYSIDE COLLECTION
16/8/98	Tel: 01451 860715

Please telephone for further information

Museum- Local History

Gloucester Old Spot Pig Show

16/8/98	COTSWOLD FARM PARK
16/8/98	Tel: 01451 850307

Can you 'spot' the champion?

Farm Parks

Sunset Cruise

16/8/98	GLOUCESTER LEISURE CRUISE
16/8/98	Tel: 01452 318054

Sit back and relax with the beautiful view, 19.00-22.00

Boat Trips

Heather - Peak in Pink - High Peak Estate

16/8/98	PEAK DISTRICT NATIONAL PARK
16/8/98	Tel: 01629 816200

A guided walk, 7 miles, to look at the management of the High Peak moors. Meet 09.00 at Bowden Bridge car park (grid ref 048869). A£2.00 C£Free. Packed lunch required, no dogs please, Call 01433 670368

National Parks

Paint the Landscape - South Peak Estate

16/8/98	PEAK DISTRICT NATIONAL PARK
16/8/98	Tel: 01629 816200

In Ilam Park. Booking and further details on 01335 350503

National Parks

The Butterflies of Hall Dale - South Peak Estate

16/8/98	PEAK DISTRICT NATIONAL PARK
16/8/98	Tel: 01629 816200

Guided Walk. Meet 10.00 Ilam Park School Visitor Room (Park NT car park - OS Outdoor Leisure 24 SK132507). Strenuous, no dogs please, packed lunch required

National Parks

Medieval Archery

16/8/98	PEVERIL CASTLE
16/8/98	Tel: 01433 620613

Please see May 17 for details

Castles

Mid-Summer Stroll

16/8/98	SNIBSTON DISCOVERY PARK
16/8/98	Tel: 01530 510851/813256

Enjoy a guided afternoon walk from Snibston Discovery Park to Donington Manor House in the company of the Rangers and learn about the local area and the countryside. Finish off the day with a relaxing visit to the Manor House tea-room. Suitable for all ages. Advance booking only. Further details available on 01530 510851 after June '98

Industrial Heritage

Outdoor Popular Concert

16/8/98	WESTON PARK
16/8/98	Tel: 01952 850207

Outdoor Pop Concert - artiste to be announced, call for further information

Historic Houses & Gardens

Tea Cruise

17/8/98	GLOUCESTER LEISURE CRUISE
17/8/98	Tel: 01452 318054

Enjoy tea on the river, 15.00-17.00

Boat Trips

The full information on the venues listed can be found in the main classified section under the classification shown under the entry. Please mention Best Guides when calling or visiting.

Children's Activity Afternoon

19/8/98 FORD GREEN HALL
19/8/98 Tel: 01782 233195

Creative 'drop-in' activities for children, 13.00-16.30. Please contact the Hall for further details

Historic Houses

Noon and Sunset Cruises

19/8/98 GLOUCESTER LEISURE CRUISE
19/8/98 Tel: 01452 318054

11.30-14.30 & 19.00-22.00

Boat Trips

Land Rover Safaris - South Peak Estate

20/8/98 PEAK DISTRICT NATIONAL PARK
20/8/98 Tel: 01629 816200

Accompany a National Trust warden patrolling Dovedale. 09.30 at Ilam Hall. A£2.00. Booking essential. Call 01335 350503

National Parks

Ragrugmaking Demonstration

21/8/98 COTSWOLD COUNTRYSIDE COLLECTION
21/8/98 Tel: 01451 860715

Please telephone for further information

Museum- Local History

Alice in Wonderland

21/8/98 PACKWOOD HOUSE
21/8/98 Tel: 01564 782024

Performed by Ilyria at 19.30, A£8.00, reduction for children, for tickets please send a cheque payable to 'National Trust (Enterprises)' and s.a.e. to the property

Historic Houses & Gardens

Cheltenham Art Club Summer Exhibition

21/8/98 COTSWOLD COUNTRYSIDE COLLECTION
6/9/98 Tel: 01451 860715

The annual exhibition by members of the Cheltenham Art Club. There will be items for sale

Museum- Local History

Swinging 6oos

22/8/98 CLUMBER PARK
22/8/98 Tel: 01909 476592

An open-air concert with firework finale. Featuring The Searchers, The Tremeloes and The Bruvvers. Gates open 16.00 for 19.00 start. £15.00 in advance, £17.00 on the day. Call Box Office on 01909 511061 Mar-Apr Mon-Fri 09.00-17.00, May-end Aug Mon Fir 09.00-17.30 Sat 09.00-15.00

Historic Houses & Gardens

Orienteering for All

22/8/98 ILAM PARK
22/8/98 Tel: 01335 350245/350503

Bring the family to try a fun day of Orienteering in Ilam Park. £2.00 per person, booking essential

Country Parks

Taming of the Shrew

22/8/98 PACKWOOD HOUSE
22/8/98 Tel: 01564 782024

Performed by Ilyria at 19.30, A£8.00, reduction for children, for tickets please send a cheque payable to 'National Trust (Enterprises)' and s.a.e. to the property

Historic Houses & Gardens

Orienteering for All

22/8/98 PEAK DISTRICT NATIONAL PARK
22/8/98 Tel: 01629 816200

In Ilam Park. From 11.00 £2.00 per person. Booking and details on 01335 350503

National Parks

Last Night of the Proms with Firework Finale

22/8/98 SHUGBOROUGH ESTATE
22/8/98 Tel: 01889 881388

Proms Concerts have now established themselves firmly in the outdoor concert calendar, giving many of the audience a chance to return to a favourite venue for one final concert before the end of the summer. After last year's brilliant success, Jayne Carpenter once again leads the audience in the singing of 'Jerusalem' and 'Rule Britannia.' Rousing, singing, waving flags, terrific atmosphere and stunning fireworks all add up to a breathtaking finale, as the orchestra plays 'Land of Hope and Glory.' Proms concerts tend to sell out early: please reserve tickets in good time, especially group bookings. Tickets A£16.50 C(5-18)£9.00. Ticket Hotline: 01625 56 00 00

Country Estates

Mothing by Moonlight

22/8/98 WWT SLIMBRIDGE
22/8/98 Tel: 01453 890333 ext. 223

Join our moth expert to see what our (non-lethal) trap catches for you tonight. Slimbridge is home to an impressive variety of species so you could be in for a surprise. Includes tea/coffee and biscuits. Time: 21.30, £5.50 (£3.50 WWT members) at the entrance

Wildlife Reserves

Wynndebagge the Piper

22/8/98 BOLSOVER CASTLE
23/8/98 Tel: 01246 823349

Lively 17th century tunes on the English bagpipes and the chance to learn popular period dances. From 12.00. Normal admission prices, EH Members Free

Castles

The History Man
22/8/98 GOODRICH CASTLE
23/8/98 Tel: 01600 890538
Enjoy unusual guided tours by the presenter of the BBC's every popular History Man programmes, Brian McNerney. But be warned, his enthusiasm is notoriously contagious and there is no antidote! Performing without costumes, props or even a safety net, he brings the past to life before your very eyes! From 12.00. A£3.00 C£1.50 Concessions£2.30. EH Members Free
Castles

Medieval Entertainment
22/8/98 KENILWORTH CASTLE
23/8/98 Tel: 01926 852078
Fighting knights, dancing, stories, children's games and juggling. Normal admission price. From 12.00. EH Members Free
Castles

Tresham Trail Guided Tours
22/8/98 RUSHTON TRIANGULAR LODGE
23/8/98 Tel: 01536 710761
See 20-21 June for details
Historic Houses

Silverstone Summer Fest '98
22/8/98 SILVERSTONE CIRCUIT
23/8/98 Tel: 01327 857271
Please call for further information.
Motor Racing Circuit

Tudor Living History
22/8/98 STOKESAY CASTLE
23/8/98 Tel: 01588 672544
Enjoy Elizabethan entertainments including music, dance, song and games with the Tudors and Stuarts Living History Society. From 12.00. A£3.00 C£1.50 Concessions£2.30. EH Members Free
Castles

The Castle Garrison
22/8/98 WARWICK CASTLE
23/8/98 Tel: 01926 406600
Witness the 15th century Knights, sworn to protect their Earl, in hand to hand combat, young masters and mistresses can join the knights as they train and drill.
Castles

British National Ballooning Championship
22/8/98 LUDLOW TOURIST INFORMATION CENTRE
29/8/98 Tel: 01584 875053
Venue: Ludlow C of E School, Brimfield Road, Ludlow, Shropshire. Organised by the Competitions Club section of the British Balloon and Airship Club. For further details please contact Neil Gabriel Tel: 01773 531551
Tourist Information Centres

Finds from the Witham
22/8/98 GRANTHAM MUSEUM
21/11/98 Tel: 01476 568783
Archeological finds
Museum- Local History

Sunset Cruise
23/8/98 GLOUCESTER LEISURE CRUISE
23/8/98 Tel: 01452 318054
Sit back and relax with the beautiful view, 19.00-22.00
Boat Trips

Motorcycle New Era Event
23/8/98 MALLORY PARK
23/8/98 Tel: 01455 842931
Please call for further information
Motor Racing Circuit

Midlands Austin 7 Car Club Rally
23/8/98 STANFORD HALL
23/8/98 Tel: 01788 860250
A small gathering of about 60 Austin 7 cars which starts 11.00. Prizes awarded 16.00. Normal opening times and admission prices apply
Historic Houses

Salmons Tickford Enthusiasts Club Rally
23/8/98 STANFORD HALL
23/8/98 Tel: 01788 860250
Telephone 01788 860250 for more details
Historic Houses

Wader Walk
23/8/98 WWT SLIMBRIDGE
23/8/98 Tel: 01453 890333 ext. 223
A warden will help you get the very best views of waders passing through on their autumn migration. Time 08.00 at the entrance. £5.50 (£3.50 WWT members) includes tea/coffee and biscuits
Wildlife Reserves

Pony Club Championships
25/8/98 WESTON PARK
27/8/98 Tel: 01952 850207
Three days of Dressage, Showjumping and Cross Country for youngsters. A must for Equestrian lovers
Historic Houses & Gardens

Children's Activity Afternoon
26/8/98 FORD GREEN HALL
26/8/98 Tel: 01782 233195
Creative 'drop-in' activities for children, 13.00-16.30. Please contact the Hall for further details
Historic Houses

Noon and Sunset Cruises
26/8/98 GLOUCESTER LEISURE CRUISE
26/8/98 Tel: 01452 318054
11.30-14.30 & 19.00-22.00
Boat Trips

The full information on the venues listed can be found in the main classified section under the classification shown under the entry. Please mention Best Guides when calling or visiting.

Land Rover Safaris - South Peak Estate
27/8/98 PEAK DISTRICT NATIONAL PARK
27/8/98 Tel: 01629 816200
Accompany a National Trust warden patrolling Dovedale. 09.30 at Ilam Hall. A£2.00. Booking essential. Call 01335 350503

National Parks

Exhibition of Agricultural Bygones
29/8/98 COTSWOLD FARM PARK
31/8/98 Tel: 01451 850307
A chance to see a variety of old farming implements ranging from Milking Machines to Vintage Tractors, all in working order. Their owners will be on hand to explain all about them

Farm Parks

Woodland Weekend
29/8/98 DEAN HERITAGE CENTRE
31/8/98 Tel: 01594 822170
A celebration of modern and traditional woodland life including demonstrations of pole-lathe turning, bee keeping, basket making, charcoal making, displays of forestry machinery, guided walks and talks, and much more

Heritage Centres

Craft Show
29/8/98 KEDLESTON HALL AND PARK
31/8/98 Tel: 01332 842191
Working Craft Show in the park, fun for the whole family, call for further details

Historic Houses

Shugborough Summer Craft Festival
29/8/98 SHUGBOROUGH ESTATE
31/8/98 Tel: 01889 881388
A major craft show with something of interest for all the family. An excellent selection of contemporary crafts, with interesting demonstrations and skills on display

Country Estates

Bank Holiday Weekend Floral Displays
29/8/98 TAMWORTH CASTLE
31/8/98 Tel: 01827 63563
Beautiful fresh floral display throughout the Castle by Tamworth Flower Club

Castles

Mediaeval Festival
29/8/98 WARWICK CASTLE
31/8/98 Tel: 01926 406600
A melee of mediaeval combat and entertainment rounds off this summer's events over the Bank Holiday weekend. Champion your knight at the jousting contest, see the mediaeval craftsmen at work and watch as the birds of prey circle the Castle ramparts.

Castles

Bank Holiday Weekend
29/8/98 WEDGWOOD VISITOR CENTRE
31/8/98 Tel: 01782 204141/204218
Entertainment and fun for all the family. Try your hand at the various skills demonstrated in the Visitor Centre and make those special purchases in the shop and gift boutique

Factory Tours and Shopping

Picasso's Etchings
29/8/98 ALFRED EAST ART GALLERY AND MANOR
26/9/98 HOUSE MUSEUM
Tel: 01536 534381/534219
On a visit to the Alfred East Art Gallery as part of a National Tour.

Art Galleries

British F3 Championship
30/8/98 DONINGTON COLLECTION OF GRAND PRIX RACING CARS
Tel: 01332 811027
BRDC championship racing with a host of support races.

Museum- Motor

Sunset Cruise
30/8/98 GLOUCESTER LEISURE CRUISE
30/8/98 Tel: 01452 318054
Sit back and relax with the beautiful view, 19.00-22.00

Boat Trips

Paint The Landscape
30/8/98 ILAM PARK
30/8/98 Tel: 01335 350245/350503
Join a professional artist and try your hand at artwork in Ilam Park. Small charge for materials. Booking essential

Country Parks

Fete Champere
30/8/98 PAINSWICK ROCOCO GARDEN
30/8/98 Tel: 01452 813204
A day of 18th century music and theatre, please telephone for further information

Gardens

Sunset at Edale Cross - High Peak Estate
30/8/98 PEAK DISTRICT NATIONAL PARK
30/8/98 Tel: 01629 816200
An evening guide walk 4-5 miles, to the summit of an old packhorse route. Meet 19.00 at Bowden Bridge car park (grid ref 048869) A£2.00 C£free. No dogs please. Call 0433 670368

National Parks

Paint the Landscape
30/8/98 PEAK DISTRICT NATIONAL PARK
30/8/98 Tel: 01629 816200
Join a professional artist and create your own artwork if Ilam Park. Small charge for materials. Booking essential 01335 350503

National Parks

Medieval Murder Mystery - Knights in Battle

30/8/98 ASHBY-DE-LA-ZOUCH CASTLE
31/8/98 Tel: 01530 413343

A 'whodunnit' that enfolds as suspicion between two opposing factions grows. From Noon. A£3.00 Concessions£2.30 C£1.50 EH Members Free

Castles

The Fury of the Norsemen

30/8/98 BOLSOVER CASTLE
31/8/98 Tel: 01246 823349

From 12.00. Viking encampment and ferocious battle at 15.00. Normal admission prices. EH Members Free

Castles

The Fury of the Norsemen!

30/8/98 BOLSOVER CASTLE
31/8/98 Tel: 01246 823349

Living History and ferocious military action by The Vikings

Castles

Medieval Family Entertainers

30/8/98 BOSCOBEL HOUSE
31/8/98 Tel: 01902 850244

Games, have-a-go archery, costumes for children to try on and talks on weaponry. Normal admission price. Members Free

Historic Houses

August Bank Holiday Frolics

30/8/98 BROADFIELD HOUSE GLASS MUSEUM
31/8/98 Tel: 01384 812745

Family activities and entertainment, indoors and out

Museum- Glass

Medieval Combat

30/8/98 GOODRICH CASTLE
31/8/98 Tel: 01600 890538

13th century knights in combat, archery contest, have-a-go archery and games. From 11.00. A£3.00 C£1.50 Concessions£2.30. EH Members Free

Castles

Medieval Weekend

30/8/98 HOLDENBY HOUSE, GARDENS AND FALCONRY CENTRE
31/8/98 Tel: 01604 770074

Medieval times at Holdenby House. Living History Camp with combat demonstrations, Dressing the Knight, Cooking and Clothing with much more. Along with our resident pine workshop and bodger, children's farm, tearoom, shop and play area to fill at day at Holdenby

Historic Houses & Gardens

Medieval Music, Surgery and Entertainments

30/8/98 KENILWORTH CASTLE
31/8/98 Tel: 01926 852078

Gruesome cures for wounds and ailments, offset by lively medieval music and monastic entertainments. From 12.00. A£3.50 C£1.80 Concessions£2.50. EH Members Free

Castles

Teddy Bear Weekend

30/8/98 MIDDLETON HALL
31/8/98 Tel: 01827 283095

Entertainment for the family. Magician, special children's entertainment. Rupert Bear and friends, painted eggs and valuations

Historic Houses & Gardens

The Bard and the Blade - Running Wolf Productions

30/8/98 STOKESAY CASTLE
31/8/98 Tel: 01588 672544

Dramatic duels and dialogue from some of Shakespeare's most famous plays. From 12.00. A£3.50 C£1.80 Concessions£2.50. EH Members Free

Castles

Town & Country Fayre

30/8/98 WESTON PARK
31/8/98 Tel: 01952 850207

Two days of arena demonstrations and family entertainment including: Monster Trucks, Shire Horses and Traction. Fun Fair

Historic Houses & Gardens

Medieval Entertainment

30/8/98 WITLEY COURT
31/8/98 Tel: 01299 896636

Music, dance and archery from 12.00 with drama and combat from 14.30. A£4.00 C£2.00 Concessions£3.00. EH Membersbers Free

Historic Houses & Gardens

Roman Festival

30/8/98 WROXETER ROMAN CITY
31/8/98 Tel: 01743 761330

Learn how to cook or make a pot Roman Style, or find out about herbs and make-up. Meet 1st century legionaries, watch 5th century soldiers at drill and in combat against barbarian raiders, plus cooking, mosaic making and a down trodden slave bemoaning his lot! From 12.00. A£4.00 C£2.00 Concessions£3.00. EH Mem Free

Roman Remains

National Model Flying Championships

31/8/98 GRANTHAM TOURIST INFORMATION CENTRE
31/8/98 Tel: 01476 566444

RAF Barkston Heath, Tel 0116 2440 028 for further information

Tourist Information Centres

The full information on the venues listed can be found in the main classified section under the classification shown under the entry. Please mention Best Guides when calling or visiting.

Brass Rubbing & Writing Experience
31/8/98
31/8/98
ILAM PARK
Tel: 01335 350245/350503
with Derek Hanley. Everyone welcome, small charge for materials. Ilam Stableblock at 11.00. Booking essential
Country Parks

Eurocar Event
31/8/98
31/8/98
MALLORY PARK
Tel: 01455 842931
BRSCC. Please call for further information
Motor Racing Circuit

Brass Rubbing - South Peak Estate
31/8/98
31/8/98
PEAK DISTRICT NATIONAL PARK
Tel: 01629 816200
Brass Rubbing and Writing Experience. Small charge for materials. 11.00 at Ilam Stableblock
National Parks

Sunset Cruise
2/9/98
2/9/98
GLOUCESTER LEISURE CRUISE
Tel: 01452 318054
Sit back and relax with the beautiful view, 19.00-22.00
Boat Trips

Last Night of the Proms with Firework Finale
4/9/98
4/9/98
RAGLEY HALL
Tel: 01789 762090
Proms Concerts have now established themselves firmly in the outdoor concert calendar, giving many of the audience a chance to return to a favourite venue for one final concert before the end of the summer. After last year's brilliant success, Jayne Carpenter once again leads the audience in the singing of 'Jerusalem' and 'Rule Britannia.' Rousing, singing, waving flags, terrific atmosphere and stunning fireworks all add up to a breathtaking finale, as the orchestra plays 'Land of Hope and Glory.' Proms concerts tend to sell out early: please reserve tickets in good time, especially group bookings. Tickets A£16.50 C(5-18)£9.00. Ticket Hotline: 01625 56 00 00
Historic Houses & Gardens

Bargain Weekend Three
4/9/98
6/9/98
BILLING AQUADROME LIMITED
Tel: 01604 408181
Tel 01604 408181 for more details
Country Leisure Parks

Friends of Thomas the Tank Engine
4/9/98
6/9/98
DEAN FOREST RAILWAY
Tel: 01594 843423 info line
Come along and see Thomas in full steam and a special visit from Wilbert the Forest Engine
Railways

FIA International GT Championship
4/9/98
6/9/98
DONINGTON COLLECTION OF GRAND PRIX RACING CARS
Tel: 01332 811027
The second and final UK appearance this year of this international series.
Museum- Motor

Silverstone SuperBike International
4/9/98
6/9/98
SILVERSTONE CIRCUIT
Tel: 01327 857271
Please call for further information.
Motor Racing Circuit

Open Day
5/9/98
5/9/98
BELTON HOUSE
Tel: 01476 566116
Gardens are open today in aid of the National Gardens Scheme - proceeds will be given to the Scheme which helps to preserve and restore some of the finest gardens in the country
Historic Houses

Last Night of the proms
5/9/98
5/9/98
BELVOIR CASTLE
Tel: 01476 870262
Stirring music accompanied by 200 strong cannon firing across the lake. Music by the Midlands Symphony Orchestra and fireworks create an unforgettable evening.
Castles

All Day Round Trip To Tewkesbury
5/9/98
5/9/98
GLOUCESTER LEISURE CRUISE
Tel: 01452 318054
Please see 5 April entry for details
Boat Trips

Country Fair
5/9/98
6/9/98
CHATSWORTH
Tel: 01246 582204/565300
Two day event for all the family, including massed pipe and military bans, hot-air balloons, free-fall parachuting and over 100 trades stands, House and Garden open to Country Fair visitors only
Historic Houses & Gardens

Steaming Weekends
5/9/98
6/9/98
ETRURIA INDUSTRIAL MUSEUM
Tel: 01782 287557
Princess, an 1820s beam engine drives the original 1856 grinding machinery; a coal fired 1903 boiler supplies the steam. 13.00-16.30
Museum- Industrial

The International 4x4 & Military Show
5/9/98
6/9/98
WESTON PARK
Tel: 01952 850207
For all 4x4 and Military vehicle enthusiasts. Mud Run, Public Off Road Course. Trade stands
Historic Houses & Gardens

Wolverhampton Festival of Transport
5/9/98
6/9/98
WOLVERHAMPTON TOURIST INFORMATION CENTRE
Tel: 01902 312051
Transport Festival held at East Park, Wolverhampton
Tourist Information Centres

"Castles in the Air"
5/9/98
4/10/98
COTSWOLD COUNTRYSIDE COLLECTION
Tel: 01451 860715
An exhibition in the Reception Gallery of stitched textile and mixed media pieces based on the theme of the castle and its place in our tradition and imagination by local artist Liz Harding. There will be items for sale
Museum- Local History

Craft Demonstration
6/9/98
6/9/98
FORGE MILL NEEDLE MUSEUM AND BORDESLEY ABBEY VISITOR CENTRE
Tel: 01527 62509
The Bordesley Abbey Spinners
Museum- Mill

BMCRC
6/9/98
6/9/98
MALLORY PARK
Tel: 01455 842931
Please call for further information
Motor Racing Circuit

Guided Walk - South Peak Estate
6/9/98
6/9/98
PEAK DISTRICT NATIONAL PARK
Tel: 01629 816200
Copper Mines and Railways of the Manifold. Meet 13.45 at Hulme End Visitor Centre. (OS Outdoor Leisure 24 SK104593). Strenuous walk. No dogs please
National Parks

Nature Activity Day
6/9/98
6/9/98
SNIBSTON DISCOVERY PARK
Tel: 01530 510851/813256
Join the Rangers for an activity packed day exploring nature at Snibston. From 08.30-10.00 take a stroll around the site to identify birds and learn more about their habitats (free, no booking required). Find and identify creatures living in and around the ponds in the Grange nature Reserve in a pond dipping workshop between 14.00-16.00 (free, no booking required). You can also take part in a bird-table making workshop between 11.00-13.00 and take you table home (there will be a charge for each birdtable made, pre-booking is essential on 01530 560851
Industrial Heritage

Scott Motorcycle Owners Club Rally
6/9/98
6/9/98
STANFORD HALL
Tel: 01788 860250
Telephone 01788 860250 for more details
Historic Houses

Wader Walk
6/9/98
6/9/98
WWT SLIMBRIDGE
Tel: 01453 890333 ext. 223
A warden will help you get the very best views of waders passing through on their autumn migration. Time 08.00 at the entrance. £5.50 (£3.50 WWT members) includes tea/coffee and biscuits
Wildlife Reserves

Decoy Demonstration
6/9/98
6/9/98
WWT SLIMBRIDGE
Tel: 01453 890333 ext. 223
Watch this fascinating and ancient art of catching ducks in our 150 year old Decoy. See them being measured and ringed as a vital part of our on-going research. You may be able to hold a duck and help release it. Weather-dependent so times are displayed in the Centre on the day
Wildlife Reserves

Galloway Antiques Fair
11/9/98
13/9/98
FULBECK HALL
Tel: 01400 272205
High quality dateline fair. Refreshments available. Fri/Sat 10.30-18.00 Sun 10.30-17.00 A£3.00 C£Free
Historic Houses & Gardens

Behind The Scenes Days
12/9/98
12/9/98
CHATSWORTH
Tel: 01246 582204/565300
Spend a day backstage at Chatsworth and meet the people who look after the House and its collections, the Garden and Park. Book on 01246 582204 contact Mrs Sue Gregory
Historic Houses & Gardens

Drive-In-Movie
12/9/98
12/9/98
WESTON PARK
Tel: 01952 850207
Based on the America idea. Films to be announced. Call for times and prices
Historic Houses & Gardens

Granada MI and MII Drivers
12/9/98
13/9/98
BILLING AQUADROME LIMITED
Tel: 01604 408181
Tel 01604 408181 for more details
Country Leisure Parks

The Duelling Association
12/9/98
13/9/98
BOLSOVER CASTLE
Tel: 01246 823349
Dashing Regency era duellists, plots and sword fights! From 12.00. A£3.00 Concessions£2.40 C£1.50 EH Members Free
Castles

The full information on the venues listed can be found in the main classified section under the classification shown under the entry. Please mention Best Guides when calling or visiting.

Archaeology Activity Weekend
12/9/98 CHEDWORTH ROMAN VILLA
13/9/98 Tel: 01242 890256
Archaeology displays, living history, activity tent, etc. Meet members of the "Time Team"; stars from the C4 programme will be at the villa for part of this weekend. £0.50 surcharge over entry including members (tickets on gate)
Roman Sites

Heritage Open Days
12/9/98 CORINIUM MUSEUM
13/9/98 Tel: 01285 655611
Visit the museum FREE over this weekend and find out about other buildings participating in the scheme. Information available from August 1998
Museum- Roman

Heritage Open Days
12/9/98 COTSWOLD COUNTRYSIDE COLLECTION
13/9/98 Tel: 01451 860715
Visit the museum FREE over this weekend and find out about other buildings participating in the scheme. Information available from August 1998
Museum- Local History

Heritage Open Days
12/9/98 TAMWORTH CASTLE
13/9/98 Tel: 01827 63563
Come and experience Tamworth Castle for Free. Free admission all weekend
Castles

Gloucestershire Women's Institute Camera & Calligraphy Exhibition
12/9/98 COTSWOLD COUNTRYSIDE COLLECTION
4/10/98 Tel: 01451 860715
The biennial exhibition of photographs and calligraphy submitted by members of the Gloucestershire WI. There will be items for sale
Museum- Local History

Mining Paintings
12/9/98 MANSFIELD MUSEUM AND ART GALLERY
11/10/98 Tel: 01623 663088
An exhibition by Janet Buckle
Museum- Local History

Ceramics
12/9/98 THE HARLEY GALLERY
1/11/98 Tel: 01909 501700
By the celebrated Phil Rogers.
Art Galleries

Stately Sculpture
12/9/98 THE FERRERS CENTRE FOR ARTS AND CRAFTS
28/3/99 Tel: 01332 865408
A touring exhibition of sculpture set within stately homes throughout Britain
Craft Galleries

East Midlands Doll Fair
13/9/98 BIRMINGHAM TOURIST INFORMATION CENTRE
13/9/98 Tel: 0121 643 2514
Venue: The Belfry Hotel, Wishaw, Birmingham North (J9 M42). A wonderful Doll Fair with dolls houses and teddies - 'a miniature wonderland.' Top quality collectors, artists and craftspeople bring old and soft dolls, dollshouse dolls, miniatures, teddy bears, dollcraft materials, kits, magazines and juvenilia, A£2.50 Students&OAPs£1.50 AccompaniedC£Free
Tourist Information Centres

Plant Sale
13/9/98 CALKE ABBEY
13/9/98 Tel: 01332 863822
Autumn plant sale, entry £1.00 11.00-17.00, parking free
Historic Houses & Gardens

Gardens Open
13/9/98 DEENE PARK
13/9/98 Tel: 01780 450223/450278
National Gardens Scheme. Please call venue for further details
Historic Houses

Historic Car Championships
13/9/98 DONINGTON COLLECTION OF GRAND PRIX RACING CARS
13/9/98 Tel: 01332 811027
HSCC organised meeting featuring classic racing cars.
Museum- Motor

Period Garden Tour
13/9/98 FORD GREEN HALL
13/9/98 Tel: 01782 233195
Please see 10 May entry for details
Historic Houses

National Heritage Day and National Archaeology Day
13/9/98 FORGE MILL NEEDLE MUSEUM AND BORDESLEY ABBEY VISITOR CENTRE
13/9/98 Tel: 01527 62509
Free Open Day. Family activities in the Archaeological Activity Centre. Tea-room open
Museum- Mill

Veteran, Vintage & Classic Car Show
13/9/98 HERITAGE MOTOR CENTRE
13/9/98 Tel: 01926 641188
Please call for more details.
Museum- Motor

BRSCC
13/9/98 MALLORY PARK
13/9/98 Tel: 01455 842931
Please call for further information
Motor Racing Circuit

Pack horses, Pitching and Paving - High Peak Estate
13/9/98
13/9/98 PEAK DISTRICT NATIONAL PARK
Tel: 01629 816200
A guided walk, 7 miles, on some of the footpaths crossing Kinder Scout. Meet 09.00 at Bowden Bridge car park (grid ref 049968) A£2.00 C£Free. Packed lunch required. No dogs please. Call 01433 670368

National Parks

Medieval Combat
13/9/98
13/9/98 PEVERIL CASTLE
Tel: 01433 620613
Please see 26 July for details

Castles

Wedding and Home
13/9/98
13/9/98 SHUGBOROUGH ESTATE
Tel: 01889 881388
Here's your chance to meet the experts. From trade stands and fashion shows to the icing on the cake

Country Estates

Mini Owners Club National Rally
13/9/98
13/9/98 STANFORD HALL
Tel: 01788 860250
Telephone 01788 860250 for more details

Historic Houses

Free Entry Day
16/9/98
16/9/98 BELTON HOUSE
Tel: 01476 566116
Visit Belton House for absolutely nothing! FREE entry day where all are welcome and entry is FREE. Save up to £12.00 for a family ticket

Historic Houses

Coming to Light: Birmingham's Photographic Collection
16/9/98
3/1/99 BIRMINGHAM MUSEUM AND ART GALLERY
Tel: 0121 235 2834
A treasure trove of images and image-making equipment re-revealed in this exhibition which both brings to light and explores the important photographic collections held by Birmingham Central Library and Birmingham Museum and Art Gallery. The exhibition, mounted as Birmingham's contribution to Photo 98: The Year of Photography and the Electronic Image, will be accompanied by a catalogue and full programme of events

Museums

Burton Festival
17/9/98
27/9/98 THE BASS MUSEUM
Tel: 01283 511000
Please call for further details

Breweries

Ragrugmaking Demonstration
18/9/98
18/9/98 COTSWOLD COUNTRYSIDE COLLECTION
Tel: 01451 860715
Please telephone for further information

Museum- Local History

All Day Round Trip To Tewkesbury
18/9/98
18/9/98 GLOUCESTER LEISURE CRUISE
Tel: 01452 318054
Please see 5 April entry for details

Boat Trips

An Antiques Evening with Philip Taubenheim
18/9/98 WWT SLIMBRIDGE
Tel: 01453 890333 ext. 223
Philip has appeared on the "Antiques Roadshow" and has a wealth of experience to share. Bring along your favourite antique for him to talk about and value. Time: 19.30 in Slimbridge Village Hall. £4.70 (£3.20 WWT members and Friends)

Wildlife Reserves

The Burton Festival
18/9/98
27/9/98 BURTON UPON TRENT TOURIST INFORMATION CENTRE
Tel: 01283 516609
Various venues in and around Burton upon Trent. Please call 01283 563761 for further information

Tourist Information Centres

Guided Walk - South Peak Estate
19/9/98
19/9/98 PEAK DISTRICT NATIONAL PARK
Tel: 01629 816200
Ilam to Wetton. Meet 10.00 at Ilam Hall. (OS Outdoor Leisure 24 SK132507) Strenuous 10 mile walk, no dogs, packed lunch required

National Parks

National Model Power Boat Association, National Finals
19/9/98
20/9/98 GRANTHAM TOURIST INFORMATION CENTRE
Tel: 01476 566444
Wyndham Park, Grantham. Call 01476 565201 for further information

Tourist Information Centres

The Lincoln Castle Longbowmen
19/9/98
20/9/98 KENILWORTH CASTLE
Tel: 01926 852078
Restoring Order, 1471. Meet the victorious Yorkists after the battle of Tewkesbury. Includes weapon training, pay and punishment, period cooking, mumming, children's have-a-go archery and dancing. From 12.00. A£3.50 C£1.80 Concessions£2.50. EH Members Free

Castles

The full information on the venues listed can be found in the main classified section under the classification shown under the entry. Please mention Best Guides when calling or visiting.

1778 Living History - Histrionix and the 47th Foot

19/9/98
20/9/98

LYDDINGTON BEDE HOUSE
Tel: 01572 822438
Gentry and bedesmen. Redcoat encampment, drill and musket firing and a fascinating comparison between a soldier of 1778 and 1998. From 12.00. A£3.00 C£1.50 Concessions£2.30. EH Members Free

Historic Houses

Silverstone International Raceday

19/9/98
20/9/98

SILVERSTONE CIRCUIT
Tel: 01327 857271
Please call for details.

Motor Racing Circuit

The Midland Game & Country Sports Fair

19/9/98
20/9/98

WESTON PARK
Tel: 01952 850207
A true Country Sports Fair with a large collection of trade stands

Historic Houses & Gardens

Black Country Vehicle Rally

20/9/98
20/9/98

BLACK COUNTRY LIVING MUSEUM
Tel: 0121 557 9643
A treat for vehicle enthusiasts when many rare locally-made cars and motorcycles, including Sunbeam and Star converge for the rally

Industrial Heritage

East Midlands Doll Fair

20/9/98
20/9/98

ELVASTON CASTLE COUNTRY PARK
Tel: 01332 571342
Another chance to visit the Doll Fair, 10.30-16.30, A£2.50 Student&OAPs£1.50 AccompaniedC£Free, £0.50 refund on car park fee at fair.

Country Parks

All Day Round Trip To Sharpness

20/9/98
20/9/98

GLOUCESTER LEISURE CRUISE
Tel: 01452 318054
Please see 18 April entry for details

Boat Trips

Morris Minor 50th Anniversary

20/9/98
20/9/98

HERITAGE MOTOR CENTRE
Tel: 01926 641188
Bring yours, if you've got one, or come anyway and join in the fun.

Museum- Motor

EMRA Club

20/9/98
20/9/98

MALLORY PARK
Tel: 01455 842931
Please call for further information

Motor Racing Circuit

L.E. Velo Motorcycle Owners Club Rally

20/9/98
20/9/98

STANFORD HALL
Tel: 01788 860250
Telephone 01788 860250 for more details

Historic Houses

Charolais Show

20/9/98
20/9/98

THE BASS MUSEUM
Tel: 01283 511000
Please call for further details

Breweries

Decoy Demonstration

20/9/98
20/9/98

WWT SLIMBRIDGE
Tel: 01453 890333 ext. 223
A warden will help you get the very best views of waders passing through on their autumn migration. Time 08.00 at the entrance. £5.50 (£3.50 WWT members) includes tea/coffee and biscuits

Wildlife Reserves

Behind The Scenes Days

23/9/98
23/9/98

CHATSWORTH
Tel: 01246 582204/565300
Spend a day backstage at Chatsworth and meet the people who look after the House and its collections, the Garden and Park. Book on 01246 582204 contact Mrs Sue Gregory

Historic Houses & Gardens

Burton Beer Festival

24/9/98
26/9/98

BURTON UPON TRENT TOURIST INFORMATION CENTRE
Tel: 01283 516609
Beer Festival at Burton Town Hall. Please call Mr Fletcher 01283 569310 for further information

Tourist Information Centres

MCN British Super Bike Championship

25/9/98
27/9/98

DONINGTON COLLECTION OF GRAND PRIX RACING CARS
Tel: 01332 811027
Final round of this prestigious championship.

Museum- Motor

Forest Branch Line Festival

26/9/98
27/9/98

DEAN FOREST RAILWAY
Tel: 01594 843423 info line
Photographic spectacular - lineside passes available, an event for all enthusiasts not to be missed

Railways

Malvern Autumn Show
26/9/98 *MALVERN TOURIST INFORMATION CENTRE*
27/9/98 Tel: 01684 892289
Venue: TCAS Showground, Malvern. Ablaze with the colours of chrysanthemums and dahlias, and scented with the mellow fragrance of ripe fruits, the Malvern Autumn Show offers a dazzling mix of the horticultural and country skills to celebrate the season. Organised in conjunction with the Three Counties Agricultural Society, the RHS Floral Marquee is complemented by rural crafts, identification clinics for apples, pears and fungi and displays including horse logging championships and sheep dog trails. Experts will be on hand at the RHS Advisory Desk to answer your gardening queries. All advance booking must be made by 9 Sept latest. 09.00-18.00, RHS Members A£5.00 in advance, A£6.00 on the gate, Public A£6.00 in advance, A£7.00 on the gate, C(0-16)£1.00 in advance, C£2.00 on the gate, Family ticket(A2+C3)13.00 in advance, £15.00 on the gate, groups 10+ £5.00 (must be booked in advance), car parking free
Tourist Information Centres

Modellers Weekend
26/9/98 *NATIONAL WATERWAYS MUSEUM*
27/9/98 Tel: 01452 318054
Modellers of engines, boats and historical buildings. Boats out on the water. Demonstrations and working displays
Museum- Waterways

BRSCC Race Meeting
26/9/98 *SILVERSTONE CIRCUIT*
27/9/98 Tel: 01327 857271
Please call for further information.
Motor Racing Circuit

Focus on Birds Weekend - Waders
26/9/98 *WWT SLIMBRIDGE*
27/9/98 Tel: 01453 890333 ext. 223
Puzzled by which is which and where they go at different times of the year? All will be revealed! Meet at the South Lake Observatory at 11.00 or 14.00 - no need to book
Wildlife Reserves

15th-18th Century Italian Art
26/9/98 *ABINGTON MUSEUM*
15/11/98 Tel: 01604 31454
A major exhibition featuring some of the foremost artists of this period in history. The majority of the work on display will be taken from our own fine collections
Museum- Local History

World Barrel Rolling Championships
27/9/98 *BURTON UPON TRENT TOURIST INFORMATION CENTRE*
27/9/98 Tel: 01283 516609
In Burton upon Trent, please call 01283 511000 for further information
Tourist Information Centres

Living History Day
27/9/98 *FORD GREEN HALL*
27/9/98 Tel: 01782 233195
See history brought to life by the English Civil War Society, who will recreate everyday life at Ford Green Hall in the 1640's, 13.00-16.30
Historic Houses

National Garden Scheme Open Day
27/9/98 *HARLAXTON MANOR GARDENS*
27/9/98 Tel: 01476 592101
Gardens open to raise funds for the National Gardens Scheme
Historic Houses & Gardens

BARC Club
27/9/98 *MALLORY PARK*
27/9/98 Tel: 01455 842931
Please call for further information
Motor Racing Circuit

World Barrel Rolling Championships
27/9/98 *THE BASS MUSEUM*
27/9/98 Tel: 01283 511000
Join contestants from home and abroad competing for the coveted Perpetual Trophy, teams of two welcome. £1.00 admission
Breweries

History Re-enactment Workshop
3/10/98 *BOLSOVER CASTLE*
4/10/98 Tel: 01246 823349
1660's Living History. The Restoration era brought to life. From 12.00. A£3.50 Concessions£2.50 C£1.80. EH Members Free
Castles

Christmas Craft Fair
3/10/98 *EASTNOR CASTLE*
4/10/98 Tel: 01531 633160
Get those early presents - early!
Castles

Steaming Weekends
3/10/98 *ETRURIA INDUSTRIAL MUSEUM*
4/10/98 Tel: 01782 287557
Steaming Weekends: Princess, an 1820s beam engine drives the original 1856 grinding machinery; a coal fired 1903 boiler supplies the steam. 13.00-16.30
Museum- Industrial

Silverstone Autumn Gold Cup
3/10/98 *SILVERSTONE CIRCUIT*
4/10/98 Tel: 01327 857271
Please call for further information.
Motor Racing Circuit

Crafts at Stanford Hall (Lady Fayre)
3/10/98 STANFORD HALL
4/10/98 Tel: 01788 860250
Telephone 01788 860250 for more details
Historic Houses

Fly-dressing Demonstration
4/10/98 FORGE MILL NEEDLE MUSEUM AND
BORDESLEY ABBEY VISITOR CENTRE
4/10/98 Tel: 01527 62509
Please call for further information
Museum- Mill

All day round trip to Tewkesbury
4/10/98 GLOUCESTER LEISURE CRUISE
4/10/98 Tel: 01452 318054
Please see 5 April entry for details
Boat Trips

39th Mini Anniversary
4/10/98 HERITAGE MOTOR CENTRE
4/10/98 Tel: 01926 641188
Please call for more information.
Museum- Motor

National Gardens Scheme Open Day
4/10/98 KAYES GARDEN NURSERY
4/10/98 Tel: 01664 424578
All proceeds for this open day go to the
National Gardens Scheme, teas available
all day 14.00-17.00
Gardens- Botanical

East Midlands Doll Fair
4/10/98 LAMPORT HALL AND GARDENS
4/10/98 Tel: 01604 686272
Another chance to visit the Doll Fair,
10.30-16.30, A£2.70 Student&OAPs£1.50
AccompaniedC£Free, refreshments and
free parking
Historic Houses & Gardens

BRSCC
4/10/98 MALLORY PARK
4/10/98 Tel: 01455 842931
Eurocar Finals. Please call for further
information
Motor Racing Circuit

Decoy Demonstration
4/10/98 WWT SLIMBRIDGE
4/10/98 Tel: 01453 890333 ext. 223
Watch this fascinating and ancient art of
catching ducks in our 150 year old Decoy.
See them being measured and ringed as a
vital part of our on-going research. You
may be able to hold a duck and help
release it. Weather-dependent so times
are displayed in the Centre on the day
Wildlife Reserves

Corby Glen Sheep Fair
4/10/98 GRANTHAM TOURIST INFORMATION CENTRE
6/10/98 Tel: 01476 566444
Corby Glen, near Grantham. Call 01476
550502 for further information
Tourist Information Centres

Stationary Engine Winter Rally
5/10/98 GLOUCESTER LEISURE CRUISE
5/10/98 Tel: 01452 318054
Please call venue for details
Boat Trips

Burton Statutes Fair
5/10/98 BURTON UPON TRENT TOURIST
INFORMATION CENTRE
6/10/98 Tel: 01283 516609
Fun Fair in Burton Town Centre. Please call
01543 372820 for further information
Tourist Information Centres

Early Opening
7/10/98 WWT SLIMBRIDGE
7/10/98 Tel: 01453 890333 ext. 223
To coincide with the Severn Bore; high
tides bring birds closer to the Hides -
enjoy the peace and quiet of an early
opening as well as great birdwatching.
Centre opens at 08.00 ready to be in the
Holden Tower for the tide at around
08.30. Normal admission prices apply
Wildlife Reserves

**Burne-Jones New York - Birmingham -
Paris**
7/10/98 BIRMINGHAM MUSEUM AND ART GALLERY
17/1/99 Tel: 0121 235 2834
This exhibition commemorates the centenary of the death of Birmingham born Sir
Edward Burne-Jones, one of our best
known artists, and is in collaboration with
the Metropolitan Museum of Art, New
York, and the Musée d'Orsay, Paris. It will
be the first exhibition ever devoted to the
artist in the whole of America and France,
and the largest in Britain for two decades.
Over 150 works, from Pre-Raphaelite
watercolours and drawings to the stained
glass designed for his lifelong friend
William Morrs. A£5.00 Concessions£3.50
Family Ticket (A2+C2) £14.00
Museums

**The 15th National Knitting and
Needlecraft Exhibition**
8/10/98 NATIONAL EXHIBITION CENTRE
11/10/98 Tel: 0121 780 4141 X2604
Sewing, cross stitch, hand and machine
knitting, patchwork and quilting, fashion
displays, workshops, demonstrations,
talks and many other attractions. On the
door A£6.50 OAPs£5.00. £1.00 off if
ordered in advance Ticket Hotline: 0117
970 1370
Exhibition Centres

Autumn Horse Trials
9/10/98 WESTON PARK
11/10/98 Tel: 01952 850207
One of the most popular Equestrian
events in the calendar
Historic Houses & Gardens

Behind The Scenes Days
10/10/98 CHATSWORTH
10/10/98 Tel: 01246 582204/565300
Spend a day backstage at Chatsworth and meet the people who look after the House and its collections, the Garden and Park. Book on 01246 582204 contact Mrs Sue Gregory
Historic Houses & Gardens

Adult Dayschool - Cords, Ropes, Tassels & Knots
10/10/98 COTSWOLD COUNTRYSIDE COLLECTION
10/10/98 Tel: 01451 860715
This practical course allows participants to discover the different techniques in making cords, ropes and tassels for decoration and use in the home. 10.00-16.30, £20.00 (10% discount with Cotswold Museums Card)
Museum- Local History

750 Motor Club Raceday
10/10/98 SILVERSTONE CIRCUIT
10/10/98 Tel: 01327 857271
Please call for further information.
Motor Racing Circuit

Christmas Craft Show
10/10/98 SHUGBOROUGH ESTATE
11/10/98 Tel: 01889 881388
A special selection of crafts - designed for early Christmas shoppers
Country Estates

Medieval Entertainers
10/10/98 STOKESAY CASTLE
11/10/98 Tel: 01588 672544
Games, squire-training and talks on weaponry and armour. Also, try your hand at spinning, weaving and calligraphy and learn about herbal medicine. From 12.00. A£3.00 C£1.50 Concessions£2.30.
Castles

"The Cotswolds in Watercolour"
10/10/98 COTSWOLD COUNTRYSIDE COLLECTION
1/11/98 Tel: 01451 860715
Works by Joy Fereday using traditional watercolour techniques inspired by the local landscapes. There will be items for sale
Museum- Local History

Historic Car Championship
11/10/98 DONINGTON COLLECTION OF GRAND PRIX RACING CARS
11/10/98 Tel: 01332 811027
HSCC organised meeting featuring classic racing cars.
Museum- Motor

BRSCC
11/10/98 MALLORY PARK
11/10/98 Tel: 01455 842931
Please call for further information
Motor Racing Circuit

Historic Race Meeting - HSCC
11/10/98 SILVERSTONE CIRCUIT
11/10/98 Tel: 01327 857271
Please call for further information.
Motor Racing Circuit

Castle by Candlelight
15/10/98 TAMWORTH CASTLE
17/10/98 Tel: 01827 63563
A magical atmosphere created by over 300 candles in the historic period rooms. Guides in period costume, bar. Slightly higher admission charges apply
Castles

"Black & White with Colour in Between" - Fashion Show
16/10/98 COTSWOLD COUNTRYSIDE COLLECTION
16/10/98 Tel: 01451 860715
A tour of the vagaries of fashion through the ages. Doors open 19.00. Refreshments available. Tickets £3.50 (10% discount for Museum Card Holders). Hosted by Shelagh Lovett-Turner, this evening promises a pageant of colour and costume. There will be a small display of accessories to accompany the talk
Museum- Local History

Ragrugmaking Demonstration
16/10/98 COTSWOLD COUNTRYSIDE COLLECTION
16/10/98 Tel: 01451 860715
Please telephone for further information
Museum- Local History

Understanding Geese
16/10/98 WWT SLIMBRIDGE
16/10/98 Tel: 01453 890333 ext. 223
Find out how 50 years of WWT research has given an insight into the intriguing lives of the wild geese, which winter in Britain aided their conservation and defined new challenges for the future. Time: 19.30 at Slimbridge Village Hall. Cost: £4.70 (£3.20 WWT Members or Friends)
Wildlife Reserves

Mam Tor and the Winnats - High Peak Estate
17/10/98 PEAK DISTRICT NATIONAL PARK
17/10/98 Tel: 01629 816200
5 miles guided walk. Meet 10.00 at main car park, Castleton. A£2.00 C£Free. Packed lunch, no dogs required. Call 01433 670368
National Parks

Eight Clubs Raceday
17/10/98 SILVERSTONE CIRCUIT
17/10/98 Tel: 01327 857271
Please call for further information.
Motor Racing Circuit

The full information on the venues listed can be found in the main classified section under the classification shown under the entry. Please mention Best Guides when calling or visiting.

Craft Fair

17/10/98 ROCKINGHAM CASTLE

18/10/98 Tel: 01536 770240

Please call for further information.

Castles

Focus on Birds - rare ones

17/10/98 WWT SLIMBRIDGE

18/10/98 Tel: 01453 890333 ext. 223

See some of the world's rare and threatened wildfowl at Slimbridge - and discover what is being done to help conserve them. Meet in the South Lake Observatory at 11.00 or 14.00 - no need to book

Wildlife Reserves

Lydney Road and Rail Show

18/10/98 DEAN FOREST RAILWAY

18/10/98 Tel: 01594 843423 info line

A chance to visit a Preservation Rally, call for further details

Railways

Image and Identity Exhibition

18/10/98 FORGE MILL NEEDLE MUSEUM AND BORDESLEY ABBEY VISITOR CENTRE

18/10/98 Tel: 01527 62509

Activity day to launch the exhibition

Museum- Mill

Retford Motorcycle Event

18/10/98 MALLORY PARK

18/10/98 Tel: 01455 842931

Please call for further information

Motor Racing Circuit

Shoe and Leathercraft Week

19/10/98 ABINGTON MUSEUM

24/10/98 Tel: 01604 31454

An exciting week of events based around our extensive boot and shoe and leathercraft collections. Talks, workshops, demonstrations and lots more! Coincides with the St. Crispin's Day celebrations in Northampton

Museum- Local History

Behind The Scenes Days

21/10/98 CHATSWORTH

21/10/98 Tel: 01246 582204/565300

Spend a day backstage at Chatsworth and meet the people who look after the House and its collections, the Garden and Park. Book on 01246 582204 contact Mrs Sue Gregory

Historic Houses & Gardens

Samplers - An Exhibition of the Museum's Samplers

21/10/98 COTSWOLD COUNTRYSIDE COLLECTION

1/11/98 Tel: 01451 860715

This exhibition of Samplers coincides with the public demonstration of the Cotswold Museums Service's new computer system, Admuse. Staff and volunteers are currently transferring all the information about the objects in the museum onto this new computer system. Members of the public will be given the chance to use the computer systems to access more information about the samplers on display

Museum- Local History

Castle by Candlelight

22/10/98 TAMWORTH CASTLE

24/10/98 Tel: 01827 63563

A magical atmosphere created by over 300 candles in the historic period rooms. Guides in period costume, bar. Slightly higher admission charges apply

Castles

Antiques Fair - Galloway Antiques

23/10/98 DEENE PARK

25/10/98 Tel: 01780 450223/450278

Please call venue for further information

Historic Houses

The SMMT British International Motor Show

23/10/98 NATIONAL EXHIBITION CENTRE

1/11/98 Tel: 0121 780 4141 x2604

Cars, light commercial vehicles up to 3.5 tonnes, accessories and components, garage equipment, tyres, magazines and associations. 23-31 October 09.30-19.00, 1 Nov 09.30-17.30. A£10.00 C&OAPs£5.00

Exhibition Centres

Motorcycle Club Raceday - MCC

24/10/98 SILVERSTONE CIRCUIT

24/10/98 Tel: 01327 857271

Please call for further information.

Motor Racing Circuit

East Midlands Doll Fair

24/10/98 STRATFORD-UPON-AVON TOURIST INFORMATION CENTRE

24/10/98 Tel: 01789 293127

Venue: Civic Hall, Stratford-upon-Avon. A wonderful Doll Fair with dolls houses and teddies - 'a miniature wonderland.' Top quality collectors, artists and craftspeople bring old and soft dolls, dollshouse dolls, miniatures, teddy bears, dollcraft materials, kits, magazines and juvenilia, 10.30-16.30, A£2.50 Student&OAPs£1.50 AccompaniedC£Free, refreshments available

Tourist Information Centres

Puritans, Daggers and Witchcraft

24/10/98 WARWICK CASTLE
1/11/98 Tel: 01926 406600

Dare you visit during All Hallows week? Discover ghosts of Warwick Castle. See the knights compete in duels, learn about the famous witch trials of the past. Children entering the castle can accept the task of finding the witch if they dare!

Castles

Migration Magic - Half Term Activities

24/10/98 WWT SLIMBRIDGE
1/11/98 Tel: 01453 890333 ext. 223

Activities and a trail to uncover the mystery of bird migration

Wildlife Reserves

Traditional Tapestries

24/10/98 CORINIUM MUSEUM
13/12/98 Tel: 01285 655611

The Cotswolds for centuries produced the wool to make tapestries throughout Europe. This exhibition will feature modern copies of some of the great tapestries from Europe. There will be items for sale

Museum- Roman

New Era Motorcycle Event

25/10/98 MALLORY PARK
25/10/98 Tel: 01455 842931

Please call for further information

Motor Racing Circuit

Motorcycle Club Raceday - BMCRC

25/10/98 SILVERSTONE CIRCUIT
25/10/98 Tel: 01327 857271

Please call for further information.

Motor Racing Circuit

18th Century Dance

25/10/98 STOKESAY CASTLE
26/10/98 Tel: 01588 672544

Enjoy revelries with costumed dancers. From 12.00. A£3.00 C£1.50 Concessions£2.30

Castles

Halloween Spooktacular

26/10/98 ALTON TOWERS
30/10/98 Tel: 0990 204060 24hr

Dare you ride the Haunted House in the dark! The spooks will be on the loose again with the terrifying return of a selection of our scariest rides will be running until dark with cauldrons-full of ghostly goings-on. What's more, kids that dress up in creepy costumes will receive a FREE gift

Theme Parks

Ragrugmaking Demonstration

30/10/98 COTSWOLD COUNTRYSIDE COLLECTION
30/10/98 Tel: 01451 860715

Please telephone for further information

Museum- Local History

Ghost Stories and Mystery Ghost Walk

30/10/98 FORGE MILL NEEDLE MUSEUM AND BORDESLEY ABBEY VISITOR CENTRE
30/10/98 Tel: 01527 62509

Anne Bradford tells Ghost stories followed by a mystery Ghost Walk

Museum- Mill

Halloween

30/10/98 SHUGBOROUGH ESTATE
31/10/98 Tel: 01889 881388

Pumpkin lanterns light the way to a bewitching evening of spooky fun and glitzy characters. Entertainment throughout the evening. Suitable for all ages

Country Estates

Bargain weekend Four

30/10/98 BILLING AQUADROME LIMITED
1/11/98 Tel: 01604 408181

Tel 01604 408181 for more details

Country Leisure Parks

Behind The Scenes Days

31/10/98 CHATSWORTH
31/10/98 Tel: 01246 582204/565300

Spend a day backstage at Chatsworth and meet the people who look after the House and its collections, the Garden and Park. Book on 01246 582204 contact Mrs Sue Gregory

Historic Houses & Gardens

Fireworks Extravaganza

31/10/98 HERITAGE MOTOR CENTRE
31/10/98 Tel: 01926 641188

Please call for more information.

Museum- Motor

Firework & Special Effects Spectacular

31/10/98 ALTON TOWERS
1/11/98 Tel: 0990 204060 24hr

Thousands of fireworks, lasers, lights, special effects, music and stunning scenery all combine to make a show nothing short of mind-blowing!

Theme Parks

Steaming Weekends

31/10/98 ETRURIA INDUSTRIAL MUSEUM
1/11/98 Tel: 01782 287557

Princess, an 1820s beam engine drives the original 1856 grinding machinery; a coal fired 1903 boiler supplies the steam. 13.00-16.30

Museum- Industrial

The full information on the venues listed can be found in the main classified section under the classification shown under the entry. Please mention Best Guides when calling or visiting.

East Midlands Doll Fair

1/11/98 NOTTINGHAM TOURIST INFORMATION CENTRE

1/11/98 Tel: 0115 915 55330

Venue: The Dome Exhibition Hall & Conference Rooms, Kelham Hall, Nottinghamshire. A wonderful Doll Fair with dolls houses and teddies - 'a miniature wonderland.' Top quality collectors, artists and craftspeople bring old and soft dolls, dollshouse dolls, miniatures, teddy bears, dollcraft materials, kits, magazines and juvenilia. 10.30-16.30, A£2.90 Student&OAPs£1.50 AccompaniedC£Free

Tourist Information Centres

Bonfire & Firework Spectacular

1/11/98 WESTON PARK

1/11/98 Tel: 01952 850207

Complete with a Petticoat Lane style market and two stunning firework displays, call for times and prices

Historic Houses & Gardens

Decoy Demonstration

1/11/98 WWT SLIMBRIDGE

1/11/98 Tel: 01453 890333 ext. 223

Watch this fascinating and ancient art of catching ducks in our 150 year old Decoy. See them being measured and ringed as a vital part of our on-going research. You may be able to hold a duck and help release it. Weather-dependent so times are displayed in the Centre on the day

Wildlife Reserves

State Room Secrets

1/11/98 WARWICK CASTLE

30/11/98 Tel: 01926 406600

Join our guides as they take you through the Great Hall and State Rooms and share with you the secrets of the Castle on our free guided tour.

Castles

Traditional Bonfire Night

5/11/98 BLACK COUNTRY LIVING MUSEUM

5/11/98 Tel: 0121 557 9643

The most memorable bonfire night around with the added safety of no fireworks. An atmospheric evening is promised. The museum will be lit by candle and gas light

Industrial Heritage

Bonfire & Fireworks Display

5/11/98 THE ALMONRY HERITAGE CENTRE

5/11/98 Tel: 01386 446944

Evesham town bonfire and fireworks display held on the Corporation Meadow, Evesham 18.15 onwards, call for prices

Museum- Local History

Firework & Special Effects Spectacular

6/11/98 ALTON TOWERS

8/11/98 Tel: 0990 204060 24hr

Thousands of fireworks, lasers, lights, special effects, music and stunning scenery all combine to make a show nothing short of mind-blowing!

Theme Parks

Bonfire Night

7/11/98 SHUGBOROUGH ESTATE

7/11/98 Tel: 01889 881388

Annual fireworks display organised by Stafford Round Table

Country Estates

Winter Warmer Raceday - BRRDC

7/11/98 SILVERSTONE CIRCUIT

7/11/98 Tel: 01327 857271

Please call for further information.

Motor Racing Circuit

Behind The Scenes Days

10/11/98 CHATSWORTH

11/11/98 Tel: 01246 582204/565300

Spend a day backstage at Chatsworth and meet the people who look after the House and its collections, the Garden and Park. Book on 01246 582204 contact Mrs Sue Gregory

Historic Houses & Gardens

Behind The Scenes Days

12/11/98 CHATSWORTH

12/11/98 Tel: 01246 582204/565300

Spend a day backstage at Chatsworth and meet the people who look after the House and its collections, the Garden and Park. Book on 01246 582204 contact Mrs Sue Gregory

Historic Houses & Gardens

Breakfast with the Birds

12/11/98 WWT SLIMBRIDGE

12/11/98 Tel: 01453 890333 ext. 223

With the expert help of a warden, watch the White-fronted Geese on their dawn flight and discover how we manage the reserve for the benefit of wetland wildlife. Wrap up warmly and enjoy a full English breakfast. Very popular so please book early. Time: 07.00 at the entrance. £12.50 (£10.50 WWT members)

Wildlife Reserves

British Crafts

12/11/98 NATIONAL EXHIBITION CENTRE

15/11/98 Tel: 0121 780 4141 x2604

Hall 6. Over 150 top quality traditional and modern craftsmen demonstrating and selling hand made British Crafts. 09.30-17.30 17.00 on Sun. A£6.50 C(0-16)£1.00 or Free if accompanied by an Adult OAPs£5.50

Exhibition Centres

Hobbycrafts
12/11/98 NATIONAL EXHIBITION CENTRE
15/11/98 Tel: 0121 780 4141 x2604
Hall 17. Whatever your craft come and see over 100 exhibitors demonstrating, teaching and selling supplies for over 30 different hobbies. 09.30-17.30 17.00 on Sun. A£6.50 C(0-16)£1.00 or Free if accompanied by an Adult OAPs£5.50
Exhibition Centres

Ragrugmaking Demonstration
14/11/98 COTSWOLD COUNTRYSIDE COLLECTION
14/11/98 Tel: 01451 860715
Please telephone for further information
Museum- Local History

Inspector Morse At Oxford
14/11/98 GRANTHAM MUSEUM
31/12/98 Tel: 01476 568783
Could this exhibition show more of an insight into one of TV's most famous fiction detective?
Museum- Local History

Animal Kingdom
14/11/98 THE FERRERS CENTRE FOR ARTS AND
11/1/99 CRAFTS
Tel: 01332 865408
A Christmas exhibition showing mixed media animals in both wood and ceramics
Craft Galleries

Decoy Demonstration
15/11/98 WWT SLIMBRIDGE
15/11/98 Tel: 01453 890333 ext. 223
Watch this fascinating and ancient art of catching ducks in our 150 year old Decoy. See them being measured and ringed as a vital part of our on-going research. You may be able to hold a duck and help release it. Weather-dependent so times are displayed in the Centre on the day
Wildlife Reserves

Schools Art
15/11/98 THE HARLEY GALLERY
20/12/98 Tel: 01909 501700
Work by local schools & colleges.
Art Galleries

The Sights and Sounds of Scilly with John Hicks
20/11/98 WWT SLIMBRIDGE
20/11/98 Tel: 01453 890333 ext. 223
John's family have been boatmen on the Scillies for several generations - he will bring you the sights and sounds of the flora and fauna of these fascinating islands. Time: 19.30 at Slimbridge Village Hall. £4.70 (£3.20 WWT Members or Friends)
Wildlife Reserves

Wild Birds by Floodlight
21/11/98 WWT SLIMBRIDGE
21/11/98 Tel: 01453 890333 ext. 223
Enjoy an out-of-hours view of hundreds of wild birds on Swan Lake. Watch the floodlit feed and listen to live commentary from the comfort of the heated Peng Observatory. Time: 18.15 in the Peng Observatory. A£3.50 (£2.50 WWT members); C£1.50 (£1.00 WWT members). Advance booking not required
Wildlife Reserves

Derby City Open
21/11/98 DERBY MUSEUM AND ART GALLERY
10/1/99 Tel: 01332 716659
A chance to see work entered into this years competition now considered to be the regions most art important area
Museum- Regimental

East Midlands Doll Fair
22/11/98 LEICESTER TOURIST INFORMATION CENTRE
22/11/98 Tel: 0116 251 1301
Venue: Aylestone Leisure Centre, Leicester. A wonderful Doll Fair with dolls houses and teddies - 'a miniature wonderland.' Top quality collectors, artists and craftspeople bring old and soft dolls, dollshouse dolls, miniatures, teddy bears, dollcraft materials, kits, magazines and juvenilia. 10.30-16.30, A£2.30 Student&OAPs£1.20 AccompaniedC£Free
Tourist Information Centres

Network Q RAC Rally
22/11/98 SILVERSTONE CIRCUIT
22/11/98 Tel: 01327 857271
Please call for further information.
Motor Racing Circuit

Late Night Christmas Shopping
24/11/98 WWT SLIMBRIDGE
24/11/98 Tel: 01453 890333 ext. 223
The Centre is open from 09.30 until 21.00 so you can enjoy shopping for those special gifts in peaceful surroundings, and treat yourself to some festive fare in the restaurant. Admission is FREE all day
Wildlife Reserves

The NEC Antiques For Everyone Fair
26/11/98 NATIONAL EXHIBITION CENTRE
29/11/98 Tel: 0121 780 4141 x2604
400+ antiques dealers offer antiques and fine art. Exhibits datelined to 1914 in plush, stand-fitted Section One; to 1940 for all things collectable in Section Two. An enormous range of very fine quality antiques and collectibles for every pocket with prices from less than £10 to over £100,000. 20,000 visitors anticipated. Open Thur & Fri 11.00-20.00, Sat & Sun 11.00-18.00
Exhibition Centres

Stoneleigh Needlecraft and Knitting Exhibition

27/11/98
29/11/98
COVENTRY TOURIST INFORMATION CENTRE
Tel: 01203 832303/4
Held at Stoneleigh Exhibition Hall, please call 01775 722900 for further information
Tourist Information Centres

Focus on Birds Weekend - Winter Wildfowl

28/11/98
29/11/98
WWT SLIMBRIDGE
Tel: 01453 890333 ext. 223
The appearance and disappearance of wildfowl puzzled our ancestors - find out about the lives of some of the birds which spend the winter with us at Slimbridge. Meet at the Zeiss Hide at 11.00 or 14.00 - no need to book
Wildlife Reserves

A Christmas Fantasy

28/11/98
24/12/98
CLEARWELL CAVES ANCIENT IRON MINES
Tel: 01594 832535
A fantasy of light and sound with the real Father Christmas!
Caves

Craft Fair

29/11/98
29/11/98
BIRMINGHAM BOTANICAL GARDENS AND GLASSHOUSES
Tel: 0121 454 1860
The best of British craftsmanship on sale for Christmas
Gardens- Botanical

From Darkness to Light

29/11/98
29/11/98
LICHFIELD CATHEDRAL
Tel: 01543 306240
Advent Carol Service by candlelight, call for times
Cathedrals

Victorian Charity Fayre

4/12/98
4/12/98
THE BASS MUSEUM
Tel: 01283 511000
Admission by donation
Breweries

Children's Christmas Activities

5/12/98
5/12/98
COTSWOLD COUNTRYSIDE COLLECTION
Tel: 01451 860715
Activities for Children to get them ready for Christmas. More details available later in the year. Children aged 5-7 years, 10.00-12.30, £6.00, children 8-12 years, 13.30-16.00, £6.00 (10% discount with Cotswold Museums Card)
Museum- Local History

Lichfield Cathedral Special Choir

5/12/98
5/12/98
LICHFIELD CATHEDRAL
Tel: 01543 306240
Mozart's Coronation Mass and Mozart's Requiem. Tickets: £10.00, £8.00, £6.00, unreserved £5.00
Cathedrals

Victorian Christmas

5/12/98
27/12/98
WARWICK CASTLE
Tel: 01926 406600
December weekends, enjoy a traditional Victorian Christmas at the Castle, see the Victorian decorations throughout the State Rooms and Great Hall. Special Christmas Lunch packages and evening Kingmaker feasts (pre booking advised)
Castles

Christmas Craft Fair

6/12/98
6/12/98
FORGE MILL NEEDLE MUSEUM AND BORDESLEY ABBEY VISITOR CENTRE
Tel: 01527 62509
Craft Fair, the tea room will be open
Museum- Mill

Santa Specials

6/12/98
24/12/98
DEAN FOREST RAILWAY
Tel: 01594 843423 info line
Ho ho ho! Come along children and see Santa as he makes a visit to the Dean Forest Railway, mums and dads give us a ring for times and prices
Railways

Christmas Festival

7/12/98
18/12/98
THE COMMANDERY
Tel: 01905 355071
See a medieval hall decorated in the traditional medieval fashion along with various surprise events over the 11 days
Historic Buildings

Christmas at Shugborough

8/12/98
11/12/98
SHUGBOROUGH ESTATE
Tel: 01889 881388
Victorian evenings with festive decorations, candlelit Mansion House, Christmas market and a host of seasonal entertainment
Country Estates

Late Night Christmas Shopping

9/12/98
9/12/98
WWT SLIMBRIDGE
Tel: 01453 890333 ext. 223
The Centre is open from 09.30 until 21.00 so you can enjoy shopping for those special gifts in peaceful surroundings, and treat yourself to some festive fare in the restaurant. Admission is FREE all day
Wildlife Reserves

The Natural History of Christmas with Dr Patrick Harding

11/12/98
11/12/98
WWT SLIMBRIDGE
Tel: 01453 890333 ext. 223
A light-hearted but informative look at the basis for the links between Christmas and natural history - for example, the Holly and the Ivy, Mistletoe and Reindeer. Time: 19.30 at Slimbridge Village Hall, £4.70 (£3.20 WWT Members or Friends)
Wildlife Reserves

"A Traditional Christmas"
12/12/98 Cotswold Countryside Collection
12/12/98 Tel: 01451 860715
Please see 5 December entry for details
Museum- Local History

Steaming Weekend & Santa at the Mill
12/12/98 Etruria Industrial Museum
13/12/98 Tel: 01782 287557
Princess, an 1820s beam engine drives
the original 1856 grinding machinery; a
coal fired 1903 boiler supplies the steam.
13.00-16.30
Museum- Industrial

Christmas Evening
18/12/98 Black Country Living Museum
18/12/98 Tel: 0121 557 9643
Start the Christmas celebrations in a
unique, nostalgic way. The mood will be
festive with the shops, cottages and workshops lit by candle and gas light, and
carol singers, hot food and mulled wine
Industrial Heritage

Stoneleigh Fine Antiques Fair
18/12/98 Coventry Tourist Information Centre
20/12/98 Tel: 01203 832303/4
Lots of antiques on view at the N. A. C.
Stoneleigh Park. Please call 01775 712100
for further information
Tourist Information Centres

"A Traditional Christmas"
19/12/98 Cotswold Countryside Collection
19/12/98 Tel: 01451 860715
Please see 5 December entry for details
Museum- Local History

**Focus on Birds Weekend - Winter
Wildfowl**
19/12/98 WWT Slimbridge
20/12/98 Tel: 01453 890333 ext. 223
Another chance to find out more about
our winter visitors. Meet at 11.00 or 14.00
in the Zeiss Hide, no need to book
Wildlife Reserves

Cathedral Carol Service
26/12/98 Lichfield Cathedral
26/12/98 Tel: 01543 306240
The only Carol Service held on Boxing Day
in the Midlands
Cathedrals

New Era Motorcycle and Car
26/12/98 Mallory Park
26/12/98 Tel: 01455 842931
Plum Pudding Event
Motor Racing Circuit

Mince Pie Specials
27/12/98 Dean Forest Railway
1/1/99 Tel: 01594 843423 info line
Now it's almost all over treat yourself to
mince pies and piping hot drinks to help
keep out the winter chill
Railways

*The full information on the venues listed can be found in the main classified section under the
classification shown under the entry. Please mention Best Guides when calling or visiting.*

98/99 Calendar

March 1998

S	M	T	W	Th	F	S
1	2	3	4	5	6	7
8	9	10	11	12	13	14
15	16	17	18	19	20	21
22	23	24	25	26	27	28
29	30	31				

April 1998

S	M	T	W	Th	F	S
			1	2	3	4
5	6	7	8	9	10	11
12	13	14	15	16	17	18
19	20	21	22	23	24	25
26	27	28	29	30		

May 1998

S	M	T	W	Th	F	S
					1	2
3	4	5	6	7	8	9
10	11	12	13	14	15	16
17	18	19	20	21	22	23
24	25	26	27	28	29	30
31						

June 1998

S	M	T	W	Th	F	S
	1	2	3	4	5	6
7	8	9	10	11	12	13
14	15	16	17	18	19	20
21	22	23	24	25	26	27
28	29	30				

July 1998

S	M	T	W	Th	F	S
			1	2	3	4
5	6	7	8	9	10	11
12	13	14	15	16	17	18
19	20	21	22	23	24	25
26	27	28	29	30	31	

August 1998

S	M	T	W	Th	F	S
						1
2	3	4	5	6	7	8
9	10	11	12	13	14	15
16	17	18	19	20	21	22
23	24	25	26	27	28	29
30	31					

September 1998

S	M	T	W	Th	F	S
		1	2	3	4	5
6	7	8	9	10	11	12
13	14	15	16	17	18	19
20	21	22	23	24	25	26
27	28	29	30			

October 1998

S	M	T	W	Th	F	S
				1	2	3
4	5	6	7	8	9	10
11	12	13	14	15	16	17
18	19	20	21	22	23	24
25	26	27	28	29	30	31

November 1998

S	M	T	W	Th	F	S
1	2	3	4	5	6	7
8	9	10	11	12	13	14
15	16	17	18	19	20	21
22	23	24	25	26	27	28
29	30					

December 1998

S	M	T	W	Th	F	S
		1	2	3	4	5
6	7	8	9	10	11	12
13	14	15	16	17	18	19
20	21	22	23	24	25	26
27	28	29	30	31		

January 1999

S	M	T	W	Th	F	S
					1	2
3	4	5	6	7	8	9
10	11	12	13	14	15	16
17	18	19	20	21	22	23
24	25	26	27	28	29	30
31						

February 1999

S	M	T	W	Th	F	S
	1	2	3	4	5	6
7	8	9	10	11	12	13
14	15	16	17	18	19	20
21	22	23	24	25	(26)*	27
28						

The special Millennium double edition of 'The Best Guide to Days Out ever'! is on sale!